D1596391

■ The California State Constitution

The Oxford Commentaries on the State Constitutions of the United States
G. Alan Tarr, Series Editor

Professor G. Alan Tarr, Director of the Center on State Constitutional Studies at Rutgers University, serves as General Editor for this important new series which in its entirety will cover each of the 50 states. Each volume of The Oxford Commentaries on the State Constitutions of the United States contains a historical overview of the state's constitutional development, plus a section-by-section analysis of the state's current constitution. Other features included in the volumes are the text of the state's constitution, a bibliographic essay, table of cases, and index. This series provides essential reference tools for those investigating state constitutional development and constitutional law.

The California State Constitution

Joseph R. Grodin,
Calvin R. Massey, and
Richard B. Cunningham

Foreword by Malcolm M. Lucas

THE OXFORD COMMENTARIES ON THE STATE CONSTITUTIONS OF THE UNITED STATES
G. Alan Tarr, Series Editor

UNIVERSITY PRESS

Oxford University Press, Inc., publishes works that further Oxford University's objective of excellence in research, scholarship, and education.

Oxford New York
Auckland Cape Town Dar es Salaam Hong Kong Karachi Kuala Lumpur Madrid Melbourne
Mexico City Nairobi New Delhi Shanghai Taipei Toronto

With offices in
Argentina Austria Brazil Chile Czech Republic France Greece Guatemala Hungary Italy
Japan Poland Portugal Singapore South Korea Switzerland Thailand Turkey Ukraine
Vietnam

Published by Oxford University Press, Inc.
198 Madison Avenue, New York, New York 10016

Library of Congress Cataloging-in-Publication Data

The California state constitution / Joseph R. Grodin ... [et al.].
p. cm. — (The Oxford commentaries on the state constitutions of the United States)
Includes bibliographical references and index.
ISBN 978-0-19-977895-9 ((hardback) : alk. paper)
1. Constitutions—California. 2. Constitutional history—California. I. Grodin, Joseph R.
II. Title. III. Series.
KFC6801879.A6 C35 2011
342.79402'3—dc22 2011001717

---

1 2 3 4 5 6 7 8 9

Printed in the United States of America on acid-free paper

Note to Readers

To the memory of Justice Mathew O. Tobriner: eminent jurist, scholar, and humanitarian; one of the pathfinders in the development of California constitutional law; dear friend

—J.R.G.

In memory of my parents, Field William Massey and Alice Eliza Bell, and in honor of my ancestor, Nicholas Gibbs, who in 1849 died somewhere on the plains en route to the California gold fields

—C.R.M.

For Thomas James Cunningham, for whom the law was the most honorable profession

—R.B.C.

CONTENTS

Acknowledgments *xix*
Series foreword by G. Alan Tarr *xxi*
Foreword by Chief Justice Malcolm M. Lucas *xxiii*

PART ONE ■ The History of California Constitution

The American Acquisition of California: "Cry Aloud for Independence!" 3
The 1849 Constitution and California Statehood: "Born in different climes, . . . assembled . . . as Californians" 7
The 1879 Constitution: "A sort of mixture of constitution, code, stump speech, and mandamus" 13
The Progressive Movement: "Give us a square deal for Christ's sake" 23
Constitutional Change after the Progressive Movement: "Constant amendment has produced an instrument bad in form" 25
The Rise and Threatened Decline of an Independent California Constitution: "Rights guaranteed by this Constitution are not dependent on those guaranteed by the United States Constitution" 29

PART TWO ■ The California Constitution and Commentary

Preamble **41**

Article I. Declaration of Rights **43**

Section 1. Inalienable Rights 45
Section 2. Liberty of Speech and of the Press; Newspersons' Refusal to Disclose Information Sources Not Adjudged in Contempt 47
Section 3. Right to Assemble and to Petition 49
Section 4. Liberty of Conscience 50
Section 5. The Military 52
Section 6. Slavery Prohibited 52
Section 7. Due Process of Law; Use of Pupil Assignment or Pupil Transportation; Privileges and Immunities 52
Section 8. Sex, Race, etc., Not a Disqualification for Business 56
Section 9. Bill of Attainder; Ex Post Facto Law; Obligation of Contract 57

Section 10. Detention of Witnesses; No Imprisonment for Debt 57
Section 11. Suspension of Habeas Corpus 58
Section 12. Bail; Release on Own Recognizance 58
Section 13. Unreasonable Search and Seizure; Warrant 59
Section 14. Felony Defendant before Magistrate; Prosecutions 60
Section 14.1. Felony; Prosecution by Indictment 61
Section 15. Criminal Prosecutions; Rights of Defendants; Due Process of Law; Jeopardy; Depositions; Assistance of Counsel 61
Section 16. Trial by Jury 62
Section 17. Unusual Punishment and Excessive Fines 63
Section 18. Treason 64
Section 19. Eminent Domain 64
Section 20. Rights of Noncitizens 65
Section 21. Separate Property of Husband and Wife 65
Section 22. No Property Qualification for Voting or Holding Public Office 66
Section 23. Grand Juries 66
Section 24. Independence of the California Constitution; Limits on Independence in Criminal Cases; Rights Retained by the People 67
Section 25. Right to Fish 67
Section 26. Constitution Mandatory and Prohibitory 68
Section 27. Death Penalty 68
Section 28. "The Victims' Bill of Rights" 68
Section 29. Due Process of Law in Criminal Cases; Speedy and Public Trial 71
Section 30. Criminal Cases: Joinder, Hearsay Evidence, and Discovery 72

Article II. Voting, Initiative, Referendum, and Recall 73

Section 1. Purpose of Government 73
Section 2. Right to Vote 74
Section 3. Residence; Registration; Free Elections 74
Section 4. Improper Practices Affecting Elections; Disqualification of Voters 74
Section 5. Primary Elections for Partisan Offices; Open Presidential Primary 75
Section 6. Nonpartisan Offices 76
Section 7. Secret Voting 76
Section 8. Initiative 77
Section 9. Referendum 79

Section 10. Initiative and Referendum Measures: Effective Date, Conflicting Measures, Legislative Repeal or Amendment, Titles 80
Section 11. Initiative and Referendum Measures: Cities and Counties 81
Section 12. Initiative and Referendum Measures: Prohibition upon Naming Persons to Office or Corporations to Duties 81
Section 13. Recall Defined 82
Section 14. Recall Petitions 82
Section 15. Recall Elections 82
Section 16. Legislature to Provide for Recall Petitions and Elections 83
Section 17. Recall of Governor or Secretary of State 83
Section 18. Reimbursement of Recall Election Expenses 83
Section 19. Recall of local Officers 83
Section 20. Commencement of Terms of Elective Office 84

Article III. State of California **85**

Section 1. Supremacy of United States Constitution 85
Section 2. State Boundaries; Sacramento the Capital 86
Section 3. Separation of Powers 86
Section 3.5. Limits on Powers of Administrative Agencies to Declare Statutes Invalid or Unenforceable 86
Section 4. Salaries of Elected State Officers and Judges 87
Section 5. Suits against the State 88
Section 6. Official State Language 88
Section 7. Retirement Benefits for Elected Constitutional Officers 89
Section 8. California Citizens Compensation Commission 90

Article IV. Legislative **93**

Section 1. Legislative Power 94
Section 1.5. Legislative Term Limits; Restriction of Retirement Benefits; Limits on Legislative Staff and Support 94
Section 2. Senate and Assembly: Membership, Elections, Number of Terms, Qualifications, Vacancies 95
Section 3. Legislative Sessions 96
Section 4. Legislators: Conflicts of Interest, Prohibited Compensation, Earned Income, Travel and Living Expenses, Retirement 96
Section 4.5. Legislators' Retirement 98
Section 5. Legislators: Qualifications and Expulsion, Honoraria, Gifts, Conflicts of Interest, Prohibited Compensation or Activities, Lobbying 98

Section 6. Senatorial and Assembly Districts 100
Section 7. House Rules: Quorum, Journals, Public Proceedings, Closed Sessions, Recess 101
Section 7.5. Limits on Total Aggregate Expenditures for the Legislature 102
Section 8. Bills and Statutes: Thirty-Day Waiting Period, Three Readings, Effective Date, Urgency Statutes 102
Section 9. Statute Titles 104
Section 10. Gubernatorial Veto: Override and Exceptions 105
Section 11. Committees 106
Section 12. Governor's Budget; Budget Bill; Other Appropriations 107
Section 13. Legislators Ineligible for Certain Offices 108
Section 14. Legislators not Subject to Civil Process 109
Section 15. Felonious Influencing of Legislative Vote 109
Section 16. Uniform and Paramount Nature of General Laws 110
Section 17. Prohibited Extra Compensation to Public Officials or Contractors 110
Section 18. Impeachment 111
Section 19. Lotteries, Horse Racing, and Gambling 111
Section 20. Fish and Game 112
Section 21. War- or Enemy-Caused Disaster 112
Section 22. Legislative Accountability 113
Sections 23–27. [Repealed.] 113
Section 28. State Capitol Maintenance 113

Article V. Executive **115**

Section 1. Executive Power Vested in Governor 115
Section 2. Gubernatorial Qualifications, Term, Election, and Limits on Terms 116
Section 3. Gubernatorial Report to Legislature 117
Section 4. Executive Officers to Report to Governor 117
Section 5. Method of Filling Vacancies 117
Section 6. Executive Assignment and Agency Reorganization 119
Section 7. Governor as Commander of the State Militia 119
Section 8. Reprieves, Pardons, and Commutations 120
Section 9. Qualifications for and Voting Power of Lieutenant Governor 121
Section 10. Succession in Office 122
Section 11. Other State Officers: Election, Term, Limits on Terms 122
Section 12. [Repealed.] 123
Section 13. Attorney General 123
Section 14. State Officers: Conflicts of Interest, Prohibited Compensation or Activities, Earned Income, Honoraria, Gifts, Lobbying 124

Article VI. Judicial 127

Section 1. Judicial Executive Power Vested in Courts 127
Section 2. Supreme Court of California 128
Section 3. Courts of Appeal 129
Section 4. Superior Courts 129
Section 5. Municipal and Justice Courts 130
Section 6. Judicial Council: Membership and Powers 131
Section 7. Commission on Judicial Appointments 132
Section 8. Commission on Judicial Performance 133
Section 9. State Bar of California 134
Section 10. Original Jurisdiction; Judicial Power to Comment upon Evidence 134
Section 11. Appellate Jurisdiction 135
Section 12. Transfer of Causes 135
Section 13. Setting Aside of Judgments 136
Section 14. Published Judicial Opinions 137
Section 15. Judicial Eligibility 137
Section 15.5. Judicial Eligibility 138
Section 16. Judges: Elections, Terms, Vacancies 138
Section 17. Judges: Restrictions, Other Employment, Benefits 139
Section 18. Judges: Disqualification, Suspension, Removal, Retirement, or Reproval 140
Section 19. Judges: Compensation 142
Section 20. Judges: Retirement and Disability 143
Section 21. Temporary Judges 143
Section 22. Appointment of Officers to Perform Subordinate Judicial Duties 144

Article VII. Public Officers and Employees 145

Section 1. Civil Service 145
Section 2. State Personnel Board: Membership and Compensation 147
Section 3. State Personnel Board: Duties 147
Section 4. Positions Exempt from Civil Service 148
Section 5. Temporary Appointments 149
Section 6. Veterans' Preferences and Other Special Rules 150
Section 7. Dual Office Holding 150
Section 8. Disqualification from Holding Office or Jury Service 151
Section 9. Subversive Organizations 151
Section 10. Disqualification of Elected Officials for Defamatory Campaign Statements 152
Section 11. Legislators' and Judges' Retirement Systems 154

Article VIII. [Repealed.] 154

Article IX. Education 155

Section 1. Legislative Policy 155
Section 2. Superintendent of State Public Instruction: Election, Commencement of Term, Limit on Terms 156
Section 2.1. Deputy and Associate Superintendents of Public Instruction 156
Section 3. County Superintendents of Schools 157
Section 3.1. County Superintendents of Schools: Qualifications and Salaries 158
Section 3.2. Joint County Board of Education and Joint County Superintendent of Schools 158
Section 3.3. County Boards of Education: Qualification and Terms of Office 158
Section 4. [Repealed.] 159
Section 5. Common School System 159
Section 6. Public Schools: Public School System, Salaries, State Aid 160
Section 6.5. School Districts and Bonds 161
Section 7. Boards of Education 162
Section 7.5. Free Textbooks 163
Section 8. Prohibition of Aid to Sectarian Schools or Teaching of Sectarian Doctrine in Public Schools 163
Section 9. University of California 164
[Sections 10–13 have been repealed.] 168
Section 14. Organization, Incorporation, and Powers of School Districts 168
Section 15. [Repealed.] 168
Section 16. City Charter Provisions and Amendments Pertaining to Boards of Education 169

Article X. Water 171

Section 1. Eminent Domain to Acquire Frontages 172
Section 2. Conservation and Beneficial Use of Water Required 173
Section 3. Grant or Sale of Tidelands 175
Section 4. Access to Navigable Waters 178
Section 5. State Control of Water Use 180
Section 6. Water Rates Franchise 181
Section 7. Agency Acquisition of Real Property in Conformance to California Water Laws 182

Article XA. Water Resources Development 185

Article XB. Marine Resources Protection Act of 1990 187

Section 1. Title 187
Section 2. Definitions 188
Section 3. Prohibition of Gill or Trammel Nets 188
Section 4. Regulation of Gill or Trammel Nets 189
Section 5. Permits for Gill or Trammel Nets 190
Section 6. Permit Fees 190
Section 7. Compensation for Surrender of Permit 191
Section 8. Marine Resources Protection Account 192
Section 9. Marine Resources Protection Account Grants 193
Section 10. Report to Legislature 193
Section 11. Violations 193
Section 12. Monitoring of Commercial Fish Landings 194
Section 13. Penalties for Violations 194
Section 14. New Ecological Reserves 195
Section 15. No Preemptive or Superseding Effect 195
Section 16. Severability 195

Article XI. Local Government 197

Section 1. Counties: Formation and Powers 198
Section 2. Cities: Formation and Powers 200
Section 3. County and City Charters 200
Section 4. County Charter Provisions 201
Section 5. City Charter Provisions 203
Section 6. Charter City and County 207
Section 7. Local Ordinances and Regulations 208
Section 8. Counties' Performance of Municipal Functions 209
Section 9. Local Utilities 211
Section 10. Local Government: Extra Compensation, Employee Residence 214
Section 11. Private Control of Public Functions; Deposit and Investment of Public Moneys 215
Section 12. Claims against Counties and Cities 217
Section 13. Construction of Article 217
Section 14. Voter Approval of Local Taxes 218
Section 15. Vehicle License Fee Allocations 219

Article XII. Public Utilities 221

Section 1. Public Utilities Commission: Composition 222
Section 2. Public Utilities Commission: Procedures 223
Section 3. Legislative Control of Public Utilities 223
Section 4. Utility Rates 224

Section 5. Public Utilities Commission: Jurisdiction 225
Section 6. Public Utilities Commission: Powers and Duties 227
Section 7. Prohibition of Free Passes and Other Conflicts of Interest 227
Section 8. Prohibited Local Regulation of Public Utilities 228
Section 9. Construction of Article 229

Article XIII. Taxation **231**

Section 1. Uniformity of Taxation 231
Section 2. Personal Property Classification 232
Section 3. Property Tax Exemptions 233
Section 3.5. Adjustments to Assessment Ratios to Maintain Veterans' Exemptions 236
Section 4. Property Tax Exemptions 237
Section 5. Property Tax Exemption for Buildings under Construction 238
Section 6. Exemption Waivers 238
Section 7. Exemption of Low-Value Property 239
Section 8. Exemption for Open-Space Land and Historical Property 239
Section 8.5. Postponement of Property Taxes 240
Section 9. Valuation of Single-Family Dwellings 241
Section 10. Golf Course Valuation 241
Section 11. Taxation of Local Government Real Property 242
Section 12. Unsecured Property Tax Rate 244
Section 13. Separate Land and Improvements Assessment 245
Section 14. Tax Situs 245
Section 15. Disaster Relief 245
Section 16. County Boards of Equalization 245
Section 17. State Board of Equalization 246
Section 18. Intercounty Equalization 247
Section 19. State Assessment of Utilities 247
Section 20. Maximum Tax Rates and Bonding Limits for Local Governments 248
Section 21. County Levy of School District Taxes 249
Section 22. State Property Tax Limits 249
Section 23. Taxation after State Boundary Change 250
Section 24. Taxes for Local Purposes 250
Section 25. Reimbursement of Local Government for Homeowners' Tax Exemptions 250
Section 26. Income Tax 251
Section 27. Corporate Franchise Taxes 251
Section 28. Taxation of Insurance Companies 252

Section 29. Local Government Tax Sharing 255
Section 30. Tax Liens and Presumption of Payment 256
Section 31. Unhindered Power to Tax 256
Section 32. Collection Proceedings 257
Section 33. Mandate to Legislature to Implement 257

Article XIIIA. Tax Limitation **259**

Section 1. Maximum ad Valorem Tax on Real Property 259
Section 2. Valuation of Real Property 261
Section 3. Vote Requirement for Changes in State Taxes 267
Section 4. Imposition of Special Taxes 268
Section 5. Effective Date 271
Section 6. Severability 271

Article XIIIB. Government Spending Limitation **273**

Section 1. Annual Appropriations Limitation 275
Section 1.5. Audit of Annual Appropriations Limit 275
Section 2. Revenues in Excess of Limitation 276
Section 3. Adjustments to Appropriations Limit 277
Section 4. Establishment or Change of Appropriations Limit by Electors 278
Section 5. Management of Contingency Funds 279
Section 5.5. Prudent State Reserve 279
Section 6. Mandated Subventions for Local Services 280
Section 7. Bonded Indebtedness 281
Section 8. Definitions 282
Section 9. Exceptions to Appropriations Limit 284
Section 10. Effective Date 284
Section 10.5. Appropriations Limit on or after July 1, 1990 285
Section 11. Severability of Categories Added to or Removed from Appropriations Limit 285
Section 12. Tobacco Tax Exceptions 286

Article XIV. Labor Relations **287**

Section 1. Minimum Wages and General Welfare 287
Section 2. Eight-Hour Workday 288
Section 3. Mechanics' Liens 289
Section 4. Workers' Compensation 289
Section 5. Inmate Labor 291

Article XV. Usury **293**

Section 1. Rate of Interest and Exemptions to Usury Limits 293

Article XVI. Public Finance **299**

Section 1. Limitations on Creation of State Indebtedness 299
Section 1.5. General Obligation Bond Proceeds Fund 302
Section 2. Form of Voter Approval of Bond Issues 302
Section 3. Limits on Appropriations to Benefit Private Entities 303
Section 4. Loan Guarantees to Nonprofit Hospitals 305
Section 5. Grants to Religious Institutions Prohibited 306
Section 6. Prohibition of Gifts, Loans, or Pledging of Public Credit 307
Section 7. Controller's Warrants 309
Section 8. School Funding Priority 309
Section 8.5. Allocations to State School Fund 312
Section 9. Fish and Game 314
Section 10. State Cooperation with Federal Pension Assistance 314
Section 11. Relief Administration 315
Section 12. [Repealed.] 315
Section 13. Legislative Power to Release Certain Liens 315
Section 14. Revenue Bonds for Environmental Pollution Control Facilities 316
Section 14.5. Revenue Bonds for Alternative Energy Sources Facilities 317
Section 15. Parking Meter Revenues 317
Section 16. Taxation of Redevelopment Projects 318
Section 17. State's Credit and Investment of Public Pension Funds 320
Section 18. Limitation on Local Indebtedness 322
Section 19. Special Assessments by Chartered City or County 324

Article XVII. [Repealed.] **325**

Article XVIII. Amending and Revising the Constitution **327**

Section 1. Legislative Initiative 327
Section 2. Constitutional Convention 328
Section 3. Popular Initiatives 328
Section 4. Effective Date 329

Article XIX. Motor Vehicle Revenues **331**

Section 1. Use of Fuel Taxes 331
Section 2. Use of Motor Vehicle Fees and Taxes 332
Section 3. Allocation of Revenues 332
Section 4. Voter Approval for Expenditures 333
Section 5. Expenditures for Bond Payments 333
Section 6. Loans to State General Fund 334

Section 7. Scope of Article 334
Section 8. Use of Excess Lands for Parks and Recreation 334
Section 9. Transfer of Surplus State Property Located in Coastal Zone 335

Article XX. Miscellaneous Subjects 337

Section 1. Sacramento County Consolidation 337
Section 1.5. Homestead Protection 338
Section 2. Tax Exemptions for Stanford University and Huntington Library 338
Section 3. Prescribed Oath of Office 339
Section 4. Franchises 340
Section 5. Reservation of Right to Alter Corporate Laws 340
Section 6. Retirement Benefits of Legislators with Reduced Terms of Office 341
Section 7. Term Limits on Constitutional Officers 341
Sections 8–15. [Repealed or renumbered.] 342
Sections 16–21. [Repealed or renumbered.] 343
Section 22. Liquor Controls 343
Section 23. Speaker of the Assembly Declared An Ex Officio Member of the Governing Board of the State College System 347

Article XXI. Reapportionment of Senate, Assembly, Congressional, and Board of Equalization Districts 349

Section 1. Reapportionment Following National Census 351

Article XXII. [Repealed.] 353

[Articles XXIII through XXVIII have either been repealed or renumbered; there are no Articles XXIX–XXXIII. 354

Article XXXIV. Public Housing Project Law 355

Section 1. Voter Approval Required for Low-Income Housing Projects 356
Section 2. Provisions Declared to Be Self-Executing 359
Section 3. Constitutional Severability 359
Section 4. Scope of Article 360

Bibliography 361
Table of Cases 367
Index 381
About the Author 391

ACKNOWLEDGMENTS

The authors collaborated on the general style and organization of this work, but allocated the articles of the constitution according to their interests. Professor Grodin was primarily responsible for Articles I to IV, VI, XIV, and XVIII; Professor Massey for the entire history, as well as Articles V, VII, IX, XV, XX, and XXXIV; and Professor Cunningham for Articles X through XIII B, XVI, XIX, and XXI.

Many people and institutions deserve to be recognized as important contributors to this book. Hastings College of the Law provided generous support. Research assistance was provided by Hastings students Cheryl Mattson, James T. Schmid, Suzanne G. Ryder, Matthew Berger, Eric Croft, Marc A. Deiter, and Robert Timothy Reagan. Although all of our research assistants provided valuable aid, the contributions of Cheryl Mattson, Marc Deiter, and Tim Reagan deserve particular mention. The entire library staff at Hastings, particularly Laura Peritore, was most helpful in responding to numerous requests for obscure source materials. We are indebted to Fran Nowve for her assistance on early drafts of this book. We are especially grateful to Ted V. Jang for his word processing skills and patience in dealing with multiple corrections and changes to the manuscript, compilations of cases and bibliographical references, and production of the final manuscript.

Although editors and authors are often said to be natural enemies, we are especially grateful for the valuable suggestions made by both G. Alan Tarr and Mildred Vasan and for their patience.

SERIES FOREWORD

In 1776, following the declaration of independence from England, the former colonies began to draft their own constitutions. Their handiwork attracted widespread interest, and draft constitutions circulated up and down the Atlantic seaboard as constitution makers sought to benefit from the insights of their counterparts in other states. In Europe, the new constitutions found a ready audience seeking enlightenment from the American experiments in self-government. Even the delegates to the Constitutional Convention of 1787, despite their reservations about the course of political developments in the states during the decade after independence, found much that was useful in the newly adopted constitutions. And when James Madison, fulfilling a pledge given during the ratification debates, drafted the federal Bill of Rights, he found his model in the famous Declaration of Rights of the Virginia Constitution.

By the 1900s, however, few people would have looked to state constitutions for enlightenment on fundamental rights or important principles. Instead, a familiar litany of complaints was heard whenever state constitutions were mentioned. State constitutions were too long and too detailed, combining basic principles with policy prescriptions and prohibitions that had no place in the fundamental law of a state. By including such provisions, it was argued, state constitutions deprived state governments of the flexibility they needed to respond effectively to changing circumstances. This—among other factors—encouraged political reformers to look to the federal government, which was not plagued by such constitutional constraints, thereby shifting the locus of political initiative away from the states. Meanwhile, civil libertarians concluded that state bills of rights, at least as interpreted by state courts, did not adequately protect rights, and they looked to the federal courts and the federal Bill of Rights for redress. As power and responsibility shifted from the states to Washington, so too did the attention of scholars, the legal community, and the general public.

During the early 1970s, however, state constitutions were rediscovered. The immediate impetus for this rediscovery was former President Richard Nixon's appointment of Warren Burger to succeed Earl Warren as chief justice of the U.S. Supreme Court. To civil libertarians, this appointment seemed to signal a decisive shift in the Supreme Court's jurisprudence because Burger was expected to lead the Court away from the liberal activism that had characterized the Warren Court. They therefore sought ways to safeguard the gains they had achieved for defendants, racial minorities, and the poor from erosion by the Burger Court. In particular, they began to look to state bills of rights to secure the rights of defendants and to support other civil-liberties claims that they advanced in state courts.

This new judicial federalism, as it came to be called, quickly advanced beyond its initial concern to evade the Burger Court. Indeed, less than two decades after it originated, it has become a nationwide phenomenon, for when judges and scholars turned their attention to state constitutions, they discovered an unsuspected richness. They found not only provisions that paralleled the federal Bill of Rights but also constitutional guarantees—of the right to privacy and of gender equality, for example—that had no analogue in the U.S. Constitution. Careful examination of the text and history of state guarantees revealed important differences between even those provisions that most resembled federal guarantees and their federal counterparts. Looking beyond state declarations of rights, jurists and scholars discovered affirmative constitutional mandates to state governments to address such important policy concerns as education and housing. Taken altogether, these discoveries underlined the importance for the legal community of developing a better understanding of state constitutions.

The renewed interest in state constitutions has not been limited to judges and lawyers. State constitutional reformers have renewed their efforts, with notable success. Since 1960, ten states have adopted new constitutions, and several others have undertaken major constitutional revisions. These changes have usually resulted in more streamlined constitutions and more effective state governments. Also, in recent years political activists on both the left and the right have pursued their goals through state constitutional amendments, often enacted through the initiative process, under which policy proposals can be placed directly on the ballot for voters to endorse or reject. Scholars have begun to rediscover how state constitutional history can illuminate changes in political thought and practice, providing a basis for theories about the dynamics of political change in America.

Grodin, Massey, and Cunningham's fine study of the California Constitution, part of the Oxford Commentaries on the State Constitutions of the United States series, reflects this renewed interest in state constitutions and contributes to our knowledge of them. Because the constitutional tradition of each state is distinctive, this volume begins by tracing the history and development of California's constitutions. It then provides the full text of the state's current constitution, with each section accompanied by commentary that explains the provision and traces its origins and its interpretation by the courts and other governmental bodies. For readers with a particular interest in a specific aspect of California constitutionalism, this book offers a bibliography of the most important sources examining the constitutional history and constitutional law of the state. It also contains a table of cases cited and a subject index.

G. Alan Tarr

FOREWORD

The relationship between the federal and state governments in our nation has undergone constant evolution since the thirteen colonies took their first steps toward independence. From the outset, of course, state courts have been charged not only with interpreting their own state constitutions, but also with applying federal constitutional guarantees. The place of the two constitutions in state court jurisprudence has, however, undergone modifications over the years as the balance between state and federal governments and their guarantees of rights has experienced significant shifts.

Having been privileged to sit on both the state and federal benches, the interplay of these systems has been of continuing interest to me. Like the relationship between the different constitutions, my perspectives on this area have continued to change during the course of my judicial career. This book provides important assistance for jurists, lawyers, academics, and laymen who want to join in fruitful dialogue about the role and relevance of federal and state constitutions in our state courts.

Originally, the federal bill of rights imposed restrictions solely on the federal government. State constitutions included guarantees of rights for their citizens long before adoption of the due process clause of the Fourteenth Amendment in 1868 began the extension of federal restrictions to state governmental action.

Some twenty years before that date, in 1849, Californians gathered together to create their first state constitution. Eleven years after the adoption of the Fourteenth Amendment, the Constitution of 1879 was adopted in California. Although many changes were wrought at the second, and to date last, constitutional convention in California, the Declaration of Rights contained in the initial document survived largely unaltered. Despite the extensive protections contained in California and other state constitutions, however, a wider application of the Fourteenth Amendment's restrictions on states developed through the end of the nineteenth century—and continues to be refined as we approach the beginning of the twenty-first.

The federal constitution did not spring full blown out of thin air. "The fifty-five delegates who attended the 1787 Constitutional Convention already had wide experience, either directly or indirectly, with constitutional theory and constitution making."[1] The California constitutional convention was made up of men

[1] Robert F. Willams, "'Experience Must Be Our Only Guide': The State Constitutional Experience of the Framers of the Federal Constitution," Hastings Const. L.Q. 15 (Spring 1988): 403, 405.

"totally unacquainted with each other" and "entirely wanting in general concert of plans or policies of action."[2] But as had been true of the federal framers, although some delegates had little or no experience in governance, many had participated in similar or related ventures in other states. All brought with them a sense of the seriousness of their undertaking.[3]

Both conventions looked to previously created models to forge a document for their intended constituencies. The process of borrowing and reworking that occurred is often overlooked when the genesis of constitutional law is taught—but understanding the process and origins of our constitutions gives context to the intentions of the framers and the environment in which they worked.

I would venture to say that most Californians, like most citizens of the United States, have some basic familiarity with the federal constitution. I am not as convinced that our citizens are equally aware of the separately enunciated protections that lie in their state constitutions and the role that those documents can play in the judicial system that forms part of their government. In fact, many of the protections and provisions in our state constitution are unique to that document, and are either not covered at all or are differently delineated in the federal constitution. Much of the constitutional litigation in state courts relates to distinctively state issues—although the interaction of the two constitutions often is given the most prominence. This book, with its article-by-article, section-by-section review of California's constitution, provides a convenient and accessible means of understanding the background of our state constitutional rights, their scope and interpretation, and their effect on every Californian's life.

Because of the existence of two constitutions to which courts may look in determining a variety of issues, some provocative and complex issues present themselves. For example: How should redundancies in state and federal guarantees be treated? Should courts strive for consistent and coextensive interpretations when the language of particular amendments is almost identical? Should courts, in every instance, go back to the origins of each document to ascertain whether the framers had different intentions? Does the extension of the restrictions contained in the federal bill of rights to state actions affect our interpretation of state constitutional guarantees?

These are difficult questions over which reasonable men and women may disagree. But the heightened attention to state constitutional origins and law bodes well for the continued vitality of constitutional discourse. To the best of my knowledge, this is the first comprehensive review of our state's constitution.

---

[2] Joseph R. Grodin, "Commentary: Some Reflections of State Contitutions," Hastings Const. L.Q. 15 (Spring 1988): z391, 392–93, qutoing Rockwell D. Hunt, The Genesis of California's First Contitution (1846–1849) (1973), p. 37.

[3] I bid., p. 393.

Keeping citizens involved, informed, and interested in the development of the jurisprudence that affects their lives can only benefit us all. Through their efforts, the authors have provided us with a thought-provoking and readable tool to help achieve that goal.

Malcolm M. Lucas
Chief Justice

PART ONE

The History of the California Constitution

THE AMERICAN ACQUISITION OF CALIFORNIA: "CRY ALOUD FOR INDEPENDENCE!"

From European discovery in 1542 until 1769, California was subject to sporadic visitation from Europeans. Occupied by Spain in 1769, California in 1822 was a possession of Spain. Upon formal recognition of Mexican independence, Spanish authority over California was ceded to the newly established Mexican imperial government, "but the actual intervention of Mexico in the affairs of the distant province [of California] consisted in little more than the sending of governors and a few score of degraded soldiery."[1] Mexico's tenuous grasp on California no doubt excited the territorial ambitions of other nations. As early as 1812, only eight years after the intrepid western explorations of Lewis and Clark, Thomas Jefferson "looked forward with gratification to the time [when the entire Pacific Coast would be populated by] free and independent Americans, unconnected

---

[1] Charles E. Chapman, A History of California: The Spanish Period (New York: Macmillan, 1921), p. 455, quoted in Peter T. Conmy, The Constitutional Beginnings of California (San Francisco: Native Sons of the Golden West, 1959), p. 4n.2; Neal Harlow, California Conquered: The Annexation of a Mexican Province 1846–1850 (Berkeley: University of California Press, 1982), p. 22.

with us but by the ties of blood and interest, and employing like us the rights of self-government."[2]

With a trickle of American trappers and traders in the 1820s, Jefferson's vision began to glimmer faintly, but only after 1836, when American immigrants to Texas had wrested that province free from Mexico, did his prediction begin to acquire substance.[3] At the same time, native Californians felt so poorly served by the distant Mexican government that in 1836 and 1845 they set up insurgent governors in opposition to the accredited governors sent by the Republic of Mexico.[4] By 1840, in the settled and established parts of the United States, "public meetings were held to discuss . . . emigration to California." From then on, "American emigration to California assumed the character of an organized, concerted movement."[5] Whether filled with notions of self-betterment or national manifest destiny, the march of American immigrant parties to California in the 1840s sounded the inevitable death knell of Mexican hegemony in upper California.

Some immigrants came with the intention of fomenting revolt and attaching California to the United States. An example of this breed was Lansford W. Hastings, an Ohio lawyer who arrived in California in 1843, by way of Oregon, at the age of twenty-four. Hastings returned to the East to proselytize for new settlers to California in order to achieve a large enough American population in California to make a revolt a practical possibility.[6] He later represented Sacramento in the 1849 constitutional convention at Monterey.

Other American settlers preferred the separation of California from Mexico and Oregon from the United States in order to form a separate and independent "Pacific republic dominated by Americans." Even the U.S. minister to Mexico favored such a scheme; he shared the prevalent view of adherents to the Pacific Republic scheme that California and Oregon were simply "too remote from the United States to become a member of the Union."[7]

The Mexican government was not oblivious to this threat. In 1840 the government had arrested nearly a hundred "foreigners of a suspicious character . . . [on]

---

[2] Thomas Jefferson to John Jacob Astor, May 24, 1812, quoted in Joseph Ellison, "The Struggle for Civil Government in California, 1846–1850," Calif. Hist. Soc. Q. 10 (1931): 3.

[3] David J. Langum, Law and Community on the Mexican California Frontier (Norman, Okla.: University of Oklahoma Press, 1987), p. 9; Harlow, California Conquered, pp. 39–44, 49.

[4] Conmy, The Constitutional Beginnings of California, pp. 4–5; Ellison, "The Struggle for Civil Government," p. 5 n.7.

[5] Ellison, "The Struggle for Civil Government," p. 5.

[6] Ibid., pp. 6–7. Hastings published, in Cincinnati in 1845, a book which endowed the region with almost fantastic qualities. See also J. S. Holliday, The World Rushed In: The California Gold Rush Experience (New York: Simon and Schuster, 1981), p. 236n.; John Phillip Reid, Law for the Elephant: Property and Social Behavior on the Overland Trail (San Marino, Calif.: Huntington Library, 1980), p. 178 n.4.

[7] Ibid., p. 7.

the charge of fostering revolutionary designs."[8] The Mexican minister to Washington publicly declared in the American press his government's desire to deter colonization of California by foreigners, and the Mexican government considered various measures to defend against the growing American incursion. Most dramatic of these was President Santa Anna's 1843 decree expelling from California all natives of the United States, an order rescinded only after the U.S. minister delivered threats of American reprisal.

Because the Mexican government had once indicated its desire to expel Americans from California, American settlers were only too willing to believe rumors of impending expulsion. Thus, with Captain John Frémont's U.S. Army detachment near at hand, it was a propitious moment for American settlers to respond to William Ide's proposal to "cry aloud for independence" and declare California an independent republic. On June 14, 1846, at Sonoma, they seized General Mariano Vallejo, the commandante general of California, and forced him to surrender California to the revolutionaries, who declared California a free and independent "'Republican Government,' which shall secure to all, civil and religious liberty."[9] Before the California Republic could be tested in its resolve to endure, war erupted between the United States and Mexico, and between July 7 and August 13, 1846, the principal settlements of California were seized by American military forces, and the suzerainty of the California Republic was deferred to the conquering claims of the United States.

The conclusion of the Mexican-American War in 1848 left California occupied by U.S. armed forces as a military possession.[10] Many of the estimated 10,000 people did not consider themselves "conquered people" but instead sought the introduction of an American civilian government.[11] To the disappointment of American settlers and others desiring establishment of civil government, Congress was so beset by deep-seated differences over the question of slavery in the territories that it failed repeatedly to welcome California into the Union. In the interim, the governing law was of decidedly mixed pedigree.

---

[8] Ellison, "The Struggle for Civil Government," pp. 8–9.

[9] Ibid., p. 10. The most extensive account of the American conquest of California is Harlow, California Conquered, pp. 62–353.

[10] The Treaty of Guadalupe-Hidalgo was signed February 2, 1848, ratified by the U.S. Senate on March 10, 1848 and the Mexican government on May 30, 1848, and formally proclaimed on July 4, 1848. Among other provisions it ceded California to the United States. Secretary of State James Buchanan regarded the federal Constitution as having "extended over California on the 30th of May, 1848, the date on which the . . . treaty with Mexico was consummated." In re Perkins, 2 Cal. 424, 453 (1851) (quoting Buchanan's letter to William Van Vorhies of the Post Office). But see Merryman v. Bourne, 76 U.S. (9 Wall.), 592, 601 (1869) ("The conquest of California by the arms of the United States is regarded as having become complete on the 7th of July, 1846. On that day the Government of the United States succeeded to the rights and authority of the government of Mexico.").

[11] Rockwell D. Hunt, The Genesis of California's First Constitution (1846–49) (New York: Johnson Reprint Corp., 1973), p. 16.

Immediately upon military seizure of California, Commodore John Sloat declared that Californians enjoyed "the same rights and privileges as the citizens of any other portion of [the United States]."[12] Six weeks later, his successor, Commodore Robert Stockton, announced that until a territorial government was established, "military law will prevail." Despite that declaration of martial law, Stockton inconsistently declared his intent to "administer the laws according to the former [Mexican] usages of the Territory."[13] This fusion of military and Mexican law continued until the 1849 Constitution, with the result that the Mexican forms of governmental machinery were observed but given little substance. The *alcaldes* (magistrates), often American settlers, exercised vast and arbitrary power in accordance with their intuitive sense of justice rather than in conformity to any known body of law.[14] Although Mexican law was proclaimed still in force, to the extent "not in conflict with the constitution of the United States," the problem was that "American alcaldes knew nothing of the Mexican laws, nor of the customs of the country."[15]

The discovery of gold in January 1848 aggravated the problem, for it brought in thousands of gold seekers from all parts of the world, swelling the small population of about 10,000 to an estimated 50,000 to 100,000 residents by the end of 1850.[16] Because the many miners adopted their own laws and customs, disjointed, ad hoc governments developed around the mines and boom towns. The increase in crime during the gold rush helped also to fuel popular demands for an organized civil government.

Congressional paralysis and growing restiveness under military rule soon made it clear that a new regime could be achieved only through local organization. Meetings were held in various cities during the winter of 1848–1849, and resolutions were adopted calling for a general convention. On June 3, 1849, the de facto governor, General Bennett Riley, issued a proclamation calling for an elected convention to meet in Monterey (the former provincial capital) on September 1, 1849, for the purpose of "fram[ing] a State constitution or a Territorial organization, to be submitted to the people for their ratification, and then proposed to Congress for its approval."[17]

---

[12] Proclamation of July 7, 1846, quoted in Ellison, "The Struggle for Civil Government," p. 11.

[13] Ibid., p. 14.

[14] Ibid., pp. 17, 23–25.

[15] Ibid., p. 19, quoting Proclamation of General Kearny, March 1, 1847, p. 24.

[16] Ibid., p. 30. Ellison's estimate of California's population is nearly 100,000. By contrast, Carl Brent Swisher maintained that "in the latter part of 1849 there were probably not more than 50,000 people in the state." Carl B. Swisher, Motivation and Political Technique in the California Constitutional Convention of 1878–79 (Claremont, Calif.: Pomona College, 1930), p. 6. The adult male population of California in 1841 has been estimated to be 2,000. A. A. Gray, History of California (Boston: D. C. Heath & Co., 1934), p. 219.

[17] Proclamation of General Riley, June 3, 1849, reprinted in J. Ross Browne, Report of the Debates of the Convention of California on the Formation of the State Constitution (Washington, D.C., 1850), p. 3.

THE 1849 CONSTITUTION AND CALIFORNIA STATEHOOD: "BORN IN DIFFERENT CLIMES, . . . ASSEMBLED . . . AS CALIFORNIANS"

The composition of the forty-eight delegates elected to attend the convention reflected the youth and heterogeneity of California. Twenty-seven were under the age of thirty-five; only three were over fifty. Three segments of the population were represented, though not in proportion to their numbers in the general population: the native Hispano-Californians, the English-speaking pioneer settlers, and the miners. Only seven of the delegates were Hispano-Californians. The major professions represented were lawyers (fourteen), farmers (eleven), and merchants (seven). Transplanted northerners made up a majority of the population, but fifteen southerners were chosen. Natives of Switzerland, France, Scotland, Ireland, and Spain were also in attendance.[18] This diversity proved to be a safeguard and a moderating influence; all were compelled to compromise at different times. No one faction dominated the proceedings, and as a result, a moderate, judicious constitution was created.

By 1849, American states had nearly seventy-five years of experience with state constitutions. A typical pattern of the early post-Revolutionary constitutions was essential trust in the legislature, almost to the point that the legislative agent was regarded as the embodiment of popular sovereignty. Perhaps the most extreme example of the genre is the well-known Pennsylvania Constitution of 1776. But by 1845, as Bayrd Still has noted,

> the experience of state governments, so constituted, had somewhat belied the infallibility of the people's agents. Quite a different pattern of constitutional philosophy is manifested in the restrictions on government which were enacted into revised constitutions in New Jersey, Louisiana, Texas, Missouri, New York, Illinois, Kentucky, Michigan, New Hampshire, Ohio, Indiana, Maryland, and Virginia in the years from 1844 to 1851. Now legislators were condemned as rash, extravagant, and inefficient. Excess legislation was deemed a curse. Biennial meetings of legislatures, whose sessions, numbers, salaries, and powers were greatly curtailed, now replaced the annual sessions once thought the alternative to tyranny. The powers of the governor were increased as a check upon legislative excess.[19]

Thus, when the forty-eight diverse men, "born in different climes, coming from different states, . . . [but] assembled in Convention, as Californians," deliberated upon the frame of government that they sought to establish, they were confronted with a choice between two models. Did they wish to

---

[18] See Browne, Report of the Debates, pp. 478–79, for a tabular biographical sketch of the members of the 1849 convention.

[19] Bayrd Still, "California's First Constitution: A Reflection of the Political Philosophy of the Frontier," Pacific Hist. Rev. 4 (1935): 221, 222.

vest the new government with expansive legislative powers, trusting the elected representatives to aggregate accurately the will of the people, or did they prefer to trim the powers of those representatives out of a fear that they could not be relied upon to act in the best interest of the people as a whole?

On the whole, they opted for a modification of the "pioneer model" of vesting the legislature with plenary authority. Their faith in the legislature was limited, for they forbad it from enacting special legislation for private benefit or to enact legislation dealing with certain subjects. Thus, the legislature was forbidden to grant divorces (Art. IV, sec. 26), establish lotteries (Art. IV, sec. 27), charter corporations specially (Art. IV, sec. 30), establish banks (other than as pure specie depositary institutions) (Art. IV, sec. 34–35), or permit corporate shareholders to evade personal liability for corporate debts (Art. IV, sec. 36). Similarly, the legislature was not trusted to act with respect to married women's separate property, for the new constitution explicitly secured such rights (Art. XI, sec. 14). Nor was the legislature trusted to act, on its own, to exempt from a creditor's levy a portion of a debtor's property. Article XI, section 15 commanded the legislature to do so.

On the other hand, the convention opted for annual legislative sessions. Although William Gwin, an ambitious forty-four-year-old former one-term congressman from Mississippi, argued for biennial sessions on the grounds of economy and libertarian philosophy, the convention preferred annual sessions, showing faith in the legislature's ability and willingness to correct its errors. Nor did the convention restrict the people in their choices of representatives. Rodman Price considered the people "the best judges, . . . and preferred leaving the age of their representatives unrestricted." William Shannon objected to Pacificus Ord's ill-fated proposal to bar clergymen from the legislature as "anti-republican . . . and totally inconsistent with the spirit of our institutions. [The convention had] . . . no right to dictate to the people what shall be the professional character of their representatives."[20]

Fears engendered by the panic of 1837, a period of speculation and overexpansion, and the "normal frontier antipathy to monopolistic association and creditor institutions"[21] led delegates to write into the constitution stringent provisions regarding corporations, banks, and paper money. Leading the opposition to the corporate existence of banks was William Gwin, whose sentiments probably reflected many colleagues' views:

> It is folly to create associations for the deposit of gold and silver. The tens of thousands engaged in gold digging, want no such associations. It will benefit those only who live by their wits, and not the hard-handed gold digger, who by his labor enriches the country. Let us guard against infringing on the rights of the people, by

[20] Browne, Report of the Debates, pp. 77, 78, 80, 83, 136, 474.

[21] Still, "California's First Constitution," p. 228.

> legalizing the association of capital to war upon labor. This is the only country on the globe where labor has the complete control of capital. If there are to be banks in the country, let us have private bankers, who, if they abuse the confidence of the people, can be punished by the law, indicted and put in the penitentiary.[22]

Similar sentiments were voiced by Charles Botts, a forty-year-old Virginia lawyer, who declared his chief object was "to crush this bank monster."[23] Lest that "insinuating serpent, a circulating bank," establish itself, Botts proposed a stable circulating currency by the state treasurer, in receipt of equivalent deposited specie.[24] Although his proposal was withdrawn, the convention did prohibit private depositary institutions from issuing paper money (Art. IV, sec. 34–35).

The majority of delegates wanted to keep wealth evenly distributed and in the hands of individuals, not corporations, and basically sought to discourage all corporations, not only banks. Toward this end, the constitution prohibited creation of corporations by special act; they could be formed only pursuant to general laws (Art. IV, sec. 30). Article IV, section 36 established the principle of individual liability: each stockholder in a corporation became responsible for his proportion of any indebtedness. This provision of personal and proportionate liability of stockholders remained in effect until 1930, and as a result, numerous enterprises doing business in California incorporated under the laws of other states or employed a noncorporate form of business organization.[25]

The convention's willingness to trust future legislative judgment was also tested in connection with the proposal to guarantee to married women ownership of their separate property. Henry Tefft, a twenty-six-year-old lawyer recently arrived from Wisconsin, defended the proposal as consistent with California's preexisting civil law and as a liberal reform "due to every wife, and to the children of every family" and was "not willing to trust to the Legislature in this matter."[26] By contrast, Francis Lippitt thought these matters should "more safely be entrusted to the action of the Legislature, than . . . form part of the irrepealable law of the land."[27] On the merits, Henry Halleck called upon all "bachelors . . . to vote for it [as] I do not think we can offer a greater inducement for women of fortune to come to California."[28] Charles Botts declared that the measure was better left to legislative judgment but condemned it since "nature did what the

[22] Browne, Report of the Debates, p. 117.

[23] Ibid., p. 125.

[24] Ibid.

[25] William Palmer and Paul Selvin, The Development of Law in California (St. Paul, Minn.: West, 1983), p. 15.

[26] Browne, Report of the Debates, p. 258.

[27] Ibid., p. 257.

[28] Ibid., p. 259.

common law has done—put her under the protection of man . . . To make the wife independent of the husband . . . is contrary to . . . nature."[29] Lippitt echoed Botts in his ridicule of the proposal as "raising [the wife] from the condition of head clerk to partner."[30] These arguments left the delegates unmoved; a married woman's right to own her separate property became constitutionally guaranteed in Article XI, section 14.[31]

More deference to later legislative judgment was observed with respect to exemption from creditors' claims of a portion of a debtor's homestead. The convention's Committee on the Constitution proposed initially that up to 320 acres of rural land, or city lots of an unspecified dollar amount, should remain free from execution. Once again, Lippitt argued that "it belongs to the . . . Legislature . . . to say what amount, and precisely what articles, shall be exempted."[32] On this issue, legislative deference prevailed, and the legislature was simply charged, by Article XI, section 15, to protect "a certain portion" of a debtor's property from forced sale.

The delegates did not trust the legislature to set educational objectives and policy. A liberal constitutional provision provided for public education and earmarked funds for the establishment of the state university system (Art. IX). The goal was to provide a fund sufficient for the education of every child in California, thus offering an incentive to immigrant families with children to move to California and adding to the permanent settlement and prosperity of the state. This policy was in tune with national policy, which strongly encouraged public education in the states. In any case, the delegates were unwilling to leave the matter to the unfettered judgment of the legislature.

Like the thirty other state constitutions then in existence, the 1840 Constitution contains a Declaration of Rights. Significantly, it was the first substantive item of business for the convention. The committee to draft a bill of rights quickly presented a sixteen-section list, with nine based upon or verbatim copies of New York's 1846 Constitution, and seven copied from or modeled after the 1846 Iowa Constitution.[33] The list was modified when Shannon of

---

[29] Ibid., pp. 259–60.

[30] Ibid., p. 261.

[31] However, when California's first legislature implemented the community property system, it subverted the constitutional rule by granting the husband both "the entire management and control of the common property" and "the management and control of the separate property of the wife." Act of April 17, 1850, Cal. Stats. 1849–50, c. 103, sec. 6, 9, p. 254.

[32] Browne, Report of the Debates, p. 271.

[33] Christian Fritz, "More Than 'Shreds and Patches': California's First Bill of Rights," Hastings Const. L.Q. 17 (1989): 13, 19 n.32. But see Ira Reiner and George Glenn Size, "The Law Through a Looking Glass: Our Supreme Court and the Use and Abuse of the California Declaration of Rights," Pac. L.J. 23 (1992): 1183, 1272–85, in which Reiner and Size confirm that the "provenance" of the Declaration of Rights was the Iowa and New York constitutions, although they contend that the archetype of certain provisions was the U.S. Constitution's Bill of Rights.

Sacramento proposed the inclusion of two sections that survive today. The first was a straightforward embrace of natural law: "All men are by nature free and independent, and have certain inalienable rights, among which are those of enjoying and defending life and liberty, acquiring, possessing, and protecting property, and pursuing and obtaining safety and happiness." The second was a ringing affirmation of the principle of popular sovereignty: "All political power is inherent in the people. Government is instituted for the protection, security, and benefit of the people; and they have a right at all times, to alter or reform the same whenever the public good may require it."[34] Both were adopted quickly.

More surprising was the rejection of a proposal to protect all inhabitants of California from deprivation of their rights or privileges "unless by the law of the land or the judgment of his peers."[35] This guarantee, with roots dating to Magna Carta, was rejected primarily out of fear that it might be invoked to protect the rights of aboriginal people and African-Americans.[36]

A proposed eminent domain clause prescribing compensation for private property taken for public use was rejected with almost no debate. Although Henry Halleck reminded the convention that the absence of such a constitutional provision in other states had led to such "abuse of the legislative power... as to require this restraint," the convention dismissed the warning, apparently preferring the wisdom of Charles Botts's confession "that I can see no connexion between a McAdamised road and a bill of rights,"[37] or at least trusting the legislature to exercise good judgment.

A similar trust was evident in the convention's rejection of Pacificus Ord's proposal to guarantee that "every person has a right to bear arms for the defence of himself and the State." Both Winfield Sherwood and M. M. McCarver, a middle-aged farmer from Kentucky by way of Oregon, objected that "no attempt should be made to prevent the Legislature from regulating matters of this kind."[38] The argument apparently prevailed, for the convention rejected the proposal by an unrecorded vote.

Whether due to faith in legislative judgment or disagreement on the merits, the convention rejected Lansford Hastings's proposal to prohibit capital punishment. There was almost no discussion of the proposal; McCarver announced that he "would vote against the resolution, not because he was opposed to it, but because he considered it impracticable," even though he conceded "the right to take human life... is very questionable."[39]

---

[34] Browne, Report of the Debates, pp. 33–34.

[35] Ibid., p. 38.

[36] Ibid., p. 35 (remarks of L. W. Hastings).

[37] Ibid., p. 41.

[38] Ibid., p. 47.

[39] Ibid., pp. 45–46.

Perhaps most surprising was the unanimous adoption, with no debate, of William Shannon's proposal to prohibit slavery.[40] Shannon represented a mining district along the Yuba River where, after the discovery of gold, resentment grew against slave owners who located claims in the names of their slaves.[41] At the same time, Shannon appears to have genuinely deplored the loathsome state to which slavery had reduced blacks. However, much of the opposition to slavery did not stem from convictions of equality as much as pragmatic economic concerns. Many delegates believed that slavery in California would create ruinous competition for free white laborers. Motivations such as these prompted McCarver to propose prohibiting "free persons of color from immigrating to and settling in this State."[42] Argument in favor of the proposal was tinctured with an ugly and frank racism; opponents expressed astonishment at the idea "that a certain class of Americans born in the United States—their forefathers born there for many generations—shall be excluded from entering the Territory of all!" To others it was inconceivable that free blacks could be denied the rights "which you award to all mankind."[43] Although initially approved by the Committee of the Whole, after further discussion, the proposal was soundly rejected,[44] perhaps due to fear that the provision would complicate California's admission as a state.[45]

Questions of slavery and race also tinged the boundary issue, the most divisive of the entire convention, which at one point threatened to derail the proceedings. As ceded by Mexico in the Treaty of Guadalupe-Hidalgo, California encompassed not only the present state but also Nevada, Arizona, New Mexico, Utah, and part of Colorado. Some members of the convention, led by Gwin and Halleck, the latter an army captain and secretary of state under the military occupation, proposed that the new state include the entire vast ceded area within its boundaries. Gwin argued that in meeting to form a constitution for the whole of California, the convention did not possess the authority to dismember the state.[46] A number of pro-slavery delegates favored a large area, possibly because they believed that such a vast area would necessitate division, giving them another opportunity to introduce slavery.[47]

---

[40] Ibid., pp. 43–44.

[41] Woodrow Hansen, The Search for Authority in California (Oakland, Calif.: Biobooks, 1960), p. 114.

[42] Browne, Report of the Debates, pp. 48, 137, 331. Cf. p. 44.

[43] Ibid., pp. 140, 149 (remarks of Kimball Dimmick and Edward Gilbert).

[44] Ibid., pp. 152, 330. The final vote was eight in favor and thirty-one against.

[45] Ibid., pp. 143, 146, 150. It was claimed that the proposal would excite discussion in Congress and "jeopard the interests of California."

[46] Ibid., pp. 186, 188.

[47] Hunt, The Genesis of California's First Constitution, pp. 43–49.

Robert Semple, an "old settler" of five years' duration and president of the convention, proposed that the body determine the northern and southern boundaries and diplomatically leave the eastern boundary to Congress.[48] This received little support, however, primarily out of fear that an open boundary would embroil Congress in endless wrangling over slavery, frustrating the object of speedy admission into the Union.[49] Several delegates contended that California should not include the area east of the Sierra Nevada because the Mormon residents at Salt Lake had no representation at the convention,[50] and, in any case it was "a great desert . . . of no value whatever."[51] In the end, this view commanded a consensus; the boundary written into the Constitution of 1849 remains in effect today.

The convention adjourned on October 13, 1849, after six weeks of work. Its product was submitted to Californians a month later, and, by vote of 12,061 to 811, the people approved the new constitution.[52] At the same election, Peter Burnett was elected governor and assumed office on December 15, 1849, Governor Riley having resigned three days earlier. On December 20, the legislature began to function, electing John Frémont and William Gwin U.S. senators and enacting laws for the benefit of the people, including the establishment of a functioning judiciary. California was a de facto state and operated as such from December 1849. Formal admission came on September 9, 1850, and when it occurred, Congress "voted to admit the state without any question being raised as to the manner in which the constitution was made, or the election of state officers, or the calling of the convention." As Peter Conmy has summarized the process, "it was the will of the people at every step of the way."[53]

■ THE 1879 CONSTITUTION: "A SORT OF MIXTURE OF CONSTITUTION, CODE, STUMP SPEECH, AND MANDAMUS"

The three decades from 1849 to 1879 brought large changes to the social and economic fabric of California. Population increased to 865,000, 234,000 of whom were situated in San Francisco alone.[54] Southern California was a sparsely populated agricultural region. More economically important than mining were agriculture and manufacturing. These changes had not, however, brought

---

[48] Browne, Report of the Debates, p. 176.

[49] Ibid., p. 173 (remarks of Lansford Hastings). See also Hunt, The Genesis of California's First Constitution, p. 48.

[50] Ibid., pp. 170–71, 185, 191; cf. p. 421.

[51] Ibid., p. 187 (remarks of John Sutter).

[52] Conmy, The Constitutional Beginnings of California, p. 23.

[53] Ibid., pp. 23–25.

[54] Swisher, Motivation and Political Technique, p. 6. At the time the County of San Francisco included the present-day County of San Mateo.

universal prosperity. Rather, the 1870s saw large-scale unemployment, business failures, homelessness, foreclosures, bank panics and failures, and a collapse of the speculative market in mining stocks.

These maladies were aggravated by a sense of "keen outrage . . . that something had gone terribly wrong in the political process."[55] The 1849 convention's qualified faith in a democratic legislative process had soured as a result of open manipulation of corrupt legislators by the railroads, giant corporate ranchers, and other large business interests.[56] In turn, the possibility of cynical political manipulation was fueled in part by radical changes in the structure of the economy.

Large mining corporations employing individuals under a wage system had replaced the individual gold digger. The Central Pacific Railroad combination controlled 70 percent of the railroad mileage in the state and exercised that control in the ruthless fashion of classic monopoly. The rise of manufacturing created a class of wage laborers whose tenure fluctuated with the business fortunes of their employers. With the economic stagnation of the 1870s, "large numbers of [these] men were turned loose, without income and without employment, . . . to aid in the . . . agitation for political and social change."[57] In addition, farmers suffered drought conditions during the winter of 1876–1877, which drove them deeper into debt and made them ever more resentful of banks, taxation policies perceived as discriminatory, and large, wealthy landowners.[58]

The unemployed gathered and agitated in the larger cities, particularly San Francisco, some finding the Chinese an easy scapegoat. Thousands of Chinese laborers had been imported to build the railroad eastward across the Sierra Nevadas, and upon completion of the railroad, some Chinese turned to agriculture and small business. Chinese laborers generally were willing to work at lower wages than white laborers.[59] Resentment toward the Chinese was a key factor behind the formation of the Workingmen's party, an organization instrumental in calling for the 1878 convention.[60] Dennis Kearney, a charismatic thirty-one-year-old Irishman imbued with social radicalism, great oratorical skill, and

---

[55] Harry Scheiber, "Race, Radicalism, and Reform: Historical Perspective on the 1879 California Constitution," Hastings Const. L.Q. 17 (1989): 35, 37.

[56] See, e.g., Swisher, Motivation and Political Technique, p. 53, quoting newspaper editorials to the effect that "Leland Stanford and a corps of trained lieutenants openly manipulated" the legislature. See also E. B. Willis and P. K. Stockton, Debates and Proceedings of the Constitutional Convention of the State of California (Sacramento, Calif., 1880), p. 533 (hereinafter cited as Debates and Proceedings).

[57] Swisher, Motivation and Political Technique, p. 9.

[58] Ibid., p. 6.

[59] Leon David, "Our California Constitutions: Retrospections in This Bicentennial Year," Hastings Const. L.Q. 3 (1976): 697, 720.

[60] See Swisher, Motivation and Political Technique, p. 11, quoting a "manifesto" of the Workingmen's party. See generally Alexander Saxton, "The Indispensable Enemy, Labor and the Anti-Chinese Movement in California (Berkeley: University of California Press, 1971).

shrill, potent racism, spearheaded the party, which became a militant force in San Francisco and other cities.

The Workingmen promised to rid the state of the Chinese; their slogan in organizing for the convention was "The Chinese Must Go!" One savage incident took place in Los Angeles in 1871 when close to a thousand whites (almost one-sixth of the population) descended on Chinatown and all but laid it to waste, taking the lives of 22 Chinese.[61] Other attacks, almost as brutal, occurred in San Francisco in 1877.[62]

Meanwhile, among farmers, the Granger movement prospered as economic adversity and drought dramatized the need for government regulation to curb the discriminatory and monopolistic practices of railroads, steamship lines, and public utilities. Granger discontent with the railroads was but one facet of a larger backlash in public opinion toward the railroads. The need to gain control over the railroad corporations was undoubtedly a main reason for the 1878–1879 convention.

In their infancy in the early 1860s, California railroads were supported by counties, cities, and the legislature through generous subsidies and land grants for construction. But small companies increasingly came under the control of the Central Pacific Railroad, which itself was in the hands of a few powerful men: Collis Huntington, Leland Stanford, Charles Crocker, Mark Hopkins, and David Coulton. By the late 1870s, the company controlled over 85 percent of the state's rail lines and was both the largest landowner and largest employer in California.[63] Charging arbitrary freight rates, it favored certain merchants and ruined others and further undermined public opinion. Location of new routes was decided by bribery, not need, with the knowledge that whole towns could be destroyed if the railroad refused to service them.[64]

Given these social and political realities, the legislature passes a bill in February 1878 calling for 152 delegates to be elected to attend a constitutional convention: 3 from each senatorial district plus 32 at-large delegates. Such was the fear of Dennis Kearney's Workingmen that a Republican and Democratic fusion slate of at-large candidates was developed; nonpartisan and Democratic tickets also appeared. The Workingmen elected 51 of the 152 delegates, making them a force to be reckoned with but leaving them powerless to control the convention without support from other quarters. The apparent allies of the Workingmen were the small farmers, who possessed heavily mortgaged property and nursed grievances against land monopolists, banks, and other large corporations. Their natural enemies consisted of the remainder of the delegates—a mixture of large

[61] R. Harvey, The Dynamics of California Government and Politics (Monterey, Calif.: Brooks/Cole, 1985), p. 15.

[62] Swisher, Motivation and Political Technique, p. 10.

[63] Ibid., p. 45; Harvey, The Dynamics of California Government and Politics, p. 15.

[64] See Swisher, Motivation and Political Technique, p. 47.

capitalists, their lawyers, and a few great landholders. But the Workingmen delegates lacked leadership ability and never exerted the kind of influence their sheer numbers seemed to promise.[65]

Nevertheless, the influence of the Workingmen and the Grangers can be seen in all the principal issues that preoccupied the convention; controlling corporate power and rendering it accountable, reforming and distributing more equitably the burden of taxation, restricting or even expelling the Chinese, expanding women's rights, controlling the tendency of the legislature to legislate for the benefit of narrow interest groups, and even in the largely symbolic issue of the degree of autonomy possessed by California within the federal union.

Corporate Power and Privilege

During the convention, corporations were denounced as "monstrous monopolies," compared to "barnacles clinging to the body of the people,"[66] branded as unnecessary[67] and a "corrupting influence" upon the state,[68] and defined as a "corrupt combination of individuals, formed together for the purpose of escaping individual responsibility for their acts."[69] Thus, the convention's committee on corporations recommended that the new constitution include fourteen sections generally designed to curb corporate power, with another nine sections directed at the specific railroad menace.[70] The convention approved these provisions after much debate. For seventeen days the delegates debated the proposed sections regulating railroad rates, devoting 150 pages of the official record to the matter. In the end, they adopted provisions that created an elected railroad commission to establish rates (Art. XII, sec. 22), prevented railroads from raising rates without the consent of the commission (Art. XII, sec. 20), and prohibited railroads from discrimination in rates (Art. XII, sec. 21).

These provisions were "not as severe as the workingmen would have" desired but "went much farther than most corporation sympathizers would have" preferred. They were sufficiently antagonistic to corporate interests that they "marked the beginning of hostility to all acts of the convention by a large section of the press," presaging the bitter fight to prevent popular adoption of the new constitution.[71] In the end, the railroad commission proved inefficacious, for its commissioners, including such erstwhile Workingmen stalwarts as

---

[65] Ibid., pp. 17–28.

[66] Debates and Proceedings, p. 402 (remarks of Mr. Dowling).

[67] Ibid., p. 385 (remarks of Volney Howard).

[68] Ibid., p. 377 (remarks of Morris Estee).

[69] Ibid., p. 388 (remarks of C. C. O'Donnell).

[70] Ibid., p. 235.

[71] Swisher, Motivation and Political Technique, p. 64.

Charles Beer-stecher, proved easily susceptible "to the blandishments of corporate influence."[72]

Taxation and Land Reform

The 1849 Constitution had little to say on taxation, providing only that all property should be taxed "in proportion to its value" and requiring that "taxation shall be equal and uniform throughout the state."[73] Since the term *property* was not defined, the legislature and the courts were free to inject substance into the term. This became most contentious in the context of taxation of mortgaged farmland and the mortgages themselves.

California legislation and a series of decisions of the California Supreme Court interpreting the 1849 Constitution's taxation provisions had resulted in the taxation of mortgaged farmland at its total value without regard to the mortgage indebtedness encumbering the land, while the mortgage loan itself, in the hands of the lender, entirely escaped taxation. These conditions were "widely and bitterly criticized . . . by debtors and tax payers, for it was recognized that creditors were . . . escaping their share of the burden of taxes."[74] From the perspective of farmers, the fiscal demands of the state were satisfied disproportionately out of the already thin pockets of the small, indebted landowners. A new device was needed, one that would ensure that creditors paid taxes on their property and prevent them from shifting the burden of those taxes to their borrowers through contractual conditions or higher interest rates.

The Grangers and the Workingmen set about to accomplish this task, but "knotty problems of finance were too much for most of them."[75] The convention ultimately adopted a series of provisions designed to accomplish the ends of the Granger-Workingmen alliance, which proved inefficacious. Although the Grangers and Workingmen obtained constitutional provisions altering the specific practices they regarded as the source of their misery, they failed to secure the enactment of a usury limitation, thus allowing lenders to raise interest rates by an amount sufficient to pay the taxes imposed on the creditors by the constitutional changes.

Other taxation devices were adopted in an attempt to break or weaken large corporate landholdings, especially by railroads. The problem was acute; small farmers paid taxes at the rate of $125 million annually, while large landowners paid taxes of only $38 million on four times the acreage.[76] The Grangers and Workingmen sought to equalize land taxation in the hope that the large land

[72] Ibid., p. 112.

[73] 1849 Const., Art. XI, sec. 13.

[74] Swisher, Motivation and Political Technique, p. 69.

[75] Ibid., p. 73.

[76] Hubert Bancroft, History of California (San Francisco: History Company, 1888), 7:383 n. 14.

speculators, whose holdings lay fallow, would pay at the same rate as the small yeoman farmers who tilled the soil. Another provision sought to impose higher taxes on railroads by denying them certain deductions available to nonrailroad landowners. This attempt to punish railroad corporations failed as a result of prolonged, and ultimately successful, litigation by the railroads.[77]

These provisions were simply the substantive counterparts to the hortatory condemnation of "land monopoly" contained in Article XVII, section 2, which declared that "the holding of large tracts of land, . . . by individuals or corporations, is against the public policy and should be discouraged by all means not inconsistent with the rights of public property." No doubt it was the wholly aspirational nature of declarations of this sort that led Henry George, the land reformer and advocate of a single tax on land, to label the convention's effort as "a sort of mixture of constitution, code, stump speech, and mandamus."[78] Yet coupled with such empty rhetoric were more meaningful devices to curb the power of wealth, such as Article XIII, section 11's grant to the legislature of the power to tax individual and corporate incomes.

Anti-Chinese Racism

The Workingmen's refrain, "The Chinese must go," led the convention quickly to establish a standing committee to draft an article dealing with Chinese settlers.[79] The committee "agreed that something ought to be done," but there "was strenuous disagreement . . . as to what should be done."[80] The able and conservative lawyers on the committee recognized that the U.S. Supreme Court had already precluded the possibility that California could impose unilateral barriers to Chinese immigration,[81] a fact that, in their view, left California in the position of supplicant to Congress for national legislation to prohibit further Chinese entry into the United States. More radical elements of the committee insisted that California had the power to prohibit Chinese immigration and offered a proposed section directing the legislature to do just that. Other proposed provisions would have stripped corporations of their charters and individuals of their vote if they employed Chinese, prohibited Chinese from the right to sue, catch fish, own property, make contracts, or obtain employment.[82]

The package proposal was attacked as an indefensible "denial of [Chinese] right[s] to the protection of the law" and "as a plan of starvation by

---

[77] Swisher, Motivation and Political Technique, p. 112.

[78] Henry George, "The Kearney Agitation in California," Popular Sci. Monthly 17 (1880): 433, 445, quoted in ibid., p. 105.

[79] Debates and Proceedings, p. 77.

[80] Ibid., p. 86.

[81] Chy Lung v. Freeman, 92 U.S. 275, 23 L. Ed. 550 (1875).

[82] Swisher, Motivation and Political Technique, p. 87.

constitutional provision."[83] Moreover, such proposals were dismissed as violative of U.S. treaty obligations with China. As the debate wore on, the advocates of radical action lost ground, and the delegates heeded conservative pleas not to include provisions that would probably be declared unconstitutional. However, the delegates did not abandon their racist impulses, for the final draft included Article XIX, consisting of four sections designed to make life more difficult for Chinese-Californians.

Section 1 was a directive to the legislature to "prescribe all necessary regulations" to protect the state "from the burdens and evils arising from the presence of aliens who are or may become vagrants, paupers, mendicants, criminals, or . . . otherwise dangerous . . . to the state, and to impose conditions upon which such persons may reside in the state, and to provide the means and mode of their removal from the state." In its emasculated form, the section amounted more to a racist plea for legislative action than a self-executing prohibition of Chinese-Californians.

In a similar vein was section 4, which declared that "the legislature shall discourage [Chinese] immigration by all the means within their power" and directed the legislature to "prohibit the introduction into this state of Chinese." At once more specific and enigmatic was the section's pronouncement that "Asiatic coolieism is a form of human slavery, . . . is forever prohibited . . . and all contracts for coolie labor shall be void." To the extent the provision had any independent force to exclude Chinese immigrants, it was swiftly declared unconstitutional.[84]

Not all of Article XIX was hortatory. Section 2 prohibited corporations from employing "any Chinese or Mongolian" but depended on the legislature to enforce the prohibition. Ultimately, however, the federal courts declared the prohibition invalid as violative of federal treaty obligations with China.[85] Section 3, which prohibited Chinese from employment on public works, was similarly invalidated.[86]

The Workingmen championed the cause of the underdog with a great deal of selectivity; only the Caucasian underdog had a friend in the Workingmen's caucus. In the end, this blind fervor of racism bore no legal fruit, although "the article seemed to provide greater temptations to oratorical display than that of any other topic considered by the convention."[87]

---

[83] Debates and Proceedings, p. 630 (remarks of John F. Miller).

[84] State v. Steamship "Constitution," 42 Cal. 578 (1872); Ex parte Ah Fook, 49 Cal. 402 (1874); In re Parrott, 1 F. 481 (C.C.D. Cal. 1880); Baker v. City of Portland, 2 F. Cas. 472 (C.C.D. Or. 1879) (No. 777).

[85] See In re Parrott, 1 F. 481 (C.C.D. Cal. 1880); Baker v. City of Portland, 2 F. Cas. 472 (C.C.D. Or. 1879) (No. 777).

[86] Baker v. City of Portland, 2 F. Cas. 472 (C.C.D. Or. 1879) (No. 777).

[87] Swisher, Motivation and Political Technique, p. 92.

Women's Rights

The 1849 Constitution's provision protecting a married woman's right to her separate property was the first instance of a state constitution's recognizing a married woman's separate property;[88] by 1879, it was so commonly accepted that it was not questioned during the 1879 convention.

By contrast, a spirited debate over women's suffrage occurred. Some argued that political participation of women would help to purge corruption in government. Others asserted that allowing women in politics would taint their moral character.[89] Although the delegates repeatedly flirted with the idea of female suffrage, in the end an overwhelming majority of delegates accepted the circumscribed domestic role already established by societal customs and legal precedents and denied women the right to vote.[90] It would not be until 1911 that voters, by constitutional amendment, would give California women the right to vote, revising Article II, section 1 of the 1879 Constitution.[91]

Given the defeat of women's suffrage, it seems paradoxical that the following provision received so little opposition: "No person shall, on account of sex, be disqualified from entering upon or pursuing any lawful business, vocation or profession" (Art. XX, sec. 18). A possible explanation, offered by at least one authority, is that the delegates assumed that only a handful of unmarried or widowed women would be interested in pursuing a career.[92] More likely, the provision was spawned by a celebrated lawsuit, occurring at the same moment in 1879, in which Clara Shortridge Foltz and Laura De Force Gordon sought to compel Hastings College of the Law, a unit of the University of California, to admit them.[93] Six days after the adoption of section 18, the convention approved, by a vote of 103 to 20, Article IX, section 9, which declared: "No person shall be

[88] Hunt, The Genesis of California's First Constitution, p. 45.

[89] Debates and Proceedings, pp. 1004–16; Swisher, Motivation and Political Technique; Noel Sargent, "The California Constitutional Convention of 1878–79," Calif. L. Rev. 6(1917): 1, 17–19.

[90] Debates and Proceedings, p. 1016. Professor Barbara Babcock has pointed out that the cause of women's suffrage came much closer to fruition than the final vote would suggest. See Barbara Babcock, "Clara Shortridge Foltz: Constitution-Maker," Ind. L.J. 66 (1991): 849, 879–901.

[91] See Sally Furay, " Women's Rights under the California Constitution," in Law and California Society: 100 Years of the State Constitution (San Diego, Calif.: San Diego Union, 1980), p. 14.

[92] Ibid., pp. 14–15.

[93] See Barbara Babcock, "Clara Shortridge Foltz: 'First Woman,'" Ariz. L. Rev. 30 (1988): 673, 707–8; "Clara Shortridge Foltz: Constitution-Maker," pp. 849, 893–901. Professor Babcock also contends that "the easy passage of [the section] served as a sort of consolation prize for the failure of suffrage" (p. 899). Article XX, section 18 was introduced and adopted by the convention, without debate, during a continuance in the Gordon/Foltz litigation with Hastings. The section was introduced on February 17, 1879, and adopted on February 20. Debates and Proceedings, pp. 1395, 1424. Although Foltz ultimately failed in her effort to complete her law studies at Hastings, she was awarded her degree posthumously by Hastings in 1991.

debarred admission to any of the collegiate departments of the University [of California] on account of sex." When introduced, one delegate objected that the clause was unnecessary, since "both [sexes] are taught there now." Joseph Ayers responded by acidly observing that "recent history points to the fact that there is a necessity for it."[94] The connection between the highly publicized suit by Foltz and Gordon for admission to a unit of the University of California and the constitutional provision seems undeniable. Nearly a century later, in 1976, voters would extend the prohibition against discrimination in employment because of sex to include race, creed, color, or national or ethnic origin (Art. I, sec. 8).

Generalized Distrust of the Legislature

In addition to specific bias against railroads, financial institutions, and business corporations, the delegates of 1878–1879 evidenced a far deeper distrust of the legislature than their counterparts of thirty years earlier had, typified by the remark of one delegate "that there is a widespread sentiment among the people, opposed to legislation generally."[95] This view manifested itself most clearly in Article IV, section 25, which barred the legislature from enacting "local or special laws" in any of thirty-three "enumerated cases," including "the punishment of crimes . . ., assessment or collection of taxes . . .," adjustment of debts due to the state, and "in all other cases where a general law can be made applicable."

Further distrust of both legislators and the interest groups seeking special laws can be seen in Article IV, section 35, which declared lobbying—seeking "to influence the vote of a [legislator] by bribery, promise of reward, intimidation, or other dishonest means"—a felony. Legislators who succumbed to these illicit temptations were not only felons but were also "disfranchised and forever disqualified from holding any office or public trust."

The Independent Role of the California Constitution

Delegates clashed sharply over an issue that was largely beyond their control: the classic problem of how much autonomy California possessed within the federal Union. The clashes surfaced in two distinct contexts. The first appears to be completely instrumental: whether California possessed any unilateral authority to expel lawfully resident Chinese-Californians or to prohibit unilaterally the further immigration of Chinese to California. Only the most violent and radical exponents of anti-Chinese racism held to the view that California possessed any such unilateral authority, typified by the extreme declaration that "if our government don't protect us, and if our government is to make this State a China

---

[94] Debates and Proceedings, p. 1476.

[95] Ibid., p. 744.

Empire, I say we have a right to secede."[96] The other context was less instrumental but even more symbolic.

As adopted, Article I, section 3 of the 1879 Constitution provided that "the State of California is an inseparable part of the American Union, and the Constitution of the United States is the supreme law of the land." The initial proposal had further declared that the U.S. Constitution was "the great charter of our liberties."[97] Not so, cried delegate Rolfe, for "we had State charters before there was any Constitution of the United States."[98] Others echoed him, asserting "that the State Constitution is as much or more the charter of our liberties than the Constitution of the United States."[99] Even the conservative delegates conceded that reliance on the federal Constitution as the principal author of liberties was "a mistake historically, a mistake in law, and it is a blunder all around."[100] Thus, the convention's refusal to label the federal Constitution "the great charter of our liberties" provided a clear indicator "that the idea of rights rooted in the state's own constitution was a robust one,"[101] a sentiment that found even clearer expression with the adoption in 1974 of Article I, section 24: "Rights guaranteed by this Constitution are not dependent on those guaranteed by the United States Constitution."

When the work of the convention was done and its product submitted to the people, reactionary interests lobbied hard for its defeat. The proposed constitution was described as a document propelled by "all the prejudices and passions of the hour," one that "places railroads and other corporations at the mercy of those whose interest it will be to steal from them; that makes it almost impossible for banks and corporations to exist, and that threatens the rights of private property."[102] Despite these characterizations, from the vantage point of today it seems clear that its regulations upon private enterprise "were well within the ambit of the emerging legislative and constitutional tendencies"[103] of the late nineteenth and twentieth centuries. But at the time, it was denounced as "the work of a clamorous mob of ignorant foreign miscreants, who desire . . . to plunder the accumulations of industry."[104]

---

[96] Ibid., p. 1186.

[97] Ibid., pp. 237–43.

[98] Ibid., p. 238.

[99] Ibid., p. 1182 (remarks of Mr. Howard).

[100] Ibid., p. 238 (remarks of Mr. Howard).

[101] Scheiber, "Race, Radicalism, and Reform," p. 78.

[102] Swisher, Motivation and Political Technique, p. 105, quoting the San Francisco Argonaut, March 8, 1879.

[103] Scheiber, "Race, Radicalism, and Reform," p. 60.

[104] San Francisco Argonaut, March 15, 1879, quoted in Swisher, Motivation and Political Technique, p. 124 n.29.

On May 7, 1879, over 145,000 Californians (90 percent of the electorate) voted on the question of adopting the new constitution. Nearly 78,000 favored adoption, while a shade more than 67,000 were opposed.[105] The cities of northern and central California opposed adoption; rural districts favored it. Southern California, rural and urban, favored adoption. Thus, in a reversal of today's California electoral patterns, the populous and urban north was the agent of conservative reaction, while the rural districts and the south were the seedbeds of more radical political experimentation.

■ THE PROGRESSIVE MOVEMENT: "GIVE US A SQUARE DEAL FOR CHRIST'S SAKE"

For the most part, the 1879 Constitution failed to solve the problems behind the constitutional revision of 1878–1879. The legislature avoided the new constitutional prohibitions on special legislation, corporations successfully challenged many of the taxation features of the new constitution, and the lack of usury limits permitted creditors to raise interest rates in order to pass their new tax burdens on to debtors.[106]

Most important, the Southern Pacific–Central Pacific Railroad continued to have a stranglehold on the economic and political life of California. As the largest landowner in California and Nevada and with almost a virtual monopoly on California's transportation facilities, the railroad had enormous economic power and did not hesitate to use it to further its interests. It "charged all the traffic would bear," forced towns on prospective routes to pay a heavy tribute or be bypassed, demanded the right to examine the books of private companies in order to increase their rates when their profits increased, and gave rate favors only to other large corporations like Standard Oil.[107] The railroad translated its economic power into political power by purchasing the services of legislators, judges, and commissioners, both state and national,[108] and controlling the political parties and conventions in the state.[109] Even the Railroad Commission

[105] Swisher, Motivation and Political Technique, p. 109. The precise vote was 77,959 in favor, 67,134 opposed.

[106] Ibid., pp. 112–13. But see David, "Our California Constitutions Retrospections in This Bicentennial Year," pp. 751–52.

[107] George S. Mowry, The California Progressives (Berkeley, Calif.: University of California Press, 1951), pp. 10–11.

[108] Ibid., p. 13: There existed "long lists of state and national officeholders who were little more than hired servants of the railroad, to be elevated or dismissed from public life according to their zeal in promoting the company's interest."

[109] Ibid., p. 16. The power of the Southern Pacific-Central Pacific Railroad "was evident in almost every party convention during the period and in practically every election." See also Gerald D. Nash, State Government and Economic Development (New York: Arno Press, 1964), p. 159: "By awarding

established by the Constitution of 1879 quickly came under the control of the railroad interests.[110]

Around the turn of the century, however, the Southern Pacific-Central Pacific Railroad's heavy-handed use of power began to backfire. Outrages accumulated: the Mussel Slough incident, publicized in Frank Norris's *The Octopus*, in which five settlers who resisted the railroad were murdered; the railroad's attempt to force Los Angeles to move its harbor from San Pedro to Santa Monica where the railroad controlled most of the land;[111] the railroad's cynical and open manipulation of the state Republican nominating convention held in Santa Cruz in 1906; and the conduct of the legislature of 1907, "which set a new record for wastefulness, unscrupulousness, and subservience to the [Railroad's] machine."[112]

Resentment against railroad dominance in California inspired a number of reform movements within both the Republican and Democratic parties, eventually coalescing around the Progressive movement. After some preliminary skirmishes, the Progressives won a near majority in the legislature of 1909. Poor organization and the lack of a definite plan hampered their efforts in the legislature, resulting only in the enactment of a direct primary law and a law giving the Railroad Commission limited new powers.[113]

In 1910, the Progressive candidate for governor, Hiram Johnson, won the Republican primary and the general election. Victory was most sobering to Johnson. During the campaign, he had remarked to an aide that he had no idea what he would do if he was elected governor. The aide replied that "they could institute a system of direct legislation . . . so that when they were defeated at some inevitable date in the future, the old machine would never again have the power over the people of California it once enjoyed. Johnson . . . confess[ed] that he did not know what direct legislation was, . . . [and asked for an explanation] how the initiative, referendum and recall worked."[114] It is hardly surprising that "the chaplain opened the first session of the 1911 California legislature with an extraordinary plea: 'Give us a square deal for Christ's sake.' "[115]

The Progressive movement stressed the declaration of Article I, section 2 of the 1849 and 1879 Constitutions: "All political power is inherent in the people."

---

legal fees, by contributions to both major political parties, by granting special favors, free passes, and discriminations, the Southern Pacific gained influence over officials in strategic positions."

[110] Swisher, Motivation and Political Technique, pp. 112–13. See also Mowry, The California Progressives, p. 18.

[111] Spencer C. Olin, Jr., California's Prodigal Sons: Hiram Johnson and the Progressives, 1911–1917 (Berkeley, Calif.: University of California Press, 1968), p. 5.

[112] John W. Caughey, California (Englewood Cliffs, N.J.: Prentice-Hall, 1953), p. 461.

[113] Olin, California's Prodigal Sons, pp. 12–17. On the legislation giving limited additional powers to the Railroad Commission, see also Franklin Hichborn, Story of the Session of the California Legislature of 1911 (San Francisco: James H. Barry Co., 1911), pp. 143ff.

[114] Mowry, The California Progressives, p. 135.

[115] Ibid., p. 139.

To that end, they sought to bypass the perceived corrupt and lax legislature by the initiative: a device for direct legislation and amendment of the constitution that would ultimately add dozens of amendments to California's Constitution. The Progressives believed such "direct democracy" would mean the public could check the power of the legislature and lobbyists, as well as address controversial measures that the legislature was unwilling or unable to address.

With an ardent advocate of reform as governor and a sizable majority of the legislature belonging to the Progressive movement, the legislature of 1911 proposed twenty-three constitutional amendments during its first session, incorporating these structural reforms, women's suffrage, and social reforms such as workmen's compensation.[116] All but one of these proposed amendments were approved by the voters at a special election on October 10,1911. Taken as a whole, the actions of the legislature and the people during 1911 constituted the most sweeping revision of the California Constitution in the twentieth century.

■ CONSTITUTIONAL CHANGE AFTER THE PROGRESSIVE MOVEMENT: "CONSTANT AMENDMENT HAS PRODUCED AN INSTRUMENT BAD IN FORM"

The 1879 Constitution permitted narrow and specific amendment of the constitution to occur by legislative initiative approved by the voters. More sweeping constitutional change or revision could occur; only by constitutional convention, proposed by the legislature and approved by the voters. This distinction between amendment and revision was recognized as early as 1894 by the California courts and was explicitly invoked in *McFadden v. Jordan* (1948) to preclude revision by amendment.[117] While the Progressives had successfully amended the constitution to permit amendments to occur by popular initiative, the distinction between amendments and revision remained (as it does today) a fixture of California constitutional law. From 1879 to 1962 the result was a constant parade of amendments and proposed amendments, punctuated by unheeded cries for a convention to revise the awkward document produced by the 1878–1879 convention and regularly amended thereafter.

Dissatisfaction with the 1879 Constitution manifested itself in a proposal of the 1897 legislature to submit to the people the question of whether to call a new constitutional convention. It is unclear whether the people regarded this as but another attempt by the railroad cabal more firmly to control the processes of government or as an ill-advised scheme to inject more radical notions into the

[116] California Secretary of State, A Study of Ballot Measures: 1884–1986 (unpaginated) (Sacramento, Calif.: Secretary of State, n.d.) (hereinafter cited as Ballot Measures). See also David, "Our California Constitutions," pp. 752–54.

[117] See McFadden v. Jordan, 32 Cal. 2d 330, 196 P. 2d 787 (1948); Livermore v. Waite, 102 Cal. 113, 36 P. 424 (1894).

frame of government. Whatever the motivation, 60 percent of the electorate rejected the idea in November 1898.[118] The 1913 session of the legislature again submitted to the people the question of a constitutional convention, and in the general election of November 3, 1914, the proposal was soundly defeated.[119] It is possible that the defeat was partly attributable to the recent adoption of the popular constitutional initiative, for the 1914 ballot carried eight such proposals, three of which succeeded.

The idea of a third constitutional convention persisted. The 1919 legislature proposed a convention, and the voters rejected it at the 1920 general election.[120] However, as the number of constitutional amendments mounted, the Constitution of 1879 seemed obsolete in certain areas and swollen with minutiae in others. By 1929, nearly 200 amendments to the 1879 Constitution had been approved.[121] In that year the legislature both asked the people again to approve another convention and authorized the governor to appoint a fifteen-member commission to investigate the need for revision and the calling of a constitutional convention. The ballot question was soundly defeated again on November 4, 1930,[122] but the commission began its work.

The commission report, which included a draft of a revised constitution, was submitted in December 1930. The thrust of the proposed revision was to simplify the from of the constitution, reducing the document from 65,000 to 27,000 words by deleting obsolete provisions, inconsistencies, and statutory-type detail.[123] The commission concluded that the substance of existing provisions adequately preserved the "natural rights" of the people, but "when it comes to the from of the Constitution, we find that its constant amendment has produced an instrument bad in from, inconsistent, . . . loaded with unnecessary detail, encumbered with provisions of no permanent value, and replete with matter . . . more properly . . . contained in the statute law of the State."[124] Since the voters had recently rejected a call for a constitutional convention, there was no constitutional vehicle by which a comprehensive revision could be submitted to the people. In any case, the legislature was paralyzed due to the fear of radical

---

118 Ballot Measures, results of election of November 8, 1898 (42,556 for, 65,007 against) (not paginated).

119 Ibid., results of election of November 3, 1914 (180,111 for, 442,687 against) (not paginated).

120 Ibid., results of election of November 2, 1920 (203, 240 for, 428,002 against) (not paginated).

121 Ibid., tabular summation of election results from 1884 through 1986 (not paginated).

122 Ibid., results of election of November 4, 1930 (263,683 for, 585, 089 against) (not paginated).

123 Proposed Revision of the California Constitution, Report to the California Legislature of the California Constitution Revision Commission, Part 1 (Sacramento, Calif.: Calif. Const. Revision Comm., 1970), p. 11 (hereinafter cited as Revision Commission Report).

124 Report of the California Constitutional Commission, December 1930, p. 9, quoted in Revision Commission Report, p. 12.

sentiments prevailing in any constitutional alteration attempted during the depression years.[125]

By 1933 the political winds had shifted abruptly, and the legislature proposed with near unanimity that the people again consider a constitutional convention.[126] This time it succeeded, with slightly over 51 percent of the electorate voting to approve such a convention in November 1934.[127] Inexplicably, however, the 1935 legislature failed to pass any enabling legislation, and the matter died.[128]

Revision fever struck anew in 1947 when the legislature created the Joint Interim Committee on Constitutional Revision. Hopes for a streamlined version of the 1879 document were smothered as various private interest groups, fearing that revision would be prejudicial to their interests, persuaded the commission to limit itself to removing obsolete material.[129] The commission's final report, adopted by the legislature in 1949 and substantially approved by the voters, reduced the constitution by approximately 14,500 words but without substantive alteration.

In 1959, the California Assembly commissioned a study of techniques and procedures that could be used to revise the constitution, resulting in a recommendation that the constitution be amended to authorize the legislature to submit an entire revision to the people. An amendment to this effect was proposed and approved by the voters in November 1962. To implement the mandate, the 1963 legislature created the California Constitution Revision Commission, a sixty-member committee that included distinguished state leaders drawn from virtually every sector. Some pruning of the constitutional orchard was clearly in order since the California Constitution then contained more than 75,000 words—ten times longer than the U.S. Constitution and longer than any other state constitution except that of Louisiana.[130]

The work of the revision commission began in 1964 and was not completed until the election of June 1976. Ultimately, all but two articles of the constitution

---

[125] Bernard Hyink, "California Revises Its Constitution," W. Pol. Q. 22 (1969): 637, 639.

[126] Ernest A. Engelbert and John G. Gunnell, State Constitutional Revision in California: An Analysis Prepared for the Citizens Legislative Advisory Commission (Sacramento, Calif., 1961), p. 11. The Assembly approved the resolution 64–0; the Senate approved it by a vote of 29–9.

[127] Ballot Measures, results of election of November 6, 1934 (705, 915 for, 668,080 against) (not paginated).

[128] Engelbert and Gunnell cite an unpublished paper by J. M. Ellis at the University of Southern California for the proposition that "the inaction of the Legislature was . . . likely a manifestation of political conflict." Engelbert and Gunnell, State Constitutional Revision in California, p. 13. The nature of the conflict is not specified, although the close margin of victory of the call for a convention may have triggered some friction.

[129] Revision Commission Report, p. 12.

[130] W. Crouch, J. Bollens, S. Scott, and D. McHenry, California Government and Politics, 4th ed. (Englewood Cliffs, N.J.: Prentice-Hall, 1967), p. 37.

were revised, and some 40,000 words were deleted. The process proved to be intensely political, time-consuming, demanding of great skill in negotiation, compromise, and leadership from both legislature and governor, with success at the polls contingent on an effective political campaign.[131]

Proposition 1-a, the first product of the revision commission, was approved by the voters in November 1966, resulting in the elimination of some 16,000 of the 22,000 words in selected sections. Three major substantive changes were approved: provision for annual legislative sessions, a technical change to the initiative process to encourage the use of statutory rather than constitutional popular initiatives, and elimination of the indirect initiative.

Proposition 1, submitted to the voters in 1968, constituted the second group of recommendations of the revision commission. Substantial revision of seven articles was proposed, involving the transfer of much detail to statutes with the effect of reducing 14,000 words to 2,000. The primary substantive change proposed was to remove selection of the superintendent of public instruction from electoral politics and to permit the legislature and governor to decide on a new method of selection, most likely appointment by the State Board of Education, as in many other states.[132]

Proposition 1 was unexpectedly rejected by the voters. There were several reasons for its defeat, including the complexity of the revision (making informing oneself quite time-consuming), the lack of publicity, an unenthusiastic legislature, the lack of an endorsement by Governor Ronald Reagan, the controversial superintendent issue, and the negative coverage by the *Los Angeles Times*.[133] The Times advised a "no" vote on Proposition 1, which probably accounted for much of the heavy negative vote in southern California. Perhaps most damaging was the perception by many voters that the method of selecting the education superintendent basically took power away from the people.

Despite the defeat of Proposition 1, the California Constitutional Revision Committee proceeded. The 1970 elections produced voter approval of revisions to articles dealing with local government, the civil service, amendment procedures, and further elimination of obsolete provisions.[134] The revision commission issued its final report in 1971, and its recommendations were incorporated into three ballot propositions approved in the 1972 elections, eliminating yet more obsolete verbosity and including the addition of a privacy right to Article I, section 1's enumeration of "inalienable rights."[135] The 1974 elections

[131] Eugene C. Lee, "The Revision of California's Constitution," California Policy Seminar Brief 3 (April 1991) (No. 3): n.p.

[132] Hyink, "California Revises Its Constitution," pp. 648–50.

[133] Ibid., pp. 651–54.

[134] Lee, "The Revision of California's Constitution," n.p.

[135] Ballot Measures, results of election of November 7, 1972 (Proposition 11: 4,861,225 for, 2,871,342 against) (not paginated).

produced approval of five more measures: a clarified restatement and augmentation of the Declaration of Rights, a concise reorganization of the taxation provisions, revision of the recall right, revision of provisions dealing with public utilities, and the substitution of sex-neutral language for masculine pronouns. Finally, voters in 1976 approved a measure reordering and renumbering many of the previously revised articles.[136]

The most significant alterations of this last round of constitutional revision were to the Declaration of Rights, Article I of the constitution. Important additions to the declaration were a prohibition on legislation "respecting an establishment of religion" and a clause granting to all persons the protections of equal protection and due process of law.[137] Finally, in express recognition of both California and constitutional history and the legal role of the California Constitution in federal constitutional law, Article I, section 24 was altered to declare that the "rights guaranteed by this Constitution are not dependent on those guaranteed by the United States Constitution."

The record of constitutional revision since 1879 is spotty at best. Despite repeated attempts to convene a constitutional convention, none has occurred. Piecemeal revision in 1949 and comprehensive revision in the period from 1962 to 1976 complete the picture. The work of the constitutional revision commission in the 1960s and 1970s is especially impressive, since its efforts toward constitutional reform resulted in substantial revision of virtually all of California's Constitution.

On the other hand, the pace of constitutional amendment has rocketed along at a dizzying pace. Through 1986, the California Constitution had been amended 460 times. According to one historian, "The consequences of this mass exercise of the amending power have been to lengthen the ballot beyond the limen of wise discrimination for practically all the voters, to make the constitution into a patchwork miscellany, and to write into it a multitude of special interest provisions."[138]

■ THE RISE AND THREATENED DECLINE OF AN INDEPENDENT CALIFORNIA CONSTITUTION: "RIGHTS GUARANTEED BY THIS CONSTITUTION ARE NOT DEPENDENT ON THOSE GUARANTEED BY THE UNITED STATES CONSTITUTION"

It is abundantly clear that the draftsmen of the 1849 and 1879 constitutions regarded the California Constitution as the principal bulwark protecting the liberties of Californians from governmental encroachment. This attitude, a staple of American constitutional thought from the beginning of the nation, began to

[136] David, "Our California Constitutions," p. 759.

[137] Calif. Const., Art. I, sec. 7.

[138] Caughey, California, p. 568.

dissipate in the twentieth century as the U.S. Supreme Court expanded the doctrine of "selective incorporation" to make most of the guarantees of the federal Bill of Rights applicable to the states via the medium of the due process clause of the Fourteenth Amendment to the federal Constitution. For a considerable period of time, the federally guaranteed rights seemed far more expansive and protective than their state analogues. Accordingly, the independent status of state constitutional rights became a largely forgotten concept. But in recent decades, California, along with many other states, has experienced a renascence of the independent state constitution. The California story, however, carries with it a contrapuntal theme: public misunderstanding of or lack of concern for an independent state constitution coupled with an expendient rejection of the substantive differences from the federal Constitution.

No single event can be identified as the origin of the modern sense of the California Constitution as a document independent of the federal Constitution. Nevertheless, a series of events in the early 1970s provide clear evidence of the development. In 1972 the California Supreme Court, in *People v. Anderson,*[139] invalidated California's death penalty on the ground that it violated Article I section 6's prohibition of cruel *or* unusual punishment. The court expressly made clear that it was not adjudicating the separate issue of whether the death penalty statute was violative of the federal Constitution's prohibition of cruel *and* unusual punishment. Although this was not the first instance in which the court had relied exclusively on the state constitution, eschewing a federal analogue, nor was it the first instance in which the court had interpreted the California Constitution in a fashion more protective of human liberty than the U.S. Constitution,[140] it was perhaps the most dramatic recent declaration of independence from the prevalent federal constitutional norm.

Two years later Californians overwhelmingly approved a restatement and revision of the Declaration of Rights that added to Article I, section 24 an explicit statement of constitutional independence from the federal Constitution: "Rights guaranteed by this Constitution are not dependent on those guaranteed by the United States Constitution."[141] Although the amendment did no more than restate the existing legal condition, its explicit declaration undoubtedly served to galvanize the development of a body of California constitutional law independent of the federal Constitution. This development has occurred with respect to the entire constitution but has been most pronounced in four major areas, in

[139] 6 Cal. 3d 628, 493 P. 2d 880, cert. denied, 406 U.S. 958 (1972).

[140] See, e.g., People v. Clark, 61 Cal. 2d 870, 402 P.2d 856 (1965), and Jerome Falk, "Foreword: The State Constitution: A More Than 'Adequate' Nonfederal Ground," Calif. L. Rev. 61 (1973): 273, 277–79.

[141] Ballot Measures, results of election of November 5, 1974 (Proposition 7: 3,567,443 for; 1,495,929 against) (not paginated).

one of which the retrograde movement away from constitutional independence has almost triumphed.

Rights of the Accused

From the 1960s until the 1980s, the provisions of the California Declaration of Rights pertinent to criminal defendants acquired a substance considerably more protective of the accused than the federal analogues. For example, as early as 1955, in *People v. Cahan*,[142] the California Supreme Court concluded that evidence seized in violation of the search and seizure provisions of the California Constitution must be excluded from subsequent legal proceedings. Because the Cahan court had treated the exclusionary rule it created "as a judicially declared rule of evidence,"[143] it was uncertain whether the California exclusionary rule was merely part of the judiciary's supervisory power of the courts or compelled by the California Constitution.[144] Whatever its true origin, the *Cahan* exclusionary rule soon spawned a considerable body of California exclusionary rule law that differed in substance from the federal exclusionary rules, first adopted in 1961.[145] In almost every instance of difference, the California constitutional rule was more protective of an accused's rights than under the analogous federal constitutional guarantee.

These developments eventually motivated a ballot initiative, entitled the "Victims' Bill of Rights," which appeared on the June 1982 ballot. It was approved by a considerable margin[146] and added Article I, section 28 to the constitution, subsection (d) of which provides that "relevant evidence shall not be excluded in any criminal proceeding." The provision was plainly intended to abrogate all California exclusionary rule decisions based solely on the California Constitution or other California law and establishing stricter standards than those required under the federal Constitution.

This countertrend away from an independent state constitution accelerated tremendously with another ballot initiative, Proposition 115, on the June 1990 ballot. California voters approved the initiative, which, among other things, added to Article I, section 24 of the constitution a provision that the California constitutional rights of an accused shall be "construed by the courts of this state in a manner consistent with the Constitution of the United States." Lest there be any residual doubt about the intended consistency, the new language added that

---

[142] 44 Cal. 2d 434, 282 P.2d 905 (1955).

[143] Ibid., p. 442.

[144] See, e.g., Kaplan v. Superior Court, 6 Cal. 3d 150, 161, 491 P.2d 1 (1971) (suggesting that *Cahan* was "constitutionally compelled").

[145] Mapp v. Ohio, 376 U.S. 643 (1961).

[146] Ballot Measures, results of election of June 8, 1982 (Proposition 8: 2,826,081 for, 2,182,710 against) (not paginated).

"this Constitution shall not be construed by the courts to offer greater rights to criminal defendants than those afforded by the Constitution of the United States."

There could hardly be a plainer renunciation of the independence of the California Constitution. Indeed, the California Supreme Court considered it so radical a transformation of the constitution that in *Raven v. Deukmejian,*[147] decided in December 1990, only six months after adoption of the amendment, it invalidated the provision on the ground that the measure constituted a revision, rather than an amendment, to the constitution. The court took this action because Article XVIII permits popular initiative measures to amend but not revise the constitution. In *Raven* the court first concluded that a measure making substantial qualitative changes to the constitutional scheme could amount to a revision and then determined that the new version of Article I, section 24 constituted a revision since it "would substantially alter the substance and integrity of the state Constitution as a document of independent force and effect."[148]

Of course, there remains the possibility that the legislature, acting pursuant to Article XVIII, section 1, which permits the legislature to propose constitutional revisions, may submit the same measure to the voters. There is as yet no certainty that the movement to reject the independence of the California Constitution has died. However, this nascent countertrend has been limited to the constitutional rights of criminal defendants. Unfortunately, there is no reason to suppose that the interests of other minorities are any safer at the hands of an aroused California electorate indifferent to the integrity of the California Constitution and determined to squeeze as dry as possible the constitutional rights of some disfavored minority.

The Right of Privacy

In November 1972 Californians overwhelmingly approved an amendment to Article I, section 1 of the Declaration of Rights declaring that privacy is one of the inalienable rights secured to Californians. This straightforward and explicit statement contrasts starkly with the implicit and penumbral right of privacy in the U.S. Constitution.[149] Moreover, the privacy initiative was, according to the ballot arguments supporting its passage, intended to protect two aspects of privacy: personal autonomy and prevention of disclosure of personal information.[150]

---

[147] 52 Cal. 3d 336, 801 P.2d 1077, 276 Cal. Rptr. 326 (1990).

[148] Ibid., p. 352.

[149] See Griswold v. Connecticut, 381 U.S. 479, 85 S. Ct. 1678 (1965).

[150] Margaret Crosby, "New Frontiers: Individual Rights under the California Constitution," Hastings Const. L.Q. 17 (1989): 81, 95.

Because ballot arguments "are an important aid in determining the intent of the voters in adopting a constitutional amendment,"[151] the California courts have sought to breathe life into both objectives. Unlike the federal privacy right, which contains little protection for personal information,[152] the California right protects employment records,[153] health records,[154] financial records,[155] scholastic records,[156] and an individual's sexual history.[157]

With respect to autonomy, the California privacy right has been consistently interpreted more generously than its federal analogue. The federal right does not protect one's choice to live with persons unconnected by marriage, biology, or other legal ties,[158] while the California right protects such unconventional living arrangements.[159] While the federal privacy right still includes a woman's choice to terminate an unwanted pregnancy,[160] it does not bar governments from eliminating abortion from a publicly financed program of medical assistance.[161] By contrast, the independent California right forbids precisely this conduct.[162]

While there may be a federal right to refuse to accept life-sustaining medical treatment[163] it is certainly more limited in scope than the California right. The California Constitution protects both the right of competent adults to discontinue life-sustaining treatment[164] and of family members to discontinue food and water for a patient in a persistent vegetative state.[165]

The federal Constitution's Fourth Amendment provides only limited protection for persons who refuse to undergo random drug testing of their urine or blood.[166] The California Constitution's privacy guarantee affords vastly more

---

[151] Lungren v. Deukmejian, 45 Cal. 3d 727, 729, 755 P. 2d 299 (1988).

[152] See, e.g., Whalen v. Roe, 429 U.S. 589, 97 S. Ct. 869 (1977).

[153] See, e.g., Payton v. City of Santa Clara, 132 Cal. App. 3d 152, 183 Cal. Rptr. 17 (1982).

[154] See, e.g., Planned Parenthood Affiliates v. Van de Kamp, 181 Cal. App. 3d 245, 226 Cal. Rptr. 361 (1986).

[155] See, e.g., Valley Bank v. Superior Court, 15 Cal. 3d 652, 542 P.2d 977 (1975).

[156] Porten v. University of San Francisco, 64 Cal. App. 3d 825, 134 Cal. Rptr. 839 (1976).

[157] See, e.g., Vinson v. Superior Court, 43 Cal. 3d 833, 740 P.2d 404 (1987).

[158] Village of Belle Terre v. Boraas, 416 U.S. 1, 94 S. Ct. 1536 (1974).

[159] City of Santa Barbara v. Adamson, 27 Cal. 3d 123, 134, 610 P.2d 436 (1980).

[160] Roe v. Wade, 420 U.S. 113, 93 S. Ct. 705 (1973).

[161] See Harris v. McRae, 448 U.S. 297, 100 S. Ct. 2671 (1980).

[162] See Committee to Defend Reproductive Rights v. Myers, 29 Cal. 3d 252, 625 P.2d 779 (1981).

[163] See Cruzan v. Director, Missouri Dept. of Health, 110 S. Ct. 2841 (1990).

[164] Bouvia v. Superior Court, 179 Cal. App. 3d 1127, 225 Cal. Rptr. 297 (1986)(healthy but seriously disabled young woman held entitled to disconnect her forced feeding tube); Bartling v. Superior Court, 163 Cal. App. 3d 186, 209 Cal. Rptr. 220 (1984) (competent older man with serious but nonterminal illness held entitled to disconnect a life-sustaining ventilator).

[165] Conservatorship of Drabick, 200 Cal. App. 3d 185, 245 Cal. Rptr. 840, cert. denied, 488 U.S. 958, 109 S. Ct. 399 (1988).

[166] See National Treasury Employees Union v. Von Raab, 489 U.S. 656 (1989); Skinner v. Railway Labor Executives' Ass'n, 489 U.S. 602 (1989).

protection by requiring that a compelling interest be shown before the fundamental privacy right may be invaded.[167] Accordingly, the privacy right protects against random drug testing as a condition of maintaining most jobs[168] and of performing in intercollegiate athletic events[169] but not as a condition of obtaining employment.[170]

Finally, and perhaps of most significance, the federal right applies only as a barrier to governmental action, but the California privacy right applies to "both governmental and nongovernmental conduct."[171] The apparent abandonment of the state action doctrine in the area of privacy has caused some commentators to question whether the doctrine has any remaining utility with respect to other California guarantees of individual rights.[172] Whatever its future in other areas, the state action doctrine is currently no impediment to the enforcement of California's privacy right against both private and public actors.

The backlash against an independent constitution has not been felt quite as harshly in the privacy area. However, Proposition 115, passed in June 1990, amended Article I, section 24 to require that the privacy right in criminal cases be construed no more broadly than under the federal Constitution. Until this measure was struck down as part of an invalid attempt to revise the constitution by initiative, this threatened to be a major rupture of the independence of the California privacy right. For example, should the U.S. Supreme Court conclude that a woman's right to terminate her pregnancy is not within the federal privacy right and the California legislature imposes criminal sanctions on abortion, Californians would be unable to assert the broader California privacy right as a defense in a resulting criminal prosecution.[173] Indeed, all that might be

---

[167] See, e.g., Hill v. National Collegiate Athletic Association, 223 Cal. App. 3d 1642, 273 Cal. Rptr. 402, 410 (1990); Luck v. Southern Pacific Transportation Co., 218 Cal. App. 3d 1, 20, 267 Cal. Rptr. 618 (1990).

[168] Luck v. Southern Pacific Transportation Co., 218 Cal. App. 3d 1, 267 Cal. Rptr. 618(1990).

[169] Hill v. National Collegiate Athletic Association, 223 Cal. App. 3d 1642, 273 Cal. Rptr. 402 (1990).

[170] Wilkinson v. Times Mirror Corp., 215 Cal. App. 3d 1034, 264 Cal. Rptr. 194 (1989).

[171] Hill v. National Collegiate Athletic Association, 223 Cal. App. 3d 1642, 273 Cal. Rptr. 402, 408 (1990). See also Luck v. Southern Pacific Transportation Co., 218 Cal. App. 3d 1, 267 Cal. Rptr. 618 (1990); Wilkinson v. Times Mirror Corp., 215 Cal. App. 3d 1034, 1041–43, 264 Cal. Rptr. 194 (1989); Porten v. University of San Francisco, 64 Cal. App. 3d 825, 829, 134 Cal. Rptr. 839 (1976).

[172] See, e.g., Jennifer Friesen, "Should California's Constitutional Guarantees of Individual Rights Apply against Private Actors?" Hastings Const. L.Q. 17 (1989): 111.

[173] It is possible that a person desiring to obtain an abortion could institute a civil proceeding seeking a declaration of the invalidity of the criminal sanctions under the independent California constitutional guarantee of privacy. It seems absurd that the breadth of the right should depend on the label attached to the legal proceeding, but that might have been the effect of Proposition 115. See also Calvin R. Massey, "California's Privacy Right: Independence Threatened," State Const. Notes & Comment. 1 (Spring 1990): 4,6.

necessary to strip the independence from the California privacy right would be legislative action to impose criminal sanctions on conduct protected by the California right but unprotected by the federal version. If this provision should be revived as part of a valid revision to the constitution, the continued independence of the California privacy right would appear to be in a parlous state.

Religion and Government

The California Constitution contains a far more detailed set of provisions protecting religious liberty and ensuring separation of church and state than the federal Constitution.

The California free exercise clause was part of the 1849 Constitution and provides that "free exercise and enjoyment of religion without discrimination or preference are guaranteed."[174] This provision is stronger than the federal counterpart "because preference is forbidden, even when there is no discrimination."[175] Thus, the California attorney general has formally opined that the California Constitution requires strict government neutrality regarding religious sects.[176] In the wake of the virtual demise of the federal free exercise clause,[177] the California version is likely to assume new importance.

California's establishment clause, contained in Article I, section 4, mirrors the federal language but was added in 1974 as part of the same package that included in the constitution the reminder that rights secured under the California Constitution are not dependent on the federal Constitution. In addition, Article IX, section 8 of the constitution prohibits the teaching in the public schools of "any sectarian or denominational doctrine" and also forbids public subsidy to any nonpublic school.[178] Finally, the California Constitution's firm commitment to the principle of separation of church and state is revealed by Article XVI, section 5, which prohibits governments from granting "anything to or in aid of any religious sect, church, creed, or sectarian purpose." This section "thus forbids more than appropriation of payment of public funds to support sectarian institutions"[179] it also forbids aid "in the form of prestige and intangible power."[180]

---

[174] Calif. Const., Art. I, sec. 4.

[175] Feminist Womens' Health Center, Inc. v. Philibosian, 157 Cal. App. 3d 1076, 1092, 203 Cal. Rptr. 918 (1984), cert. denied, 470 U.S. 1052 (1985).

[176] 25 Op. Cal. Att'y Gen. 309, 313 (1955).

[177] See Employment Division, Dept. of Human Resources of Oregon v. Smith, 110 S. Ct. 1595 (1990).

[178] See California Teachers Ass'n v. Riles, 29 Cal. 3d 794 (1981).

[179] California Educ. Facilities Auth. v. Priest, 122 Cal. 3d 593, 605 n.12, 526 P.2d 513 (1974).

[180] Fox v. City of Los Angeles, 22 Cal. 3d 792, 802, 587 P.2d 663 (1978) (Bird, C. J., concurring).

The result of these textual commitments to separation of church and state has been that the California Supreme Court has struck down such forms of aid as a loan program of public school textbooks to parents of children attending parochial schools[181] while the U.S. Supreme Court has upheld a virtually identical program against a challenge made under the federal establishment clause.[182] Moreover, the explicit clarity of the California prohibitions makes it far more difficult for the California courts to permit governmental aid to sectarian groups for nominally nonsectarian purposes than it has proved to be for the U.S. Supreme Court under the federal Constitution.[183]

There does not yet appear to be any movement towards evisceration of the independence of the California Constitution on this subject.

Freedom of Expression

There are several ways in which the California Constitution offers more protection to expression than does the federal counterpart. Under federal constitutional law, there is no right to express one's views in privately owned shopping centers that invite the public to enter.[184] By contrast, the California Supreme Court determined, in *Robins v. Pruneyard Shopping Center* (1979),[185] that the California Constitution protected such a right. Although the shopping center industry detests *Robins* and "has launched a massive resistance to the decision [by] promulgating burdensome and restrictive rules"[186] relating to the exercise of expression rights, these attempts have proved unsuccessful.[187]

Under federal constitutional law, governments, as owners of property, are forbidden from denying expressive activity in traditional public forums (such as streets and parks) but are permitted to do so with respect to other property that they have declared closed to expressive purposes.[188] Under the California Constitution, "public property must be available for expressive purposes that are

[181] California Teachers Ass'n v. Riles, 29 Cal. 3d 794, 632 P.2d 953 (1981).

[182] Board of Educ. v. Allen, 392 U.S. 236, 88 S. Ct. 1923 (1968).

[183] See, e.g., Bowen v. Kendrick, 487 U.S. 589, 108 S. Ct. 2562 (1988) (approving grants made to religiously affiliated groups for the purpose of counseling teenagers to abstain from sex and to forgo abortion).

[184] See Lloyd Corp. v. Tanner, 407 U.S. 551, 92 S. Ct. 2219 (1972); Hudgens v. NLRB, 424 U.S. 507, 96 S. Ct. 1029 (1976).

[185] 23 Cal. 3d 899, 592 P.2d 341 (1979), aff'd, 447 U.S. 74, 100 S. Ct. 2035 (1980).

[186] Crosby, "New Frontiers: Individual Rights under the California Constitution," p. 84.

[187] See, e.g., Westside Sane/Freeze v. Ernest W. Hahn, Inc., 224 Cal. App. 3d 546, 274 Cal. Rptr. 51 (1990) (rejecting a contention that Pruneyard permitted only the gathering of signatures for petitions and concluding that Pruneyard established the principle that the expression rights protected in shopping centers are not less than those available in public fora).

[188] See Perry Education Ass'n v. Perry Local Educators' Ass'n, 460 U.S. 37, 103 S. Ct. 948 (1983).

not inconsistent with the [government's primary] use"[189] of the property.[190] The difference is that the California Constitution does not permit the creation of "limited public forums" to which access may be conditioned or denied. Accordingly, Californians possess a greater freedom to express their opinions, especially when they desire to do so directly to some governmental entity.

As with the religious clauses, there does not yet appear to be any perceptible movement toward curtailing the independent status of the California Constitution. It is to be hoped that this deplorable countertrend is sparked entirely by public unhappiness about crime and will not soon manifest itself in more restrictive proposals to curb the liberties of the citizens by tying them exclusively to the protections of the federal Constitution. To do so would be to ignore the history of California's Constitution. If there is a single theme that exemplifies that historical development, it is the clear statement that the California Constitution is an invaluable charter of rights and liberties separate and independent from the federal charter.

---

[189] Crosby, "New Frontiers: Individual Rights under the California Constitution," p. 84.

[190] University of California Nuclear Weapons Labs Conversion Project v. Lawrence Livermore Laboratory, 154 Cal. App. 3d 1157, 201 Cal. Rptr. 837 (1984).

■ PART TWO

The California Constitution and Commentary

PREAMBLE

> We, the People of the State of California, grateful to Almighty God for our freedom, in order to secure and perpetuate its blessings, do establish this Constitution.

This has been the preamble to the constitution since 1849. The 1879 Constitution added only the words "and perpetuate" to the third clause. The 1878–1879 convention's Committee on the Preamble and the Bill of Rights thought that the 1849 preamble "expresses, in brief and appropriate language, the people's gratitude to the Supreme Being for their freedom, and their desire and determination to secure and perpetuate its blessings by the establishment of constitutional government. This is all that seems to be required, without loading it down with unnecessary recitals."[1]

Note: With rare exceptions, the California Constitution does not include titles to its sections. The titles used throughout this book are descriptive of each section but are not part of the text of the constitution.

---

[1] E. B. Willis and P. K. Stockton, Debates and Proceedings of the Constitutional Convention of the State of California (Sacramento, Calif.: State Printing, 1880), pp. 178, 230 (hereafter cited as Debates).

Article I

Declaration of Rights

Article I was the first substantive item on the agenda of the 1849 Constitutional Convention. At that time, the provisions of the federal Bill of Rights did not impose limits on the states, so this article constituted the primary, if not the only, protection California would have against abuse of power by the state and local governments.

The Declaration of Rights survived the 1878–1879 Constitutional Convention virtually intact, except for the addition of provisions prohibiting the legislature from granting unrevokable or preferential "privileges of immunities" (now part of sec. 1), prohibiting property qualifications for voting (now sec.22), and stating a rule of constitutional construction (now sec.24).

There were few important changes in Article I until 1972, when initiative measures added privacy to the list of inalienable rights protected under section 1 and added what is now section 27, sanctioning the death penalty. In its 1971 report, however, the Constitution Revision Commission recommended a number of changes, some of them cosmetic but others substantive. The state constitution, for example, contained no explicit clause guaranteeing equal protection of the laws or prohibiting the establishment of religion such as are contained in the federal Constitution. Throughout the state's history, courts had relied on other provisions to provide equivalent or, in some cases, more protective doctrine, but the commission recommended inclusion of these specific clauses. The legislature agreed, and the voters enacted the changes into law in 1974.

The 1974 revision also confirmed the independence of the state constitution through addition of a new provision (sec. 24) declaring that the "rights guaranteed by this Constitution are not dependent on those guaranteed by the United States Constitution." Indeed, from the 1920s through the 1940s, California courts would typically discuss a constitutional claim as if it made no difference whether the claim was under the state or federal constitution and would typically refer to decisions of the U.S. Supreme Court as if controlling.

Beginning in the 1950s, however, California courts began to chart a more independent course. In *People v. Cahan* (1955), six years before the federal Supreme Court required the exclusion from evidence of unconstitutionally seized information or materials, the state supreme court concluded that evidence seized in violation of the search and seizure provisions of the California Constitution was inadmissible in a criminal proceeding. In subsequent cases, state courts continued to provide greater protection of privacy interests than did the federal courts counterpart. (See the discussion under sec. 13 below.) In *Cardenas v. Superior Court* (1961), the supreme court, rejecting federal constitutional law to the contrary, held that retrying a criminal defendant after a mistrial granted on the court's own motion would violate the state constitution's ban on double jeopardy. (See the discussion under sec. 15 below.) In 1972 in *People v. Anderson*, the California Supreme Court, expressly declining to pass on the application of the federal cruel or unusual punishment clause, invalidated California's death penalty statute on the ground that it violated the state constitutional prohibition of "cruel or unusual punishment." (See the discussion under sec. 6 below.) In the years following, California courts built on these foundations to provide a variety of safeguards in criminal trials in addition to those required by the federal Constitution. California courts staked out the independence of the state constitution in other areas as well. The privacy clause, added in 1972, has been accorded a more generous scope and application than the implied privacy right of the federal Constitution. (See the discussion under sec. 1.) Due process and equal protection principles have been applied in broader fashion than their federal counterparts. (See the discussion under sec. 7.) The distinctive language of the California Constitution protective of free expression has been read more broadly than the First Amendment, and in *Robins v. Pruneyard Shopping Center* (1979), the California Supreme Court held, contrary to the federal rule, that under the state's constitution, the owner of a shopping center was required to permit the distribution of handbills containing a political message. (See the discussion under sec. 2.) Indeed, independence runs both ways: California's constitutional guarantee of a speedy trial, for example, has been construed to provide less protection than the federal Constitution requires.

Judicial decisions relying on the state constitution to provide additional protection beyond the federal Constitution did not meet with universal acceptance. In two areas—the rights of defendants in criminal trials and the rights of minorities to integrated schools—the voters came to reject such decisions and to insist, through initiative constitutional amendments, that rights be limited to the federally mandated floor. In 1972, they added section 27 to declare that the death penalty did not constitute cruel or unusual punishment under the state constitution. In 1979, they amended section 7, removing the authority of California courts to order busing as a remedy for school segregation except to the extent that the remedy was required by federal law. Three years later, they approved an initiative measure entitled Victims' Bill of Rights (now sec. 28), which made sweeping changes in criminal procedure. In 1990, voters approved another broad measure, Proposition 115, that (among other things) would have prohibited courts from affording "greater rights to criminal defendants than those afforded by the Constitution of the United States" and would have required courts to construe virtually all of Article I, as applied to criminal cases, "in a manner consistent with the Constitution of the United States." The state supreme court, however, has held that such sweeping changes could be adopted only through the process of constitutional revision. (See the discussion under Article XVIII.)

SECTION I

Inalienable rights. All people are by nature free and independent and have inalienable rights. Among these are enjoying and defending life and liberty, acquiring, possessing, and protecting property, and pursuing and obtaining safety, happiness, and privacy. [Nov. 5, 1974]

Except for a 1972 amendment substituting the word *people* for the original *men* and adding *Privacy* to the list of protected rights, this provision remains as it was first adopted in 1849. California courts have viewed it from the outset as a positive protection against interference with the enumerated rights. The supreme court said of Article I, section 1 in 1857: "It was not lightly incorporated into the Constitution of this State as one of those political dogmas designed to tickle the popular ear, and conveying no substantial meaning or idea; but as one of those fundamental principles of enlightened government, without a rigorous observance of which there could be neither liberty nor safety to the citizen" (*Billings v. Hall*, 1857).

Initially the supreme court rejected attempts to invoke section 1, and its protection for "liberty" and "property," as a basis for attacking regulation of business, and it adopted a generous view of legislative authority to decide "what is or is not hurtful" to society (*Exparte Andrews*, 1861). But in 1890 the supreme court held that an ordinance prohibiting the employment of any person to work more than eight hours a day (and, incidentally, the employment of Chinese labor) on city contracts interfered impermissibly with the right to contract embraced within "liberty" (*Ex parte Kuback*). Over the next few years, the court invalidated a provision of the state's mechanic's lien law requiring liens to be paid in money rather than in kind (*Stimson Mill Company v. Braun*, 1902) and a statute prohibiting the sale of theater tickets in excess of the original price (*Exparte Quarg*, 1906). By 1909, the court had became so enamored of the property and liberty rights protected by section 1 that it held the legislature may not prohibit a person from building a fire on his property without a permit (*In re McCapes*).

In 1925, however, the supreme court upheld a residential zoning ordinance against property and liberty claims in an opinion that emphasized the need of the police power to meet changing conditions and the subordination of property rights to societal interests (*Miller v. Board of Public Works*), and by the mid–1930s it had returned to its former posture of deference to legislative judgment. Except in the case of regulations that implicate other constitutional rights, such as freedom of speech, neither the liberty nor property clauses of Article I, section 1 have been relied upon since to invalidate regulation of business or property.

It is the right to privacy that has generated most litigation under section 1. The inclusion of that right among the inalienable rights secured to Californians contrasts starkly with the implicit and penumbral right of privacy in the federal Constitution. Moreover, the ballot arguments in support of its passage reflect concern with both confidentiality and personal autonomy and with intrusions by private institutions as well as government. California courts, respecting these concerns, have given the provision effect well beyond the boundaries of its federal counterpart.

Courts have held that the privacy provision is self-enforcing—it does not require implementing legislation (*White v. Davis*, 1975)—and that in the light of the language of section 1 (which makes no reference to governmental action), as well as the ballot argument in support of the initiative measure (which referred to invasions of privacy by private industry as well as by government), the provision protects against actions of private as well as governmental entities (*Porten v. University of San Francisco*, 1976).

Unlike the federal privacy right, which contains little protection for personal information, the California provision has been held to apply in a variety of contexts involving intrusion upon confidentiality—for example, surveillance of college classrooms by police serving as secret informers (*White v. Davis*, 1975); the release by a bank of a customer's financial records to a third party's investigators (*Burrows v. Superior Court*, 1974); disclosure by a private university of a student's grades without his permission (*Porten v. University of San Francisco*, 1976); and the public disclosure of nonnewsworthy facts about a person's private affairs (*Forsher v. Bugliosi*, 1980). The constitutional right to privacy has also been held to be implicated in polygraph testing of employees (*Long Beach City Employees Association v. City of Long Beach*, 1986) and in drug testing (*Luck v. Southern Pacific Railway*, 1990).

The state privacy right protects interests in personal autonomy, such as the right to make choices in matters involving living arrangements (*Robbins v.*

Superior Court, 1985), and in matters relating to medical treatment (*Bouvia v. Superior Court,* 1986). Contrary to federal principles, it protects the right of poor people to funding for abortions under a system in which the state funds other medical procedures (*Committee to Defend Reproductive Rights v. Myers,* 1981) and the right of unrelated persons to live together in a household unit (*City of Santa Barbara v. Adamson,* 1980). As with other constitutional rights deemed to be fundamental, intrusions upon privacy can be justified only by a compelling interest (*White v. Davis,*1975).

The "safety" clause of section 1 has so far received no judicial attention. The "happiness" clause has been relied on as an independent basis for decision only once, in a case involving what would now be regarded as an invasion of privacy (*Melvin v. Reid,* 1931). The unusual phrasing of section 1—guaranteeing the right both to pursue and obtain safety and happiness (as well as privacy)—has not been the subject of judicial comment. What could be the largest class action in history—with all unhappy people joined as plaintiffs—has yet to be filed.

SECTION 2

Liberty of speech and of the press; newspersons' refusal to disclose information sources not adjudged in contempt. (a) Every person may freely speak, write and publish his or her sentiments on all subjects, being responsible for the abuse of this right. A law may not restrain or abridge liberty of speech or press. [June 3, 1980]

Subsection (a) stems from section 9 of the 1849 Constitution, with the nonsubstantive changes in wording adopted as part of the 1974 constitutional revision. The pharase "being responsible for the abuse of this right" was intended to distinguish between prior restraints on speech and the imposition of consequences through the law of defamation.

An early case under this provision involved an attempt by the defendant in a celebrated murder case to enjoin performance of a theater production that was based on the facts of his case, on the ground that the performance would deprive him of the opportunity for a fair trial. The trial court granted the injunction as requested, but the supreme court reversed. Acknowledging that the purpose of this provision was to abolish censorship, the court said that although the provision's language differed from the First Amendment, "it works no harm to this petitioner, for the provision here considered is the broader, and gives him greater liberty in the exercise of the right granted" (*Dailey v. Superior Court,* 1896).

In succeeding years, as First Amendment jurisprudence blossomed in the U.S. Supreme Court, California courts downplayed the independent significance of the state free speech provision, focusing instead on federal cases and referring to the two provisions interchangeably (e.g., *American Civil Liberties*

Union v. Board of Education, 1961). By the 1970s, however, state court opinions began to echo the earlier cases, referring to the state provision as being "more definitive and inclusive than the First Amendment." And in 1979 the California Supreme Court broke with federal precedent to hold that the owners of the Pruneyard Shopping Center in San Jose could not prevent high school students from peacefully soliciting signatures, in the central courtyard of the center, for a petition expressing opposition to a United Nations resolution against "Zionism." While the U.S. Supreme Court had held that the First Amendment did not apply to a shopping center because it was private property, the California court held that this section and Article I, section 3 (right to petition) were not limited in their application by federal state action concepts (*Robins v. Pruneyard Shopping Center*, 1979). The U.S. Supreme Court affirmed this ruling, finding no "taking" contrary to federal law and acknowledging the right of states to accord their citizens greater rights so long as federally protected rights were respected.

Pruneyard does not necessarily stand for the proposition that California's free speech protection limits all private actors. The court emphasized the important role that the shopping center plays in modern suburban life as a kind of community. Whether and to what extent the *Pruneyard* principle might apply to other communities—for example, the private sector workplace—remains to be seen.

Since *Pruneyard*, California courts have relied frequently on this provision as an independent ground for deciding free speech issues. It appears, for example, that California courts may have a broader, and more functional, view of what constitutes a public forum for free speech purposes, allowing peaceful expression on public property that is not a traditional or historical forum for speech so long as there is no undue interference with the property's intended purposes (e.g., *Prisoners Union v. Department of Corrections*, 1982).

(b) A publisher, editor, reporter, or other person connected with or employed upon a newspaper, magazine, or other periodical publication, or by a press association or wire service, shall not be adjudged in contempt by a judicial, legislative, or administrative body, or any other body having the power to issue subpoenas, for refusing to disclose the source of any information procured while so connected or employed for publication in a newspaper, magazine or other periodical publication, or for refusing to disclose any unpublished information obtained or prepared in gathering, receiving or processing of information for communication to the public.

Nor shall a radio or television news reporter or other person connected with or employed by a radio or television station, or any person who has been so connected or employed, be so adjudged in contempt for refusing to disclose the source of any information procured while so connected or employed for news or news commentary purposes on radio or television, or for refusing to disclose any unpublished information obtained or prepared in gathering, receiving or processing of information for communication to the public.

> As used in this subdivision, "unpublished information" includes information not disseminated to the public by the person from whom disclosure is sought, whether or not related information has been disseminated and includes, but is not limited to, all notes, out takes, photographs, tapes or other data of whatever sort not itself disseminated to the public through a medium of communication, whether or not published information based upon or related to such material has been disseminated.

This subsection, added by constitutional amendment in 1980, was designed to provide greater protection to news reporters and editors against compelled disclosure of their sources than appears to be provided by the federal Constitution. On its face, the language only protects newspersons (or others covered by its terms) from being held in contempt, by a governmental body, for refusing to obey an order requiring disclosure. When the newsperson is a party to an action, however, such an order may carry with it sanctions other than contempt; for example, in a civil action, the refusal of a party to respond to interrogatories proposed by an opponent may lead to dismissal of that party's case. The supreme court has held that in a civil action, Article I, section 2 gives rise to an implied qualified constitutional privilege that allows a reporter, editor, or publisher to withhold disclosure of the identity of confidential sources, based upon a judicial balancing of factors such as the nature of the litigation, the relevance of the information sought, whether it is obtainable from other sources, and the importance of protecting confidentiality in the particular case (*Mitchell v. Superior Court*, 1984).

SECTION 3

> **Right to assemble and to petition**. The people have the right to instruct their representatives, petition government for redress of grievances, and assemble freely to consult for the common good. [Nov. 5, 1974]

Article I, section 10 of the 1849 Constitution, from which this section derives, referred to the right to petition the legislature for redress of grievances. The language was amended to its present form in 1974. The commission report explained that the section was being broadened to clarify that the right of petition extends beyond the legislature to the government.

The earliest application of this provision came at the turn of the century, in connection with an 1899 primary election law that prohibited the election of delegates to a convention of any political party not representing 3 percent of the votes cast at the previous election. Characterizing the law as a discrimination against minority parties, the supreme court relied upon this provision (along with the privileges and immunities clause and the provision requiring laws of a general nature to have uniform application) to strike it down (*Britton v. Board of Election Commissioners*, 1900).

For the next three-quarters of a century, California courts treated section 3 as if it merely replicated analogous provisions of the First Amendment, sometimes citing the state provisions but relying primarily on U.S. Supreme Court decisions for the analysis. In *Robins v. Pruneyard Shopping Center* (1979), however, the supreme court relied on section 3 (along with the free speech provision), holding that under the California Constitution (unlike the federal Constitution), citizens have a right of access to a privately owned shopping center for the purpose of peacefully soliciting signatures for a petition to the government. The court emphasized the significance of the right of petition as a means of instituting California's system of direct democracy, including initiative, referendum, and recall.

Several years later, the court relied on section 3 and the First Amendment as grounds for holding that the right to petition encompasses the act of filing a lawsuit against a government entity, though the suit pertains solely to compensation for individualized wrongs, so that the plaintiff cannot be sued for malicious prosecution. The U.S. Supreme Court vacated the opinion and sent the case back for clarification as to whether it was decided on state or federal grounds. On remand, the California Supreme Court declared that section 3 provided an independent basis for the decision (*City of Long Beach v. Bozek*, 1983).

SECTION 4

Liberty of conscience. Free exercise and enjoyment of religion without discrimination or preference are guaranteed. This liberty of conscience does not excuse acts that are licentious or inconsistent with the peace or safety of the state. The legislature shall make no law respecting an establishment of religion.

A person is not incompetent to be a witness or juror because of his or her opinions on religious beliefs. [Nov. 5, 1974]

Except for the clause prohibiting establishment of religion, the language is similar to section 4 of the 1849 Constitution and is based on the constitution of New York. Charles Botts, a delegate to the 1849 convention, opposed the exception for acts that are "licentious or inconsistent with the peace or safety of the state," arguing that the language was ambiguous and could be interpreted to permit outlawing of the Catholic church. He suggested instead the "most eloquent and beautiful language" from his home state, Virginia. Winfield Sherwood, who had served in the New York legislature, rose to observe that the gentleman from Virginia was evidently not acquainted with the "new religious sects" in New York, or he would see the propriety of the proposed language. There were, said Mr. Sherwood, "fanatical sects," which have been known to "discard all decency and admit spiritual wives, where men and women have herded together, without any regard to the established usages of society." The exception was retained. Later in the convention, Mr. Botts inquired of another provision whether it emanated from New York; if so, he intended to vote for it so that he could be "in the majority for a change."

The first judicial gloss on section 4 came in 1859 and 1861 with a pair of cases involving the constitutionality of a Sunday closing law. The supreme court first held the law unconstitutional, in part on the ground that it discriminated among religious beliefs, but two years later (with a changed composition) it disapproved the earlier decision and upheld the statute (*Ex parte Andrews*, 1861).

In its original form, section 4 provided that the free exercise and enjoyment of religious profession and worship, without discrimination or preference, "shall forever be allowed in this State." The 1878–1879 convention changed the word *allowed to guaranteed* in order to make clear that the right to disallow or deny did not exist. At the same time, the delegates displayed their opposition to government involvement with religion by rejecting proposals to acknowledge God as the source of civil authority, to prohibit "blasphemy," and to allow Bible reading in public schools. Instead, they adopted two provisions prohibiting government aid of religious enterprises. One of these, now Article XVI, section 5, prohibits in broad language any public aid to religion or religious institutions. The other, now Article IX, section 8, specifically bans state aid to sectarian schools.

The language prohibiting "establishment" of religion was added in the 1974 constitutional revision. Even before that amendment, however, the supreme court had construed section 4 to prohibit governmental action that "favors, fosters [or] establishes any religion" (*California Educational Facilities Authority v. Priest*, 1974). And subsequently, in concluding that the presence of a cross on public land violates section 4, the court suggested that the language of the section prohibiting both preference and discrimination may go further than the federal establishment clause in its preclusion of government involvement (*Fox v. City of Los Angeles*, 1978). Lower courts have relied on section 4 (often in conjunction with Art. IX, sec. 8 and Art. XVI, sec. 5) as an independent constitutional basis for invalidating such governmental acts as an order by the governor to close state offices between noon and 3 P.M. on Good Friday (*Mandel v. Hodges*, 1976) and the participation by a district attorney in the plans of a religious organization to bury aborted fetuses in a memorial park and to conduct a religious ceremony in connection with the burial (*Feminist Women's Health Center, Inc. v. Philibosian*, 1984). More recently, the supreme court ruled that the practice of providing a religious invocation at a high school graduation ceremony was unconstitutional, although only three justices relied squarely on the state constitution for that result (*Sands v. Morongo School District*, 1991).

Section 4 has not so far played an independent role in free exercise claims. The supreme court, in concluding that a tribe of native Americans who relied on peyote as a central feature of their religion could not be prosecuted for that activity, mentioned the section but relied mainly upon the First Amendment (*People v. Woody*, 1964). Now that the U.S. Supreme Court has reached an opposite conclusion under the First Amendment—and in the process narrowed the scope of the federal free exercise clause considerably (*Employment Division v. Smith*, 1990)—the state constitutional provision may play a greater role in such cases.

The witness clause of section 4 has no express federal counterpart. In 1887 the supreme court relied on that clause to hold that a criminal defendant was not entitled to seek to establish that the prosecution witness was an atheist (*People v, Copsey*, 1887). Since then, the clause has not been litigated.

SECTION 5

The military. The military is subordinate to civil power. A standing army may not be maintained in peacetime. Soldiers may not be quartered in any house in wartime except as prescribed by law, or in peacetime without the owner's consent. [Nov. 5, 1974]

The language is identical to the original 1849 provision (Art. I, sec. 12), except for minor editorial changes in 1974. The "military" refers, presumably, to the National Guard (see Art. 5, sec. 7). The third sentence tracks the Third Amendment to the federal Constitution. There have been no decisions of significance applying the provision.

SECTION 6

Slavery prohibited. Slavery is prohibited. Involuntary servitude is prohibited except to punish crime. [Nov. 5, 1974]

The language is substantially identical to that contained in Article I, section 18 of the 1849 Constitution. (See Constitutional History section for the background of its adoption.)

In an early case, the supreme court held that the provision is self-executing in that it requires no legislation for its application (*In re Archy*, 1858).

The "involuntary servitude" provision has potential application beyond the context of slavery. The court of appeal has held, for example, that the state would violate section 6 were it to incarcerate a person as punishment for failure to comply with a court order requiring support payments to a former spouse, where die person had no funds to make the payments and the order was entered as a means of forcing him to take a job (*In re Jennings*, 1982).

SECTION 7

Due process of law; use of pupil assignment or pupil transportation; privileges and immunities. (a) A person may not be deprived of life, liberty, or property without due process of law or denied equal protection of the laws; provided, that nothing contained herein or elsewhere in this Constitution imposes upon the State of California or any public entity, board or official any obligations or responsibilities which exceed those imposed by the Equal Protection Clause of the 14th Amendment to the United States Constitution with respect to the use of public school assignment or pupil transportation. In enforcing this subdivision or any other provisions of this Constitution, no court of this state may impose upon the State of California or any public entity, board, or official any obligation or responsibility with respect to the use of public school assignment or pupil transportation, (1) except to remedy a specific violation by such party that would also constitute a violation of the Equal Protection Clause of the 14th Amendment to the United States Constitution, and (2) unless a federal court would be permitted under federal decisional law to impose that obligation or responsibility upon such party to remedy the specific violation of the Equal Protection Clause of the 14th Amendment of the United States Constitution.

Except as may be precluded by the Constitution of the United States, every existing judgment, decree, writ, or other order of a court of this state, whenever rendered, which includes provisions regarding public school assignment or pupil transportation, or which requires a plan including any such provisions shall, upon application to a court having jurisdiction by any interested person, be modified to conform to the provisions of this subdivision as amended, as applied to the facts which exist at the time of such modification. In all actions or proceedings arising under or seeking application of the amendments to this subdivision proposed by the Legislature at its 1979–80 Regular Session, all courts, wherein such actions or proceedings are or may hereafter be pending, shall give such actions or proceedings first precedence over all other civil actions therein.

Nothing herein shall prohibit the governing board of a school district from voluntarily continuing or commencing a school integration plan after the effective date of this subdivision as amended.

In amending this subdivision, the Legislature and people of the State of California find and declare that this amendment is necessary to serve compelling public interests, including those of making the most effective use of the limited financial resources now and prospectively available to support public education, maximizing the educational opportunities and protecting the health and safety of all public school pupils, enhancing the ability of parents to participate in the educational process, preserving harmony and tranquility in this state and its public schools, preventing the waste of scarce fuel resources, and protecting the environment.

(b) A citizen or class of citizens may not be granted privileges or immunities not granted on the same terms to citizens. Privileges or immunities granted by the Legislature may be altered or revoked. [Nov. 6, 1979]

The 1849 Constitution contained a proscription against deprivation of life, liberty, or property without due process of law, as part of a section dealing with safeguards in criminal proceedings but no equal protection clause and no privileges-and-immunities clause. The privileges-and-immunities clause (now subsection (b) was added through the constitution of 1879. The first part of subsection (a), protecting against deprivation of life, liberty, or property without due process of law and denial of equal protection of the laws, was added in 1974. The balance of subsection (a) was added by initiative amendment in 1978.

Due Process

Until 1974, the only due process language in the California Constitution appeared in a section on criminal procedure. Even so, California courts read it as applicable to the civil context as well (*Kruger v. Wells Fargo*, 1974), and the constitutional revision of 1974 replicated the clause in this section.

One of the first issues to arise after the 1974 revision was whether the due process principle applied only to actions by government or whether it had some application to nongovernmental action as well. In 1978 the supreme court, reaffirming a pre-1974 ruling, held that the clause did not apply to actions by private banks. In reaching that conclusion, the court rejected an argument that the wording of the 1974 amendment, and specifically its lack of explicit reference to governmental action, signified an intent to dispense with the traditional state action requirement. Rather, the court reasoned, the 1974 amendment was intended to conform the protection of rights to those protected by the federal Constitution (*Garfinkle v. Superior Court*, 1978).

Notwithstanding that reasoning, California courts in a number of cases have departed from federal precedent in applying the due process requirement. In *People v. Ramirez* (1979), the court held that a person excluded from treatment at the California Rehabilitation Center has a right under the state due process clause to at least minimal due process in the form of a statement of reasons and an opportunity to respond. The plurality opinion explicitly rejected the analysis of the U.S. Supreme Court that due process is required only when there is an "entitlement" that can be defined as "liberty" or "property," contending that the federal approach "undervalued important due process interests in recognizing the dignity and worth of the individual by treating him as an equal, fully participating and responsible member of society."

Equal Protection of the Laws

While the early constitutions lacked an explicit equal protection clause, California courts nonetheless found in those documents language to support and equal protection principle. For example, in *Britton v. Board of Commissioners of the City and County of San Francisco* (1900), the supreme court relied on former Article 1, section 11 (now Art. IV, sec. 16(a)), requiring laws of a general nature to have uniform application, and on former Article IV, section 25 (now Art. IV, sec. 16(b)), barring special legislation, to strike down a statute that prohibited the election of delegates to a convention of any political party that did not represent at least 3 percent of the votes cast at the previous election. In subsequent cases, the privileges-and-immunities clause also came to be relied on, in combination with these other provisions, to provide what the supreme court characterized in relation to the federal equal protection clause as "generally equivalent but independent protections" (*Department of Mental Hygiene v. Kirchner*, 1965).

Beginning in the 1970s, California courts began to regard the California constitutional equal protection principle (now buttressed by an explicit equal protection clause) as providing broader protection than its federal counterpart. The supreme court's declaration of independence was articulated in *Serrano v. Priest* (1976): "Our state equal protection provisions, while 'substantially the equivalent of the guarantees contained in the Fourteenth Amendment' are possessed of an independent vitality which, in a given case, may demand an analysis different from that which would obtain if only the federal standard were applicable."

While California courts accept the federal principle that classifications affecting fundamental interests or suspect classes will receive strict scutiny, they do not regard themselves as bound by the federal definition of the fundamental interests category. In Serrano, the court, departing from federal precedent, found education to be such an interest in California, and on that basis it held the state's system for financing public schools (allowing more money for schools in wealthier districts) to be invalid. Similarly, the court has held that application of the state's equal protection principle is not limited by federally defined requirements for state action. In *Gay Law Students v. Pacific Telephone & Telegraph Company* (1979), the court held that a public utility's policy of discriminating against homosexuals violated this provision. How far equal protection principle may extend to private actors remains to be seen.

California courts have also held that under the state constitution (unlike the federal Constitution), the equal protection principle is offended not only by intentional (de jure) discrimination, but—as in the case of segregated schools where no intentional discrimination was shown—by de facto discrimination as well (*Crawford v. Board of Education*, 1976). Insofar as this conclusion entailed the use of busing to remedy segregation, it was "overruled" by the voters in 1978 through adoption of an initiative measure amending section 7(a) by adding the language that follows the semicolon. The amendment does not preclude the California courts from continuing to apply a different standard as to what violates the equal protection principle; it simply precludes them from imposing busing as a remedy for such a violation in the context of segregated schools unless that remedy is required by the federal Constitution. When a school district fails to fulfill its state constitutional obligation, California courts retain power to bring other remedies to bear, including school closure, school site selection, creation of special magnet schools, curriculum changes, or other steps to overcome the adverse effects (*McKinney v. Board of Trustees*, 1982).

SECTION 8

Sex, race, etc., not a disqualification for business. A person may not be disqualified from entering or pursuing a business, profession, vocation, or employment because of sex, race, creed, color, or national or ethnic origin. [Nov. 5, 1974]

In its original form, as Article XX, section 18 of the Constitution of 1879, this provision read: "No person shall on account of sex be disqualified from entering upon or pursuing any lawful business, vocation, or profession." In 1974 the provision was renumbered as Article 1, section 8 and changed to its current reading.

In 1881, the supreme court relied upon it to invalidate a San Francisco ordinance prohibiting the employment of women as waitresses in places that serve alcoholic drinks.

Soon, however, the court began to backtrack. In *Ex parte Felchlin* (1892), it upheld a city licensing scheme that imposed a license fee of $150 per month on bars that employed women in any capacity, while imposing a fee of only $30 per quarter on other bars, and in *Ex parte Hayes* (1893), the court declared broadly that the provision limits legislation regulating employment conditions in places that sell intoxicating beverages. When, in 1915, the court upheld a law providing for an eight-hour day for women in certain occupations, it declared that the provision is "subject to such reasonable regulations as may be imposed in the exercise of police powers" (*In re Miller*, 1915).

In 1971 the court returned to its original understanding of the provision. Overruling *Hayes* and declaring that the general hazards of an occupation "cannot be a valid ground for excluding [women] from those occupations," it held that the long-standing prohibition against the employment of women as bartenders was invalid under this provision. In addition, and in a departure from federal constitutional precedent, it relied on this provision to declare that classifications based on sex are subject to strict scrutiny review under the state constitution, so that they may be justified only by a showing of a compelling state interest and the lack of feasible alternatives to achieve legislative policy (*Sail'er Inn Inc. v. Kirby*, 1971).

The current language prohibiting discrimination on the basis of creed has been held to require a school district to make reasonable accommodation to the religious practices of employees (*Rankins v. Commission on Professional Competence*, 1979). And the Supreme Court has suggested that Article I, section 8 covers private as well as state action. The court found it unnecessary to decide that issue, however, holding instead that this section declares a "fundamental public policy against discrimination in employment—public or private—on account of sex"—so that it is unlawful for an employer to terminate an employee for refusing to submit to sexual harassment (*Rojo v. Kliger*, 1990).

SECTION 9

Bill of attainder; ex post facto law; obligation of contract. A bill of attainder, ex post facto law, or law impairing the obligation of contracts may not be passed. [Nov. 5, 1974]

This section is based on Article 1, section 16 of the 1849 Constitution, with only insignificant semantic changes.

As the revision commission observed in its report: "A bill of attainder is a legislative finding that an act which was legal when committed is to be punished as a crime. An ex post facto law is one which retroactively affects legal relationships. A law impairing the obligation of contracts is one which retroactively affects contractual agreements. The application of these classic prohibitions in changing fact situations is a source of chronic litigation."

In an early case, the supreme court observed that these provisions were the "same . . . in substance" as analogous provisions of the federal Constitution (*Robinson v. Magee*, 1858), and the "chronic litigation" that followed failed to produce any significant differences in application. In a pair of early ex post facto challenge cases, the court referred only to the federal provision (*People v. Mortimer*, 1873; *People v. Gutierrez*, 1873). By 1980, in a case applying the obligation-of-contracts principle to invalidate legislation reducing salaries and pensions for state judges, the state constitutional provision achieved honorable mention, along with the federal Constitution (*Olson v. Cory*, 1980). The spirit of independence that has infused other provisions of the state constitution has yet to reach section 9.

SECTION 10

Detention of witnesses; no imprisonment for debt. Witnesses may not be unreasonably detained. A person may not be imprisoned in a civil action for debt or tort, or in peacetime for a militia fine. [Nov. 5, 1974]

These provisions derive from the Constitution of 1849. The prohibition against unreasonable detention of witnesses is largely anachronistic, dating from a period in which witnesses at preliminary hearings in criminal cases could be detained if they failed to post security ensuring their appearance at trial. Legislation to that effect, authorizing detention for up to ten days, is still on the books but seldom used.

It has been held that the ban on imprisonment for debt may not be circumvented by the adoption of a statute making the mere act of failing to pay a debt a crime (*People v. Beggs,* 1918). An early case held, however, that the provision does not bar imprisonment for failing to obey a court order directing a husband to pay the costs of a divorce proceeding, because the obligation was not a "debt" (*In re Perkins,* 1861), and that reasoning was subsequently utilized to uphold imprisonment for failure to pay a court's order for spousal support (*Application of Wilson,* 1888).

SECTION 11

Suspension of habeas corpus. Habeas corpus may not be suspended unless required by public safety in cases of rebellion or invasion. [Nov. 5, 1974]

This provision derives from Article I, section 5 of the 1849 Constitution, with only nonsubstantive changes from the 1974 constitution revision. The function of the "Great Writ" of habeas corpus is, generally, to permit a person whose liberty is constrained by the state to challenge the constraint by filing a petition with a court. The procedures for the filing and consideration of such a petition are governed by statute. Never in California history has the writ been suspended.

SECTION 12

Bail; release on own recognizance. A person shall be released on bail by sufficient sureties, except for:

(a) capital crimes when the facts are evident or the presumption great;
(b) felony offenses involving acts of violence on another person when the facts are evident or the presumption great and the court finds based upon clear and convincing evidence that there is a substantial likelihood the person's release would result in great bodily harm to others;
(c) felony offenses when the facts are evident and the presumption great and the court finds based on clear and convincing evidence that the person has threatened another with great bodily harm and that there is a substantial likelihood that the person would carry out the threat if released.

Excessive bail may not be required. In fixing the amount of bail, the court shall take into consideration the seriousness of the offense charged, the previous criminal record of the defendant, and the probability of his or her appearing at the trial or hearing of the case.

A person may be released on his or her own recognizance in the court's discretion. [June 8, 1982]

The Constitutions of 1849 and 1879 provided for a right of bail except "in capital crimes when the proof is evident or the presumption great," and they prohibited "excessive bail." The provision authorizing a person's release on his or her own recognizance was added in 1974. The present language is the product of an initiative amendment in 1982.

The prohibition on excessive bail tracks the federal Constitution, but the former guarantee of a right to bail in all but certain capital cases had no federal constitutional counterpart. As the supreme court observed, that guarantee was "consciously added . . . in order to make clear that, unlike the federal rule, all except the one class of defendants [i.e., those defined by the exception] were to be bailable." Thus, the court held in 1973, there was no room for an implied "public safety" exception to the state constitutional mandate (*In re Underwood*, 1973).

The 1982 initiative measure was directed in part toward overturning that holding and permitting the denial of bail to be used as a form of preventive detention in some cases. It provides for the denial of bail not only in capital cases but also in other felony cases "when the facts are evident or the presumption great" and the court finds either that there is substantial likelihood that release would result in great bodily harm to others or that the person has threatened another with great bodily harm and there is substantial likelihood that the person would carry out the threat if released.

The "when the facts are evident or the presumption great" standard has been held, in the capital context, to be a lenient one, requiring only such evidence as would be sufficient to sustain a capital verdict (*Ex parte Curtis*, 1891). Whether that lenient interpretation will carry over to the preventive detention context remains to be seen. The finding of probable harm from release requires, in any event, "clear and convincing evidence."

There are no clear standards for determining when bail is excessive, although the provision sets out criteria to be taken into account. Procedures for "own recognizance" release have been adopted by the legislature.

SECTION 13

Unreasonable search and seizure; warrant. The right of the people to be secure in their persons, houses, papers, and effects against unreasonable seizures and searches may not be violated; and a warrant may not issue except on probable cause, supported by oath or affirmation, particularly describing the place to be searched and the persons and things to be seized. [Nov. 5, 1974]

This provision derives from Article I, section 19 of the 1849 Constitution, with minor nonsubstantive change in wording as a result of the 1974 revision. While similar in language to the Fourth Amendment, it has been held to impose a "more exacting standard" than the federal Constitution (*People v. Brisendine*, 1975). The provision provides protection against a variety of governmental intrusions that might be permissible under the Fourth Amendment—for example, the warrantless search of a garbage can (*People v. Krivda*, 1973), the warrantless surveillance of a backyard from a police helicopter (*People v. Cook*, 1985), or the warrantless search of an arrestee prior to booking in the absence of probable cause and exigent circumstances (*People v. Laiwa*, 1983). In addition, under some circumstances, searches by privately employed store guards will trigger application of the state search and seizure provision even when the Fourth Amendment might not apply (*People v. Zelinski*, 1979).

The protection of privacy interests afforded by this provision is buttressed by Article I, section 1, protecting the right of privacy, so that in passing upon the constitutionality of a particular intrusion, the courts may look to the two provisions in tandem (*In re William G.*, 1985).

It is important to distinguish between the substantive right to be free of government or governmentlike intrusions and the remedies for an unconstitutional intrusion. Article I, section 28, subsection (e) now limits use of the exclusionary rule as a means of enforcing the constitutional guarantee. As a result, California courts may not exclude evidence that would be admissible by federal standards. But the adoption of that provision does not alter the substance of the protection afforded otherwise by the state constitution, nor does it affect other remedies, such as damages, injunction, or declaratory relief (*People v. Cook*, 1985).

SECTION 14

Felony defendant before magistrate; prosecutions. Felonies shall be prosecuted as provided by law, either by indictment or, after examination and commitment by a magistrate, by information.

A person charged with a felony by complaint subscribed under penalty of perjury and on file in the county where the felony is triable shall be taken without unnecessary delay before a magistrate of that court. The magistrate shall immediately give the defendant a copy of the complaint, inform the defendant of the defendant's right to counsel, allow the defendant a reasonable time to send for counsel, and on the defendant's request read the complaint to the defendant. On the defendant's request the magistrate shall require a peace officer to transmit within the county where the court is located a message to counsel named by defendant.

A person unable to understand English who is charged with a crime has a right to an interpreter throughout the proceedings. [Nov. 5, 1974]

This section, as elaborated by section 14A, has had a pendulumlike history. The 1849 Constitution required the prosecution, in the case of any "capital or otherwise infamous crime," to seek a grand jury indictment. The 1879 Constitution abandoned that requirement and permitted the prosecution to proceed, in the alternative, through the filing of charges (an "information") after examination and commitment by a magistrate. The two procedures are quite different. In the information procedure, the defendant receives a preliminary hearing at which he or she is entitled to be present, to be represented by counsel, and to present evidence in his or her own behalf; in the indictment procedure, the grand jury meets behind closed doors, and none of these safeguards applies. For these reasons, the supreme court ruled in 1978 that a defendant is entitled by due process guarantees under the state constitution to a preliminary hearing even when a grand jury returns an indictment against him or her (*Hawkins v. Superior Court*, 1978). The practical effect of that ruling was to eliminate the use of grand juries in nearly all criminal proceedings. In 1990, however, as part of an omnibus criminal reform initiative of that year, section 14.1 was added to Article I, and the pre-*Hawkins* state of affairs was restored.

A 1934 amendment added an elaborate statement of the procedure applicable to arraignment, but as part of the constitutional revision in 1974, those details were streamlined into the language of the current second paragraph. At the same time, the interpreter requirement was added.

SECTION 14.1

Felony; prosecution by indictment. If a felony is prosecuted by indictment there shall be no postindictment preliminary hearing. [June 5, 1990]

This section, added by initiative amendment in 1990, has the effect of overruling the Supreme Court's decision in *Hawkins v. Superior Court*, discussed in section 14. As a result, the dual system of felony prosecutions through indictment or information that existed pre-*Hawkins* has been restored.

SECTION 15

Criminal prosecutions; rights of defendants; due process of law; jeopardy; depositions; assistance of counsel. The defendant in a criminal case has the right to a speedy public trial, to compel attendance of witnesses in the defendant's behalf, to have the assistance of counsel for the defendant's defense, to be personally present with counsel, and to be confronted with the witnesses against the defendant. The legislature may provide for the deposition of a witness in the presence of the defendant and the defendant's counsel.

Persons may not twice be put in jeopardy for the same offense, be compelled in criminal cause to be a witness against themselves, or be deprived of life, liberty, or property without due process of law. [Nov. 5, 1974]

This provision derives from Article I, section 8 of the 1849 Constitution, later Article I, section 13 of the 1879 Constitution. Language added in 1934, permitting comment on and consideration of a defendant's "failure to explain or to deny by his testimony any evidence or facts in the case against him," whether the defendant testified or not, was deleted in 1974 as violative of the defendant's right to remain silent under the Fifth Amendment to the federal Constitution. The language pertaining to the right of a defendant to counsel was added in 1972, along with language (deleted in 1974) authorizing the legislature to require the defendant in a felony case to have the assistance of counsel. While the guarantees of this provision have counterparts in the federal Constitution, some of them have been the subject of disparate judicial gloss. The speedy trial provision, for example, is interpreted differently in two respects, one favoring the defendant and the other the prosecution. The right under the state constitution attaches upon the filing of a complaint against the accused, whereas the comparable federal right does not attach until arrest; but contrary to federal law, the defendant has the burden of demonstrating prejudice attributable to delay (*Serna v. Superior Court,* 1985). And the prohibition against double jeopardy prohibits retrial of a defendant after the grant of a mistrial without the defendant's consent. In *Cardenas v. Superior Court* (1961), the supreme court declined to apply federal precedent allowing retrial when the grant of a mistrial was deemed in the defendant's interest, observing that the federal rule "does not accord with the uniform construction placed by this court upon the jeopardy provision of the California Constitution."

SECTION 16

Trial by jury. Trial by jury is an inviolate right and shall be secured to all, but in a civil cause three-fourths of the jury may render a verdict. A jury may be waived in a criminal cause by the consent of both parties expressed in open court by the defendant and the defendant's counsel. In a civil cause a jury may be waived by the consent of the parties expressed as provided by statute.

In civil causes the jury shall consist of twelve persons or a lesser number agreed on by the parties in open court. In civil causes in municipal or justice court the Legislature may provide that the jury shall consist of eight persons or a lesser number agreed on by the parties in open court.

In criminal actions in which a felony is charged the jury shall consist of twelve persons. In criminal actions in which a misdemeanor is charged the jury shall consist of twelve persons or a lesser number agreed on by the parties in open court. [Nov. 4, 1980]

This provision derives from Article I, section 3 of the 1849 Constitution and survived intact in the 1879 Constitution despite an attempt by some delegates to the 1878–79 constitutional convention to dispense with jury trials in misdemeanor cases. The provision authorizing the legislature to provide for fewer than twelve jurors in certain civil cases was added in 1980.

This provision has been construed to require jury trial (unless waived) in all proceedings in which criminal sanctions can be imposed, including proceedings not labeled as criminal (such as a contempt proceeding in which there is the potential for imposing the equivalent of misdemeanor sanctions) and proceedings that (because of the relatively light sanction) would not require a jury trial under the federal Constitution (*Mitchell v. Superior Court,* 1984). In its application to civil cases, the provision guarantees the right to jury trial as that right existed at common law in 1850 in California. Since juries were used for civil actions "at law" but not "in equity," juries are not required in what would have been considered equitable proceedings, such as proceedings for injunctive relief (*C & K Engineering Contractors v. Amber Steel Co.,* 1978). Nor are they required in small claims proceedings, since there was no right to a jury trial in comparable proceedings in 1850 (*Crouchman v. Superior Court,* 1988).

The right to a jury trial in civil cases may be implicated when a statute authorizes an administrative agency to decide disputes ordinarily resolved through the judicial process. The supreme court has held that whether the exercise of such power offends this section is to be determined by the nature of the remedy available through the agency and by the scope of judicial review (*McHugh v. Santa Monica Rent Control Board,* 1989).

SECTION 17

Unusual punishment and excessive fines. Cruel or unusual punishment may not be inflicted or excessive fines imposed. [Nov. 4, 1974]

The substance of the prohibition against cruel or unusual punishment and excessive fines was contained in the Constitutions of 1849 and 1879. The 1974 revision allocated the prohibition to a separate section.

Early decisions viewed the ban on cruel or unusual punishment as prohibiting only "barbarous" punishments unknown to the common law (*State v. McCauley & Tevis,* 1860), and on that basis, the death penalty was initially upheld (*People v. Oppenheimer,* 1909). In 1972, however, the supreme court in *People v. Anderson* held that the death penalty as then administered in California violated this provision. Noting that the state constitution uses the word or (unlike the federal Constitution, which speaks of cruel and unusual punishment), the court emphasized the lack of standards to guide the sentence in deciding whether to impose the death penalty and the lack of swiftness or certainty in its application.

This decision aroused a storm of popular protest, and an initiative measure amending the constitution to reverse the *Anderson* decision was adopted by overwhelming vote. (See Art. I, sec. 27.)

Outside the death penalty arena, this section has been used on occasion to strike down sentences that appear, in the particular case, to be excessive. In *In re Lunch* (1972), the court held that a sentence of one year to life for a second crime of indecent exposure was excessive, taking into account (1) the nature of the offense and/or the offender, with particular regard to the degree of danger both present to society; (2) a comparison of the challenged penalty with those imposed in the same jurisdiction for more serious crimes; and (3) a comparison of the challenged penalty with those imposed for the same offense in different jurisdictions. Applying these criteria, the court has also invalidated the imposition of a life sentence on a seventeen-year-old with no prior criminal record who shot impulsively in the course of robbery from the victim's marijuana farm (*People v. Dillon*, 1983) and a requirement that all persons convicted of soliciting to engage in or engaging in "lewd or dissolute conduct" must register with the chief of police in the city in which they reside. No fines have been invalidated under the "excessive fines" clause.

SECTION 18

Treason. Treason against the state consists only in levying war against it, adhering to its enemies, or giving them aid and comfort. A person may not be convicted of treason except on the evidence of two witnesses to the same overt act or by confession in open court. [Nov. 5, 1974]

This provision derives from Article I, section 20 of the 1849 Constitution, with minor nonsubstantive modification through the 1974 revision. Its function is merely to limit the number of offenses that can be punishable as treason under the common law and not to limit the power of the legislature to provide for punishment of acts "inimical to the public welfare" that might have been punished as "constructive treason"; accordingly, the provision was no bar to the enactment of a criminal syndicalism statute (*People v. Steelik*, 1921).

SECTION 19

Eminent domain. Private property may be taken or damaged for public use only when just compensation, ascertained by a jury unless waived has first been paid to, or into court for, the owner. The Legislature may provide for possession by the condemnor following commencement of eminent domain proceedings only upon deposit in court and prompt release to the owner of money determined by the court to be the probable amount of just compensation. [Nov. 5, 1974]

The 1849 Constitution contained a simple declaration against taking of private property for public use without just compensation. This was expanded in the 1879 Constitution (Art. I, sec. 14) to include damage as well as taking and to prohibit the appropriation of any right of way "to the use of any corporation other than municipal" without compensation to the owner. In 1911, the section was amended to include the taking of property for a railraod run for logging or lumbering purposes. The section was amended in 1918 to provide for immediate possession by the condemning agency upon the giving of security. After other, less substantive amendments in 1928 and 1934, the section was lengthy and prolix. It was amended to its present, relatively brief, form in 1974.

SECTION 20

Rights of noncitizens. Noncitizens shall have the same property rights as citizens. [Nov. 5, 1974]

The 1849 Constitution provided that foreigners who become residents of the state "shall enjoy the same rights in respect to the possession, enjoyment, and inheritance of property, as native born citizens." The 1879 Constitution continued that language but with two important qualifications: to receive equal treatment with citizens, foreigners had to be "of the white race or of African descent" (thereby ruling out Asians), and they had to be "eligible to become citizens of the United States under the naturalization laws there of." In 1894, the right to equal treatment itself was restricted to "property, other than real estate" (with the proviso that aliens owning real estate at the time of the amendment could remain owners), and the legislature was authorized to provide for the disposition of real estate there after acquired "by descent or devise" (i.e., by reason of the death of the owner).

It was not until 1954 that the language referring to "the white race or of African descent" was deleted; the remainder of the section remained until 1974, when it was amended to its present, unqualified guarantee of equal treatment for noncitizens.

SECTION 21

Separate property of husband and wife. Property owned before marriage or acquired during marriage by gift, will, or inheritance is separate property. [Nov. 5, 1974]

This provision derives from Article 11, section 14 of the 1849 Constitution. While the debates made clear it was intended to protect a woman's property owned before marriage, as well as her postmarriage inheritances and gifts, from the common law's coverture system, the legislature adopted a statute declaring the rents and profits from a woman's separate property to be subject to her husband's creditors as well. In 1860, the supreme court held the statute unconstitutional (*George v. Ransom*, 1860). The current language is the product of amendment in 1970.

SECTION 22

No property qualification for voting or holding public office. The right to vote or hold office may not be conditioned by a property qualification. [Nov. 5, 1974]

This provision was introduced through the 1879 Constitution. Most of the litigation concerning it has involved property qualifications for voters in special districts, such as irriagation districts, that provide services pertaining to land in exchange for assessments payable by property owners. In an early irrigation district case, the supreme court intimated that a statute limiting voting rights to property owners would violate this section (*In re Madera Irrigation District*, 1891), but six years later, the court upheld a property qualification for voting in a reclamation district (*People v. Reclamation District*, 1897). After unsuccessfully attempting to distinguish the two types of districts, the court abandoned it in 1923, reasoning that by prescribing property qualifications for voting in special districts, the legislature "is not dealing with elections, with suffrage, or with the ballot, within the meaning of the Constitution and the elections, laws of the State. The formation of this and similar districts is a function pertaining purely to the legislative branch of government . . . wherefore it may do so by giving such persons as it may think best an opportunity to be heard" (*Tarpey v. McClure*, 1923).

SECTION 23

Grand juries. One or more grand juries shall be drawn and summoned at least once a year in each county. [Nov. 5, 1974]

Grand juries in California have historically performed both criminal functions (investigation of criminal charges and issunace of indictments) and civil functions (investigations of local government administration and recommendations to the governing bodies). Formerly, this section provided for the drawing and summoning of a grand jury, but in 1974 it was amended to allow the creation of separate criminal and civil grand juries. A few counties have adopted the dual grand jury system.

While the section refers to grand juries being "drawn," the practice pursuant to statute is that members of the grand jury are selected by individual members of the county board of supervisors.

SECTION 24

Independence of the California Constitution; limits on independence in criminal cases; rights retained by the people. Rights guaranteed by this Constitution are not dependent on those guaranteed by the United States Constitution. This declaration of rights may not be construed to impair or deny others retained by the people. [June 5, 1990]

The second sentence derives from Article I, section 21 of the 1849 Constitution, the only change being the substitution (in 1974) of the word *declaration* for the original *enumeration*. The concept of unenumerated rights has not played a significant role in state constitutional history. In 1900 the supreme court gave the sentence passing mention in a decision invalidating the state's primary election law, principally on other grounds, and it has not been invoked since as a basis for invalidating legislation. In its report underlying the 1974 revision, the revision commission characterized this sentence as protecting "other inherent rights retained by the people."

The first sentence was added in 1974, upon recommendation of the revision commission, to underscore the independent nature of the state's Declaration of Rights. Although the sentence did not alter existing law, courts have referred to it frequently in decisions that depart from federal precedent.

In 1990, the voters approved an initiative measure, Proposition 115, which among other things amended this section to require state courts in criminal proceedings to adhere to federal rulings under the U.S. Constitution. The supreme court, however, ruled that portion of Proposition 115 invalid as a constitutional revision, capable of enactment only through legislative proposal or constitutional convention (*Raven v. Deukmajian*, 1990, see Art. XVIII).

SECTION 25

Right to fish. The people shall have the right to fish upon and from the public lands of the State and in the waters thereof, excepting upon lands set aside for fish hatcheries, and no land owned by the State shall ever be sold or transferred without reserving in the people the absolute right to fish thereupon; and no law shall ever be passed making it a crime for the people to enter upon the public lands within this State for the purpose of fishing in any water containing fish that may have been planted therein by the State; provided, that the Legislature may by statute, provide for the season when and the conditions under which the different species of fish may be taken. [Nov. 8, 1910]

This ringing endorsement of the constitutional right to fish was adopted by amendment in 1910. It has been construed to mean that the right to fish upon public lands (such as a reservoir) may not be prohibited unless recreational fishing is incompatible with the land's primary purpose (*State v. San Luis Obispo Sportsman's Association*, 1978).

SECTION 26

Constitution mandatory and prohibitory. The provisions of this Constitution are mandatory and prohibitory, unless by express words they are declared to be otherwise. [June 8, 1976]

This section was added in 1870 for the purpose of overruling prior court decisions that had held certain provisions of the 1849 Constitution regarding the title of legislative acts to be directory rather than mandatory and therefore not subject to judicial enforcement. It has been said that this declaration "applies to all sections of the Constitution alike, and is binding upon any department of the state government, legislative, executive or judicial" (*People ex rel. Webb v. California Fish Co.*, 1913). It represents a declaration by the people that " we mean what we say"(*Matter of Maguire*, 1881).

SECTION 27

Death penalty. All statutes of this state in effect on February 17, 1972 requiring, authorizing, imposing, or relating to the death penalty are in full force and effect, subject to legislative amendment or repeal by statute, initiative or referendum. The death penalty provided for under those statutes shall not be deemed to be, or to constitute, the infliction of cruel or unusual punishments within the meaning of Article 1, Section 6 nor shall such punishment for such offenses be deemed to contravene any other provision of this Constitution. [Nov. 7, 1972]

In *People v. Anderson* (1972), the supreme court held California's death penalty statute invalid under the state Constitution. (See Art. 1, sec. 17.) This provision, adopted later the same year, was aimed at overturning that decision and insulating existing statutes from state constitutional attack. At about the same time, however, the U.S. Supreme Court reached the same conclusion as the California court with respect to a similar statute under the federal Constitution (*Furman v. Georgia*, 1972). In 1977, the California legislature enacted a new death penalty statute, and in 1978 the people adopted an even stricter death penalty statute by initiative. Both statutes have subsequently been upheld against attack under both federal and state constitutions.

SECTION 28

"The Victims' Bill of Rights." (a) The People of the State of California find and declare that the enactment of comprehensive provisions and laws ensuring a bill of rights for victims of crime, including safeguards in the criminal justice system to fully protect those rights, is a matter of grave statewide concern.

The rights of victims pervade the criminal justice system, encompassing not only the right to restitution from the wrongdoers for financial losses suffered as a result of criminal acts, but also the more basic expectation that persons who commit felonious acts causing injury to innocent victims will be appropriately detained in custody, tried by the courts, and sufficiently punished so that the public safety is protected and encouraged as a goal of highest importance.

Such public safety extends to public primary, elementary, junior high, and senior high school campuses, where students and staff have the right to be safe and secure in their persons.

To accomplish these goals, broad reforms in the procedural treatment of accused persons and the disposition and sentencing of convicted persons are necessary and proper as deterrents to criminal behavior and to serious disruption of people's lives.

(b) *Restitution.* It is the unequivocal intention of the People of the State of California that all persons who suffer losses as a result of criminal activity shall have the right to restitution from the persons convicted of the crimes for losses they suffer.

Restitution shall be ordered from the convicted persons in every case, regardless of the sentence or disposition imposed, in which a crime victim suffers a loss, unless compelling and extraordinary reasons exist to the contrary. The Legislature shall adopt provisions to implement this section during the calendar year following adoption of this section.

(c) *Right to Safe Schools.* All students and staff of public primary, elementary, junior high and senior high schools have the inalienable right to attend campuses which are safe, secure, and peaceful.

(d) *Right to Truth-in-Evidence.* Except as provided by statute hereafter enacted by a two-thirds vote of the membership in each house of the Legislature, relevant evidence shall not be excluded in any criminal proceeding, including pretrial and post conviction motions and hearings, or in any trial or hearing of a juvenile for a criminal offense, whether heard in juvenile or adult court. Nothing in this section shall affect any existing statutory rule of evidence relating to privilege or hearsay, or Evidence Code, Sections 352, 782, or 1103. Nothing in this section shall affect any existing statutory or constitutional right of the press.

(e) *Public Safety Bail.* A person may be released on bail by sufficient sureties, except for capital crimes when the facts are evident or the presumption great. Excessive bail may not be required. In setting, reducing or denying bail, the judge or magistrate shall take into consideration the protection of the public, the seriousness of the offense charged, the previous criminal record of the defendant, and the probability of his or her appearing at the trial or hearing of the case. Public safety shall be the primary consideration.

A person may be released on his or her own recognizance in the court's discretion, subject to the same factors considered in setting bail. However, no person charged with the commission of any serious felony shall be released on his or her own recognizance.

Before any person arrested for a serious felony may be released on bail, a hearing may be held before the magistrate or judge, and the prosecuting attorney shall be given notice and reasonable opportunity to be heard on the matter.

When a job or magistrate grants or denies bail or release on a person's own recognizance, the reasons for that decision shall be stated in the record and included in the court's minutes.

(f) *Use of Prior Convictions.* Any prior felony conviction of any person in any criminal proceeding, whether adult or juvenile, shall subsequently be used without limitation for purposes of impeachment or enhancement of sentence in any criminal proceeding. When a prior felony conviction is an element of any felony offense, it shall be proven to the trier of fact in open court.

(g) As used in this article, the term "serious felony" is any crime defined in Penal Code, Section 1192.7 (c). [June 8, 1972]

This section was added to the constitution by an initiative amendment (the "Victims' Bill of Rights") in 1982. Its backers, which included organizations of crime victims and many prosecutors, argued that the measure was necessary to overturn court decisions, based on the state constitution, that they considered to be overly favorable toward criminal defendants. Its opponents argued that it would remove important protections established over years of constitutional development. Despite the variety of topics addressed by the measure, the supreme court held it did not violate the "single subject" requirement of Article II, section 8, and the measure became law (*Brosnahan v. Brown*, 1982).

Subsection (a) sets forth the findings and declarations of policy that underlie the measure.

Subsection (b) commands the legislature to adopt provisions requiring resti- tution from persons convicted of crime for losses incurred by the victims. The legislature has complied with that mandate.

Subsection (c) declares that public school students and staff have the "inalienable right to attend campuses which are safe, secure and peaceful." Persons injured through violence on school campuses have relied on this subsection as declaring a duty of care on the part of school administrators.

Subsection (d) provides, in effect, that evidence obtained in violation of the California Constitution—for example, through an unlawful search or seizure or through violation of a person's right to counsel or to be free from self-incrimination—shall nevertheless be admissible in a criminal proceeding unless its exclusion is required by the federal Constitution (*In re Lance W.*, 1985). Since the California Constitution had been interpreted in many contexts to provide greater protection for such rights, the impact of this subsection on criminal trials has been substantial. The subsection does not otherwise affect the scope of rights under the state constitution, however, and leaves available remedies for their protection (such as injunction or damages) other than the exclusion of evidence illegally obtained.

The mandate of subsection (d) that relevant evidence not be excluded in criminal proceedings is subject to certain exceptions traditional to the law of evidence. Evidence that is the subject of a privilege, such as that between doctor and patient, or hearsay evidence may still be excluded. The retention of Evidence Code sections 352, 781, and 1103 empowers courts to exclude evidence that, though relevant, may be unfairly prejudicial. And the subsection is subject to override by legislative enactment adopted by two-thirds vote in both legislative houses.

Subsection (e) of the Victims' Bill of Rights as adopted by the voters contained provisions relating to bail, but another measure on the same ballot, dealing exclusively with that topic through amendment of Article I, section 12, received more votes. The California Constitution provides that where proposed amendments conflict, the measure receiving the higher affirmative vote prevails (Art. II, sec. 10; Art. XVII, sec. 4). Consequently, it is the language of Article I, section 12 that governs bail.

Subsection (f) pertains to the use of a criminal defendant's prior felony convictions in a current trial. When a criminal defendant chooses to testify on his or her own behalf, the prosecutor may seek to discredit (impeach) his or her testimony by submitting evidence that the defendant had been convicted of a prior felony. This provision eliminated judicially constructed barriers to the use of such evidence. However, the supreme court has held that a judge still has discretion under Evidence Code section 352 to exclude evidence of prior convictions when the evidence is more prejudicial than it is relevant, and the prior conviction must be one involving moral turpitude (*People v. Castro*, 1985). Subsection (f) has a similar effect on former barriers to the consideration of prior felony convictions for the purpose of determining the appropriate sentence. The last sentence of subsection (f) pertains to those cases in which the commission of a prior felony is an element of a currently charged crime—for example, the use of a gun by a felon. Even if the defendant is willing to stipulate to the prior felony conviction, this section insists that the prosecutor be permitted to establish the circumstances, before the jury, in open court.

Subsection (g) refers to a statutory listing of felonies for definition of the term *serious felony*. In section 28, the term appears only in subsection (e), and that subsection is superseded by the bail provisions of section 8, which do not contain that language.

SECTION 29

Due process of law in criminal cases; speedy and public trial. In a criminal case, the people of the State of California have the right to due process of law and to a speedy and public trial. [June 5, 1990]

This section was added through initiative measure, Proposition 115, in 1990. It was apparently intended as a counterbalance to the due process and speedy and public trial rights of criminal defendants, but its meaning in practice has yet to be determined.

SECTION 30

Criminal cases: joinder, hearsay evidence, and discovery. (a) This Constitution shall not be construed by the courts to prohibit the joining of criminal cases as prescribed by the Legislature or by the people through the initiative process.
(b) In order to protect victims and witnesses in criminal cases, hearsay evidence shall be admissible at preliminary hearings, as prescribed by the Legislature or by the people through the initiative process.
(c) In order to provide for fair and speedy trials, discovery in criminal cases shall be reciprocal in nature as prescribed by the Legislature or by the people through the initiative process. [June 5, 1990]

This section, among those added by initiative measure (Proposition 115) in 1990, is aimed at overturning prior court decisions that, on constitutional grounds, (a) restricted the joinder of more than one criminal defendant in a single trial when joinder would be prejudicial to any of the defendants, (b) restricted the use of hearsay evidence in preliminary hearings, and (c) prohibited discovery by the prosecutor of the elements of the defendant's case prior to trial. Each subsection was accompanied, in the initiative measure, by an implementing statutory amendment. The precise scope of the constitutional and statutory amendments has yet to be determined.

Article II

Voting, Initiative, Referendum, and Recall

Article II has its roots in the Constitutions of 1849 and 1879, but it has been amended so frequently—with deletions, additions, and incorporation from other articles—that the heritage is barely recognizable. In its original form, the article was entitled "Suffrage" and contained provisions relating to voter eligibility. Over the years, those provisions were elaborated, and new provisions, including those relating to primary elections and nonpartisan offices, were added. In 1972, in accordance with recommendations of the California Constitution Revision Commission, provisions imposing a literacy requirement and a ninety-day waiting period for naturalized citizens were deleted, and other provisions were relegated to legislative action. In addition, at that time, the provisions for initiative, referendum, and recall, formerly contained in other articles, were relocated into Article II.

SECTION 1

Purpose of government. All political power is inherent in the people. Government is instituted for their protection, security, and benefit, and they have the right to alter or reform it when the public good may require. [June 8, 1976]

This provision sets forth the basic Lockean premise as to the justification for government. A corollary premise—that when an individual becomes a member of organized society he or the surrenders "only so much of his personal rights as may be considered essential to the furtherance of the objects for which it exists"—has occasionally found its way into judicial reasoning (e.g., *Ex parte Quarg*, 1906).

SECTION 2

Right to vote. A United States citizen 18 years of age and resident in this state may vote. [June 8, 1976]

The clarity and simplicity of this provision belies its complex and awkward ancestry. Former versions contained various limitations—sex (male), residence period (one year), literacy (English), and the like—together with detailed prescriptions relating to residence, registration, and absentee voting. Some limitations came into conflict with the federal Constitution and were removed or held unconstitutional. The 1972 revision pared down the rest, through deletions or relegation to legislative action, and changed the voting age from twenty-one to eighteen.

SECTION 3

Residence; registration; free elections. The Legislature shall define residence and provide for registration and free elections. [June 8, 1976]

This section, a product of the 1972 revision, supplants former provisions that specified certain voting requirements (as in the case of voters who move from one precinct or county to another) and authorized legislative enactments covering various aspects of elections. One important consequence of the revision was to eliminate the requirements for absence or physical disability as a condition to voting by absentee ballots. The legislature has responded by authorizing absentee ballots on request, with the result that increasing percentages of the electorate are voting absentee ballots rather than going to the polls.

SECTION 4

Improper practices affecting elections; disqualification of voters. The Legislature shall prohibit improper practices that affect elections and shall provide for the disqualification of electors while mentally incompetent or imprisoned or on parole for the conviction of a felony. [June 8, 1976]

Prior to 1972, Article II, section 1 provided for constitutional disqualification of any "idiot," "insane person," or person convicted of any "infamous crime," including embezzlement or misappropriation of public money. The "infamous crime" disqualification was challenged in the 1960s under the due process and equal protection clauses of the Fourteenth Amendment to the U.S. Constitution; as a means of preserving its constitutionality, the California Supreme Court construed the term to require a showing of threat to the integrity of the elective process (*Otsuka v. Hite*, 1966). As a result of the 1972 revision (which also exchanged the *word idiot* for the term *severely mentally deficient person*, the legislature was directed to prescribe for disqualification of persons within the designated categories.

The current language was the product of amendment in 1974. Despite its reference to legislative action, the section insofar as it relates to persons imprisoned or on parole for the conviction of a felony has been held to be selfexecuting, in the face of legislative inaction (*Flood v. Riggs*, 1978). The provision directing the legislature to prohibit improper practices has not been the subject of adjudication.

SECTION 5

Primary elections for partisan offices; open presidential primary. The Legislature shall provide for primary elections for partisan offices, including an open presidential primary whereby the candidates on the ballot are those found by the Secretary of State to be recognized candidates throughout the nation or throughout California for the office of President of the United States, and those whose names are placed on the ballot by petition, but excluding any candidate who has withdrawn by filing an affidavit of noncandidacy. [June 8, 1976]

The first phrase of this provision derives from former Article II, section 2½, initially adopted in 1900, which granted the legislature sweeping authority to "enact laws relative to the election of delegates to conventions of political parties," to determine "the tests and conditions upon which electors, political parties, or organizations of electors may participate in any such primary election," and to make primary elections obligatory. The courts construed the new provision broadly, upholding legislative enactments (for example) that required a person in whose primary he or she votes to declare allegiance to the party (*Rebstock v. Superior Court*, 1905) and limited use of the primary election to parties that polled 3 percent or more of the vote in the previous election (*Katz v. Fitzgerald*, 1907). But legislative authority over primaries is not unlimited. In 1942 the supreme court struck down a provision excluding any party that used the word *communist* in its designation on the ground that it exceeded legislative authority under section 2½ (*Communist Party v. Peek*, 1942).

The current language of the first phrase, simply directing the legislature to "provide for primary elections for partisan, offices," was the product of a 1972 amendment, recommended by the revision commission on the ground that further specification of authority was unnecessary in the light of the general power of the legislature to provide for elections (Art. I, sec. 2) and what the commission characterized as the legislature's "inherent power."

The remainder of this provision, pertaining to presidential primaries, was adopted in November 1972 to replace Article II, section 8, to the same effect, that had been adopted in the June election of that year. A 1974 amendment substituted "of noncandidacy" for "that he is not a candidate."

In 1913 the Progressive movement, with its distrust of political parties, led the legislature in adopting the controversial system of cross-filing, which dominated primary politics in California for the next forty-six years. That system permitted a candidate to run in the primaries of both his or her own and the opposition party and, if the candidate received a plurality in both parties, to become the nominee of both, thus rendering the general election superfluous. Many prominent California politicians, including Governor Earl Warren, achieved office in that manner. The cross-filing system was ultimately abandoned by adoption of a statutory initiative in 1959.

SECTION 6

Nonpartisan offices. (a) All judicial, school, county, and city offices shall be nonpartisan.

(b) No political party or central committee may endorse, support, or oppose a candidate for nonpartisan office. [June 3, 1986]

Subsection (a), declaring certain offices to be nonpartisan, was adopted in 1902, the product of an early Progressive reform movement aimed at correcting what were perceived to be the excesses of partisan politics. As a consequence, candidates for such offices are not nominated by political parties, there is no primary election for such offices, and party designations do not appear on the ballot.

Long after adoption of the amendment, questions arose as to whether a political party could endorse, or otherwise support or oppose, a candidate in a primary election. In 1984, the supreme court held that section 6 did not by its own force preclude a political party from declaring its views in that manner (*Unger v. Superior Court*, 1984), but two years later, the voters adopted an initiative measure to override *Unger* by the addition of subsection (b). It appears, however, that subsection (b)'s sweeping ban on endorsement, support, or opposition of a candidate by a political party or central committee may violate First Amendment free expression guarantees (*Renne v. Geary*, 1991).

SECTION 7

Secret voting. Voting shall be secret. [June 8, 1976]

The 1849 Constitution (Art. 2, sec. 6) provided that "all elections by the people shall be by ballot." The requirement for secrecy was added in 1879. In 1972 the current succinct language was substituted, and in 1976 the section was renumbered.

There is some tension between the secrecy requirement and the increased use of absentee ballots and (in the case of some local political units) mail ballots, especially when candidates or their supporters visit voters in their homes or at meetings to "assist" in voting. The supreme court, however, has upheld the use of mail ballots despite these problems, on the ground that the secrecy requirement was not intended to preclude reasonable measures designed to facilitate voting (*Peterson v. City of San Diego*, 1983). The court has also held that it does not violate this provision for someone to assist in the marking of ballots, so long as the assistance is given at the voter's request and without fraud or coercion (*Wilks v. Mouton*, 1986).

SECTION 8

Initiative. (a) The initiative is the power of the electors to propose statutes and amendments to the Constitution and to adopt or reject them.

(b) An initiative measure may be proposed by presenting to the Secretary of State a petition that sets forth the text of the proposed statute or amendment to the Constitution and is certified to have been signed by electors equal in number to 5 percent in the case of a statute, and 8 percent in the case of an amendment to the Constitution, of the votes for all candidates for Governor at the last gubernatorial election.

(c) The Secretary of State shall then submit the measure at the next general election held at least 131 days after it qualifies or at any special statewide election held prior to that general election. The Governor may call a special statewide election for the measure.

(d) An initiative measure embracing more than one subject may not be submitted to the electors or have any effect. [June 8, 1976]

The initiative, along with the referendum (Art. II, sec. 9) and the recall (Art. II, sec. 13), is the product of a movement toward direct democracy that was led by the Progressive faction of the Republican party around the turn of the century. Put forward as a means of counteracting the political machine then controlled by the Southern Pacific Railroad Company and adopted through constitutional amendment in 1911 by overwhelming vote of the people, the initiative process has increasingly come to dominate California political culture. Among the states that use the initiative process, California is by far the most active. It is one of the few states in which the initiative can be used to amend the constitution and the only one in which a statutory amendment adopted by initiative cannot be modified by the legislature unless the initiative so provides.

Subsection (a) refers to both statutory and constitutional initiatives. The original 1911 direct democracy package included also provision for indirect statutory initiatives, by which voters could submit a measure to the legislature for adoption, with the proviso that the measure would appear on the ballot if the legislature failed to enact it. Used only four times in California history, the indirect statutory initiative was eliminated in 1966.

Subsection (b) prescribes the number of signatures that must be obtained in order to place an initiative measure on the ballot. Prior to 1966, the number for statutory and constitutional initiatives was the same: 8 percent of the total number of votes cast for gubernatorial candidates in the previous election. In that year, in an effort to encourage the use of statutory initiatives rather than constitutional initiatives, the percentage for statutory initiatives was reduced to 5 percent. Obtaining signatures on petitions has become big business, with firms hired by proponents to solicit signatures, charging as much as two dollars for each signature obtained.

Under subsection (c), an initiative measure that obtains the requisite number of signatures is submitted to the voters at the next general election, unless the governor calls for a special statewide election—a rare event. The secretary of state is responsible for determining whether the requisite number of signatures has been obtained but otherwise has no discretion to keep an initiative measure off the ballot. On occasion the supreme court has ordered the secretary of state not to place a measure on the ballot, on the ground that it is not the proper subject of the initiative process (*American Federation of Labor v. Eu*, 1982). The courts will not intervene prior to an election, however, to consider whether the measure, if adopted, would be constitutional (*Brosnahan v. Eu*, 1982).

The single-subject rule imposed by subsection (d) has given rise to a good deal of litigation but has proved to be a toothless tiger. A similar rule exists for legislative enactments, and in that context it has been loosely applied, but there is good reason to construe the rule more stringently in the case of initiative measures, where the opportunities for amendment and compromise do not exist. Some supreme court justices have suggested from time to time that the rule in the initiative context should be construed to require that the provisions of the measure be functionally related to one another, but the court has rejected that suggestion in favor of a test that inquires simply whether the provisions are "reasonably germane to each other, and to the general purpose or object of the initiative" (*Brosnahan v. Brown*, 1982). The court has reasoned that in order to protect and favor the initiative, the voters must be able to deal "comprehensively and in detail with an area of the law" (*Fair Political Practices Commission v. Superior Court*, 1979). On that basis, the court has upheld (for example) the Victims' Bill of Rights (Art. I, sec. 28), which provides for sweeping changes in various aspects of criminal law and criminal procedure, ranging from the definition of insanity to the admissibility of illegally obtained evidence, along with a declaration in favor of "safe schools" (*Brosnahan v. Brown*, 1982). If a measure affects various parts of the constitution, it may be invalid as a "constitutional revision," which can be accomplished only through constitutional convention or legislative proposal. (See Art. XVIII.)

SECTION 9

Referendum. (a) The referendum is the power of the electors to approve or reject statutes or parts of statutes except urgency statutes, statutes calling elections, and statutes providing for tax levies or appropriations for usual current expenses of the State.

(b) Areferendum measure may be proposed by presenting to the Secretary of State, within 90 days after the enactment date of the statute, a petition certified to have been signed by electors equal in number to 5 percent of the votes for all candidates for Governor at the last gubernatorial election, asking that the statute or part of it be submitted to the electors. In the case of a statute enacted by a bill passed by the Legislature on or before the date the Legislature adjourns for a joint recess to reconvene in the second calendar year of the biennium of the legislative session, and in the possession of the Governor after that date, the petition may not be presented on or before January 1 next following the enactment date unless a copy of the petition is submitted to the Attorney General pursuant to subdivision (d) of Section 10 of Article II before January 1.

(c) The Secretary of State shall then submit the measure at the next general election held at least 31 days after it qualifies or at a special statewide election held prior to that general election. The Governor may call a special statewide election for the measure. [June 6, 1990]

The referendum, along with the initiative, was part of the direct democracy package that the voters adopted in 1911. (For additional history, see Art. II, sec. 8.) Passage of a referendum measure does not result in the adoption of any law; rather, it operates to prevent a statute adopted by the legislature from having legal effect. The filing of a duly qualified referendum challenging a statute normally stays implementation of the statute until the election (*Assembly v. Deukmejian*, 1982).

The statewide referendum has fallen into disuse for a number of reasons, the major one being that with the growth in the state's population, obtaining the necessary number of signatures is exceedingly difficult. The fact that the legislature now meets almost continuously throughout the year (instead of biannually, as was the case prior to 1966) facilitates the seeking of amendments or repeal through the legislative process itself. Even before these changes, the legislature could avoid a referendum by declaring a measure to be urgent, and courts were disinclined to interfere with such a determination (*Davis v. County of Los Angeles*, 1938). The referendum has not been used statewide in California since 1952.

The second sentence of subsection (b) was added in 1990 as part of a constitutional amendment that extends the governor's time to review bills in his or her possession after the adjournment of the first year of the legislative session.

SECTION 10

Initiative and referendum measures: effective date, conflicting measures, legislative repeal or amendment, titles. (a) An initiative statute or referendum approved by a majority of votes thereon takes effect the day after the election unless the measure otherwise provides. If a referendum petition is field against a part of the statute the remainder shall not be delayed from going into effect.
(b) If provisions of 2 or more measures approved at the same election conflict, those of the measure receiving the highest affirmative vote shall prevail.
(c) The Legislature may amend or repeal referendum statutes. It may amend or repeal an initiative statute by another statute that becomes effective only when approved by the electors unless the initiative statute permits amendment or repeal without their approval.
(d) Prior to circulation of an initiative or referendum petition for signatures, a copy shall be submitted to the Attorney General who shall prepare a title and summary of the measure as provided by law.
(e) The Legislature shall provide the manner in which petitions shall be circulated, presented, and certified, and measures submitted to the electors. [June 8, 1976]

Former law provided that an initiative or referendum measure would take effect five days after the official declaration of vote by the secretary of state. The official declaration was often delayed for an unpredictable period, however. As a result of a 1970 amendment, subsection (a) now provides that the measure will become effective the day after election.

Subsection (b) deals with the increasingly common situation in which two or more initiatives, each bearing on the same subject matter, appear on the same ballot. Its directive—that in the event of conflict, the provisions of the measure receiving the highest affirmative vote shall prevail—has been read by the supreme court as meaning that if the measures are "competing initiatives," either because they are expressly offered as all-or-nothing alternatives or because each creates a comprehensive regulatory scheme related to the same subject, then unless a contrary intent is apparent in the ballot measures themselves, only the provisions of the measure receiving the highest number of affirmative votes will be enforced. The court chose this interpretation over one that would invalidate only the "conflicting"provisions of the measure receiving fewer votes, which would allow the remaining provisions to stand. To permit that result, the court reasoned, would impose upon the electorate a mixed regulatory scheme, which they neither understood or intended (*Taxpayers to Limit Campaign Spending v. Fair Political Practices Commission*, 1990).

Subsection (c) states the unusual California rule that the legislature may not directly amend a statute adopted by an initiative unless the measure so provides. This rule permits use of the statutory initiative to place matters beyond legislative control, much as a constitutional amendment would do. Often initiative measures will authorize legislative modification but only by a supermajority (two-thirds or three-fourths) vote.

Subsection (d) calls upon the attorney general to prepare a title and summary of each measure that appears on the ballot. This official's duties in that regard are ministerial; he or she cannot refuse to prepare a summary, for example, because he or she believes the measure to be invalid (*Warner v. Kenny*, 1946).

Subsection (e) authorizes the legislature to provide, by statute, for the procedures associated with the initiative and referendum process.

SECTION 11

Initiative and referendum measures: cities and counties. Intiative and referendum powers may be exercised by the electors of each city or county under procedures that the Legislature shall provide. This section does not affect a city having a charter. [June 8, 1976]

As adopted in 1911, this section delegated to local governments the power to regulate procedural aspects of local initiative and referendum elections. The chartered government exception, which then embraced chartered counties as well as cities, was adopted in deference to local entities whose charters already provided for the initiative and referendum and was intended to authorize charters to expand upon, but not to limit, the use of those processes (*Hunt v. Mayor*, 1948). In 1966, the section was amended to provide for control of local initiative and referendum procedures by the legislature, except in the case of chartered cities.

SECTION 12

Initiative and referendum measures: prohibition upon naming persons to office or corporations to duties. No amendment to the Constitution, and no statute proposed to the electors by the Legislature or by initiative, that names any individual to hold any office, or names or identifies any private corporation to perform any function or to have any power or duty, may be submitted to the electors or have any effect. [June 8, 1976].

This section, aimed at preventing the initiative from being used to confer special privilege or benefit, derives from two separate constitutional amendments.

The first, adopted in 1950 as Article IV, section 1(d), provided that any initiative, statute, or constitutional amendment "which names any individual . . . to hold any office"shall have no effect. The second, adopted in 1964, extended that principle to any constitutional amendment "which names any private corporation." In 1966, in response to recommendations by the constitutional revision commission, the two measures were merged into a single provision. At the same time, the language was expanded to apply to initiative measures as well as constitutional amendments in the case of corporations and to measures that identify as well as name particular beneficiaries.

This section restricts only the power of the voters; it has no application to statutes adopted by the legislature. The supreme court has held that this section is not limited to profit corporations or to entities in existence at the time of the initiative (*Calfarm Insurance Co. v. Deukmejian*, 1989). Whether inclusion of a prohibited naming or identification invalidates an entire measure or only a portion of it depends on whether the court deems the prohibited portion "severable."

SECTION 13

Recall defined. Recall is the power of the electors to remove an elective officer. [June 8, 1976]

SECTION 14

Recall petitions. (a) Recall of a State officer is initiated by delivering to the Secretary of State a petition alleging reason for recall. Sufficiency of reason is not reviewable. Proponents have 160 days to file signed petitions.

(b) A petition to recall a statewide officer must be signed by electors equal in number to 12 percent of the last vote for the office, with signatures from each of 5 counties equal in number to 1 percent of the last vote for the office in the county. Signatures to recall Senators, members of the assembly, members of the Board of Equalization, and judges of courts of appeal and trial courts must equal in number 20 percent of the last vote for the office.

(c) The Secretary of State shall maintain a continuous count of the signatures certified to that office. [June 8, 1976]

SECTION 15

Recall elections. An election to determine whether to recall an officer and, if appropriate, to elect a successor shall be called by the Governor and held not less than 60 days nor more than 80 days from the date of certification of sufficient signatures. If the majority vote on the question is to recall, the officer is removed and, if there is a candidate, the candidate who receives a plurality is the successor. The officer may not be a candidate, nor shall there be any candidacy for an office filled pursuant to subdivision (d) of Section 16 of Article VI. [June 8, 1976]

SECTION 16

Legislature to provide for recall petitions and elections. The Legislature shall provide for circulation, filing, and certification of petitions, nomination of candidates, and the recall election. [June 8, 1976]

SECTION 17

Recall of governor or secretary of state. If recall of the Governor or Secretary of State is initiated, the recall duties of that office shall be performed by the Lieutenant Governor or Controller, respectively. [June 8, 1976]

SECTION 18

Reimbursement of recall election expenses. A state officer who is not recalled shall be reimbursed by the State for the officer's recall election expenses legally and personally incurred. Another recall may not be initiated against the officer until six months after the election. [June 8, 1976]

SECTION 19

Recall of local officers. The Legislature shall provide for recall of local officers. This section does not affect counties and cities whose charters provide for recall. [June 8, 1976]

The power of recall was added to the constitution in 1911 as Article XXIII, section 1. The original provisions contained considerable detail as to procedures. In 1974, as part of the revision of that year, Article XXIII, section 1 was repealed, most of the procedural detail was relegated to the Elections Code, and the remaining provisions were revamped and retained as Article XXIII. In 1976, Article XXIII was renumbered as Article II, sections 13–19, without any textual changes, rewritten to their current form, and adopted as Article XX.

Section 13 defines the power of recall; section 14 sets forth the requirements for a recall petition; section 15 provides for recall elections; section 16 authorizes the legislature to adopt more specific recall procedures; section 17 stipulates the order of succession in the event of recall of the governor or secretary of state; section 18 provides that a state officer who is not recalled shall be reimbursed by the state for recall expenses; and section 19 provides for recall of local officers pursuant to procedures adopted by the legislature—with the exception of chartered counties and cities, which may provide their own procedures. While there have been several attempts, no recall of a statewide officer has succeeded. Recall of local officials has been successful on occasion.

SECTION 20

Commencement of terms of elective office. Terms of elective offices provided for by this Constitution, other than Members of the Legislature, commence on the Monday after January 1 following election. The election shall be held in the last even-numbered year before the term expires. [June 8, 1976]

The 1849 Constitution did not specify the terms of elective offices. This section was originally adopted (as Art. XX, sec. 20)in 1870. The exception for members of the legislature was added in 1972; their terms are specified in Article IV, sections 2(a) and (b).

Article III

State of California

This catchall article contains provisions relating to state governance that do not fit easily within the other, more specific articles. In the 1849 and 1879 constitutions, it consisted only of what is now section 3, providing for separation of powers. Sections 1,2, and 5 were contained elsewhere in the early constitutions and were transferred to this article as part of the revision of 1972. Section 3.5 and sections 6–8 were adopted by later amendment.

SECTION 1

Supremacy of United States Constitution. The State of California is an inseparable part of the United States of America, and the United States Constitution is the supreme law of the land. [Nov. 7, 1972]

This section was initially part of the 1879 Constitution, where the term *Union* was used instead of *United States of America*. Readopted in 1972 with minor changes, its twin declarations—that California is an inseparable part of the United States and that the federal Constitution is the supreme law of the land—are redundant truisms.

SECTION 2

State boundaries; Sacramento the capital. The boundaries of the state are those stated in the Constitution of 1849 as modified pursuant to statute. Sacramento is the capital of California. [Nov. 7, 1972]

The Constitution of 1849 (Art. XII, sec. 1) defined California's boundaries by reference to geographic parallels and meridians, the Colorado River, the Pacific Ocean, and the Mexican border. The application of such a description to the earth's surface and its changing contours can be problematic, as evidenced by the fact that the U.S. Supreme Court was called upon to resolve a border dispute between California and Nevada as late as 1980. (*California v. Nevada,* 1980). Hence, the reference to modifying legislation. Consistent with general principles of international law, California's territory includes ocean waters within three nautical miles off the coast (*Ex parte Marincovich,* 1920).

Prior to statehood, the de facto capital of California was Monterey. The 1849 Constitution designated Pueblo de San Jose as the seat of government, subject to change by two-thirds vote of the legislature. Thereafter, the capital was moved first to Vallejo, then to Sacramento, then to Benecia, and finally (in 1853) back to Sacramento again, where its location was permanently established in the Constitution of 1879.

SECTION 3

Separation of powers. The powers of state government are legislative, executive, and judicial. Persons charged with the exercise of one power may not exercise either of the others except as permitted by this Constitution. [Nov. 7, 1972]

This section, stating the basic principle of separation of powers, stems directly from identical language in the Constitution of 1849. Judicial elaboration upon that principle as it applies to the legislative, executive, and judicial branches is reflected in the commentary to Articles IV, V, and VI.

SECTION 3.5

Limits on powers of administrative agencies to declare statutes invalid or unenforceable. An administrative agency, including an administrative agency created by the Constitution or an initiative statute, has no power:

(a) To declare a statute unenforceable, or refuse to enforce a statute, on the basis of its being unconstitutional unless an appellate court has made a determination that such statute is unconstitutional;
(b) To declare a statute unconstitutional;

(c) To declare a statute unenforceable, or to refuse to enforce a statute on the basis that federal law or federal regulations prohibit the enforcement of such statute unless an appellate court has made a determination that the enforcement of such statute is prohibited by federal law or federal regulations. [June 6, 1978]

This unusual provision forbids any state agency from declaring a state law unconstitutional or refusing to enforce a state law on that basis, or on the basis that it conflicts with federal law, unless an appellate court first makes such a determination. It was adopted as a legislatively proposed amendment in 1978 in response to a supreme court decision holding that an administrative agency with constitutional status (in that case, the Public Utilities Commission) had the power to decide that it would not implement a particular statutory provision it considered to be unconstitutional (*Southern Pacific Transportation Co. v. PUC*, 1976). Legislative proponents of the 1978 ballot measure argued that the supreme court's ruling enabled an administrative agency to thwart the legislative will. The supreme court has since held that the section does not prohibit the legislature itself from restricting the scope of a statute through a provision that it is not to be applied where its application would be unconstitutional (*Reese v. Kizer*, 1988).

SECTION 4

Salaries of elected state officers and judges. (a) Except as provided in subdivision (b), salaries of elected state officers may not be reduced during their term of office. Laws that set these salaries are appropriations.

(b) Beginning on January 1, 1981, the base salary of a judge of a court of record shall equal the annual salary payable as of July 1, 1980, for that office had the judge been elected in 1978. The Legislature may prescribe increases in those salaries during a term of office, and it may terminate prospective increases in those salaries at any time during a term of office, but it shall not reduce the salary of a judge during a term of office below the highest level paid during that term of office. Laws setting the salaries of judges shall not constitute an obligation of contract pursuant to Section 9 of Article I or any other provision of law. [Nov. 4, 1980]

Subsection (a), as adopted in 1972, provided that the legislature could fix salaries and expenses of state officers, that salaries of elected state officers may not be reduced during their term of office, and that laws setting these salaries are appropriations—meaning that they require two-thirds vote for adoption.

In 1980 subsection (b) was adopted through a legislatively proposed amendment relating to judicial salaries, and subsection (a) was amended to make reference to that addition. Prior to 1976, judges' salaries automatically rose each year with increases in the cost of living index. In the inflationary period of the 1970s, that resulted in substantial increases. In 1976 the legislature passed a law freezing judges' salaries for eighteen months from January 1, 1977, and limiting future increases to a maximum of 5 percent. The supreme court, however, ruled that the law was unconstitutional as applied to incumbent judges. (*Olson v. Cory*, 1980). Subsection (b), enabling the legislature to limit increases in salaries for incumbent judges, was designed to overcome that ruling. As applied to judges then in office, however, the attempt failed; a court of appeal held that as so applied, the provision violated the federal Constitution's prohibition of impairment of contracts and deprivation of property without due process of law (*Olson v. Cory*, 1982). Due to deaths and retirements, the issue is largely moot.

In 1990, when a new system for determining legislative salaries through the California Citizens Compensation Commission was adopted (Art. 3, sec. 12), subsection (a) was amended to delete reference to the legislature's fixing its own salaries.

SECTION 5

Suits against the state. Suits may be brought against the state in such manner and in such courts as shall be directed by law. [Nov. 7, 1972]

This section stems from identically worded provisions in the 1849 and 1879 Constitutions. While it might be viewed as a constitutional prohibition against suing the state without its permission, the courts have not so viewed it. In *Muskopf v. Corning Hospital District* (1961), the supreme court abolished the common law rule of sovereign immunity, which held that the state may not be sued without its consent, and interpreted this section as an enabling provision, permitting the legislature to consent to be sued. The legislature responded by passing the California Tort Claims Act (Gov. Code sec. 810 et seq.) prescribing the conditions under which suit may be maintained against the state.

SECTION 6

Official state language. (a) Purpose. English is the common language of the people of the United States of America and the State of California. This section is intended to preserve, protect and strengthen the English language, and not to supersede any of the rights guaranteed to the people by this Constitution.

(b) English as the Official Language of California. English is the official language of the State of California.

(c) Enforcement. The Legislature shall enforce this section by appropriate legislation. The Legislature and officials of the State of California shall take all steps necessary to insure the role of English as the common language of the State of California is

preserved and enhanced. The Legislature shall make no law which diminishes or ignores the role of English as the common language of the State of California.
(d) Personal Right of Action and Jurisdiction of Courts. Any person who is a resident of or doing business in the State of California shall have standing to sue the State of California to enforce this section, and the Courts of record of the State of California shall have jurisdiction to hear cases brought to enforce this section. The Legislature may provide reasonable and appropriate limitations on the time and manner of suits brought under this section. [Nov. 4, 1986]

This unfortunate provision, reflecting voter impatience with the necessity of accommodating to increased numbers of non-English-speaking residents, was adopted as an initiative measure in 1986. What legal effect it was supposed to have is unclear from the ballot arguments, and the courts have yet to provide an authoritative interpretation.

SECTION 7

Retirement benefits for elected constitutional officers. (a) The retirement allowance for any person, all of whose credited service in the Legislators' Retirement System was rendered or was deemed to have been rendered as an elective officer of the state whose office is provided for by the California Constitution, other than a judge and other than a Member of the Senate or Assembly, and all or any part of whose retirement allowance is calculated on the basis of the compensation payable to the officer holding the office which the member last held prior to retirement, or for the survivor or beneficiary of such a person, shall not be increased or affected in any manner by changes on or after November 5, 1986, in the compensation payable to the officer holding the office which the member last held prior to retirement.
(b) This section shall apply to any person, survivor, or beneficiary described in subdivision (a) who receives, or is receiving, from the Legislators' Retirement System a retirement allowance on or after November 5, 1986, all or any part of which allowance is calculated on the basis of the compensation payable to the officer holding the office which the member last held prior to retirement.
(c) It is the intent of the people, in adopting this section, to restrict retirement allowances to amounts reasonably to be expected by certain members and retired members of the Legislators' Retirement System and to preserve the basic character of earned retirement benefits while prohibiting windfalls and unforeseen advantages which have no relation to the real theory and objective of a sound retirement system. It is not the intent of this section to deny any member, retired member, survivor, or beneficiary a reasonable retirement allowance. Thus, this section shall not be construed as a repudiation of a debt nor the impairment of a contract for a

substantial and reasonable retirement allowance from the Legislators' Retirement System.

(d) The people and the Legislature hereby find and declare that the dramatic increase in the retirement allowances of persons described in subdivision (a) which would otherwise result when the compensation for those offices increases on November 5, 1986, or January 5, 1987, are not benefits which could have reasonably been expected. The people and the Legislature further find and declare that the Legislature did not intend to provide in its scheme of compensation for those offices such windfall benefits. [Nov. 4, 1986]

Prior to 1986, retirement benefits for constitutional officers who took office before 1974 were geared to current salaries, so that upon retirement such an officer received an increase in benefits whenever salary was increased for incumbents. In 1986, the legislature provided for substantial salary increases for incumbents to take effect in 1987. The legislature, considering that application of the former rule would result in a windfall to retired officers, proposed, and the voters adopted, this section. Its effect, applicable to only a handful of persons, is to eliminate the connection between future increases in the salaries and the retirement benefit of such officers.

SECTION 8

California Citizens Compensation Commission. (a) The California Citizens Compensation Commission is hereby created and shall consist of seven members appointed by the Governor. The commission shall establish the annual salary and the medical, dental, insurance, and other similar benefits of state officers.

(b) The commission shall consist of the following persons:

(1) Three public members, one of whom has expertise in the area of compensation, such as an economist, market researcher, or personnel manager; one of whom is a member of a nonprofit public interest organization; and one of whom is representative of the general population and may include, among others, a retiree, homemaker, or person of median income. No person appointed pursuant to this paragraph may, during the 12 months prior to his or her appointment, have held public office, either elective or appointive, have been a candidate for elective public office, or have been a lobbyist, as defined by the Political Reform Act of 1974.

(2) Two members who have experience in the business community, one of whom is an executive of a corporation incorporated in this state which ranks among the largest private sector employers in the state based on the number of employees employed by the corporation in this state and one of whom is an owner of a small business in this state.

(3) Two members, each of whom is an officer or member of a labor organization.

(c) The Governor shall strive insofar as practicable to provide a balanced representation of the geographic, gender, racial, and ethnic diversity of the state in appointing commission members.

(d) The Governor shall appoint commission members and designate a chairperson for the commission not later than 30 days after the effective date of this section. The terms of two of the initial appointees shall expire on December 31, 1992, two on December 31, 1994, and three on December 31, 1996, as determined by the Governor. Thereafter, the term of each member shall be six years. Within 15 days of any vacancy, the Governor shall appoint a person to serve the unexpired portion of the term.

(e) No current or former officer or employee of this state is eligible for appointment to the commission.

(f) Public notice shall be given of all meetings of the commission, and the meetings shall be open to the public.

(g) On or before December 13, 1990, the commission shall, by a single resolution adopted by a majority of the membership of the commission, establish the annual salary and the medical, dental, insurance, and other similar benefits of state officers. The annual salary and benefits specified in that resolution shall be effective on and after December 3, 1990.

Thereafter, at or before the end of each fiscal year, the commission shall, by a single resolution adopted by a majority of the membership of the commission, adjust the annual salary and the medical, dental, insurance, and other similar benefits of state officers. The annual salary and benefits specified in the resolution shall be effective on and after the first Monday of the next December.

(h) In establishing or adjusting the annual salary and the medical, dental, insurance, and other similar benefits, the commission shall consider all of the following:

(1) The amount of time directly or indirectly related to the performance of the duties, functions, and services of a state officer.

(2) The amount of the annual salary and the medical, dental, insurance, and other similar benefits for other elected and appointed officers and officials in this state with comparable responsibilities, the judiciary, and, to the extent practicable, the private sector, recognizing, however, that state officers do not receive, and do not expect to receive, compensation at the same levels as individuals in the private sector with comparable experience and responsibilities.

(3) The responsibility and scope of authority of the entity in which the state officer serves.

(i) Until a resolution establishing or adjusting the annual salary and the medical, dental, insurance, and other similar benefits for state officers takes effect, each state officer shall continue to receive the same annual salary and the medical, dental, insurance, and other similar benefits received previously.

(j) All commission members shall receive their actual and necessary expenses, including travel expenses, incurred in the performance of their duties. Each member shall be compensated at the same rate as members, other than the chairperson, of the

Fair Political Practices Commission, or its successor, for each day engaged in official duties, not to exceed 45 days per year.

(k) It is the intent of the Legislature that the creation of the commission should not generate new state costs for staff and services. The Department of Personnel Administration, the Board of Administration of the Public Employees' Retirement System, or other appropriate agencies, or their successors, shall furnish, from existing resources, staff and services to the commission as needed for the performance of its duties.

(l) "State officer," as used in this section, means the Governor, Lieutenant Governor, Attorney General, Controller, Insurance Commissioner, Secretary of State, Superintendent of Public Instruction, Treasurer, member of the State Board of Equalization, and Member of the Legislature. [June 6, 1990]

This section, part of Proposition 112 on the November 1990 ballot, removes from the legislature the power to set salaries and benefits of state officers (including members of the legislature itself) and allocates that power to a seven-person commission consisting of three public members, two members with experience in the business community, and two members with ties to labor organizations, all appointed by the governor with staggered initial terms and ultimate terms of six years. The commission has authority to establish the annual salary and the medical, dental, insurance, and other similar benefits of state officers. The term *state officer* is defined to include, in addition to members of the legislature, the principal elective executive officers of the state. The section directs the commission to consider various criteria, including the amount of time the officer spends on state duties, comparable salaries in public and private employment, and the responsibility and scope of authority of the entity in which the state officer serves.

Article IV

Legislative

Unlike the federal Congress, which has only those powers enumerated in the Constitution, the state legislature has plenary authority subject to constitutional limitations. From the outset, however, the constitutional framers were suspicious of the legislative branch and placed numerous restrictions on its powers and procedures.

The 1960s brought revolutionary changes in the composition of the legislature and in its functioning. Pursuant to the one-person, one-vote rulings of the U.S. Supreme Court, the apportionment of senatorial districts based largely on county lines was abandoned in favor of apportionment based on population. This shifted the balance of political power away from the rural areas and to the cities. During the same period, as a result of constitutional amendments, the legislature became a relatively full-time and continuous body and was permitted to establish its own salaries. Legislative staffs were increased in such a way as to enable the legislature to deal with the governor on equal terms in the development of the annual budget and in the drafting of legislation. In 1971 the Citizens Conference on State Legislatures judged the California legislature to be the best in the Union.

Over the next two decades, however, public dissatisfaction led, in 1990, to the adoption of two constitutional amendments. Proposition 112, proposed by the legislature on the June ballot as a means of warding off more severe measures, prohibited members of the legislature and certain other officers from receiving honorariums; imposed restrictions on gifts, lobbying activity, and sources of income; and created a Citizens Compensation Commission with exclusive power to set salaries and fringe benefits, except retirement, for such officers. In the November election, however, the voters approved Proposition 140, an initiative measure that effected more far-reaching changes: limitations on terms of elected state officials, limitations on the legislature's institutional budget, and limitations on retirement benefits for legislators.

SECTION 1

Legislative power. The legislative power of this State is vested in the California Legislature which consists of the Senate and Assembly but the people reserve to themselves the power of initiative and referendum. [Nov. 8, 1966]

The drafters of the 1849 Constitution followed the prevailing model in providing for a bicameral legislature. The phrase referring to the initiative and referendum was added in 1911, when those procedures were established.

Under the doctrine of separation of powers, explicitly set forth in Article III, the legislative branch may not delegate its authority to make laws to either courts or administrative agencies. In early cases, the courts applied that principle strictly. By the 1930s, however, confronted with growing legislative reliance upon rule making by administrative agencies, courts came to accept delegations of power so long as they were accompanied by some standards to guide administrative discretion and permit judicial review.

SECTION 1.5

Legislative term limits; restriction of retirement benefits; limits on legislative staff and support. The people find and declare that the Founding Fathers established a system of representative government based upon free, fair, and competitive elections. The increased concentration of political power in the hands of incumbent representatives has made our electoral system less free, less competitive and less representative.

The ability of legislators to serve unlimited number of terms, to establish their own retirement system and to pay for staff and support services at State expense contribute heavily to the extremely high number of incumbents who are reelected. These unfair incumbent advantages discourage qualified candidates from seeking public office and create a class of career politicians, instead of the citizen representatives envisioned by the Founding Fathers. These career politicians become representatives of the bureaucracy, rather than of the people whom they are elected to represent.

To restore a free and democratic system of fair elections and to encourage qualified candidates to seek public office the people find and declare that the powers of incumbency must be limited. Retirement benefits must be restricted, state-financed incumbent staff and support services limited, and limitations placed upon the number of terms which may be served. [Nov. 6, 1990]

Section 1.5 is the preamble to Proposition 140, the sweeping initiative measure adopted by the voters in 1990 that altered the nature of the California legislature by restricting retirement benefits, limiting amounts that could be spent on staff and support services, and limiting legislative terms.

SECTION 2

Senate and Assembly: membership, elections, number of terms, qualifications, vacancies. (a) The Senate has a membership of 40 Senators elected for 4-year terms, 20 to begin every 2 years. No Senator may serve more than 2 terms.

The Assembly has a membership of 80 members elected for 2-year terms. No member of the Assembly may serve more than 3 terms.

Their terms shall commence on the first Monday in December following their election.

(b) Election of members of the Assembly shall be on the first Tuesday after the first Monday in November of even-numbered years unless otherwise prescribed by the Legislature. Senators shall be elected at the same time and places as members of the Assembly.

(c) A person is ineligible to be a member of the Legislature unless the person is an elector and has been a resident of the legislative district for one year, and a citizen of the United States and a resident of California for 3 years, immediately preceding the election.

(d) When a vacancy occurs in the Legislature the Governor immediately shall call an election to fill the vacancy. [Nov. 6, 1990)

In the 1849 Constitution, the composition of the two houses was left flexible. The assembly could have from twenty-four to thirty-six until the state's population reached 100,000; thereafter the limits were to be from thirty to eighty. The number of senators was limited to from one-third to one-half the number in the assembly. The 1879 Constitution fixed the numbers at forty and eighty for the senate and assembly, respectively. The four-year and two-year terms have been in effect since 1862.

The two-term limit for members of the senate and the three-term limit for members of the assembly were established by initiative amendment in 1990. The limitation applies to terms in the same office; it does not preclude a member of the assembly, for example, from running for the senate after two terms.

SECTION 3

Legislative sessions. (a) The Legislature shall convene in regular sessions on the first Monday in December of each even-numbered years and each house shall immediately organize. Each session of the Legislature shall adjourn sine die by operation of the Constitution at midnight on November 30 of the following even-numbered year.
(b) On extraordinary occasions the Governor by proclamation may cause the Legislature to assemble in special session. When so assembled it has power to legislate only on subjects specified in the proclamation but may provide for expenses and other matters incidental to the session. [June 8, 1976]

How frequently and for what periods of time the legislature should meet in session has been a matter of controversy since the formation of the state. In the 1849 constitutional convention the proponents of annual sessions won out, on the basis that in the early years of the new state, there would be a great deal of legislation. The new constitution also provided no limits as to the duration of a session. There then followed a bewildering variety of experiments: sessions every other year, limited to 120 days each (1863–1878); sessions every other year with no limit as to duration (1880–1911); sessions every other year, each session bifurcated by a 30-day recess between the introduction of bills and their consideration (1913–1945); sessions every year, bifurcated in odd-numbered years, with even-numbered years being restricted to fiscal matters and limited to 30 days (1947–1950); the same system with a 120-day limitation on the bifurcated sessions (1951–1958); annual sessions but limited to 120 days in odd-numbered years (1959–1966); annual sessions of unlimited duration with no special budget session (1967–1972); and, finally, the biennial system.

Under the current system, there are two kinds of legislative session: regular and special. The regular session convenes at noon on the first Monday in December of each even-numbered year and is automatically adjourned on November 30 of the following even-numbered year, so that it has a life span of just short of two years. The governor is vested with the power to call the legislature into special session by proclamation.

SECTION 4

Legislators: conflicts of interest, prohibited compensation, earned income, travel and living expenses, retirement. (a) To eliminate any appearance of a conflict with the proper discharge of his or her duties and responsibilities, no Member of the Legislature may knowingly receive any salary, wages, commissions, or other similar earned income from a lobbyist or lobbying firm, as defined by the Political Reform Act of 1974, or from a person who, during the previous 12 months, has been under a contract with the Legislature. The Legislature shall enact laws that define earned income. However, earned income does not include any community property interest in the income of a spouse. Any Member who knowingly receives any salary, wages, commissions, or other similar earned income from a lobbyist employer, as defined by the Political Reform Act of 1974, may not, for a period of one year following its receipt, vote upon or make, participate in making, or in any way attempt to use his or her official position to influence an actor or decision before the Legislature, other than an action or decision involving a bill described in subdivision (c) of Section 12 of this article, which he or she knows, or has reason to know, would have a direct and significant financial impact on the lobbyist employer and would not impact the public generally or a significant segment of the public in a similar manner. As used in this subdivision, "public generally" includes an industry, trade, or profession.

(b) Travel and living expenses for Members of the Legislature in connection with their official duties shall be prescribed by statute passed by rollcall vote entered in the journal, two-thirds of the membership of each house concurring. A Member may not receive travel and living expenses during the times that the Legislature is in recess for more than three calendar days, unless the Member is traveling to or from, or is in attendance at, any meeting of a committee of which he or she is a member, of a meeting, conference, or other legislative function or responsibility as authorized by the rules of the house of which he or she is a member, which is held at a location at least 20 miles from his or her place of residence.

(c) The Legislature may not provide retirement benefits based on any portion of a monthly salary in excess of five hundred dollars ($500) paid to any Member of the Legislature unless the Member receives the greater amount while serving as a Member in the Legislature. The Legislature may, prior to their retirement, limit the retirement benefits payable to Members of the Legislature who serve during or after the term commencing in 1967.

When computing the retirement allowance of a Member who serves in the Legislature during the term commencing in 1967 or later, allowance may be made for increases in cost of living if so provided by statute, but only with respect to increases in the cost of living occurring after retirement of the Member. However, the Legislature may provide that no Member shall be deprived of a cost of living adjustment based on a monthly salary of five hundred dollars ($500) which has accrued prior to the commencement of the 1967 Regular Session of the Legislature. [June 5, 1990]

Subsection (a), added by Proposition 112 in 1990, is aimed at eliminating the appearance of conflict of interest on the part of legislators. It prohibits a legislator from receiving earned income (such as salary or commission) from any lobbyist or lobbying firm and disqualifies any legislator who receives such income for a period of one year from participating in certain legislative actions or decisions. The scope of matters in which such a legislator may not participate is defined narrowly, however; action or decision must be one that has a direct and significant financial impact on the lobbyist and would not affect the public generally, or a significant segment of the public, in a similar manner. Most legislative actions do not meet those criteria.

Subsection (b) continues the constitutional formula, in effect since 1972, that allows legislators to establish levels of reimbursement for travel and living expenses by two-thirds vote, with limitations during any period in which the legislature is in recess for more than three calendar days. Prior to 1972, the constitution specified levels of reimbursement.

Subsection (c) continues the constitutional formula, in effect since 1966, limiting the extent to which retirement benefits for legislators may be based on income earned outside the legislature and in other ways. In the November 1990 election, the voters amended the constitution by the adoption of section 4.5, eliminating legislative retirement benefits except for social security.

SECTION 4.5

Legislators' retirement. Notwithstanding any other provision of this Constitution or existing law, a person elected to or serving in the Legislature on or after November 1,1990, shall participate in the Federal Social Security (Retirement, Disability, Health Insurance) Program and the State shall pay only the employer's share of the contribution necessary to such participation. No other pension or retirement benefit shall accrue as a result of service in the Legislature, such service not being intended as a career occupation. This Section shall not be construed to abrogate or diminish any vested pension or retirement benefit which may have accrued under an existing law to a person holding or having held office in the Legislature, but upon adoption of this Act no further entitlement to nor vesting in any existing program shall accrue to any such person, other than Social Security to the extent herein provided. [Nov. 6, 1990]

This section, added by Proposition 140 in 1990, prohibits legislators from accruing pension or retirement benefits (other than social security) as a result of their service after November 1,1990. The justification asserted for the prohibition is that as a result of term limitations adopted at the same time, legislative service is no longer a "career occupation."

The supreme court has held that the federal constitutional prohibition on impairment of contracts renders this section invalid as applied to incumbent legislators. (*Legislature v. Eu*, 1991). Accordingly, section 4.5 applies only to legislators elected for the first time after its adoption.

SECTION 5

Legislators: qualifications and expulsion, honoraria, gifts, conflicts of interest, prohibited compensation or activities, lobbying. (a) Each house shall judge the

qualifications and elections of its Members and, by rollcall vote entered in the journal, two thirds of the membership concurring, may expel a Member.
(b) No Member of the Legislature may accept any honorarium. The Legislature shall enact laws that implement this subdivision.
(c) The Legislature shall enact laws that ban or strictly limit the acceptance of a gift by a Member of the Legislature from any source if the acceptance of the gift might create a conflict of interest.
(d) No Member of the Legislature may knowingly accept any compensation for appearing, agreeing to appear, or taking any other action on behalf of another person before any State government board or agency. If a Member knowingly accepts any compensation for appearing, agreeing to appear, or taking any other action on behalf of another person before any local government board or agency, the Member may not, for a period of one year following the acceptance of the compensation, vote upon or make, participate in making, or in any way attempt to use his or her official position to influence an action or decision before the Legislature, other than an action or decision involving a bill described in subdivision (c) of Section 12 of this article, which he or she knows, or has reason to know, would have a direct and significant financial impact on that person and would not impact on that person and would not impact the public generally or a significant segment of the public in a similar manner. As used in this subdivision, "public generally" includes an industry, trade, or profession. However, a Member may engage in activities involving a board or agency which are strictly on his or her own behalf, appear in the capacity of an attorney before any court or the Workers' Compensation Appeals Board, or act as an advocate without compensation or make an inquiry for information on behalf of a person before a board or agency. This subdivision does not prohibit any action of a partnership or firm of which the Member is a member if the Member does not share directly or indirectly in the fee, less any expenses attributable to that fee, resulting from that action.
(e) The Legislature shall enact laws that prohibit a Member of the Legislature whose term of office commences on or after December 3, 1990, from lobbying, for compensation, as governed by the Political Reform Act of 1974, before the Legislature for 12 months after leaving office.
(f) The Legislature shall enact new laws, and strengthen the enforcement of existing laws, prohibiting Members of the Legislature from engaging in activities or having interests which conflict with the proper discharge of their duties and responsibilities. However, the people reserve to themselves the power to implement this requirement pursuant to Article II. [June 5, 1990]

Subsection (a), authorizing each house of the legislature to judge the qualifications and elections of its member and to expel a member by two-thirds vote, is an amalgam of provisions contained in the Constitution of 1879. In 1966, these provisions were consolidated into section 5, together with a provision mandating the legislature to enact laws to prohibit members from engaging in activities or having interests that conflict with the proper discharge of their duties and responsibilities.

Proposition 112, enacted against a background of public displeasure with the activities of certain legislators, strengthened and particularized the conflict of interest principle in a variety of ways. Subsection (b) now prohibits legislators from accepting honoraria, and it mandates implementing legislation. Subsection (c) mandates legislation limiting acceptance of gifts that might create a conflict of interest. Subsection (d) prohibits legislators from appearing or representing other persons before state boards or agencies, other than the Workers Compensation Appeals Board for compensation, subject to a one-year disqualification from undertaking certain legislative activities connected with the subject matter. Subsection (e) mandates legislation prohibiting legislators from lobbying for compensation before the legislature for a period of twelve months after leaving office. Finally, subsection (e) calls upon the legislature to enact new laws, and strengthen the enforcement of existing laws, relating to conflict of interest.

SECTION 6

Senatorial and Assembly districts. For the purpose of choosing members of the Legislature, the State shall be divided into 40 Senatorial and 80 Assembly districts to be called Senatorial and Assembly Districts. Each Senatorial district shall choose one Senator and each Assembly district shall choose one member of the Assembly. [June 3, 1980]

Prior to 1926 this section provided for division of the state into forty senatorial districts and eighty assembly districts "as nearly equal in population as may be." In 1926, however, the voters, through an initiative measure, adopted a so-called federal plan under which each county was limited to one senator. The result was that by 1962, the rural counties dominated the senate.

In 1964, the U.S. Supreme Court, in *Reynolds v. Sims*, declared that the federal Constitution required that the seats in both houses of a bicameral state legislature be apportioned on a population basis. Under prodding by the state supreme court, the California legislature adopted a reapportionment plan that was used in the 1966 legislative elections and gave increased representation to urban areas, particularly in southern California. There were reapportionment battles in succeeding years, with the state supreme court acting as referee, but the constitutional provision remained unchanged until 1980. In that year, this section was amended to its present, neutral language, and Article XXI, providing for reapportionment on the basis of population, was adopted.

SECTION 7

House rules: quorum, journals, public proceedings, closed sessions, recess. (a) Each house shall choose its officers and adopt rules for its proceedings. A majority of the membership constitutes a quorum but a smaller number may recess from day to day and compel the attendance of absent members.

(b) Each house shall keep and publish a journal of its proceedings. The rollcall vote of the members on a question shall be taken and entered in the journal at the request of 3 members present.

(c) (1) The proceedings of each house and the committees thereof shall be open and public. However, closed sessions may be held solely for any of the following purposes:

(A) To consider the appointment, employment, evaluation of performance, or dismissal of a public officer or employee, to consider or hear complaints or charges brought against a Member of the Legislature or other public officer or employee, or to establish the classification of an employee of the Legislature.

(B) To consider matters affecting the safety and security of Members of the Legislature or its employees or the safety and security of any buildings and grounds used by the Legislature.

(C) To confer with, or receive advice from, its legal counsel regarding pending or reasonably anticipated, or whether to initiate, litigation when discussion in open session would not protect the interests of the house or committee regarding the litigation.

(2) A caucus of the Members of the Senate, the Members of the Assembly, or the Members of both houses, which is composed of the members of the same political party, may meet in closed session.

(3) The Legislature shall implement this subdivision by concurrent resolution adopted by rollcall vote entered in the journal, two-thirds of the membership of each house concurring, or by statute, and shall prescribe that, when a closed session is held pursuant to paragraph (1), reasonable notice of the closed session and the purpose of the closed session shall be provided to the public. If there is a conflict between a concurrent resolution and statute, the last adopted or enacted shall prevail.

(d) Neither house without the consent of the other may recess for more than 10 days or to any other place. [June 5, 1990]

Subsections (a), (b), and (d) are based on provisions of the 1879 Constitution, with minor changes. While permitting each house of the legislature generally to choose its officers and adopt rules for its proceedings, they establish certain minimal ground rules: the definition of a quorum, the requirement for a journal of proceedings, and a reciprocal obligation that neither house recess for more than ten days (formerly three days) or to any other place without the consent of the other.

Both the 1849 and 1879 constitutions required open legislative meetings. Until 1974 the legislature could meet in closed sessions by majority vote. A 1974 amendment changed this requirement to a two-thirds vote. As a result of Proposition 112 (1990), the section now mandates that proceedings be public subject to certain narrow exceptions for the consideration of personnel matters or charges against a legislator, safety and security matters, legal litigation questions, and party caucuses.

SECTION 7.5

Limits on total aggregate expenditures for the legislature. In the fiscal year immediately following the adoption of this Act, the total aggregate expenditures of the Legislature for the compensation of members and employees of, and the operating expenses and equipment for, the Legislature may not exceed an amount equal to nine hundred fifty thousand dollars ($950,000) per member for that fiscal year or 80 percent of the amount of money expended for those purposes in the preceding fiscal year, whichever is less. For each fiscal year thereafter, the total aggregate expenditures may not exceed an amount equal to that expended for those purposes in the preceding fiscal year, adjusted and compounded by an amount equal to the percentage increase in the appropriations limit for the State established pursuant to Article XIII B. [Nov. 6, 1990]

This section limits the total amount of expenditures by the legislature for salaries and operating expenses, beginning in the 1991–1992 fiscal year. In that year, expenditures were limited to the lower of two amounts: (1) a total of $950,000 per member or (2) 80 percent of the total amount of money expended in the previous year for these purposes. In future years, the measure limits expenditure growth to an amount equal to the percentage change in the state's appropriations limit.

The impact of these limitations on legislative resources is substantial. In the first year, it required a 38 percent reduction in budget and the elimination of more than 640 staff employees. In *Legislature v. Eu* (1991), the legislature argued that the impact of this provision, coupled with the term limitations imposed by Proposition 140, were so substantial as to alter the nature of the institution and render the proposition of a revision rather than merely an amendment, which could be adopted by initiative. The supreme court disagreed and upheld all of Proposition 140 except for the restrictions on retirement benefits as applied to incumbent members.

SECTION 8

Bills and statutes: thirty-day waiting period, three readings, effective date, urgency statutes. (a) At regular sessions no bill other than the budget bill may be

heard or acted on by committee or either house until the 31st day after the bill is introduced unless the house dispenses with this requirement by rollcall vote entered in the journal, three fourths of the membership concurring.
(b) The Legislature may make no law except by statute and may enact no statute except by bill. No bill may be passed unless it is read by title on 3 days in each house except that the house may dispense with this requirement by rollcall vote entered in the journal, two thirds of the membership concurring. No bill may be passed until the bill with amendments has been printed and distributed to the members. No bill may be passed unless it is read by title on 3 days in each house except that the house may dispense with this requirement by rollcall vote entered in the journal, two thirds of the membership concurring. No bill may be passed until the bill with amendments has been printed and distributed to the members. No bill may be passed unless, by rollcall vote entered in the journal, a majority of the membership of each house concurs.
(c) (1) Except as provided in paragraphs (2) and (3) of this subdivision, a statute enacted at a regular session shall go into effect on January 1 next following a 90-day period from the date of enactment of the statute and a statute enacted at a special session at which the bill was passed.

(2) A statute, other than a statute establishing or changing boundaries of any legislative, congressional, or other election district, enacted by a bill passed by the Legislature on or before the date the Legislature adjourns for a joint recess to reconvene in the second calendar year of the biennium of the legislative session, and in the possession of the Governor after that date, shall go into effect on January 1 next following the enactment date of the statute unless, before January 1, a copy of a referendum petition affecting the statute is submitted to the Attorney General pursuant to subdivision (d) of Section 10 of Article II, in which event the statute shall go into effect on the 91st day after the enactment date unless the petition has been presented to the Secretary of State pursuant to subdivision (b) of Section 9 of Article II.

(3) Statutes calling elections, statutes providing for tax levies or appropriations for the usual current expenses of the State, and urgency statutes shall go into effect immediately upon their enactment.

(d) Urgency statutes are those necessary for immediate preservation of the public peace, health, or safety. A statement of facts constituting the necessity shall be set forth in one section of the bill. In each house the section and the bill shall be passed separately, each by rollcall vote entered in the journal, two thirds of the membership concurring. An urgency statute may not create or abolish any office or change the salary, term, or duties of any office, or grant any franchise or special privilege, or create any vested right or interest. [June 5, 1990]

Subsection (a) establishes the general rule that there must be a thirty-one-day waiting period between the introduction of a bill and action on the bill. The rule does not apply to emergency sessions, to the budget bill, or when the house in which the bill is pending dispenses with the requirement by two-thirds vote.

Subsection (b) establishes further procedural safeguards with respect to the legislative process: laws can be made only through the adoption of bills that have been printed and distributed to the members, read on three days in each house (unless the house dispenses with the readings by two-thirds vote), and adopted by a majority of the membership in both houses, through roll call vote entered in the journal. As a practical matter, bills are read by simply calling the number of the bill, and roll call is taken by electronic means.

Subsection (c) specifies the date on which legislation becomes effective. Ordinarily, that date is the first day of January following a ninety-day waiting period after enactment, or, in the case of a special session, ninety days from enactment. The purpose of the ninety-day waiting period is to allow opportunity for the filing of a referendum petition to block the legislation.

In three categories of legislation—statutes calling elections, statutes providing for tax levies or appropriations for current expenses, and urgency statutes—there is no waiting period, and the statute becomes effective immediately upon adoption. Under subsection (d) an urgency statute—defined as one "necessary for immediate preservation of the public peace, health, or safety"—must be accompanied by a statement of the facts constituting the necessity and must be adopted by two-thirds vote in both houses. The last sentence of subsection (d) prohibits the use of urgency statutes in certain cases. Courts have uniformly deferred to legislative judgment as to when urgency legislation is required.

SECTION 9

Statute titles. A statute shall embrace but one subject, which shall be expressed in its title. If a statute embraces a subject not expressed in its title, only the part not expressed is void. A statute may not be amended by reference to its title. A section of a statute may not be amended unless the section is re-enacted as amended. [Nov. 8, 1966]

The single subject and title requirements were contained in the 1849 Constitution but were held by the courts to be merely directory and thus not subject to judicial enforcement. The 1879 Constitution changed that interpretation (see Art. 1, sec. 26), while adding the condition that only the portion of the statute not expressed in the title was invalid.

The two aspects of this section are independent provisions that serve separate purposes. The single subject clause is designed to minimize logrolling—the combination of several proposals in a single bill so that legislators, by combining their votes, obtain a majority for a measure that would not have been approved if divided into separate bills—and the titling requirement is designed to prevent legislators or the public from being misled by misleading or inaccurate titles. In practice, however, both provisions are accorded an interpretation so loose as to be almost meaningless; the legislature may insert in a single act all legislation "reasonably germane" to the title of a statute (*Harbor v. Deukmejian*, 1987).

The requirement that an amendment to a statute reenact the statute as amended was also contained in the 1849 Constitution and remains essentially unchanged. A provision in the 1849 Constitution requiring statutes to be published in both Spanish and English was changed in 1879 to require publication in English only, and in the 1966 constitutional revision, that requirement was deleted as obsolete.

SECTION 10

Gubernatorial veto: override and exceptions. (a) Each bill passed by the Legislature shall be presented to the Governor. It becomes a statute if it is signed by the Governor. The Governor may veto it by returning it with any objections to the house of origin, which shall enter the objections in the journal and proceed to reconsider it. If each house then passes the bill by rollcall vote entered in the journal, two thirds of the membership concurring, it becomes a statute.

(b) (1) Any bill, other than a bill which would establish or change boundaries of any legislative, congressional, or other election district, passed by the Legislature on or before the date the Legislature adjourns for a joint recess to reconvene in the second calendar year of the biennium of the legislative session, and in the possession of the Governor after that date, that is not returned within 30 days after that date becomes a statute.

(2) Any bill passed by the Legislature before September 1 of the second calendar year of the biennium of the legislative session and in the possession of the Governor on or after September 1 that is not returned on or before September 30 of that year becomes a statute.

(3) Any other bill presented to the Governor that is not returned within 12 days becomes a statute.

(4) If the Legislature by adjournment of a special session prevents the return of a bill with the veto message, the bill becomes a statute unless the Governor vetoes the bill within 12 days after it is presented by depositing it and the veto message in the office of the Secretary of State.

(5) If the 12th day of the period within which the Governor is required to perform an act pursuant to paragraph (3) or (4) of this subdivision is a Saturday, Sunday, or holiday, the period is extended to the next day that is not a Saturday, Sunday, or holiday.

(c) Any bill introduced during the first year of the biennium of the legislative session that has not been passed by the house of origin by January 31 of the second calendar year of the biennium may no longer be acted on by the house. No bill may be passed by either house on or after September 1 of an even-numbered year except statutes calling elections, statutes providing for tax levies or appropriations for the usual current expenses of the State, and urgency statutes, and bills passed after being vetoed by the Governor.

(d) The Legislature may not present any bill to the Governor after November 15 of the second calendar year of the biennium of the legislative session.

(e) The Governor may reduce or eliminate one or more items of appropriation while approving other portions of a bill. The Governor shall append to the bill a statement of the items reduced or eliminated with the reasons for the action. The Governor shall transmit to the house originating a bill a copy of the statement and reasons. Items reduced or eliminated shall be separately reconsidered and may be passed over the Governor's veto in the same manner as bills. [June 5, 1990]

Subsection (a) requires that each bill passed by the legislature be presented to the governor for signature or veto and provides that the legislature may override a veto by two-thirds vote in both houses. That basic format has been in effect since 1849. Subsection (b) provides that under certain circumstances—when the governor has had the bill in his or her possession for a specified period and does nothing—a bill may become law even without the governor's signature. That principle has also been operative since 1849, although the time within which the governor is required to act has varied.

Subsection (c) states certain limitations on legislative action, designed to facilitate gubernatorial consideration. A bill that is introduced in the first year of the biennial legislative session must be acted upon by January 31 of the following year, or it dies; and with certain exceptions, no bill may be passed by either house on or after September 1 of an even-numbered year, which is the second year of the biennial.

Subsection (d) provides that the legislature may not present any bill to the governor after November 15 of the second calendar year of the biennium. These limitations on legislative action were added by amendment in 1972.

The governor's authority to veto individual items of an appropriation bill, provided for in subsection (e), was established in 1908 and substantially increased the governor's power over the budget. Prior to that time, the governor's only options were to accept or veto the entire bill as passed by the legislature. In 1922 the governor's authority over the budget was amplified by amendment of this section to allow the governor to reduce items of appropriation (instead of eliminating them) and by adoption of what is now section 12, providing for an executive budget. Items reduced or eliminated by the governor may be restored by two-thirds vote in both houses, as with the veto generally.

SECTION 11

Committees. The Legislature or either house may by resolution provide for the selection of committees necessary for the conduct of its business, including committees to ascertain facts and make recommendations to the Legislature on a subject within the scope of legislative control. [Nov. 7, 1972]

When the legislature was a part-time body, it developed the practice of appointing committees to act during the interim periods, but in 1939 the supreme court held that a single house could not authorize an interim committee (*Special Assembly Interim Committee v. Southard,* 1939). In 1940, the constitution was amended to enable the legislature "or either house" to appoint committees and to authorize them to act in the interim. When, in 1972, the legislature became virtually continuous, the paragraph authorizing interim committees was deleted. What is now the language of this section was retained, though it is probably superfluous.

SECTION 12

Governor's budget; budget bill; other appropriations. (a) Within the first 10 days of each calendar year, the Governor shall submit to the Legislature, with an explanatory message, a budget for the ensuing fiscal year containing itemized statements for recommended State expenditures and established State revenues. If recommended expenditures exceed estimated revenues, the Governor shall recommend the sources from which the additional revenues should be provided.

(b) The Governor and the Governor-elect may require a State agency, officer or employee to furnish whatever information is deemed necessary to prepare the budget.

(c) The budget shall be accompanied by a budget bill itemizing recommended expenditures. The bill shall be introduced immediately in each house by the persons chairing the committees that consider appropriations. The Legislature shall pass the budget bill by midnight on June 15 of each year. Until the budget bill has been enacted, the Legislature shall not send to the Governor for consideration any bill appropriating funds for expenditure during the fiscal year for which the budget bill is to be enacted, except emergency bills recommended by the Governor or appropriations for the salaries and expenses of the Legislature.

(d) No bill except the budget bill may contain more than one item of appropriation, and that for one certain, expressed purpose. Appropriations from the General Fund of the State, except appropriations for the public schools, are void unless passed in each house by rollcall vote entered in the journal, two thirds of the membership concurring.

(e) The Legislature may control the submission, approval, and enforcement of budgets and the filing of claims for all State agencies. [June 4, 1974; Nov. 5, 1974]

Prior to 1922, appropriation bills were adopted by the legislature in an ad hoc fashion, and the governor had little control. In 1922, the predecessor to this section (Art. IV, sec. 34) was amended to provide for the submission by the governor of an executive budget, thereby increasing the governor's power in relation to the legislature and executive agencies.

Subsection (a) requires the governor to include in his or her budget itemized statements of estimated revenues and recommended expenditures, together with a recommendation of sources for additional revenues to cover any projected deficit. Subsection (b) authorizes the governor to require from state officers and employees whatever information is required for preparation of the budget. Sub- section (c) requires the governor to accompany the budget with a budget bill, which is then introduced into both houses of the legislature by the chair of their respective appropriations committees. The legislature is required to act on the budget bill by June 15 and until then may not adopt any bill requiring appropriations during the fiscal year covered by the proposed bill, except for emergency appropriations. Even after the budget bill is adopted, no bill may contain more than one item of appropriation (subsec. [d]).

The other major change in the state's budgetary process, apart from adoption of provision for the executive budget, came during the Great Depression, amid concern over rising expenditures. The 1933 legislature submitted, and the voters adopted, a constitutional amendment requiring a two-thirds vote in both houses for any appropriation (other than for public schools) exceeding by more than 5 percent the equivalent appropriation in the previous biennium. In 1962, the 5 percent provision was eliminated so as to require two-thirds vote for all appropriations from the general fund.

Subsection (e), giving the legislature control over the submission, approval, and enforcement of budgets and the filing of claims for all state agencies, was added by amendment in 1974.

SECTION 13

Legislators ineligible for certain offices. A member of the Legislature may not, during the term for which the member is elected, hold any office or employment under the State other than an elective office. [Nov. 5, 1974]

The 1849 and 1879 constitutions prohibited appointment of a legislator to "any civil office of profit" that was created, or the salary for which was increased, during the legislator's term. In the face of court decisions that construed the term narrowly, the section was amended in 1916 to prohibit a legislator from holding any nonelective "office, trust, or employment under this State." The 1966 revision dropped the word *trust* and made other nonsubstantive changes.

Whether an office or employment is elective depends on the character of the office, not on whether the legislator was in fact appointed to it, so that a legislator could be appointed during his or her term to a vacancy on the supreme court

(*Carter v. Commission on Qualifications of Judicial Appointments*, 1939). A separate constitutional provision (Art. VI, sec. 17) prohibits judges from holding other public office or employment at the same time.

SECTION 14

Legislators not subject to civil process. A member of the Legislature is not subject to civil process during a session of the Legislature or for 5 days before and after a session. [Nov. 8, 1966]

The 1849 and 1878 Constitutions provided that legislators "shall, in all cases, except treason felony, and breach of the peace, be privileged from arrest, and shall not be subject to civil process during the session of the Legislature, nor for 15 days before the commencement and after the termination of each session." The immunity conferred by this section extended to protect the chairman of the Senate Fact Finding Committee on Un-American Activities from liability for inducing an employer to fire witnesses who invoked the privilege against self-incrimination (*Hancock v. Burns*, 1958). The immunity from arrest, however, was interpreted to apply only to civil arrest and thus to have no application to a member of the assembly who punched a police officer in the face after the officer stopped him for jaywalking (*In re Emmett*, 1932). By the time of the constitution revision of 1966, civil arrest had fallen into disuse, and the present language (which also changed the timing on immunity from civil process to reflect the speed of modern transportation) was substituted.

SECTION 15

Felonious influencing of legislative vote. A person who seeks to influence the vote or action of a member of the Legislature in the member's legislative capacity by bribery, promise of reward, intimidation, or other dishonest means, or a member of the Legislature so influenced, is guilty of a felony. [Nov. 5, 1974]

This language originated in the 1879 Constitution and described in the case of the influencing party what the constitution called the offense of lobbying. The turn-of-the-century view of the nature of that offense is described by the court of appeal in *Le Tourneux v. Gillis* (1905), holding that a contract to pay a lobbyist was void as against public policy, despite the lack of evidence that any dishonest means were used:

> It is not the policy of the law that the members of the legislature should be subjected to the personal solicitation during the session of experienced and paid lobbyists. Men who are paid to influence legislation and who become acquainted with and cultivate the friendship of members through dinners, wines, cigars, and personal attention are

> certainly not assisting the state in procuring good legislation. . . . If such persons escape punishment through a public prosecution they may consider themselves fortunate.

The term *lobbyist,* apparently having lost its offensive character, was deleted in 1962. Lobbying activities are extensively regulated through the California Fair Political Practices Act.

The original provision treated severely those legislators who allowed themselves to be influenced by prohibited conduct. In addition to being guilty of a felony, such a legislator would, upon conviction, "be disenfranchised and forever disqualified from holding any office or public trust." That provision was eliminated in 1966 upon recommendation of the revision commission, which characterized it as overly harsh and inflexible. The 1966 revision also made minor language changes, and in 1974 the provision was made gender neutral.

SECTION 16

Uniform and paramount nature of general laws. (a) All laws of a general nature have uniform operation.

(b) A local or special statute is invalid in any case if a general statute can be made applicable. [Nov. 5, 1974]

Subsection (a) derives from former Article I, section 11 of the 1849 Constitution, which provided, "All laws of a general nature shall have a uniform operation." Prior to the 1974 revision, which added an explicit equal protection clause to the constitution, the language was relied upon as establishing a constitutional requirement similar to the equal protection principle. (See Art. I, sec. 7.) Despite deletion of the word *shall* in 1966, courts still rely on the language of subsection (a) for that purpose (*People v. Soto*, 1985).

Subsection (b) derives from former Article 4, section 25, which provided that the legislature shall not pass "local or special laws" in thirty-two enumerated areas and "in all other cases where a general law can be made applicable." That section, like former Article I, section 11, was relied on as embodying an equal protection principle similar to that contained in the federal Constitution. The 1966 revision retained the general prohibition of former Article 4, section 25 while eliminating the detailed recitation.

SECTION 17

Prohibited extra compensation to public officials or contractors. The Legislature has no power to grant, or to authorize a city, county, or other public body to grant, extra compensation or extra allowance to a public officer, public employee, or contractor after service has been rendered or a contract has been entered into and performed in whole or in part, or to authorize the payment of a claim against the State or a city, county, or other public body under an agreement made without authority of law. [Nov. 8, 1966]

According to an early decision of the supreme court, the purpose behind this section, which appeared for the first time in the Constitution of 1879, was to correct "abuses which had crept into legislation by reason of the unlimited power therefore exercised by the legislature in determining what individual claims should be recognized by private act, and to relieve in some degree legislators from the importunities of persons interested in securing such appropriations that the power of the legislature was thus limited by the present constitution of this state" (*Stevenson v. Colgan*, 1891). The effect is to prohibit the legislature from recognizing "moral obligations" growing out of service to the state (*Veterans' Welfare Board v. Riley*, 1922).

SECTION 18

Impeachment. (a) The assembly has the sole power of impeachment. Impeachment shall be tried by the Senate. A person may not be convicted unless, by rollcall vote entered in the journal, two thirds of the membership of the Senate concurs.
(b) State officers elected on a statewide basis, members of the State Board of Equalization, and judges of State courts are subject to impeachment for misconduct in office. Judgment may extend only to removal from office and disqualification to hold any office under the State, but the person convicted or acquitted remains subject to criminal punishment according to law. [Nov. 8, 1966]

The 1849 Constitution contained similar language, except that it required only two-thirds of the senators present to concur in the impeachment vote. The current requirement for two-thirds of the membership of the senate was introduced in the 1879 Constitution, paralleling a similar change in the veto override majority. Both early constitutions provided for impeachment for misdemeanor in office. The 1966 revision substituted the word *misconduct* and provided for general categories of impeachable offices in place of an enumerated list.

There have been only four instances of impeachment in the state, and only two resulted in conviction. In 1857 the state treasurer, Henry Bates, was impeached for having defrauded the state, and in 1862 Judge James H. Hardy was impeached for using profane language out of court and indulging in expressions of sympathy for the Confederacy.

SECTION 19

Lotteries, horse racing, and gambling. (a) The Legislature has no power to authorize lotteries and shall prohibit the sale of lottery tickets in the State.

(b) The Legislature may provide for the regulation of horse races and horse race meetings and wagering on the results.
(c) Notwithstanding subdivision (a) the Legislature by statute may authorize cities and counties to provide for bingo games, but only for charitable purposes.
(d) Notwithstanding subdivision (a), there is authorized the establishment of a California State Lottery.
(e) The Legislature has no power to authorize, and shall prohibit casinos of the type currently operating in Nevada and New Jersey. [Nov. 6, 1984]

The prohibition on lotteries contained in subsection (a) dates back to the 1849 Constitution, which provided, "No lottery shall be allowed by this State, nor shall the sale of lottery tickets be allowed." Subsection (b), authorizing state-regulated horse racing and wagering, was adopted by amendment in 1933. Subsection (c), authorizing legislation to provide for charitable bingo games by local option, was added in 1976. Finally, an initiative measure in 1984 authorizing establishment of a state lottery (subsec. (d)) while prohibiting "casinos of the type currently operating in Nevada and New Jersey" (subsec. (e)) was passed over the vigorous opposition of most elected officials.

SECTION 20

Fish and game. (a) The Legislature may provide for division of the State into fish and game districts and may protect fish and game in districts or parts of districts.
(b) There is a Fish and Game Commission of 5 members appointed by the Governor and approved by the Senate, a majority of the membership concurring, for 6-year terms and until their successors are appointed and qualified. Appointment to fill a vacancy is for the unexpired portion of the term. The Legislature may delegate to the commission such powers relating to the protection and propagation of fish and game as the Legislature sees fit. A member of the commission may be removed by concurrent resolution adopted by each house, a majority of the membership concurring. [Nov. 8, 1966]

SECTION 21

War- or enemy-caused disaster. To meet the needs resulting from war-caused or enemy-caused disaster in California, the Legislature may provide for:

(a) Filling the offices of members of the Legislature should at least one fifth of the membership of either house be killed, missing, or disabled, until they are able to perform their duties or successors are elected.

(b) Filling the office of Governor should the Governor be killed, missing, or disabled, until the Governor or the successor designated in this Constitution is able to perform the duties of the office of Governor or a successor is elected.
(c) Convening the Legislature.
(d) Holding elections to fill offices that are elective under this Constitution and that are either vacant or occupied by persons not elected thereto.
(e) Selecting a temporary seat of State or county government. [Nov. 5, 1974]

The predecessor to this section was added to the constitution in 1958, apparently in anticipation of nuclear attack. Its language was streamlined as part of the 1966 revision and made gender neutral in 1974.

SECTION 22

Legislative accountability. It is the right of the people to hold their legislators accountable. To assist the people in exercising this right, at the convening of each regular session of the Legislature, the President pro Tempore of the Senate, the Speaker of the Assembly, and the minority leader of each house shall report to their house the goals and objectives of that house during that session and, at the close of each regular session, the progress made toward meeting those goals and objectives. [June 5, 1990]

This section was part of an initiative measure (Proposition 140) adopted in 1990. Evidencing uncommon faith in rhetoric, it requires the principal officers and minority leaders in both houses to make reports at the beginning and at the end of each legislative session with respect to goals and achievements.

[SECTIONS 23–27 HAVE BEEN REPEALED.]

SECTION 28

State capitol maintenance. (a) Notwithstanding any other provision of this Constitution, no bill shall take effect as an urgency statute if it authorizes or contains an appropriation for either (1) the alteration or modification of the color, detail, design, structure or fixtures of the historically restored areas of the first, second, and third floors and the exterior of the west wing of the State Capitol from that existing upon the completion of the project of restoration or rehabilitation of the building conducted pursuant to Section 9124 of the Government Code as such section read upon the effective date of this section, or (2) the purchase of furniture of different design to replace that restored, replicated, or designed to conform to the historic period of the historically restored areas specified above, including the legislators' chairs and desks in the Senate and Assembly Chambers.

(b) No expenditures shall be made in payment for any of the purposes described in subdivision (a) of this section unless funds are appropriated expressly for such purposes.

(c) This section shall not apply to appropriations or expenditures for ordinary repair and maintenance of the State Capitol building, fixtures and furniture. [June 3, 1980]

This section was adopted in 1980 to protect the restoration work and structural repairs made to the state capitol building in Sacramento during the late 1970s by requiring that the public be informed of proposals for future modifications in advance and have opportunity to respond. Opponents described the measure as "a perfect example of misuse of the Constitution by ballot measure."

Article V

Executive

Article V establishes the executive branch of California government. It creates and describes the duties of the principal executive officers of the state, the qualifications for holding certain of these offices, and the terms of the offices, and it imposes certain standards for succession to these offices in the case of vacancy during a term of office. A substantial portion of the current version of Article V is the product of the work of the California Constitutional Revision Commission in the 1960s and 1970s. Most of Article V as it now stands was adopted by the voters' approval of Proposition 1-a at the November 1966 general election.

SECTION 1

Executive power vested in governor. The supreme executive power of this State is vested in the Governor. The Governor shall see that the law is faithfully executed. [Nov. 5, 1974]

This provision originated in the 1849 Constitution. Because most of the governor's authority derives from statutes, one California Court of Appeal labeled the predecessor version of this section as simply descriptive, granting no inherent authority (*People v. Brophy*, 1942). A series of early California Supreme Court decisions reached the conclusion that the governor's executive authority was susceptible to judicial mandamus in those instances in which the governor lacked discretion but was required by law to perform purely ministerial functions (*McCauley v. Brooks*, 1860; *Middletown v. Low*, 1866; *Harpending v. Haight*, 1870). Thus, the governor's status as chief executive officer of the state does not insulate the incumbent from judicial control. Nonetheless, the provision does establish that the ultimate responsibility for the direction of the executive branch of California government rests with the governor. A 1981 decision of the California Supreme Court, *People ex rel. Deukmejian v. Brown*, which involved a sharp disagreement between the governor and the attorney general, confirmed that whenever conflict erupts among members of the executive branch concerning matters of public policy or fidelity to law, the governor's position prevails.

SECTION 2

Gubernatorial qualifications, term, election, and limits on terms. The Governor shall be elected every fourth year at the same time and places as members of the Assembly and hold office from the Monday after January 1 following the election until a successor qualifies. The Governor shall be an elector who has been a citizen of the United States and a resident of this State for 5 years immediately preceding the Governor's election. The Governor may not hold other public office. No Governor may serve more than 2 terms. [Nov. 7, 1990]

This section, which sets forth the term of office of the governor and the minimum requirements for holding the office, is an amalgamation of three sections from the 1849 Constitution.

Prior to revision in 1966, the constitution established a minimum age of twenty-five for the office of governor. The current version would permit an eighteen-year-old to hold the office. The precondition of U.S. citizenship for holding elective office has been determined to be consistent with the U.S. Constitution's equal protection clause:[2] "Within broad boundaries [including state elective office] a State may establish its own form of government and limit the right to govern to those who are full-fledged members of the political community" (*Bernal v. Fainter*, 1984).

It is not clear whether the prohibition on the governor's holding other public office applies only to public offices of California and its political subdivisions or includes federal public offices. The issue could arise if a governor held a reserve military commission in the U.S. armed forces. An analogous problem under the federal Constitution, relating to members of Congress, has never been

[2] See, e.g., Sugarman v. Dougall, 413 U.S. 634, 93 S. Ct. 2842 (1973) (state civil service); Bernal v. Fainter, 467 U.S. 216, 104 S. Ct. 2312 (1984) (notary public).

definitively resolved by the courts.[3] The last sentence, limiting gubernatorial service to two terms, was added as part of Proposition 140, a 1990 ballot initiative that imposed limits on terms of service of legislators as well as the governor. (See also Art. IV, sec. 2.)

SECTION 3

Gubernatorial report to legislature. The Governor shall report to the Legislature each calendar year on the condition of the State and may make recommendations. [Nov. 7, 1972]

This provision, derived from the 1849 Constitution, is analogous to Article II, section 3 of the U.S. Constitution, which imposes on the president the obligation "from time to time to give to the Congress information of the state of the union, and recommend to their consideration such measures as he shall judge necessary and expedient."

SECTION 4

Executive officers to report to governor. The Governor may require executive officers and agencies and their employees to furnish information relating to their duties. [Nov. 8, 1966]

This provision, derived from the 1849 Constitution, is analogous to Article II, section 2, clause 1 of the U.S. Constitution, which vests in the president the authority to "require the opinion, in writing, of the principal officer in each of the executive departments, upon any subject relating to the duties of their respective offices." Its effect is augmented by Government Code sections 11090 and 11091, which require state agencies to provide periodic reports to the governor, and Government Code sections 12010 and 12011, which require the governor to "supervise the official conduct of all executive and ministerial officers" and to be certain "that all offices are filled and their duties performed."

SECTION 5

Method of filling vacancies, (a) Unless the law otherwise provides, the Governor may fill a vacancy in office by appointment until a successor qualifies.

---

[3] See Schlesinger v. Reservists Committee to Stop the War, 418 U.S. 208, 94 S. Ct. 2925 (1974) (respondents held to lack standing to raise the substantive issue of whether members of Congress serving in the armed forces reserve violates the incompatibility clause of the U.S. Constitution, Art. I, sec. 6, cl. 2).

(b) Whenever there is a vacancy in the office of the Superintendent of Public Instruction, the Lieutenant Governor, Secretary of State, Controller, Treasurer, or Attorney General, or on the State Board of Equalization, the Governor shall nominate a person to fill the vacancy who shall take office upon confirmation by a majority of the membership of the Senate and a majority of the membership of the Assembly and who shall hold office for the balance of the unexpired term. In the event the nominee is neither confirmed nor refused confirmation by both the Senate and the Assembly within 90 days of the submission of the nomination, the nominee shall take office as if he or she had been confirmed by a majority of the Senate and Assembly; provided, that if such 90-day period ends during a recess of the Legislature, the period shall be extended until the sixth day following the day on which the Legislature reconvenes. [Nov. 2, 1976]

The prior provision, Article V, section 8, which originated in the 1849 Constitution, vested the governor with the authority to fill any vacant office where "no mode is provided by the Constitution and law for filling such vacancy." The courts read the term "Constitution *and* law" to mean "Constitution or law" and thus concluded that whenever the legislature prescribed some mode of filling vacant offices other than by gubernatorial appointment, the governor lacked appointive power to fill the vacant offices (*Woodmansee v. Lowery*, 1959; *People ex rel. Mattison v. Nye*, 1908). Subsection (a) of this section, added as part of the 1966 revision as a replacement for the prior Article V, section 8, was intended to express more directly this judicial interpretation of the gubernatorial power to fill vacancies.

Subsection (b), added in 1976, was modeled after the Twenty-fifth Amendment to the U.S. Constitution, which provides that the president may nominate a person for the vice-presidency in case of a vacancy in that office, subject to the approval of both the Senate and the House of Representatives. Similarly, section 5(b) was intended to give the governor authority to nominate replacements for the offices enumerated in the event of a vacancy, subject to the general requirement that both the senate and the assembly approve the nominee. This is plainly the main premise of the subsection and is articulated unambiguously in the first sentence of section 5(b). The second sentence, however, injects ambiguity by creating an exception to the normal procedure of bicameral approval expressed in the first sentence.

This ambiguity became the subject of debate when Jesse Unruh, the incumbent treasurer, died in 1987, and Governor George Deukmejian nominated Dan Lun-gren as his successor. The assembly approved, but the senate rejected the nomination. Lungren contended that because his nomination had not literally "been confirmed nor refused confirmation by both the Senate and the Assembly within 90 days of the submission of the nomination," he was entitled to take office. In *Lungren v. Deukmejian* (1988), the California Supreme Court rejected that interpretation. Instead, the court concluded that the second sentence was intended merely to provide that if the legislature failed to act on a nomination within ninety days after submission, the nominee would be deemed confirmed. In essence, the second sentence operates to prevent either house of the legislature from exercising a pocket veto over a gubernatorial nomination. The court concluded that the more expansive interpretation offered by Lungren would eviscerate the major premise of the subsection: bicameral approval.

SECTION 6

Executive assignment and agency reorganization. Authority may be provided by statute for the Governor to assign and reorganize functions among executive officers and agencies and their employees, other than elective officers and agencies administered by elective officers. [Nov. 8, 1966]

This section was inserted by the legislature into the 1966 constitutional revision package presented to the voters so that it could vest in the governor extensive authority to alter the mode of operation of state agencies. In 1967, relying on this section, the legislature added Article 7.5 to the Government Code,[4] giving the governor wide latitude to reorganize the executive branch.[5] The legislature, however, retained the power to veto any proposed gubernatorial reorganization plan by resolution of either house of the legislature adopted within sixty days of submission of the plan to the legislature.[6]

SECTION 7

Governor as commander of the state militia. The Governor is commander-in-chief of a militia that shall be provided by statute. The Governor may call it forth to execute the law. [Nov. 5, 1974]

This power has existed since the constitutional beginnings of California. The militia of the state, the National Guard, is by federal statute also part of the U.S. armed services. The governor's power to direct the National Guard is thus subordinate to the supervening authority of the president and the executive officers of the Defense Department to activate the National Guard and direct its units in furtherance of federal objectives (*Perpich v. Department of Defense*, 1990).

The California Supreme Court has ruled that the governor's authority over the militia is not, however, exclusive. In *Martin v. Riley* (1942), it upheld the

---

[4] Calif. Stat. 1967, ch. 1540, sec. 2, codified in Calif. Government Code sec. 12080–81.2 (Deering's 1982).

[5] Calif. Government Code sec. 12080.3–4.

[6] Calif. Government Code sec. 12080(c), 12080.5.

validity of the "California State Guard Act of 1942," a wartime emergency measure that specified various aspects of the equipment, pay, training, and support of the militia.

SECTION 8

Reprieves, pardons, and commutations. (a) Subject to application procedures provided by statute, the Governor, on conditions the Governor deems proper, may grant a reprieve, pardon, and commutation, after sentence, except in case of impeachment. The Governor shall report to the Legislature each reprieve, pardon, and commutation granted, stating the pertinent facts and the reasons for granting it. The Governor may not grant a pardon or commutation to a person twice convicted of a felony except on recommendation of the Supreme Court, 4 judges concurring.
(b) No decision of the parole authority of this state with respect to the granting, denial, revocation, or suspension of parole of a person sentenced to an indeterminate term upon conviction of murder shall become effective for a period of 30 days, during which the Governor may review the decision subject to procedures provided by statute. The Governor may only affirm, modify, or reverse the decision of the parole authority on the basis of the same factors which the parole authority is required to consider. The Governor shall report to the Legislature each parole decision affirmed, modified or reversed, stating the pertinent facts and the reasons for the action. [Nov. 9, 1988]

This section is derived from provisions originating in the 1849 Constitution. The question of whether the governor posseses exclusive authority to pardon, reprieve, or commute sentences has never been definitively resolved by the California Supreme Court. However, in *Way v. Superior Court* (1977), the California Court of Appeal delivered a thorough and convincing opinion that the pardon authority is exclusively gubernatorial based upon the clear rejection of legislative pardons by the 1879 constitutional convention.

The rationale of *Way* was expressly adopted by the California Supreme Court in *Younger v. Superior Court* (1978), upholding legislation that permitted certain drug offenders who had completed their punishment to obtain destruction of the arrest and conviction records. Any infringement on the governor's clemency powers, the court held, was "purely incidental to the main purpose of the statute—which is well within the province of the Legislature—and hence does not violate the separation of powers." Although the court was not required to rule on the issue of the governor's exclusive possession of the clemency powers, its endorsement of *Way* suggests it agreed with *Way* on that point as well.

People v. Odle (1951) suggests that the judiciary also lacks any power to pardon, reprieve, or commute sentences. The court construed an amendment to Penal Code section 1260 empowering courts to "reduce the degree of the offense or the punishment imposed"[7] to mean only that courts could correct legal errors but not to "vest power in the court to modify a judgment in the absence of error in the proceedings." The *Odle* court thought that any more expansive interpretation would "raise serious constitutional questions relating to the separation of powers." Recent California decisions have accepted the *Odle* dictum as a firm statement of constitutional principle.[8]

In 1983, three weeks before the scheduled parole date of Archie Fain, a notorious murderer, rapist, and kidnapper, Governor Deukmejian asserted the power to suspend Fain's release. The governor based his action on the clemency powers of Article V, section 8 and Penal Code section 3062. Fain sought review of this action, and the court of appeal concluded both that the Penal Code did not grant to the governor the power to rescind or suspend a parole granted by the parole authorities and that the governor's constitutional clemency powers do not extend to the granting or rescinding of parole (*In re Fain*, 1983). Fain was paroled.

In apparent response to the *Fain* decision, California voters in 1988 added subsection (b). The added language makes plain that the governor may review parole decisions of the state parole authorities de novo, using the same statutory criteria mandated for use by the parole authorities.

SECTION 9

Qualifications for and voting power of lieutenant governor. The Lieutenant Governor shall have the same qualifications as the Governor.

The Lieutenant Governor is President of the Senate but has only a casting vote. [Nov. 5, 1974]

This provision, derived from the 1849 Constitution, establishes the qualifications for lieutenant governor, and, in imitation of the federal Constitution, the senate permits the lieutenant governor to preside over and cast tie-breaking votes in that chamber.

---

[7] Cal. Stat. 1949, ch. 1309, sec. 1.

[8] See, e.g., People v. Enriquez, 173 Cal. App. 3d 990, 998, 219 Cal. Rptr. 325, 330 (1985); In re Fain, 145 Cal. App. 3d 540, 548, 193 Cal. Rptr. 483, 488 (1983). But see People v. Lucero, 44 Cal. 3d 1006, 1034–36, 750 P.2d 1342, 245 Cal. Rptr. 185 (1988) (Mosk, J. concurring and dissenting); People v. Adcox, 47 Cal. 3d 207, 277, 763 P.2d 906, 253 Cal. Rptr. 55 (1990) (Mosk, J., dissenting) for a view that, under Penal Code 1260, the courts have the power to vacate imposition of the death penalty and to remand with instructions to impose a penalty of life imprisonment.

SECTION 10

Succession in office. The Lieutenant Governor shall become Governor when a vacancy occurs in the office of Governor.

The Lieutenant Governor shall act as Governor during the impeachment, absence from the State, or other temporary disability of the Governor or of a Governor-elect who fails to take office.

The Legislature shall provide an order of precedence after the Lieutenant Governor for succession to the office of Governor and for the temporary exercise of the Governor's functions.

The Supreme Court has exclusive jurisdiction to determine all questions arising under this section.

Standing to raise questions of vacancy or temporary disability is vested exclusively in a body provided by statute. [Nov. 5, 1974]

This section, which originated in the 1849 Constitution, authorizes the lieutenant governor to succeed the governor in the event of a vacancy in the office. Before revision in 1966, the predecessor section spelled out a detailed line of succession following the lieutenant governor, but this line of succession is now contained in the Government Code.[9]

The issue of the extent of the lieutenant governor's powers when the governor is physically absent from the state has proved somewhat troublesome. In 1979 Lieutenant Governor Mike Curb, a Republican, appointed a judge during a forty-hour absence from the state of Governor Edmund G. Brown, Jr., a Democrat. Upon his return, Governor Brown rescinded the appointment, and litigation ensued. The supreme court concluded that the lieutenant governor possessed all the powers of the governor during any absence from the state of the governor but also determined that Governor Brown was entitled to rescind the appointment made during his absence. (*In re Petition of Commission on the Governorship of California,* 1979). In so doing, the court explicitly rejected the "effective-absence" test—the concept that some absences are so inconsequential as not to constitute "temporary disability" under Article V, section 10.

SECTION 11

Other state officers: election, term, limits on terms. The Lieutenant Governor, Attorney General, Controller, Secretary of State, and Treasurer shall be elected at the same time and places and for the same term as the Governor. No Lieutenant Governor, Attorney General, Controller, Secretary of State, or Treasurer may serve in the same office for more than 2 terms. [Nov. 7, 1990]

---

[9] Calif. Government Code sec. 12058–59.

This section, originating in two portions of the 1849 Constitution, merely serves to make identical the terms of all the constitutional officers of the state. The final sentence, added in 1990, was part of Proposition 140's set of broad restrictions on continuous office-holding by the legislators and executive officers of the state.

SECTION 12

This section was repealed June 6, 1990.

SECTION 13

Attorney general. Subject to the powers and duties of the Governor, the Attorney General shall be the chief law officer of the State. It shall be the duty of the Attorney General to see that the laws of the State are uniformly and adequately enforced. The Attorney General shall have direct supervision over every district attorney and sheriff and over such other law enforcement officers as may be designated by law, in all matters pertaining to the duties of their respective offices, and may require any of said officers to make reports concerning their investigation, detection, prosecution, and punishment of crime in their respective jurisdictions as to the Attorney General may seem advisable. Whenever in the opinion of the Attorney General any law of the State is not being adequately enforced in any county, it shall be the duty of the Attorney General to prosecute any violations of law of which the superior court shall have jurisdiction, and in such cases the Attorney General shall have all the powers of a district attorney. When required by the public interest or directed by the Governor, the Attorney General shall assist any district attorney in the discharge of the duties of that office. [Nov. 5, 1974]

This provision, originally added by a popular initiative amendment in November 1934, was designed to increase the efficiency of law enforcement by enlarging the attorney general's duties to supervise and coordinate the activities of county district attorneys.

The attorney general's powers are, of course, subordinate to those of the governor. In the 1981 case of *People ex rel. Deukmejian v. Brown*, the California Supreme Court rejected the claim of the attorney general that, "as 'the People's legal counsel' . . . the Attorney General may determine, contrary to the views of the Governor, wherein lies the public interest." According to the court, "The constitutional pattern is crystal clear: if a conflict between the Governor and the Attorney General develops over the faithful execution of the laws of this state, the Governor retains the 'Supreme executive power' to determine the public interest; the Attorney General may act only 'subject to the powers' of the Governor."

Subject to this limitation and in the absence of specific legislative restriction, however, the attorney general has broad power to file any civil action thought necessary for enforcement of the law or protection of the public (*People v. New Perm Mines, Inc.*, 1963). Moreover, the attorney general and the district attorneys of each county possess the exclusive responsibility for initiating criminal prosecutions. Private individuals may not do so without the concurrence of the relevant district attorney (*People v. Shults*, 1978).

Despite the clear intent of the proponents of the 1934 amendment, the attorney general's power to intervene in the operations of the county district attorneys has rarely been invoked. Such intervention is politically charged, and, given the section's grant of discretion to the attorney general concerning the necessity of intervention, it is predictable that the principal result of any such intervention would be political acrimony.

SECTION 14

State officers: conflicts of interest, prohibited compensation or activities, earned income, honoraria, gifts, lobbying. (a) To eliminate any appearance of a conflict with the proper discharge of his or her duties and responsibilities, no state officer may knowingly receive any salary, wages, commissions, or other similar earned income from a lobbyist or lobbying firm, as defined by the Political Reform Act of 1974, or from a person who, during the previous 12 months, has been under a contract with the state agency under the jurisdiction of the state officer. The Legislature shall enact laws that define earned income. However, earned income does not include any community property interest in the income of a spouse. Any state officer who knowingly receives any salary, wages, commissions, or other similar earned income from a lobbyist employer, as defined in the Political Reform Act of 1974, may not, for a period of one year following its receipt, vote upon or make, participate in making, or in any way attempt to use his or her official position to influence an action or decision before the agency for which the state officer serves, other than an action or decision involving a bill described in subdivision (c) of Section 12 of Article IV, which he or she knows, or has reason to know, would have direct and significant financial impact on the lobbyist employer and would not impact the public generally or a significant segment of the public in a similar manner. As used in this subdivision, "public generally" includes an industry, trade, or profession.

(b) No state officer may accept any honorarium. The Legislature shall enact laws that implement this subdivision.

(c) The Legislature shall enact laws that ban or strictly limit the acceptance of a gift by a state officer from any source if the acceptance of the gift might create a conflict of interest.

(d) No state officer may knowingly accept any compensation for appearing, or agreeing to appear, or taking any other action on behalf of another person before any state government board or agency. If a state officer knowingly accepts any compensation for appearing, or agreeing to appear, or taking any other action on behalf of another person before any local government board or agency, the state officer may not, for a period of one year following the acceptance of the compensation, make, participate in making, or in any way attempt to use his or her official position to influence an action or decision before the state agency for which the state officer serves, other than an action or decision involving a bill described in subdivision (c) of Section 12 of Article IV, which he or she knows, or has reason to know, would have direct and significant financial impact on the lobbyist employer and would not impact the public generally or a significant segment of the public in a similar manner. As used in this subdivision, "public generally" includes an industry, trade, or profession. However, a state officer may engage in activities involving a board or agency which are strictly on his or her own behalf, appear in the capacity of an attorney before any court or the Workers' Compensation Appeals Board, or act as an advocate without compensation or make an inquiry for information on behalf of a person before a board or agency. This subdivision does not prohibit any action of a partnership or firm of which the state officer is a member if the state officer does not share directly or indirectly in the fee, less any expenses attributable to that fee, resulting from that action.

(e) The Legislature shall enact laws that prohibit a state officer, or a secretary of an agency or director of a department appointed by the Governor, who has not resigned or retired from state service prior to January 7, 1991, from lobbying, for compensation, as governed by the Political Reform Act of 1974, before the executive branch of state government for 12 months after leaving office.

(f) "State officer," as used in this section, means the Governor, Attorney General, Controller, Insurance Commissioner, Secretary of State, Superintendent of Public Instruction, Treasurer, and member of the State Board of Equalization. [Dec. 3, 1990]

This section, championed by such advocates of good government as Common Cause and the League of Women Voters, was adopted in June 1990 as part of Proposition 112. It was intended to limit the possibilities for corruption of office by prohibiting legislators from receiving honoraria or compensation from lobbyists and requiring the enactment of legislation restricting legislators from accepting gifts or lobbying the legislature within twelve months of their departure from that body, and restricting executive officers from lobbying the executive branch within twelve months following their cessation of executive service. A comprehensive statute implementing this section was enacted in 1990.[10]

[10] Cal. Stat. 1990, ch. 84 (SB 1738).

There appears to be at least one drafting error of potential substance.[11] Subsection (d) prohibits state officers from knowingly accepting compensation for appearances on behalf of others before "state government boards or agencies." However, the penalty of disqualification for one year applies only if the state officer has knowingly accepted compensation to appear for another before "any local government board or agency." Read literally, the subsection does not penalize that which it prohibits. It is possible that, notwithstanding the apparent sloppiness, the provision will be interpreted like the otherwise linguistically parallel subsection (a).

The provision is also unusual in that it refers specifically to a statute, the Political Reform Act of 1974.[12] Incorporated into section 14 are definitional terms contained in the act. Thus, an interesting question is presented: whether the legislature could, by amendment or repeal of the incorporated statutory definitions, effectively alter the constitution. Should a future legislature employ this gambit, this ambiguous possibility invites future litigation.

[11] The section twice employs the deplorable and ungrammatical practice of converting the noun *impact* into a verb. The only remedy for this offense is to point out the malfeasance and thus expose the section's unschooled drafters to deserved ridicule.

[12] Government Code sec. 81000 et seq.

Article VI

Judicial

This article was formerly much longer and full of detail. The streamlining is the product of a revision recommended by the California Constitution Revision Commission, proposed by the legislature, and adopted by the voters in 1966.

SECTION 1

Judicial executive power vested in courts. The judicial power of this State is vested in the Supreme Court, courts of appeal, superior courts, municipal courts, and justice courts. All courts are courts of record. [Nov. 9, 1988]

The 1849 Constitution established a two-tier judicial system. At the bottom were the trial courts, consisting of district courts, county courts, and justices of the peace. At the top was the supreme court, consisting of three justices. (Its composition was later expanded to five and then its present complement of seven; see sec. 2). What is now the middle tier—the court of appeal—was not created until 1904.

Amendments and revisions subsequent to 1849 tinkered with the trial court structure in various ways. An amendment in 1862 added probate courts to the list and authorized the legislature to provide for other inferior courts, but the 1879 Constitution eliminated the reference to probate courts and replaced "district courts" with "superior courts." In 1924, municipal courts, which had existed only in some cities by legislative grace, acquired constitutional status independent of legislative control pursuant to an amendment that authorized their creation as a matter of municipal option. A further amendment in 1950 established the current trial-level structure of superior courts (at the county level) and mu- nicipal and justice courts (at the city level), and it froze that structure into the constitution by mandating municipal and justice courts on the basis of population (sec. 5) and by eliminating the power of the legislature to provide for courts other than those identified in the constitution.

Until recently, justice courts have had a unique status. Historically staffed by nonlawyers, they were not regarded as courts of record, which meant that their judgments were more vulnerable to attack and could not be enforced in other states. In 1974 the supreme court dealt justice courts a blow by holding that a criminal defendant has a constitutional right to be tried by a judge who is a lawyer. (*Gordon v. Justice Court,* 1974). In 1988 section 15 of this article was amended to require judges of justice courts to be lawyers, and in the same year this section was amended to provide that all courts are courts of record.

In addition to identifying the various courts of constitutional status, this section serves as a limitation on the exercise of judicial power by other tribunals or branches of government. The supreme court has held that an administrative agency may be authorized to adjudicate disputes and make restitutive money awards only where that authority is reasonably necessary to effectuate the administrative agency's primary, legitimate regulatory purpose and subject to ultimate judicial review (*McHugh v. Santa Monica Rent Control Board,* 1989). Applying these criteria, the court had concluded (over vigorous dissent) that an agency charged with responsibility for remedying and deterring housing discrimination could not constitutionally be given power to award damages for emotional damages suffered by victims of discrimination (*Walnut Creek Manor v. Fair Employment and Housing Commission,* 1991). The court has acknowledged that these standards are different from those applicable to separation-of-power questions under the federal Constitution.

SECTION 2

Supreme Court of California. The Supreme Court consists of the Chief Justice of California and 6 associate justices. The Chief Justice may convene the court at any time. Concurrence of 4 judges present at the argument is necessary for a judgment.

An acting Chief Justice shall perform all functions of the Chief Justice when the Chief Justice is absent or unable to act. The Chief Justice or, if the Chief Justice fails to do so, the court shall select an associate justice as acting Chief Justice. [Nov. 5, 1974]

The 1849 Constitution provided for a supreme court consisting of a chief justice and two associate justices. An 1862 amendment added two justices, and the 1879 Constitution established the current total of seven. That constitution divided the court into two departments, each consisting of three associate justices with the chief justice presiding, and it provided for in bank (full court) consideration in the event of disagreement. This arrangement was designed to enable the court to fulfill the onerous burden, which existed at the time, of deciding all appeals.

After the intermediate appellate court was created in 1904 and the supreme court's jurisdiction became largely discretionary, the departmental structure proved neither necessary nor desirable. By 1914 the court had abandoned it in practice, deciding almost all cases in bank, and in 1966 it was formally abandoned.

SECTION 3

Courts of appeal. The Legislature shall divide the State into districts each containing a court of appeal with one or more divisions. Each division consists of a presiding justice and 2 or more associate justices. It has the power of a court of appeal and shall conduct itself as a 3-judge court. Concurrence of 2 judges present at the argument is necessary for a judgment.

An acting presiding justice shall perform all functions of the presiding justice when the presiding justice is absent or unable to act. The presiding justice or, if the presiding justice fails to do so, the Chief Justice shall select an associate justice of that division as acting presiding justice. [Nov. 5, 1974]

A 1904 amendment established, for the first time, an intermediate appellate court (then called the district court of appeal) consisting of three appellate districts with three justices each in specified geographical areas. As the state's population increased over the next sixty-two years, there were frequent amendments providing for additional districts and divisions. Finally, as part of the 1966 constitutional revision, this section was amended to authorize the legislature to decide the number and location of districts and divisions of what was then renamed the "court of appeal."

There are six districts of the court of appeal. District 2 in Los Angeles-Santa Barbara is the largest, with seven divisions of three or four justices each. District 6 in San Jose, with a single division of six justices, is the smallest. There are nearly ninety appellate justices throughout the state. Each division of the court of appeal is a separate court, free to reject decisions of other divisions, even in the same appellate district.

SECTION 4

Superior courts. In each county there is a superior court of one or more judges. The Legislature shall prescribe the number of judges and provide for the officers and employees of each superior court. If the governing body of each affected county concurs, the Legislature may provide that one or more judges serve more than one superior court.

The county clerk is ex officio clerk of the superior court in the county. [Nov. 5, 1974]

The superior court was created by the Constitution of 1879 as a court of general jurisdiction at the county level. This section, which derived from former section 6 of this article, acquired its current language and form as a result of the 1966 revision.

Superior courts have original jurisdiction over all cases other than those allocated by the legislature to municipal or justice courts (see sec. 10) and appellate jurisdiction over cases decided by those "inferior" tribunals (see sec. 11). There are nearly 800 superior court judges throughout the state, their number ranging from 1 in some counties to more than 200 in Los Angeles County.

SECTION 5

Municipal and justice courts. (a) Each county shall be divided into municipal court and justice court districts as provided by statute, but a city may not be divided into more than one district. Each municipal and justice court shall have one or more judges.

There shall be a municipal court in each district of more than 40,000 residents and a justice court in each district of 40,000 residents or less. The number of residents shall be ascertained as provided by statute.

The Legislature shall provide for the organization and prescribe the jurisdiction of municipal and justice courts. It shall prescribe for each municipal court and provide for each justice court the number, qualifications, and compensation of judges, officers, and employees.

(b) Notwithstanding the provisions of subdivision (a), any city in San Diego County may be divided into more than one municipal court or justice court district if the Legislature determines that unusual geographic conditions warrant such division. [June 8, 1976]

Section 11 of this article, from which this section derived, replaced the legislative discretion that previously existed in the creation of municipal and justice courts with a constitutionally prescribed formula, based on population. It retained legislative authority, however, to provide for the organization and prescribe the jurisdiction of such courts and "to prescribe [for each such court] the employees." The 1966 constitutional revision substituted the current language of subsection (a). Subsection (b), authorizing the legislature to depart from the prescribed formula in the case of San Diego County, so as to divide cities within that county into more than one judicial district, was added in 1976.

By statute, the legislature has delegated to the board of supervisors of each county the power to define judicial districts (Gov. Code sec. 71040), but it is the legislature that determines the jurisdiction of each court. In 1976, the legislature significantly reduced the relevance of the distinction between municipal and justice courts by according them the same jurisdiction and subject to the same procedures on appeal. Municipal and justice courts now have jurisdiction in civil cases in which the amount in controversy does not exceed $15,000 (Cal. Code Civ. Proc. sec. 86) and in criminal cases in which only a misdemeanor is charged (Cal. Penal Code sec. 1462).

SECTION 6

Judicial Council: membership and powers. The Judicial Council consists of the Chief Justice and one other judge of the Supreme Court, 3 judges of courts of appeal, 5 judges of superior courts, 3 judges of municipal courts, and 2 judges of justice courts, each appointed by the Chief Justice for a 2-year term; 4 members of the State Bar appointed by its governing body for 2-year terms; and one member of each house of the Legislature appointed as provided by the house.

Council membership terminates if a member ceases to hold the position that qualified the member for appointment. A vacancy shall be filled by the appointing power for the remainder of the term.

The council may appoint an Administrative Director of the Courts, who serves at its pleasure and performs functions delegated by the council or the Chief Justice, other than adopting rules of court administration, practice and procedure.

To improve the administration of justice the council shall survey judicial business and make recommendations to the courts, make recommendations annually to the Governor and Legislature, adopt rules for court administration, practice and procedure, not inconsistent with statute, and perform other functions prescribed by statute.

The Chief Justice shall seek to expedite judicial business and to equalize the work of judges. The Chief Justice may provide for the assignment of any judge to another court but only with the judge's consent if the court is of lower jurisdiction. A retired judge who consents may be assigned to any court.

Judges shall report to the Judicial Council as the Chief Justice directs concerning the condition of judicial business in their courts. They shall cooperate with the council and hold court as assigned. [Nov. 5, 1974]

The Judicial Council was created by constitutional amendment in 1926 in order, its proponents said, to put the courts on a "business basis." Initially, it was composed of eleven judges chosen by the chief justice. An amendment in 1960 increased the membership of the council by adding four appointees of the state bar, one member of each house of the legislature, and a second municipal court judge. The 1960 amendment also authorized the position of administrative director. In 1966, council membership was again increased, to its present complement of twenty-one.

The Judicial Council is charged by this section with responsibility for performing a variety of functions to ensure the proper functioning of the judicial branch. The council supervises an annual survey of the work of the courts, including caseloads, and submits an annual report to the governor and the legislature containing statistical information and recommendations relating to the administration of justice. Typically, such reports advise the other branches regarding such matters as the necessity for additional courts or judges, the allocation of jurisdiction among courts, and the need for physical expansion or renovation of court facilities. The Judicial Council also represents the judicial branch in its dealings with the governor and the legislature over budgetary matters and legislation relating to the courts. In cooperation with the California Judges Association, it provides for the training of new judges and the continued education of existing judges by means of educational programs and materials, through an independent entity, the California Center for Judicial Education and Research (CJER).

The council is assisted in these various activities by an Administrative Office of the Courts (AOC), headed by the administrative director. The AOC also assists the chief justice with the administrative responsibilities of that office for expediting judicial business and equalizing the work of the courts, including the assignment of judges to fill needs created by temporary vacancy or overload.

The Judicial Council has responsibility, of a quasi-legislative nature, for adopting rules with respect to court administration, practice, and procedure within the framework of statutory guidelines. The council also prescribes uniform legal forms as a means of simplifying and standardizing certain routine legal transactions.

SECTION 7

Commission on Judicial Appointments. The Commission on Judicial Appointments consists of the Chief Justice, the Attorney General, and the presiding justice of the court of appeal of the affected district or, if there are 2 or more presiding justices, the one who has presided longest or, when a nomination or appointment to the Supreme Court is to be considered, the presiding justice who has presided longest on any court of appeal. [Nov. 8, 1966]

The Commission on Judicial Appointments was created in 1934 as part of a new system for the appointment of appellate judges. Its function is to pass upon gubernatorial nominees to the supreme court and the court of appeal. (See sec. 16.)

The constitution specifies neither the procedure that the commission is to use nor the criteria that it is to apply. Early in its history, the commission acted privately, voting in the chambers of the chief justice, but in recent years it has held public hearings and has invited written or oral participation by persons with relevant information or opinion about the candidate.

Only rarely has the commission rejected a nominee.

SECTION 8

Commission on Judicial Performance. (a) The Commission on Judicial Performance consists of 2 judges of courts of appeal, 2 judges of superior courts, and one judge of a municipal court, each appointed by the Supreme Court; 2 members of the State Bar of California who have practiced law in this State for 10 years, appointed by its governing body; and 2 citizens who are not judges, retired judges, or members of the State Bar of California, appointed by the Governor and approved by the Senate, a majority of the membership concurring. Except as provided in subdivision (b), all terms are 4 years. No member shall serve more than 2 4-year terms.

Commission membership terminates if a member ceases to hold the position that qualified the member for appointment. A vacancy shall be filled by the appointing power for the remainder of the term. A member whose term has expired may continue to serve until the vacancy has been filled by the appointing power.

(b) To create staggered terms among the members of the Commission on Judicial Performance, the following members shall be appointed as follows:

(1) The court of appeal member appointed to immediately succeed the term that expired on November 8, 1988, shall serve a 2-year term.

(2) Of the State Bar members appointed to immediately succeed terms that expire on December 31, 1988, one member shall serve for a 2-year term. [Nov. 9, 1988]

Created by constitutional amendment in 1960, the constitutional function of the Commission on Judicial Performance (then called the Commission on Judicial Qualifications) is to investigate and make recommendations to the supreme court concerning the retirement of a judge for disability or the censure or removal of a judge for various reasons. (See sec. 18 of this article) In the performance of these functions, the commission has statutory authority to conduct hearings, subpoena witnesses, and the like (Gov. Code sec. 67570). The commission processes nearly 1,000 complaints annually, most of them resulting in dismissal after preliminary investigation or in private admonishment. The legislature has delegated certain functions to the commission in addition to those constitutionally specified—for example, to pass upon applications by judges for disability retirement (Cal. Govt. Code sec. 75060).

This section describes the composition of the commission. Its provisions have remained substantially unchanged since 1960, except for the creation of staggered terms and the two-term limitation, both a product of amendment in 1988.

SECTION 9

State Bar of California. The State Bar of California is a public corporation. Every person admitted and licensed to practice law in this State is and shall be a member of the State Bar except while holding office as a judge of a court of record. [Nov. 8, 1966]

The State Bar Act of 1927 created an "integrated bar," which means that all lawyers are automatically members, upon admission to practice, and must pay annual dues prescribed by the State Bar Board of Governors. This section gives that principle constitutional status.

The state bar regulates admission to the bar, prescribes rules of professional conduct, and maintains special courts for the consideration of charges against lawyers and the imposition of discipline subject to review by the supreme court. Pursuant to statute, it administers a system for the arbitration of fee disputes and for the reimbursement of clients injured through wrongdoing by their attorneys.

SECTION 10

Original jurisdiction; judicial power to comment upon evidence. The Supreme Court, courts of appeal, superior courts, and their judges have original jurisdiction in habeas corpus proceedings. Those courts also have original jurisdiction in proceedings for extraordinary relief in the nature of mandamus, certiorari, and prohibition.

Superior courts have original jurisdiction in all causes except those given by statute to other trial courts.

The court may make such comment on the evidence and the testimony and credibility of any witness as in its opinion is necessary for the proper determination of the cause. [Nov. 8, 1966]

A court is said to have original jurisdiction in cases that can be brought to the court's attention directly rather than by appeal from a decision of some lower court. The first two paragraphs of this section list the kinds of cases over which various courts have that sort of jurisdiction. By statute, municipal courts and justice courts have jurisdiction over civil cases in which the amount in controversy is less than a specified sum (currently $15,000) and over criminal cases in which the defendant is charged with a misdemeanor rather than a felony. These are the principal dividing lines between municipal and justice court jurisdiction on one hand, and superior court jurisdiction on the other.

The third paragraph, authorizing courts to comment on the evidence and the testimony and credibility of witnesses, derives from a constitutional amendment in 1934. The 1849 and 1879 Constitutions stated that judges should not "charge" juries with respect to matters of fact but may "state the testimony" and "declare the law." The purpose of the current language is to allow the trial court to use its experience and training in analyzing evidence in order to assist the jury. The provision does not permit a court to suggest that the jury return a particular verdict or (in a criminal case) to express its opinion on the ultimate fact of guilt or innocence (*People v. Cook*, 1983).

SECTION 11

Appellate jurisdiction. The Supreme Court has appellate jurisdiction when judgment of death has been pronounced. With that exception courts of appeal have appellate jurisdiction when superior courts have original jurisdiction and in other causes prescribed by statute.

Superior courts have appellate jurisdiction in causes prescribed by statute that arise in municipal and justice courts in their counties.

The Legislature may permit appellate courts to take evidence and make findings of fact when jury trial is waived or not a matter of right. [Nov. 8, 1966]

This section describes the appellate jurisdiction of the various courts. In general, appeals from decisions of municipal or justice courts are heard by an appellate division of the superior court and are considered by higher courts only on a discretionary basis. Appeals from decisions of the superior courts are heard by the court of appeal except in cases in which the death penalty is imposed; those decisions are appealed automatically to the supreme court. With the exception of death penalty cases, the supreme court's jurisdiction is discretionary; it grants review in those cases it considers sufficiently important to warrant its attention. (See sec. 12.)

SECTION 12

Transfer of causes. (a) The Supreme Court may, before decision, transfer to itself a cause in a court of appeal. It may, before decision, transfer a cause from itself to a court of appeal or from one court of appeal or division to another. The court to which a cause is transferred has jurisdiction.

(b) The Supreme Court may review the decision of a court of appeal in any cause.

(c) The Judicial Council shall provide, by rules of court, for the time and procedure for transfer and for review, including, among other things, provisions for the time and procedure for transfer with instructions, for review of all or part of a decision, and for remand as improvidently granted.

(d) This section shall not apply to an appeal involving a judgment of death. [May 6, 1985]

This section describes the options the supreme court has in the exercise of its appellate jurisdiction. Subsections (b) through (d) were added in 1985.

On occasion, under subsection (a), the court will transfer to itself a case pending for decision elsewhere in the system, either to decide the case itself—usually because it considers speedy decision of the issue important—or to transfer the case to some other court for decision, usually when that court has already decided some previous issue in the case.

More typically, however, the court will wait until the case has been decided by the court of appeal and then determine whether to grant review under subsection (b). Subsection (c) allows for other options, such as limiting review to a portion of the appellate court's opinion, subject to rules adopted by the Judicial Council.

Subsection (d) makes clear that the supreme court alone has responsibility, under the existing system, for deciding death penalty cases. The court has been inundated with such cases in recent years, however, and it is likely that at some point, there will be an effort to amend the constitution so as to permit the supreme court to share that jurisdiction with the court of appeal.

SECTION 13

Setting aside of judgments. No judgment shall be set aside, or new trial granted, in any cause, on the ground of misdirection of the jury, or of the improper admission or rejection of evidence, or for any error as to any matter of pleading, or for any error as to any matter of procedure, unless, after an examination of the entire cause, including the evidence, the court shall be of the opinion that the error complained of has resulted in a miscarriage of justice. [Nov. 8, 1966]

This section is based on a 1911 amendment, amended further in 1914. Its purpose is to prevent an appellate court from overturning the judgment of a lower court unless it finds that there has been a miscarriage of justice. In other words, the court may not set aside the judgment simply because some legal error was committed or simply because the court would have reached a different conclusion on the facts presented.

Generally, the miscarriage-of-justice standard has been interpreted to mean that reversal is appropriate only when it appears likely that, absent the error, the jury itself (or the trial judge) would have reached a different result (*People v. Watson*, 1956). Otherwise, the error is deemed "harmless," and the judgment is affirmed. When the error is of federal constitutional dimension, however, state courts are obliged to follow the federal standard, which requires reversal unless it can be said that no reasonable trier of fact would have reached a different result absent the error (*Chapman v. California*, 1968). Even under California law, if the error is so fundamental as to deprive the defendant of a fair trial, courts will say that the error is itself a miscarriage of justice, and reverse (*People v. Modesto*, 1963).

SECTION 14

Published judicial opinions. The Legislature shall provide for the prompt publication of such opinions of the Supreme Court and courts of appeal as the Supreme Court deems appropriate, and those opinions shall be available for publication by any person.

Decisions of the Supreme Court and courts of appeal that determine causes shall be in writing with reasons stated. [Nov. 8, 1966]

Copies of all appellate opinions are available to the public, and all supreme court opinions are published in official reports. Only a fraction—less than 20 percent—of court of appeal opinions are so published, however. Pursuant to rules adopted by the Judicial Council, the court of appeal may decide that parts or all of its opinion are not sufficiently significant to merit publication. And the supreme court may order all or part of a court of appeal opinion "depublished," for that or other reasons, with the result that it is not published in the official reports and cannot be cited as authority. The depublication option has been used by the supreme court increasingly in recent years as a way of controlling the development of the law without granting review in a case and has been the subject of steady criticism from segments of the bar and the lower courts.

Prior to the 1879 Constitution, the supreme court would often decide cases without opinion or explanation, and when the legislature attempted to impose an opinion requirement, the court held that it had no power to do so (*Houston v. Williams*, 1859). The last sentence of section 14 requires that California appellate courts—unlike the U.S. Supreme Court and the courts of most other states—may not determine a cause without a statement of reasons in writing.

SECTION 15

Judicial eligibility. A person is ineligible to be a judge of a court of record unless for 5 years immediately preceding selection to a municipal or justice court or 10 years immediately preceding selection to other courts, the person has been a member of the State Bar or served as a judge of a court of record in this State. A judge eligible for municipal court service may be assigned by the Chief Justice to serve on any court. [Nov. 9, 1988]

Prior to 1966, the constitution prescribed only five years' state bar membership or judicial service for all judges; in that year, the requirement was increased to ten years for all judges other than those of the municipal court. Formerly, a judge of a justice court was not required to be a lawyer, but an amendment in 1988 made the five-year requirement for municipal court judges prospectively applicable to justice courts as well.

SECTION 15.5

Judicial eligibility. The 5-year membership or service requirement of Section 15 does not apply to justice court judges who held office on January 1, 1988.

This section shall be operative only until January 1, 1995, and as of that date is repealed. [Nov. 9, 1988]

This section granted incumbent justice court judges a temporary exemption from the previous section's five-year membership or service requirement.

SECTION 16

Judges: elections, terms, vacancies. (a) Judges of the Supreme Court shall be elected at large and judges of courts of appeal shall be elected in their districts at general elections at the same time and places as the Governor. Their terms are 12 years beginning the Monday after January 1 following their election, except that a judge elected to an unexpired term serves the remainder of the term. In creating a new court of appeal district or division the Legislature shall provide that the first elective terms are 4, 8, and 12 years.

(b) Judges of other courts shall be elected in their counties or districts at general elections. The Legislature may provide that an unopposed incumbent's name not appear on the ballot.

(c) Terms of judges of superior courts are 6 years beginning the Monday after January 1 following their election. A vacancy shall be filled by election to a full term at the next general election after the January 1 following the vacancy, but the Governor shall appoint a person to fill the vacancy temporarily until the elected judge's term begins.

(d) Within 30 days before August 16 preceding the expiration of the judge's term, a judge of the Supreme Court or a court of appeal may file a declaration of candidacy to succeed to the office presently held by the judge. If the declaration is not filed, the Governor before September 16 shall nominate a candidate. At the next general election, only the candidate so declared or nominated may appear on the ballot, which shall present the question whether the candidate shall be elected. The candidate shall be elected upon receiving a majority of the votes on the question.

A candidate not elected may not be appointed to that court but later may be nominated and elected.

The Governor shall fill vacancies in those courts by appointment. An appointee holds office until the Monday after January 1 following the first general election at which the appointee had the right to become a candidate or until an elected judge qualifies. A nomination or appointment by the Governor is effective when confirmed by the Commission on Judicial Appointments.

Electors of a county, by majority of those voting and in a manner the Legislature shall provide, may make this system of selection applicable to judges of superior courts. [Nov. 5, 1974]

Under the Constitutions of 1849 and 1879, all judges were subject to contested elections at the expiration of their respective terms. This is still the arrangement for judges of the municipal, justice, and superior courts and is reflected in subsections (b) and (c).

In 1934, the constitution was amended to insulate judges of the court of appeal and the supreme court from contested elections and to provide for "retention elections" after appointment by the governor and confirmation by the Commission on Judicial Appointments. In a retention election, the judge appears on the ballot unopposed, and the voters vote "yes" or "no" on the question whether the judge should be retained. This section sets forth the terms of office and the timing of both contested and retention elections. The 1934 amendments are reflected in subsections (a) and (d). Subsection (d) authorizes counties, by popular vote, to adopt retention elections for superior court judges, but to date no county has exercised that option.

The backers of the 1934 initiative measure saw it as a means of insulating judges from the electoral process. This effort succeeded until 1978 when Chief Justice Rose Bird, the first woman justice on the supreme court and a controversial figure from the outset of her tenure, was subjected to a well-organized and well-funded opposition campaign from which she emerged with a narrow margin of votes. Eight years later, she and two associate justices (Joseph R. Grodin and Cruz Reynoso) were voted out of judicial office—the first occurrence of that sort since 1934—after a campaign that focused on the court's frequent overturning of death penalty judgments.

SECTION 17

Judges: restrictions, other employment, benefits. A judge of a court of record may not practice law and during the term for which the judge was selected is ineligible for public employment or public office other than judicial employment or judicial office, except that a judge of a court of record may accept a part-time teaching position that is outside the normal hours of his or her judicial position and that does not interfere with the regular performance of his or her judicial duties while holding office. A judge of a trial court of record may, however, become eligible for election to other public office by taking a leave of absence without pay prior to filing a declaration of candidacy. Acceptance of the public office is a resignation from the office of judge.

A judicial officer may not receive fines or fees for personal use.

A judicial officer may not earn retirement service credit from a public teaching position while holding judicial office. [Nov. 9, 1988]

The prohibition against judges' practicing law and holding other than judicial office stems from the 1849 Constitution and appears aimed at avoiding conflict of interest and maintaining separation of powers. Superior and municipal court judges, however, may take an unpaid leave of absence in order to run for other nonjudicial office without risking their judicial position.

In the 1980s, question arose whether this section prohibited judges from teaching part-time in public institutions. A 1988 amendment expressly permits such activity so long as it does not interfere with judicial duties and the judges do not accrue dual retirement credit.

SECTION 18

Judges: disqualification, suspension, removal, retirement, or reproval. (a) A judge is disqualified from acting as a judge, without loss of salary, while there is pending (1) an indictment or an information charging the judge in the United States with a crime punishable as a felony under California or federal law, or (2) a recommendation to the Supreme Court by the Commission on Judicial Performance for removal or retirement of the judge.

(b) On recommendation of the Commission on Judicial Performance or on its own motion, the Supreme Court may suspend a judge from office without salary when in the United States the judge pleads guilty or no contest or is found guilty of a crime punishable as a felony under California or federal law or of any other crime that involved moral turpitude under the law. If the conviction is reversed suspension terminates, and the judge shall be paid the salary for the judicial office held by the judge for the period of suspension. If the judge is suspended and the conviction becomes final the Supreme Court shall remove the judge from office.

(c) On recommendation of the Commission on Judicial Performance the Supreme Court may (1) retire a judge for disability that seriously interferes with the performance of the judge's duties and is or is likely to become permanent; and (2) censure or remove a judge for action occurring not more than 6 years prior to the commencement of the judge's current term that constitutes willful misconduct in office, persistent failure or inability to perform the judge's duties, habitual intemperance in the use of intoxicants or drugs, or conduct prejudicial to the administration of justice that brings the judicial office into disrepute. The Commission on Judicial Performance may privately admonish a judge found to have engaged in an improper action or dereliction of duty, subject to review in the Supreme Court in the manner provided for review of causes decided by a court of appeal.

(d) A judge retired by the Supreme Court shall be considered to have retired voluntarily. A judge removed by the Supreme Court is ineligible for judicial office and pending further order of the court is suspended from practicing law in this State.

(e) A recommendation of the Commission on Judicial Performance for the censure, removal or retirement of a judge of the Supreme Court shall be determined by a tribunal of 7 court of appeal judges selected by lot.

(f) If, after conducting a preliminary investigation, the Commission on Judicial Performance by vote determines that formal proceedings shall be instituted:

(1) The judge or judges charged may require that formal hearings be public, unless the Commission on Judicial Performance by vote finds good cause for confidential hearings.

(2) The Commission on Judicial Performance may, without further review in the Supreme Court, issue a public reproof with the consent of the judge for conduct warranting discipline. The public reproof shall include an enumeration of any and all formal charges brought against the judge which have not been dismissed by the commission.

(3) The Commission on Judicial Performance may in the pursuit of public confidence and the interests of justice, issue press statements or releases or, in the event charges involve moral turpitude, dishonesty, or corruption, open hearings to the public.

(g) The Commission on Judicial Performance may issue explanatory statements at any investigatory stage when the subject matter is generally known to the public.

(h) The Judicial Council shall make rules implementing this section and providing for confidentiality proceedings. [Nov. 9, 1988]

Prior to 1960, the constitution provided for the supreme court, on its own motion or on the motion of any person, to remove a judge who had been convicted of a crime involving moral turpitude, but otherwise judges could be removed from office, or otherwise disciplined, only by action of the other branches, through impeachment or similar process. In 1960, the constitution was amended to create the Commission on Judicial Qualifications (now the Commission on Judicial Performance; see sec. 8) and to provide for discipline or removal of judges by the supreme court, acting on recommendations of the commission for designated offenses or in the event of disability. Several subsequent amendments produced the existing language.

Subsection (a) provides for temporary automatic disqualification of a judge who has been formally charged with a felony or is subject to a recommendation by the commission that he or she be removed or retired. Subsection (b) provides for formal suspension of a judge who has been vindicated of (or pleads no contest to) a crime that is either a felony or involves moral turpitude.

Subsection (c) provides for involuntary retirement of a judge, through action by the supreme court on recommendation by the commission, for disability that seriously interferes with the performance of the judge's duties. The most notable example is the removal of Justice Marshall McComb from the supreme court in 1977, after contested hearings before the commission and a decision by a seven-judge tribunal composed of appeal judges selected by lot.

Subsection (c) provides also for the censure or removal of a judge for various offenses, including "conduct prejudicial to the administration of justice that brings the judicial office into disrepute." That language has been used as a basis for disciplining judges who, for example, used abusive, racist, or sexist language toward attorneys or parties in the courtroom. Under subsection (c) the commission may on its own authority privately admonish a judge without prior approval by the supreme court but subject to review by that court on petition by the admonished judge.

Subsection (d) distinguishes between involuntary retirement and removal. A judge who is retired by the supreme court is treated like any other judge who retires; a judge who is removed by the supreme court may not hold further judicial office and may not practice law in California.

Subsection (e) provides a special procedure when proposed discipline against a justice of the supreme court is under consideration; the matter is heard by a tribunal of justices from the court of appeal selected by lot.

Prior to 1988, subsection (f) provided that the council "shall make rules implementing this section and providing for confidentiality of proceedings." That language is now contained in subsection (h). Subsection (f) was amended in that year to make certain exceptions to the rule of confidentiality. A judge may now require that formal hearings against him or her be public unless the commission for good cause decides otherwise. In addition, the commission on its own motion may open hearings to the public in the case of charges involving moral turpitude, dishonesty, or corruption. With the permission of the judge found guilty of conduct warranting discipline, and commission may issue a public reproof without further review in the supreme court. The commission is also permitted to issue press statements or releases, to explain what it is doing. Subsection (g), also added in 1988, permits the commission to issue explanatory statements at any investigatory stage of its proceedings when the subject matter is generally known to the public.

SECTION 19

Judges: compensation. The Legislature shall prescribe compensation for judges of courts of record.

A judge of a court of record may not receive the salary for the judicial office held by the judge while any cause before the judge remains pending and undetermined for 90 days after it ha been submitted for decision. [Nov. 5, 1974]

The 1849 Constitution prescribed the salary of supreme court justices, leaving the salaries of lower court judges to the legislature. Subsequent amendments modified the salaries of supreme court justices and (after establishment of the court of appeal) all appellate justices until 1934, when the constitution was amended to permit the legislature to fix the salaries of all judges.

The second sentence of this section—regarding withholding salary from judges who fail to decide matters within ninety days of submission—was added in 1879 as a prod to prompt decision making by both the trial courts and the supreme court. In the trial courts, a case is submitted when all the evidence is in and the arguments heard. As applied to the court of appeal, "submission" usually means the time scheduled for oral argument, and the section has been construed to mean that if an opinion is not filed within ninety days of the date, no judge who heard the case may draw salary, even though responsibility for drafting the opinion may have been assigned to some other judge.

The supreme court for many years resisted that application of the ninety-day requirement, taking the position that a case was submitted for decision only when an order to that effect was filed, typically with the opinion itself. Following litigation in the 1980s in which the plaintiff sought to suspend the pay of supreme court justices under this section, the court announced that it would comply with the section by filing opinions within ninety days of oral argument, unless the case was not ripe for decision at that time. Pursuant to this commitment, the court typically waits until proposed opinions in a case have been circulated before it schedules oral argument. Whether that results in the speedier decision of cases after briefing seems doubtful.

SECTION 20

Judges: retirement and disability. The Legislature shall provide for retirement, with reasonable allowance, of judges of courts of record for age or disability. [Nov. 8, 1966]

Pursuant to the mandate of this section, the legislature has provided for a retirement system for all judges. There is no mandatory retirement, but by statute a judge who fails to retire by age seventy forfeits one-half of his or her retirement pay.

SECTION 21

Temporary judges. On stipulation of the parties litigant the court may order a cause to be tried by a temporary judge who is a member of the State Bar, sworn and empowered to act until final determination of the cause. [Nov. 8, 1966]

Under this section, any attorney may be appointed to serve as a judge pro tempore, provided the parties consent. This practice is often used in small claims courts and as a means of relieving the workload of congested courts.

SECTION 22

Appointment of officers to perform subordinate judicial duties. The Legislature may provide for the appointment by trial courts of record of officers such as commissioners to perform subordinate judicial duties. [Nov. 8, 1966]

The legislature has provided for the appointment of special commissioners in certain matters, such as uncontested probate or dissolution proceedings, who may take evidence and enter appropriate orders. Absent the authorization this section provides, such action by the legislature might be considered to violate theseparation-of-powers doctrine.

Article VII

Public Officers and Employees

This article establishes the constitutional structure of California's modern civil service system. The core principle is that public employees should be selected on the basis of merit. The mandate for civil service was created in 1934 by the addition of Article XXIV, in an effort to eliminate the political spoils system and to promote efficiency and economy in California's state government. The original article was systematically revised by the California Constitution Revision Commission, and its recommendations, which made no substantive changes but merely eliminated obsolete and superfluous provisions, were approved by the electorate in 1970. In 1976 the article was renumbered as Article VII.

Sections 1 through 6 derive from the previous Article XXIV. Sections 7 and 8, concerning dual office-holding, disqualification from office and juries, and the support of free suffrage, derive from the 1849 and 1879 Constitutions. More recent additions, sections 9 through 11, concern limits on subversion, campaign defamation, and state officer pensions.

SECTION 1

Civil service. (a) The Civil service includes every officer and employee of the state except as otherwise provided in this Constitution.

(b) In the civil service permanent appointment and promotion shall be made under a general system based on merit ascertained by competitive examination. [June 8, 1976]

Section 1(b) expresses the basic principle of the civil service system. Section 1(a) allows some state employees to be exempt from the system (the exemptions are described in sec. 4).

Although Article VII does not explicitly prohibit the practice of hiring private enterprises to perform state functions, the courts have implied some limitations as "an implicit necessity for protecting the policy of . . . civil service . . . against dissolution and destruction (*California State Employees' Association v. Williams,* 1970). Early cases denied the state's authority to look outside civil service for window washers (*Stockburger v. Riley,* 1937) and attorneys (*State Compensation Insurance Fund v. Riley,* 1937), except where civil service attorneys could be demonstrated to be inadequate or incompetent to provide the legal services required (*Burum v. State Compensation Insurance Fund,* 1947). In time, other exceptions to the judicially created limitation were developed. For example, the state was allowed to contract with private carriers for administrative tasks of the Medi-Cal program (California's Medicaid), because it was "a new state function not previously conducted by any state agency" (*California State Employees' Association v. Williams,* 1970). The State Personnel Board, created by Article VII, section 2 and endowed by section 3 with the power to administer and enforce legislative implementation of Article VII, also created a body of standards by which it approved the awarding of contracts to private firms in order to achieve cost savings (*California State Employees' Association v. State of California,* 1988). With the enactment of Government Code section 19130 in 1982, the legislature codified both the Personnel Board's cost-savings standards and the judicially created conditions on the award of personal service contracts outside the civil service system. In *California State Employees' Association v. State of California* (1988), the court of appeal concluded that the judicially implied limits of Article VII, section 7 did not invalidate Government Code section 19130's controlled scheme permitting the state to award private contracts in order to achieve cost savings.

From 1934 to 1961, civil service existed in the absence of collective bargaining. From 1961 to the present, the legislature "has enacted a series of . . . measures granting public employees . . . a variety of organizational and negotiating rights somewhat analogous to the rights long afforded most employees in the private sector."[13] As public employee collective bargaining increased, the legislation authorizing such collective bargaining was attacked as violative of the merit principle established by Article VII. That challenge was firmly rejected by the

[13] Pacific Legal Foundation v. Brown, 29 Cal. 3d 168, 173, 624 P.2d 1215, 172 Cal. Rptr. 487 (1981).

supreme court in *Pacific Legal Foundation v. Brown* (1981). A similar challenge to an affirmative action program was rejected by the court of appeal in the 1979 case of *Dawn v. State Personnel Board.*

SECTION 2

State personnel board: membership and compensation. (a) There is a Personnel Board of 5 members appointed by the Governor and approved by the Senate, a majority of the membership concurring, for 10-year terms and until their successors are appointed and qualified. Appointment to fill a vacancy is for the unexpired portion of the term. A member may be removed by concurrent resolution adopted by each house, two-thirds of the membership of each house concurring.
(b) The board annually shall elect one of its members as presiding officer.
(c) The board shall appoint and prescribe compensation for an executive officer who shall be a member of the civil service but not a member of the board. [June 8, 1976]

The structure of the Personnel Board was designed so that a governor in a single term will select only a minority of the board's members. This design and the requirement of senate approval were intended to make the board nonpartisan.

SECTION 3

State personnel board: duties. (a) The board shall enforce the civil service statutes and, by majority vote of all its members, shall prescribe probationary periods and classifications, adopt other rules authorized by statute, and review disciplinary actions.
(b) The executive officer shall administer the civil service statutes under rules of the board. [June 8, 1976]

By this section, the Personnel Board is granted broad authority to enforce legislation implementing the civil service system created by Article VII. Over time the functions of the Personnel Board have expanded beyond the mere administration of the merit principle. Thus, as the legislature has delegated to other agencies certain functions that overlap with those performed by the Personnel Board, litigation has arisen in which it is contended that the board's jurisdiction must prevail to the extent of the overlap, by reason of its constitutional status. Rather than indulging in an approach that would protect one legislative scheme at the expense of another, the supreme court has sought to harmonize overlapping jurisdictional grants in a way that implements the intended purpose of each. For example, in *Pacific Legal Foundation v. Brown* (1981), the court concluded that the Public Employment Relations Board's power to investigate and adjudicate unfair labor practices was not constitutionally invalidated by the Personnel Board's power under section 3(a) to "review disciplinary actions" because "each agency was established to serve a different, but not inconsistent, public purpose." For similar reasons, the supreme court has concluded that Article VII, section 3(a) did not bar the Fair Employment and Housing Commission from hearing employment discrimination complaints (*State Personnel Board v. Fair Employment and Housing Commission*, 1985), and the court of appeal has held that the Department of Personnel Administration was constitutionally entitled to hear a complaint by a state employee that his duties were above his rank (*Lund v. California State Employees' Association*, 1990).

The Personnel Board has considerable but not absolute authority over public employment. It may terminate a civil servant's employment for cause (*Batson v. State Personnel Board*, 1961), but because it is a state entity, its actions must comport with due process. Before the Personnel Board removes a person from permanent state employment, the employee must receive, at a minimum,"notice of the proposed action, the reasons therefor, a copy of the charges and materials upon which the action is based, and the right to respond, either orally or in writing, to the authority initially imposing discipline" (*Skelly v. State Personnel Board*, 1975). Decisions of the board must be upheld by a court if they are supported by "substantial evidence" (*Genser v. State Personnel Board*, 1952). The board's interpretation of statutes will be upheld by the courts unless "clearly erroneous" (*Neely v. California State Personnel Board*, 1965).

SECTION 4

Positions exempt from civil service. The following are exempt from civil service:

(a) Officers and employees appointed or employed by the Legislature, either house, or legislative committees.
(b) Officers and employees appointed or employed by councils, commissions or public corporations in the judicial branch or by a court of record or officer thereof.
(c) Officers elected by the people and a deputy and an employee selected by each elected officer.
(d) Members of boards and commissions.
(e) A deputy or employee selected by each board or commission either appointed by the Governor or authorized by statute.
(f) State officers directly appointed by the Governor with or without the consent or confirmation of the Senate and the employees of the Governor's office, and the employees of the Lieutenant Governor's office directly appointed or employed by the Lieutenant Governor.

(g) A deputy or employee selected by each officer, except members of boards and commissions, exempted under Section 4(f).

(h) Officers and employees of the University of California and the California State Colleges.

(i) The teaching staff of schools under the jurisdiction of the Department of Education or the Superintendent of Public Instruction.

(j) Member, inmate, and patient help in state homes, charitable or correctional institutions, and state facilities for mentally ill or retarded persons.

(k) Members of the militia while engaged in military service.

(l) Officers and employees of district agricultural associations employed less than 6 months in a calendar year.

(m) In addition to positions exempted by other provisions of this section, the Attorney General may appoint or employ six deputies or employees, the Public Utilities Commission may appoint or employ one deputy or employee, and the Legislative Counsel may appoint or employ two deputies or employees. [June 8, 1976]

This section specifies the categories of public employees who are exempt from civil service protections. A revision in 1970 added to exempt categories the employees of the lieutenant governor and adjusted the number of civil service exempt "deputies or employees" allowed state officers and boards. Prior to 1970, these positions were called "confidential positions." When first adopted in 1934, the predecessor section allowed the legislature to transfer to civil service any constitutionally exempt position except elected officers, persons appointed by the governor, and employees of the University of California. In 1950 a provision was added that once a position was transferred to civil service, it could not be made exempt again, unless it became an appointment by the governor. The 1970 revision eliminated the legislature's ability to transfer an exempt position to civil service, except through constitutional amendment.

State employees exempt from civil service are nevertheless subject to the legislature's authority over the conditions of their employment, such as salary and benefits (*Slivkoff v. California State University and Colleges*, 1977).

Just as the state may not ordinarily avoid civil service by contracting for labor rather than hiring as an employee (see Art. VII, sec. 1), neither is an exempt person's status contingent on whether the person is an employee or a contractor. For example, personal services by an independent contractor for the state colleges are exempt from civil service as if they were done by an employee (*California State Employees' Association v. Trustees of California State Colleges*, 1965).

SECTION 5

Temporary appointments. A temporary appointment may be made to a position for which there is no employment list. No person may serve in one or more positions under temporary appointment longer than 9 months in 12 consecutive months. [June 8, 1976]

This section, originating in 1934, was amended in 1950 by substituting "employment list" for "eligible list." Eligible lists excluded persons eligible for promotion or rehiring after layoff but who had not taken civil service examinations for a specific classification. The term "employment list" was intended to include those persons excluded from the former "eligible list" thus, the amendment further restricted bypass of civil service by temporary appointment. A second change in the 1950 amendment was the increase of the allowed temporary appointment period from six to nine months.

SECTION 6

Veterans' preferences and other special rules. (a) The Legislature may provide preferences for veterans and their surviving spouses.

(b) The board by special rule may permit persons in exempt positions, brought under civil service by constitutional provision, to qualify to continue in their positions.

(c) When the state undertakes work previously performed by a county, city, public district of this state or by a federal department or agency, the board by special rule shall provide for persons who previously performed this work to qualify to continue in their positions in the state civil service subject to such minimum standards as may be established by statute. [June 8, 1976]

The provision for veterans' preferences was part of the original 1934 civil service constitutional enactment. The provision for retaining employees when the state takes over functions previously performed by other levels of government was added in 1970. Preferences for veterans are commonly employed and have been found valid under the federal Constitution (*Personnel Administrator of Massachusetts v. Feeney*, 1979).

SECTION 7

Dual office holding. A person holding a lucrative office under the United States or other power may not hold a civil office of profit. A local officer or postmaster whose compensation does not exceed 500 dollars per year or an officer in the militia or a member of a reserve component of the armed forces of the United States except where on active federal duty for more than 30 days in any year is not a holder of a lucrative office, nor is the holding of a civil office of profit affected by this military service. [June 8, 1976]

The proscription against dual office-holding dates back to the 1849 and 1879 constitutions. It was moved from Article IV to Article VII in 1976. The only substantive change since 1849 was a 1952 amendment that made it clear that a paid state civil officer could be a member of the reserve military forces of the United States.

SECTION 8

Disqualification from holding office or jury service. (a) Every person shall be disqualified from holding any office of profit in this State who shall have been convicted of having given or offered a bribe to procure personal election or appointment.
(b) Laws shall be made to exclude persons convicted of bribery, perjury, forgery, malfeasance in office, or other high crimes from office or serving on juries. The privilege of free suffrage shall be supported by laws regulating elections and prohibiting, under adequate penalties, all undue influence thereon from power, bribery, tumult, or other improper practice. [June 8, 1976]

Section 8(a) is taken virtually verbatim from Article XI, section 17 of the 1849 Constitution, enacted as Article XX, section 10 in the 1879 Constitution. The only change from those original provisions has been substitution of the word *personal for his* as part of the 1974 gender-neutralization revision.

Section 8(b) comes from Article XI, section 18 of the 1849 Constitution, enacted as Article XX, section 11 in the 1879 Constitution. Section 8(b) originally included the right to vote as one of the privileges permanently lost by conviction of "bribery, perjury, forgery, malfeasance in office, or other high crimes." After the California Supreme Court struck the provision down as violative of the federal Constitution's equal protection clause (*Ramirez v. Brown*, 1973) and the U.S. Supreme Court reversed (*Richardson v. Ramirez*, 1974) California voters in 1974 adopted a constitutional amendment that eliminated the provision's denial of suffrage to ex-felons who had already satisfied all penalties and conditions of parole. Other changes in wording since 1849 have been purely cosmetic.

SECTION 9

Subversive organizations. Notwithstanding any other provision of this Constitution, no person or organization which advocates the overthrow of the Government of the United States or the State by force or violence or other unlawful means or who advocates the support of a foreign government against the United States in the event of hostilities shall:

(a) Hold any office or employment under this State, including but not limited to the University of California, or with any county, city or county, city, district, political or other public agency of this State; or

(b) Receive any exemption from any tax imposed by this State or any county, city or county, city, district, political subdivision, authority, board, bureau, commission or other public agency of this State. [June 8, 1976]

Section 9 was adopted in 1952 as part of the same measure that required loyalty oaths of public employees. The ballot argument in favor of adoption of this section reveals the proponents' intent: "No right thinking person should object to making a declaration that he is not a communist before receiving [benefits] from the State."

In 1967, following the U.S. Supreme Court's decision in *Keyishian v. Board of Regents* (1967), the California Supreme Court determined, in *Vogel v. Los Angeles County*, that the loyalty oath required by Article XX, section 3 violated the federal Constitution's guarantee of free expression. Although the Vogel court did not resolve the related issue of whether section 9(a) also violated the First Amendment, it is apparent that the unconstitutional loyalty oath required under Article XX, section 3 was merely a device to implement the substantive barrier erected by section 9(a). The federal constitutional doctrine of unconstitutional conditions would surely operate to invalidate this provision were litigation to arise testing its constitutionality.[14]

Section 9(b), which conditions the availability of tax exemptions upon abjuration of disloyalty, was declared unconstitutional by the U.S. Supreme Court in the 1958 case, *First Unitarian Church v. County of Los Angeles*, on the ground that the condition restricts freedom of speech.

When a veterans' group and an individual taxpayer attempted to use section 9(a) to oust Assemblyman Tom Hayden from the legislature because of his alleged support of North Vietnam against the United States during the Vietnam War, the California Supreme Court decided it was not empowered to decide the question because Article IV, section 5 assigned to the legislature the exclusive authority to expel its members (*California War Veterans for Justice v. Hayden*, 1986).

SECTION 10

Disqualification of elected officials for defamatory campaign statements. (a) No person who is found liable in a civil action for making libelous or slanderous statements against an opposing candidate during the course of an election campaign for any federal, statewide, Board of Equalization, or legislative office or for any county, city and county, city, district, or any other local elective office shall retain the seat to which he or she is elected, where it is established that the libel or slander was a major contributing cause in the defeat of an opposing candidate.

A libelous or slanderous statement shall be deemed to have been made by a person within the meaning of this section if that person actually made the

[14] See, e.g., Speiser v. Randall, 357 U.S. 513, 527 (1958).

statement or if the person actually or constructively assented to, or authorized, or ratified the statement.

"Federal office," as used in this section means the office of United States Senator and Member of the House of Representatives; and to the extent that the provisions of this section do not conflict with any provision of federal law, it is intended that candidates seeking the office of United States Senator or Member of the House of Representatives comply with this section.

(b) In order to determine whether libelous or slanderous statements were a major contributing cause in the defeat of an opposing candidate, the trier of fact shall make a separate, distinct finding on that issue. If the trier of fact finds that libel or slander was a major contributing cause in the defeat of an opposing candidate and that the libelous or slanderous statement was made with knowledge that it was false or with reckless disregard of whether it was false or true, the person holding office shall be disqualified from or shall forfeit that office as provided in subdivision (d). The findings required by this section shall be in writing and shall be incorporated as part of the judgment.

(c) In a case where a person is disqualified from holding office or is required to forfeit an office under subdivisions (a) and (b), that disqualification or forfeiture shall create a vacancy in office, which vacancy shall be filled in the manner provided by law for the filling of a vacancy in that particular office.

(d) Once the judgment of liability is entered by the trial court and the time for filing a notice of appeal has expired, or all possibility of direct attack in the courts of this state has been finally exhausted, the person shall be disqualified from or shall forfeit the office involved in that election and shall have no authority to exercise the powers or perform the duties of that office.

(e) This section shall apply to libelous or slanderous statements made on or after the effective date of this section. [June 6, 1984]

This addition to the constitution was enacted to deter persons from winning elections by defaming their opponents. Not only would such persons be susceptible to civil liability for damages, but the section provides for their removal from office. Opponents expressed concern over the difficulties of proving that an election outcome hinged on defamation and whether such proof would compromise the secrecy of popular votes.

The U.S. Supreme Court has established that defamation of public figures is protected by the federal constitutional guarantee of free expression unless such defamation occurs with "actual malice": knowledge of its falsity or with reckless disregard for its truth or falsity (*New York Times Co. v. Sullivan*, 1964). Since candidates for elective office are paradigmatic public figures, this provision is valid under the federal Constitution only to the extent that it is applied upon a finding that the defamation that triggers the section's removal-from-office penalty was the result of a knowing or reckless falsehood. Section 10(b) appears to impose explicitly the constitutionally required actual malice requirement.

SECTION 11

Legislators' and judges' retirement systems. (a) The Legislators' Retirement System shall not pay any unmodified retirement allowance or its actuarial equivalent to any person who on or after January 1, 1987, entered for the first time any state office for which membership in the Legislators' Retirement System was elective or to any beneficiary or survivor of such a person, which exceeds the higher of (1) the salary receivable by the person currently serving in the office in which the retired person served or (2) the highest salary that was received by the retired person while serving in that office.

(b) The Judges' Retirement System shall not pay any unmodified retirement allowance or its actuarial equivalent to any person who on or after January 1, 1987, entered for the first time any judicial office subject to the Judges' Retirement System or to any beneficiary or survivor of such a person, which exceeds the higher of (1) the salary receivable by the person currently serving in the judicial office in which the retired person served or (2) the highest salary that was received by the retired person while serving in that judicial office.

(c) The Legislature may define the terms used in this section.

(d) If any part of this measure or the application to any person or circumstance is held invalid, the invalidity shall not affect other provisions or applications which reasonably can be given effect without the invalid provision or application. [Nov. 7, 1990]

This section was adopted in 1986, with subsection (d) added in 1990. Because retirement benefits and current salaries are adjusted by different mechanisms, the possibility developed that, over time, retirement payments to retired officers might exceed the salaries of current officers. This section essentially places a ceiling on retirement benefits that is equivalent to current salaries of the incumbent office-holders.

ARTICLE VIII

This article was repealed November 8, 1966.

Article IX

Education

Article IX contains the principal provisions of the California Constitution concerning public education. It provides for free public education at the elementary and secondary levels according to state policies administered by local school boards and creates the framework for the administration of that school system. It also recognizes the quasi-independent status of the University of California, and section 8 contains a strong prohibition against the use of public funds to support sectarian instruction.

SECTION 1

Legislative policy. A general diffusion of knowledge and intelligence being essential to the preservation of the rights and liberties of the people, the Legislature shall encourage by all suitable means the promotion of intellectual, scientific, moral, and agricultural improvement. [May 7, 1879]

The language after the first comma was the first sentence of Article IX, section 2 of the 1849 Constitution. The rest of the 1849 Constitution's section 2, concerning property revenues to be used for schools, became section 4 in 1879 but was repealed in 1964.

This general expression of state interest in education has been used frequently to support judicial opinions but has virtually never been relied upon. The principle is aspirational in effect.

SECTION 2

Superintendent of state public instruction: election, commencement of term, limit on terms. A Superintendent of Public Instruction shall be elected by the qualified electors of the State at each gubernatorial election. The Superintendent of Public Instruction shall enter upon the duties of the office on the first Monday after the first day of January next succeeding each gubernatorial election. No Superintendent of Public Instruction may serve more than 2 terms. [Nov. 7, 1990]

The original 1849 Constitution provided for a popularly elected superintendent of public instruction, but the term of office was changed from three to four years in 1862. A limit of two terms was added in 1990 as part of Proposition 140, a general term-limit initiative measure.

The duties of the superintendent of public instruction are largely defined by statute. Under the Education Code, the superintendent is charged with the vague and general responsibility of "superintend[ing] the schools."[15] Because Article IX, section 7 of the constitution creates a State Board of Education with equally ill-defined authority, there has arisen disagreement between the superintendent and the board concerning the respective scope of their authority over education policy and program finance.

The constitutional and statutory lacunae concerning the scope of the authority vested in the superintendent and the board may be partially filled by litigation commenced in 1991, by which the board seeks to establish that the constitution and the Education Code impliedly vest it with power to determine education policy and program funding.

SECTION 2.1

Deputy and associate superintendents of public instruction. The State Board of Education, on nomination of the Superintendent of Public Instruction, shall appoint one Deputy Superintendent of Public Instruction and three Associate Superintendents of Public Instruction who shall be exempt from State civil service and whose terms of office shall be four years.

[15] Calif. Education Code sec. 33112(a).

This section shall not be construed as prohibiting the appointment, in accordance with law, of additional Associate Superintendents of Public Instruction subject to State civil service. [Nov. 5, 1946]

The purpose of this section, added by amendment in 1946, was to allow the superintendent of public instruction to select additional staff members exempt from the civil service system, above the number that would otherwise consti- tutionally be permitted. Ballot arguments made in 1946 by proponents of the amendment emphasized the need to give the superintendent great latitude in selecting his or her principal staff assistants in order to enable the superintendent to "carry[ ] out . . . more effective[ly] . . . the educational policy of his office."[16]

The State Board of Education, however, contends that the provision vests in it a mandatory obligation to appoint the deputy superintendent and the associate superintendents. Accordingly, the superintendent's failure to follow board-prescribed policies for the selection of these officials is alleged, in a currently pending case before the supreme court, to constitute a violation of this section.

SECTION 3

County superintendents of schools. A Superintendent of Schools for each county may be elected by the qualified electors thereof at each gubernatorial election or may be appointed by the county board of education, and the manner of the selection shall be determined by a majority vote of the electors of the county voting on the question; provided that two or more counties may, by an election conducted pursuant to Section 3.2 of this article, unite for the purpose of electing or appointing one joint superintendent for the counties so uniting. [Nov. 2, 1976]

Provision for county superintendents of schools was included in the 1879 Constitution and amended in 1976. Each county may select its own superintendent, or counties may join together under one superintendent. Prior to the 1976 amendment, county superintendents had to be elected in nonchartered counties but could be either elected or appointed in chartered counties. The amendment allows for either election or appointment in all counties.

The county superintendent is intended to be analogous to the state superintendent. Depending on the population and size of a county, the county superintendent may function as an administrator in charge of a number of separated school systems or as an overseer of a single school system. Since some counties are so sparsely populated that it makes little sense to employ a county superintendent in addition to other school administrators, the 1976

[16] California Voters' Pamphlet for General Election of November 5, 1946, p. 9.

amendment permits counties to unite for purposes of sharing a common county superintendent.

SECTION 3.1

County superintendents of schools: qualifications and salaries. (a) Notwithstanding any provision of this Constitution to the contrary, the Legislature shall prescribe the qualifications required of county superintendents of schools, and for these purposes shall classify the several counties in the state.
(b) Notwithstanding any provision of this Constitution to the contrary, the county board of education or joint county board of education, as the case may be, shall fix the salary of the county superintendent of schools or the joint county superintendent of schools, respectively. [Nov. 2, 1976]

Prior to 1946, county superintendents were the only professional positions in the California educational system for which there were no professional requirements. The 1946 addition of this section professionalized the position by imposing on the legislature the obligation to establish such requirements. The section originally called for the legislature to fix superintendent salaries, but that responsibility was shifted to county boards of education by amendment in 1976.

SECTION 3.2

Joint county board of education and joint county superintendent of schools. Notwithstanding any provision of this Constitution to the contrary, any two or more chartered counties, or nonchartered counties, or any combination thereof, may by a majority vote of the electors of each such county voting on the proposition at an election called for that purpose in each such county, establish one joint board of education and one joint county superintendent of schools for the counties so uniting. A joint county board of education and a joint county superintendent of schools shall be governed by the general statutes and shall not be governed by the provisions of any county charter. [Nov. 2, 1976]

Prior to the addition of this section in 1976, the constitution gave the legislature authority to permit two or more counties to unite with one superintendent of schools. This section allows counties to unite under one board of education as well.

SECTION 3.3

County boards of education: qualification and terms of office. Except as provided in Section 3.2 of this article, it shall be competent to provide in any charter framed for a county under any provision of this Constitution or by the amendment of any such charter, for the election of the members of the county board of education of such county and for their qualifications and terms of office. [Nov. 7, 1976]

This section was added in 1946 in order to provide to counties the option of selecting county boards of education by election rather than appointment. Under the education code at that time, members of the county boards of education consisted of the county superintendent and four others appointed by the county board of supervisors.[17]

SECTION 4

This section was repealed November 3, 1964.

SECTION 5

Common school system. The Legislature shall provide for a system of common schools by which a free school shall be kept up and supported in each district at least six months in every year, after the first year in which a school has been established. [May 7, 1879]

Provision for a common school system was made by Article IX, section 3 of the 1849 Constitution. The 1879 Constitution retained the provision as Article IX, section 5 but added the adjective *free* and changed the constitutional minimum of school provision from three months to six months.

Public education is a matter of state concern (*Kennedy v. Miller*, 1893) and only a matter of municipal or local concern to the extent made so by the state "in promotion and not in derogation" of the state's constitutional responsibilities (*Whitmore v. Brown*, 1929). The power of the legislature over school districts is plenary (*Pass School District v. Hollywood City School District*, 1909). As a consequence, the legislature may confer on local school districts immunity from municipal legislation (*Lansing v. Board of Education*, 1935; *Hall v. City of Taft*, 1956) and preempt contrary local legislation (*Phelps v. Prussia*, 1943). By itself, the constitutional obligation to provide free and common education does not prohibit a school financing scheme that produces substantial disparities between school districts in the revenue available for educational expenditures (*Serrano v. Priest*, 1971). Nevertheless, in a landmark 1976 decision, *Serrano v. Priest*, the supreme court held that such disparities violated the California Constitution's guarantee of equal protection. The legislature

[17] Calif. Education Code sec. 301, as enacted by Stat. 1943, cl. 71, p. 318.

responded by enacting legislation[18] that limited the amount of revenue any district could raise for educational purposes and created a set of complicated formulas designed to reduce wealth disparities among districts. This task has been rendered more difficult by the taxing and spending limitations of Article XIII A and XIII B, coupled with the mandated priority of state spending for schools contained in Article XVI, section 8 and the mandated allocation of property tax revenues to schools contained in Article XVI, section 8.5. Nevertheless, the result has been a statewide school financing scheme that has reduced the financial disparities among districts to insignificant amounts. As tax revenues have declined and the spending limitations resulting from *Serrano* and Articles XIII A and XIII B have hindered the ability of school districts to provide traditional extracurricular educational programs, such as art, music, drama, cheerleading, and athletics, school districts began to experiment with fees as a prerequisite for participation in such programs. In 1984, the supreme court, in *Hartzell v. Connell*, declared this practice violative of the "free common schools" provision of section 5.

SECTION 6

Public schools: public school system, salaries, state aid. Each person, other than a substitute employee, employed by a school district as a teacher or in any position requiring certification qualifications shall be paid a salary which shall be at the rate of an annual salary of not less than twenty-four hundred dollars ($2,400) for a person serving full time, as defined by law.

The Public School System shall include all kindergarten schools, elementary schools, secondary schools, technical schools, and State colleges, established in accordance with law and, in addition, the school districts and the other agencies authorized to maintain them. No school or college or any other part of the Public School System shall be, directly or indirectly, transferred from the Public School System or placed under the jurisdiction of any authority other than one included within the Public School System.

The Legislature shall add to the State School Fund such other means from the revenues of the State as shall provide in said fund for appointment in each fiscal year, an amount not less than one hundred eighty dollars ($180) per pupil in average daily attendance in the kindergarten schools, elementary schools, secondary schools, and technical schools in the Public School System during the next preceding fiscal year.

The entire State School Fund shall be apportioned in each fiscal year in such manner as the Legislature may provide, through the school districts and other agencies maintaining such schools, for the support of, and aid to, kindergarten schools, elementary schools, secondary schools, and technical schools except that there shall

[18] A.B. 8, Calif. Stat. 1979, ch. 232.

be apportioned to each school district in each fiscal year not less than one hundred twenty dollars ($120) per pupil in average daily attendance in the district during the next preceding fiscal year and except that the amount apportioned to each school district in each fiscal year shall be not less than twenty-four hundred dollars ($2,400).

Solely with respect to any retirement system provided for in the charter of any county or city and county pursuant to the provisions of which the contributions of, and benefits to, certified employees of a school district who are members of such system are based upon the proportion of the salaries of such certificated employees contributed by said county or city and county, all amounts apportioned to said county or city and county, or to school districts therein, pursuant to the provision of this section shall be considered as though derived from county or city and county school taxes for the support of county and city and county government and not money provided by the State within the meaning of this section. [Nov. 5, 1974]

The 1879 version of section 6 consisted of language equivalent to the first sentence of the current second paragraph describing the levels of education in the public school system, plus a requirement that state school funds be used exclusively for elementary schools. A 1902 amendment allowed the legislature to authorize a special tax for high schools and technical schools.

Specific funding minima were added in 1920 and revised in 1946, both amendments being responses to postwar teacher-shortage crises. The 1946 amendment also constitutionally raised teacher salaries to $2,400 per year. Funding minima were again raised in 1952. The California Constitution Revision Commission inexplicably left the minimum salaries unchanged, presumably having concluded that the matter of salaries is better left for legislation or the market for teachers. The mandated minimum levels of funding per pupil have effectively been eclipsed by *Serrano v. Priest* (1976) and the subsequent legislative response.

The provision requiring that no portion of the public school "system" be placed under the control of any other authority than the mandated school administrators does not prevent public schools from contracting with private firms to perform educational functions so long as that delegation of instructional responsibility is "done under the control and supervision of the school district" (*California Teachers Association v. Board of Trustees*, 1978).

SECTION 6.5

School districts and bonds. Nothing in this Constitution contained shall forbid the formation of districts for school purposes situate in more than one county or the issuance of bonds by such district under such general laws as have been or may hereafter be prescribed by the Legislature; and the officers mentioned in such laws shall be authorized to levy and assess such taxes and perform all such other acts as may be prescribed therein for the purpose of paying such bonds and carrying out the other powers conferred upon such districts; provided, that all such bonds shall be issued subject to the limitations prescribed in section 18 of article eleven hereof. [Nov. 7, 1922]

At the time section 61/2 was added to the constitution, there were over 100 school districts in the state that spanned county boundaries. The purpose of the amendment was to establish the legitimacy of such school districts and allow them to raise revenue through the issuance of bonds. This authority complements that given by Article IX, section 14, which permits the legislature to provide for the incorporation and organization of school districts.

SECTION 7

Boards of education. The Legislature shall provide for the appointment or election of the State Board of Education and a board of education in each county or for the election of a joint county board of education for two or more counties. [Nov. 2, 1976]

This section originated with the 1879 Constitution. In its original form, it contemplated the creation of local boards of education but was intended more to vest in local authorities the task of adoption of textbooks. By a 1970 amendment, the responsibility for textbook selection was shifted to Article IX, section 7.5. An 1884 amendment created the state Board of Education with a specified membership, but a 1912 amendment simply mandated that the legislature "provide for the appointment or election of a State Board of Education." Apart from the elimination of textbook selection, the section has remained substantively unchanged. The State Board of Education is empowered by statute to "determine all questions of policy within its powers"[19] and to establish "rules and regulations . . . for the government" of elementary and secondary schools.[20] Local school boards thus work within the policy guidelines that may be set by the State Board of Education and the superintendent of public instruction.

---

[19] Calif. Education Code sec. 33030.

[20] Calif. Education Code sec. 33031.

SECTION 7.5

Free textbooks. The State Board of Education shall adopt textbooks for use in grades one through eight throughout the State, to be furnished without cost as provided by statute. [June 2, 1970]

Section 7 of the 1879 Constitution provided for the selection of textbooks by local school boards. A 1912 amendment mandated the free provision of textbooks to elementary school students in order to "remove the last excuse that some selfish parents have for not sending their children to school."

The provision for textbooks became section 7.5, separate from section 7, by amendment in 1970. The State Board of Education is required to adopt textbooks for use in grades 1 through 8; it does so pursuant to provisions of the Education Code that mandate certain content and impose minimum obligations on textbook publishers as a condition of eligibility for consideration for adoption by the Board of Education.[21]

SECTION 8

Prohibition of aid to sectarian schools or teaching of sectarian doctrine in public schools. No public money shall ever be appropriated for the support of any sectarian or denominational school, or any school not under the exclusive control of the officers of the public schools; nor shall any sectarian or denominational doctrine be taught, or instruction thereon be permitted, directly or indirectly, in any of the common schools of this State. [May 7, 1879]

The language of section 8 remains unchanged from its first adoption in 1879. The section has two aims: prohibition of the use of public funds to support private education, whether secular or sectarian, and maintenance of strict separation between religion and public education. These goals are partially duplicated by the provisions of Article XVI, section 5, which prohibits public assistance of sectarian institutions, including schools, and Article I, section 4, which prohibits the legislative establishment of religion. All of these provisions were the product of the 1878–1879 constitutional convention. Unfortunately, the records of the convention reveal a paucity of debate upon these provisions, so there is no clue concerning the necessity for multiple safeguards against public subsidy of sectarian institutions.

Case law has established that a public agency may be created to issue tax-exempt bonds for the purpose of constructing facilities for private education, so long as the entire cost of the operation, including the obligation of the bonds themselves, is assumed by the private beneficiaries (*California Educational*

[21] See Calif. Education Code sec. 60000 et seq.

Facilities Authority v. Priest, 1974). The benefit conferred by the state is a lower interest rate on borrowed funds, but that benefit is created without expenditure of public funds. Another early case held that public money could be spent to pay for the care and custody of minors committed, via the penal system, to a nonsectarian charitable corporation operating a "reform school," on the ground that the character of the institution was more penal than educational (*Boys' and Girls' Aid Society v. Reis,* 1887). Public money may thus be used to support private penal institutions but not private schools.

The result of the firm textual commitment to separation of church and state in public education has been that the supreme court, in *California Teachers Association v. Riles* (1981), struck down a program by which public school textbooks were loaned to parents of children attending parochial schools. Under federal constitutional law, the practice has been declared valid (*Board of Education v. Allen,* 1977). A 1947 decision of the court of appeal, *Gordon v. Board of Education,* upheld the constitutionality of released-time programs for religious instruction, and a 1946 decision of that court, *Bowker v. Baker,* upheld the use of public funds to transport parochial schoolchildren to school. Although not overruled by *Riles,* their continued efficacy would seem to be questionable. By contrast, the supreme court's 1924 decision in *Evans v. Selma Union High School District,* upholding the acquisition of King James Version Bibles as reference works for public school libraries, would appear to be distinguishable as not being as clearly in aid of sectarian institutions.

SECTION 9

University of California. (a) The University of California shall constitute a public trust, to be administered by the existent corporation known as "The Regents of the University of California," with full powers of organization and government, subject only to such legislative control as may be necessary to insure the security of its funds and compliance with the terms of the endowments of the university and such competitive bidding procedures as may be made applicable to the university by statute for the letting of construction contracts, sales of real property, and purchasing of materials, goods, and services. Said corporation shall be in form a board composed of seven ex officio members, which shall be: the Governor, the Lieutenant Governor, the Speaker of the Assembly, the Superintendent of Public Instruction, the president and the vice president of the alumni association of the university and the acting president of the university, and 18 appointive members appointed by the Governor and approved by the Senate, a majority of the membership concurring; provided, however that the present appointive members shall hold office until the expiration of their present terms.

(b) The terms of the members appointed prior to November 5, 1974, shall be 16 years; the terms of two appointive members to expire as heretofore on

March 1st of every even-numbered calendar year, and two members shall be appointed for terms commencing on March 1, 1976, and on March 1 of each year thereafter; provided that no such appointments shall be made for terms to commence on March 1, 1979, or on March 1 of each fourth year thereafter, to the end that no appointment to the regents for a newly commencing term shall be made during the first year of any gubernatorial term of office. The terms of the members appointed for terms commencing on and after March 1, 1976, shall be 12 years. During the period of transition until the time when the appointive membership is comprised exclusively of persons serving for terms of 12 years, the total number of appointive members may exceed the numbers specified in the preceding paragraph.

In case of any vacancy, the term of office of the appointee to fill such vacancy, who shall be appointed by the Governor and approved by the Senate, a majority of the membership concurring, shall be for the balance of the term for which such vacancy exists.

(c) The members of the board may, in their discretion, following procedures established by them and after consultation with representatives of faculty and students of the university, including appropriate officers of the academic senate and student governments, appoint to the board either or both of the following persons as members with all rights of participation: a member of the faculty at a campus of the university or of another institution of higher education; a person enrolled as a student at a campus of the university for each regular academic term during his service as a member of the board. Any person so appointed shall serve for not less than one year commencing on July 1.

(d) Regents shall be able persons broadly reflective of the economic, cultural, and social diversity of the state, including ethnic minorities and women. However, it is not intended that formulas or specific ratios be applied in the selection of regents.

(e) In the selection of the Regents, the Governor shall consult an advisory committee composed as follows: The Speaker of the Assembly and two public members appointed by the Speaker, the President Pro Tempore of the Senate and two public members appointed by the Rules Committee of the Senate, two public members appointed by the Governor, the chairman of the regents of the university, an alumnus of the university chosen by the alumni association of the university, a student of the university chosen by the Council of Student Body Presidents, and a member of the faculty of the university chosen by the academic senate of the university. Public members shall serve for four years, except that one each of the initially appointed members selected by the Speaker of the Assembly, the President Pro Tempore of the Senate, and the Governor shall be appointed to serve for two years; student, alumni, and faculty members shall serve for one year and may not be regents of the university at the time of their service on the advisory committee.

(f) The Regents of the University of California shall be vested with the legal title and the management and disposition of the property of the university and of property held for its benefit and shall have the power to take and hold, either by purchase or by donation, or gift, testamentary or otherwise, or in any other manner, without restriction, all real and personal property for the benefit of the university or incidentally to its conduct; provided, however, that sales of university real property shall be subject to such competitive bidding procedures as may be provided by statute. Said corporation shall also have all the powers necessary or convenient for the effective administration of its trust, including the power to sue and to be sued, to use a seal, and to delegate to its committees or to the faculty of the university, or to others, such authority or functions as it may deem wise. The Regents shall receive all funds derived from the sale of lands pursuant to the act of Congress of July 2, 1862, and any subsequent acts amendatory thereof. The university shall be entirely independent of all political or sectarian influence and kept free therefrom in the appointment of its regents and in the administration of its affairs, and no person shall be debarred admission to any department of the university on account of race, religion, ethnic heritage, or sex.

(g) Meetings of the Regents of the University of California shall be public, with exceptions and notice requirements as may be provided by statute. [Nov. 2, 1976]

The original 1849 Constitution authorized the legislature to fund a state university, "with such branches as the public convenience may demand." The University of California was created by statute in 1868,[22] an event reflected in the language of the 1879 version of section 9.

Constitutional provision for the Regents of the University of California was added to section 9 by amendment in 1918. A 1970 amendment required that meetings of the board be ordinarily open to the public, and a 1972 amendment required senate confirmation of the governor's appointments. In 1974 two ex officio positions were removed, one was added, the number of appointive members was increased from sixteen to eighteen, and terms were reduced from sixteen to twelve years. In addition, the board was authorized to appoint one college professor and one University of California student to serve terms of at least one year.

Since its adoption in 1879, section 9 has prohibited sex discrimination in admission to the university. A 1976 amendment added race, religion, and ethnic heritage as prohibited grounds of discrimination.

By virtue of section 9, the university was invested with "constitutional" status, acquiring significant autonomy from the legislature in its governance. In this, the University of California occupies a status enjoyed by only eight other state universities.[23] The terms of the section provide that the regents are delegated "full powers of organization and government, . . . subject *only* to such legislative control as may be necessary to insure the security of its funds and compliance with"

[22] 1867–68 Calif. Stat. ch. 244.

[23] See Harold Horowitz, "The Autonomy of the University of California under the State Constitution," UCLA L. Rev. 25 (1977): 23, 24 n.l.

endowment terms and competitive bidding procedures, which might be made applicable to the university by legislative action. Moreover, the section provides that the university "shall be entirely independent of all *political* . . . influence and kept free therefrom . . . *in the administration of its affairs*." On its face the language would suggest that the university is largely immune from legislative regulation. While California judicial opinions are peppered with comments to the effect that the regents possess broad authority to administer the university as independently of the state as possible, the scope of that independence has never been precisely delineated.

In *Tolman v. Underhill* (1952), the supreme court concluded that section 9 did not bar the legislature from prescribing an oath of office applicable to all state employees, including university employees, thus preempting a university-required loyalty oath. The court reached this decision on the ground that the loyalty of university teachers was a matter of general concern to the state and not a matter exclusively of concern to the university. It did not establish the principle that any statute of general application to the state would thus also validly apply to the university, for that would have effectively repealed the autonomy conferred by section 9. Rather, it limited the zone of university autonomy to matters "exclusively [concerning] University affairs."

Similarly, in *Regents of the University of California v. Superior Court* (1976), the supreme court concluded that, in lending money commercially, the university was subject to the usury laws rather than enjoying the exemption afforded the state due to its sovereignty. Although the court declared that it did not need to decide the scope of immunity enjoyed by the university, it reached its decision on the ground that lending money commercially was "not so closely related to its educational decisions" to acquire immunity.

It thus appears that the university enjoys immunity from legislative control only with respect to "exclusively University affairs." In determining the precise boundaries of this immunity, it is necessary to consider "(1) the centrality of the subject matter [of the legislation] to the functioning of the University as a university; (2) the degree of impairment of the Regents' 'full' powers of governance; and (3) the interest advanced by the legislative enactment."[24] So, for example, the university may set salaries, but the legislature need not appropriate sufficient funds to pay such salaries (*California State Employees' Association v. Flournoy*, 1973).

There is another dimension to university autonomy. Once the regents have acted within the scope of "exclusively University affairs," such actions enjoy a status equivalent to that of state statutes. Thus, to the extent that the state is exempt from local ordinances, so is the university (*Regents of the University of California v. Santa Monica*, 1976).

[24] Horowitz, "Autonomy of the University of California," 23, 26.

SECTION 10

This section was repealed November 5, 1974.

SECTION 11

This section was repealed November 5, 1974.

SECTION 12

This section was repealed November 5, 1974.

SECTION 13

This section was repealed November 5, 1974.

SECTION 14

Organization, incorporation, and powers of school districts. The Legislature shall have power, by general law, to provide for the incorporation and organization of school districts, high school districts and community college districts, of every kind and class, and may classify such districts.

The Legislature may authorize the governing boards of all school districts to initiate and carry on any programs, activities, or to otherwise act in any manner which is not in conflict with the laws and purposes for which school districts are established. [July 1, 1973]

Section 14 was added in 1926, originally consisting of only the first paragraph. The purpose of allowing the legislature to classify school districts is to allow statutes to be sensitive to differing needs of different districts, such as small versus large or rural versus urban. The second paragraph was added by amendment in 1972 to permit school boards to initiate programs on their own.

SECTION 15

This section was repealed November 5, 1974.

SECTION 16

City charter provisions and amendments pertaining to boards of education. (a) It shall be competent, in all charters framed under the authority given by Section 5 of Article XI, to provide, in addition to those provisions allowable by this Constitution, and by the laws of the state for the manner in which, the times at which, and the terms for which the members of boards of education shall be elected or appointed, for their qualifications, compensation and removal, and for the number which shall constitute any one of such boards.

(b) Notwithstanding Section 3 of Article XI, when the boundaries of a school district or community college district extend beyond the limits of a city whose charter provides for any or all of the foregoing with respect to the members of its board of education, no charter amendment effecting a change in the manner in which, the times at which, or the terms for which the members of the board of education shall be elected or appointed, for their qualifications, compensation, or removal, or for the number which shall constitute such board, shall be adopted unless it is submitted to and approved by a majority of all the qualified electors of the school district or community college district voting on the question. Any such amendment, and any portion of a proposed charter or a revised charter which would establish or change any of the foregoing provisions respecting a board of education, shall be submitted to the electors of the school district or community college district as one or more separate questions. The failure of any such separate question to be approved shall have the result of continuing in effect the applicable existing law with respect to that board of education. [June 6, 1978]

Section 16(a), allowing chartered cities authority over composition of their school boards, is derived from previous Article XI, section 81/2, subsection 2, as adopted in 1896. In 1970 it became Article XXII, section 8, and in 1972 it became Article IX, section 16.

Section 16(b) was added in 1978 to ensure that persons living within a school district but outside the chartered city where the district's school board sits would be allowed to vote on any changes to the city's charter affecting the school district.

Article X

Water

The Constitution of 1879 had addressed the general topics of water resources, tidelands, harbors, and navigation in two distinct articles: Article XIV, "Water and Water Rights," and Article XV, unceremoniously titled "Harbor Frontages, Etc." The current constitution combines those articles, which remained essentially unaltered for nearly a hundred years, in a newly titled Article X, "Water." The single combined article includes as well two sections that had been added to the earlier articles in 1928 (sec. 2) and in 1954 (sec. 7). The addition of section 2 was the result of a prolonged and complex struggle to redefine the law of consumptive water rights; it is perhaps the most important of the sections in this article. Section 7 was added in a problematic attempt to assert state control of water resources as against the activities of the federal government's immense water delivery projects; it has received little notice and is of uncertain effect.

The current Article X was created as part of a group of relatively noncontroversial miscellaneous revisions adopted in the primary election of June 8, 1976. Although the sections are newly numbered and arranged, thus appearing to constitute modern material, they actually continue without change the meaning and effect of the predecessor sections. Both the legislature and the California Constitution Revision Commission were reluctant to recommend any substantive changes to the water provisions of former Article XIV, apparently because of the "lengthy and costly evolution of judicial precedents" that might be "jeopardized" by even minor attempts at revision.[25] Although the commission had been willing to recommend changes to former Article XV regarding harbors, tidelands, and access to navigable waters, those recommendations were not adopted by the legislature and thus were not proposed to the voters.

The arrangement of Article X alters the context of the sections as originally organized, intermixing the topics of access to waters, control of tidelands, and the substantive law of water rights. Indeed, it is still easier to understand the article by regarding sections 1,3, and 4 as dealing with control of the shoreline and beds of navigable waters, whereas sections 2, 5, 6, and 7 concern the substantive law of water allocation and quality protection.

SECTION 1

Eminent domain to acquire frontages. The right of eminent domain is hereby declared to exist in the State to all frontages on the navigable waters of this State. [June 8, 1976]

Section 1 was introduced in the 1879 version of Article XV in conjunction with current section 4.[26] The two sections reflected an intense popular concern that the state be able to assert and protect public and private rights of access to navigable waters, a topic of considerable interest in a rapidly growing state that relied heavily on water transportation.

This section, which was barely debated by the convention, has received relatively little attention since then. The purpose seems primarily to have been a cautionary reminder that the power of eminent domain, already acknowledged by the members of the convention as an attribute of the state's powers, would be available to allow the state to acquire ownership of frontage lands on any navigable waters, thus protecting the ability of the public to gain access to the waterways. More narrowly, it was intended to clarify that the state would be able to employ its eminent domain powers even against lands that had been acquired previously by those "quasi-public corporations," perhaps including railroads, that had acted under the power of eminent domain earlier delegated to them by the legislature. (In later years, both the eminent domain powers of "quasi-public entities" and the power to exercise eminent domain against land "already appropriated to a public use" were given major statutory clarification.)[27] There is no indication whether it was contemplated that the power might be employed as

---

[25] California Constitution Revision Commission, Proposed Revision of the California Constitution, Part Two 1970, p. 25 (Art. XIV, Water). Compare the "savings clauses" employed in sec. 13 of Art. XI and sec. 9 of Art. XII, in which language was changed, but the meaning was to be unaffected.

[26] Debates, pp. 110, 782.

[27] See generally Calif. Code of Civil Procedure sec. 1240.010 (Deering's 1991).

well against those lands that had already been distributed through legislative grants (see sec. 3 and 4).

As constitutional theory later developed, section 1 was to become irrelevant in those special situations where any frontage land was found to be subject to the "public trust" (or "public easement" or "servitude") that exists over navigable waters (see sec. 3 and 4). As to such land, the government may "take or damage" the land, or access to it, to the extent necessary to accomplish any recognized public trust purposes, without the necessity of exercising the power of eminent domain or paying compensation (*Colberg, Inc. v. California*, 1967).

SECTION 2

Conservation and beneficial use of water required. It is hereby declared that because of the conditions prevailing in this State the general welfare requires that the water resources of the State be put to beneficial use to the fullest extent of which they are capable, and that the waste or unreasonable use or unreasonable method of use of water be prevented, and that the conservation of such waters is to be exercised with a view to the reasonable and beneficial use thereof in the interest of the people and for the public welfare. The right to water or to the use or flow of water in or from any natural stream or water course in this State is and shall be limited to such water as shall be reasonably required for the beneficial use to be served, and such right does not and shall not extend to the waste or unreasonable use or unreasonable method of use or unreasonable method of diversion of water. Riparian rights in a stream or water course attach to, but to no more than so much of the flow thereof as may be required or used consistently with this section, for the purposes for which such lands are, or may be made adaptable, in view of such reasonable and beneficial uses; provided, however, that nothing herein contained shall be construed as depriving any riparian owner of the reasonable use of water of the stream to which the owner's land is riparian under reasonable methods of diversion and use, or as depriving any appropriator of water to which the appropriator is lawfully entitled. This section shall be self-executing, and the Legislature may also enact laws in the furtherance of the policy in this section contained. [June 8, 1976]

Section 2 is a fundamental statement of policy affecting the allocation and consumption of the state's water resources. It was added to the constitution in 1928 as an amendment specifically designed to alter the rules of state water law that had prevailed since 1886.

California's early water law was a dual system that incorporated aspects of riparian law, adopted from English and American common law, as well as aspects of appropriation law, developed in various western states in the late nineteenth century. (Riparian law governs the correlative rights of landowners to use water flowing by their lands; appropriation law gives protection, in order of seniority, to water users who divert and use waters, whether or not on lands that are contiguous to the watercourse.) The overlap in operation of the two systems allowed riparian users to oppose new uses of water by appropriation claimants, even if the result were to force vast quantities of water to continue flowing in a stream or otherwise remain underutilized. That wasteful result presented recurring difficulties for the judiciary, which nevertheless adamantly resisted modification of the rules to reflect considerations of public policy. A 1926 state supreme court decision (*Herminghaus v. Southern California Edison Co.*) prompted the legislature, after extensive consideration, to propose the amendment to the electorate, which adopted it in November 1928. The amendment's stated purpose, which was to "prevent the waste of waters" and to make possible the storage and conservation of "a great natural resource" (*Gin S. Chow v. City of Santa Barbara*, 1933), forced riparian rights to be judged by the new standard and to yield to competing claims when they could not demonstrate that a "reasonable" use was being made of claimed waters.

The adoption of section 2 reconstructed California's basic water law by imposing a standard of "reasonable use" on all users of water—whether riparian or appropriative—within the state, thus integrating many doctrinal aspects of the formerly dual system. In practice, any use of water must now be both "beneficial" in type and "reasonable" in its method of application and is subject to continued governmental supervision and regulation that may require the reconsideration and modification of permit terms to meet the "reasonable use" standard of section 2 (*National Audubon Society v. Superior Court*, 1983; *U.S. v. State Water Resources Control Board*, 1986). So pervasive is the rule that it affects all uses of water, including both private uses and those protected by the public trust (*National Audubon Society v. Superior Court*, 1983). The courts have repeatedly recognized that what is "reasonable" in any particular application is affected by an evaluation of the totality of the circumstances, including competing local factors and overall statewide considerations of public welfare (*Joslin v. Marin Municipal Water District*, 1967; *Environmental Defense Fund, Inc. v. East Bay Municipal Utility District*, 1980).

Although section 2 recites that it is a self-executing constitutional provision, statutes place the primary responsibility for its enforcement on the State Water Resources Control Board. Under the modern comprehensive regulatory scheme,[28] the board governs regulation of both the quantity and the quality of water resources (*People v. Shirokow*, 1980; *Imperial Irrigation District v. State Water Resources Control Board*, 1986). The state courts, however, retain a

[28] The modern board was created in 1967; its powers include adjudicatory and regulatory functions and responsibility for water quality. See Calif. Water Code sec. 174, 179, 1250 (appropriation), 13000 et seq. (water quality) (Deering's 1977).

concurrent power with the board in application of the standards of section 2 and retain their power to review the validity of board action.

SECTION 3

Grant or sale of tidelands. All tidelands within two miles of any incorporated city, city and county, or town in this State, and fronting on the water of any harbor, estuary, bay, or inlet used for the purposes of navigation, shall be withheld from grant or sale to private persons, partnerships, or corporations; provided, however, that any such tidelands, reserved to the State solely for street purposes, which the Legislature finds and declares are not used for navigation purposes and are not necessary for such purposes may be sold to any town, city, county, city and county, municipal corporations, private persons, partnerships or corporations subject to such conditions as the Legislature determines are necessary to be imposed in connection with any such sales in order to protect the public interest. [June 8, 1976]

For more than a century, section 3 has figured prominently in protracted and extremely complex controversies regarding the control of California's extensive tidelands. The original goal of this section appears to have been a rather narrow protection of local government prerogatives concerning access to navigation, reflecting problems similar to those addressed in sections 1 and 4. However, the underlying issues regarding tidelands have expanded over subsequent decades to include broad environmental concerns and other questions of public rights in tidelands areas. Although this article provides a partial basis for those rights, most of the applicable policy development has occurred through judicial opinions (*Marks v. Whitney*, 1971; *City of Berkeley v. Superior Court of Alameda*, 1980).

Long before the convention assembled in 1878, the control and disposition of tidelands had become one of the new state's great controversies. Several U.S. Supreme Court opinions, rendered only a few years before California's statehood, had declared that each new state would enter the Union on an equal footing with all earlier states. As such, it would automatically acquire an absolute right to the ownership and control of the land beneath its navigable waters, subject only to certain federal rights (*Martin v. Wadded*, 1842; *Pollard's Lessee v. Hagen*, 1845; *Phillips Petroleum Co. v. Mississippi*, 1988). Upon its admission to the Union on September 9, 1850, California achieved sovereign status, and in that capacity the state became owner of its tidelands, which therefore sometimes were described as "sovereignty" lands. The attributes of sovereignty were eventually understood to determine questions of ownership and also to impose a responsibility to safeguard rights of navigation, fishery, and other public uses of the tidelands. Primary among the responsibilities was the evolving doctrine variously termed "navigation easement," "tidelands trust," or "public trust," a concept of stewardship that has had profound impact on issues of environment and public use of water areas.

Also in September 1850, in a coincidental but highly significant federal action, California received potential ownership of additional lands—eventually to amount to more than 2 million acres—under a federal "Swamp Land Act,"[29] by which Congress, eager to encourage the drainage and reclamation of lands that were considered "unfit for cultivation," made available to various states huge areas of "swamp and overflowed lands." Unfortunately, little attempt was made in California to maintain a clear distinction between sovereign "tidelands" and the congressionally granted "swamplands"; the statutes regularly grouped together for sale the several categories of state-owned "swamp, overflowed, salt marsh, and tide lands." Under those provisions during the 1860s and 1870s, tens of thousands of acres of "tidelands" throughout the state were sold to private parties, including vast tracts in San Francisco Bay, San Diego Bay, and Los Angeles County; countless other acres of "swamplands" along the sea shores and interior valleys were sold as well.

The delegates to the 1878 convention were thus presented with a situation in which the sale of sovereign "tidelands" regularly had been caught up with the aggressive disposal practices designed for "swamp and overflowed" lands. The resulting confusion was substantial; legally, the "tidelands" were subject to the "trust" responsibilities of sovereignty, but "swamplands" were not (*Taylor v. Underhill*, 1871). As a result, any sales made under the numerous authorizing statutes that combined the categories were bound to create confusion as to both title and allowable use of the lands. The confusion was complicated by the definitions of each type of land. The term *tidelands* was generally understood in the 1860s to refer to a strip of land that is the margin between dry shore and deeper navigable waters, usually described as "between the lines of high and low tide." In contrast, the *swamp and overflowed lands* were best represented by the vast lands in the San Joaquin and Sacramento river basins. Unfortunately, the two categories could merge imperceptibly in many coastal and estuarine areas.

One effect of the widespread sales of tidelands was to create a "monopoly of frontage," in which strips of tidelands, bordering on navigable waters, might be held under different ownership than that of the immediately adjoining dry uplands. The sales created ripe opportunities for speculative attempts to acquire the tidal strip, thus monopolizing access from the uplands to the physically navigable portion of the waters. Even more troubling was the manner in which sales that combined tidal and swamp lands had occurred. In 1873, a state legislative committee found ample evidence that "the grossest frauds have been committed

---

[29] Act of Sept. 28, 1850, first enacted at 9 Stat. 519–20 (1850), now 43 U.S.C.A. 982–84 (West's 1986). Originally known as the Arkansas Act, the statute was quickly expanded to include numerous other states, including the new state of California.

in swamp land matters in this State," the state system for sales was infused with "corruption" and "connivance," and sales of lands had been accomplished with "utter looseness and extremely wanton manner."[30] Faced with evidence of wasteful practices but desirous of allowing some development, the delegates adopted the limited sales prohibition represented by the current language of section 3.

The land sales statutes were of statewide effect except for various exclusions or reservations—that is, withdrawals from sale—affecting certain areas. The original 1855 swamplands statute specifically excluded from sale any lands "within one mile of any . . . incorporated city or town" as well as lands within greater distances—either five miles or ten miles—from major named cities such as San Francisco, San Diego, and Oakland.[31] That pattern of exclusions reappeared sporadically in later statutes; although the reasons for the "exclusions" were not explicitly stated, the intention appears to have been to protect the several municipal and public rights "likely to become important" in the area of a growing municipality (*People ex rel. Webb v. California Fish Co.*, 1913). Thus, when section 3 was adopted by the convention in 1879, the policy of exempting from sale those tidelands within two miles of cities was characterized as merely making "permanent by placing . . . in the Constitution" what had "been the policy of the State heretofore."[32] The reason to continue to withhold the lands, the delegates were told, was that the lands were "necessary for the commerce of the state."[33]

Section 3 prohibits sale only to private entities; a sale to a municipality is clearly allowed,[34] and for many years the legislature followed a long-standing practice of granting or leasing tidelands directly to cities, often as part of their acts of incorporation (*Atwood v. Hammond*, 1935; *City of Oakland v. Oakland Water-Front Co.*, 1897). The general effect of the system was that "withheld" lands were eventually granted to the nearby municipalities, thus putting control of the tidelands in the hands of local governments rather than the state legislature. Unfortunately, a different pattern obtained in some areas; state control and sales of "withheld" lands were sometimes entrusted not to nearby cities but to special state-appointed boards. Thus, in 1868 and 1870, a special Board of Tide

---

[30] Report of the Swamp Land Investigating Committee, 4 Appendix to the Journals of the Senate and Assembly, 20th sess. 1873, pp. 3, 4.

[31] 1855 Calif. Stat., ch. 41, p. 189; sec. 1, 11, pp. 189, 190–91.

[32] Debates, p. 1039, remarks of Mr. Ayers. This answer may have been disingenuous or ill informed, since the statutory pattern had been very sporadic before the inclusion of the twomile provision in sec. 3488 of the original 1872 Political Code. Clearly, however, it indeed had been a code provision for the six years preceding the convention.

[33] Debates, p. 1039 (Remarks of Mr. Ayers). See San Pedro v. Hamilton, 161 Cal. 610,618–19 (1911).

[34] Cimpher v. City of Oakland, 162 Cal. 87, 90 (1912), upholding the practice, but noting that the city itself is prohibited from making further grants to private persons or corporations.

Land Commissioners was specifically charged by the legislature with the sales of the "swamp, overflowed, and tide lands" within the entire five-mile area around the city of San Francisco. That board disposed of more lands than were granted to the city itself, most of which were acquired eventually by private corporations (*City of Berkeley v. Superior Court of Alameda County*, 1980).

Although section 3 prohibited sales near cities, it did not bar the legislature from continuing its long-standing practice of leasing such lands (*San Pedro, LA. and S.L.R.R. v. Hamilton*, 1911) or of selling outright any lands beyond the two-mile limit. (Tidelands sales elsewhere in the state were eventually delegated to the State Lands Commission.) Not until thirty years later, in 1909, did the legislature enact a statute withholding all tidelands from sale wherever they may be located,[35] thus effectively forbidding further sales "of all such lands" (*Messenger v. Kingsbury, 1910; Newcomb v. Newport Beach*, 1936).

The language of section 3 has remained essentially unchanged since 1879, except for the prolix clause following "provided, however," which was added in 1962 to create a minor exception for certain "street sales." The amendment allowed the legislature to sell certain "tidelands" that had been designated, but never developed, as streets. It was proposed to the voters as a means of making possible "the development of vast areas of industrial land in our crowded urban communities."[36] That explanation merely repeated the policy arguments for development that had been made since the 1850s; the distinction offered by the amendment concerned those areas of privately held tidelands, lawfully conveyed prior to the restrictions of section 3, that were "surrounded," and thus made inefficient, by state-owned lands held as potential streets. Conveyance of the "streets," subject to appropriate conditions, was urged as a desirable accommodation to those private holdings. The provision appears to be consistent with restrictions otherwise imposed by the courts (*City of Long Beach v. Mansell*, 1970).

SECTION 4

Access to navigable waters. No individual, partnership, or corporation, claiming or possessing the frontage or tidal lands of a harbor, bay, inlet, estuary, or other navigable water in this State, shall be permitted to exclude the right of way to such water whenever it is required for any public purpose, nor to destroy or obstruct the free navigation of such water; and the Legislature shall enact such laws as will give the most liberal construction to this provision, so that access to the navigable waters of this State shall be always attainable for the people thereof. [June 8, 1976]

---

[35] Calif. Pub. Res. Code sec. 7991 (Deering's 1987).

[36] Argument in favor of Proposition 14, Official Ballot Pamphlet for the general election of Nov. 6, 1962, pp. 20–21.

Section 4, like sections 1 and 3, was part of the original 1879 provisions dealing with access to navigable waters. It continued an elemental rule derived from centuries of common law heritage and more recently has formed the basis for renewed assertions of a modern version of the "public trust."

Implementation of the several 1879 provisions was originally premised on section 1's power to acquire access by eminent domain and the section 3 prohibitions on sale of tidelands; section 4, however, operated only as a general proscription on activities that threatened public rights and was primarily dependent on legislative action for its operation. The most basic legislative implementation was a simple (and relatively ineffective) penal declaration, first dating from 1850, that any "obstruction of navigation" was a misdemeanor.[37] More assertive legislative action occurred in several subsequent phases.

In the late nineteenth and early twentieth centuries, the legislature relied primarily on the concept of municipal ownership and control of the lands underlying navigable waters in order to achieve the protection of public access. Thus, in 1913, the legislature authorized those cities that possessed the title to tidelands to establish "harbor lines," public streets, and public easements.[38] That authorization was consistent with the widespread practice, authorized by section 3, of making tidelands grants to municipalities. Although those provisions imposed an affirmative duty on cities that remained relevant for decades (*Lane v. City of Redondo Beach*, 1975), they were of no immediate effect beyond municipal borders.

It was not until the 1970s that the legislature, confronted with widespread private land development that diminished opportunities for public access, adopted more far-reaching provisions designed to control private activities wherever they arose, thus going considerably beyond reliance on municipal stewardship. Beginning in 1970, the legislature overtly undertook to implement section 4 by enacting a series of code provisions that controlled development of private real estate subdivisions near the seacoast or interior rivers. The first provisions required that any subdivision make provisions for "reasonable public access" from a public highway to lands on the ocean coastline or bay shore lines.[39] Those provisions were extended the following year to include public access to any river or stream banks within the subdivision, as well as requiring the subdividers to provide a public easement along the bank of the river or stream (*Kern River Public Access Committee v. City of Bakersfield*, 1985). Similar provisions were added in 1974 regarding the shorelines of lakes or reservoirs owned by a public agency.[40]

---

[37] Calif. Harbors and Navigation Code sec. 131 (Deering's 1978).

[38] Stat. 1913, ch. 272, p. 497, provisions that now appear in Calif. Government Code sec. 39930–38.

[39] Calif. Government Code sec. 66478.11 (West's 1983).

[40] Calif. Government Code sec. 66478.12 (West's 1983).

The most widely publicized implementation of section 4 began in 1972 with the creation of the California Coastal Commission. In addition to utilizing various planning techniques for preservation of coastal resources, current statutory provisions require most new development in California's coastal zone to be subjected to a variety of mandatory provision-of-access requirements[41] that were specifically intended to implement the provisions of section 4 (*Georgia-Pacific Corp. v. California Coastal Commission,* 1982). Those provisions require landowners to make easements available to the public as a condition of receiving land development approval and have formed the basis for substantial and acrimonious litigation. Generally, the power to require easements has withstood constitutional attack against state and federal "taking" questions, except where the requirement does not appear reasonably related to otherwise valid regulatory goals (*Liberty v. California Coastal Commission, 1980; Nollan v. California Coastal Commission,* 1987).

One effect of section 4 is to ensure that the public trust would remain applicable to any lands whose title had been granted to private individuals under the authorization of section 3 (*Forestier v. Johnson,* 1912). More recently, section 4 has served as a general source of public trust authority applicable to a wide variety of activities occurring on or affecting different types of navigable waters. Thus, the types of activities and interests protected by the trust—in addition to traditional matters of navigation, commerce, and fishing—have been expanded to include recreation and environmental preservation (*Marks v. Whitney,* 1971). The areas to which the trust applies incorporate not only tidal waters but were recognized by the California Supreme Court in 1981 to include the water and beds of navigable but nontidal interior lakes and rivers, although the beds may be privately owned (*State of California v. Superior Court of Lake County (Lyon),* 1981). The trust was extended to apply to activities, such as water diversion, that affect nonnavigable tributaries of navigable waterways (*National Audubon Society v. Superior Court of Alpine County,* 1983). Those decisions have greatly broadened the application, and implications, of the "free navigation" protected by section 4.

SECTION 5

State control of water use. The use of all water now appropriated, or that may hereafter be appropriated, for sale, rental, or distribution, is hereby declared to be a public use, and subject to the regulation and control of the State, in the manner to be prescribed by law. [June 8, 1976]

[41] Calif. Public Resources Code sec. 30210–14 (Deering's 1987).

The current language of section 5 continues precisely the first sentence of section 1 of Article XV as originally adopted in 1879. A lengthy passage that followed that sentence was deleted by the voters in 1972, and in its reduced form, the section was reenacted without further change in the general revision of 1976.

Both sections 5 and 6 relate to the appropriation of water for the purpose of resale, reflecting widespread concerns among delegates to the convention that water be widely available and not subjected to arbitrary corporate control. The origin of section 5 can be traced directly to the original constitutional debates, in which the delegates attempted to establish the nature of water rights, not when as held by individuals or corporations for direct use but when the holder subsequently sells or otherwise distributes that water.[42] In the latter situation, the delegates clearly wanted to make the use and sale of water subject to "state regulation and control" (*San Francisco Pioneer Woolen Factory v. Brickwedel*, 1882). Because of legal uncertainties regarding the ability of the public to regulate private contractual arrangements, the delegates believed that an express declaration of public use was required. The now-omitted language of the original section went on in great detail to provide that the local governing body would annually pass ordinances to set appropriate water rates.

That early regulatory scheme was fraught with uncertainties and beset with constant litigation (e.g., *Spring Valley Water Works v. City and County of San Francisco*, 1890). Advancements in regulatory theory, represented by the 1911 revisions to Article XII, resulted in a provision of the new Public Utility Act in 1913 that subjected any entity that sells water to regulation as a public utility.[43] Presumably it was the existence of PUC regulatory authority that made possible the eventual 1972 deletion of detailed provisions for local government regulation.

Given the transition from local control to Public Utilities Commission regulation, section 5 now appears to be merely a redundant anachronism of little present value.

SECTION 6

Water rates franchise. The right to collect rates or compensation for the use of water supplied to any county, city and county, or town, or the inhabitants thereof, is a franchise, and cannot be exercised except by authority of and in the manner prescribed by law. [June 8, 1976]

---

[42] Debates, p. 1021, remarks of Mr. Tinnin; Debates, pp. 1372, 1472.

[43] Now codified in Calif. Public Utility Code sec. 2701 (Deering's 1990). See also sec. 3 of Art. XII.

Section 6 continues unchanged the original language of section 2 of former Article XIV and was reenacted in its entirety as part of the 1976 revision. Like section 5, this section also reflects intense concern with regulation of water companies.

Extensive litigation contemporaneous with the 1878 convention dealt with the attempts by cities to regulate the rates charged by politically powerful water distribution companies. In 1877 the supreme court had specifically held that the power to charge rates for water was in the nature of a government franchise and thus appropriately subject to government control (*Spring Valley Water Works v. Bryant*). This section appears to be an outright adoption of that decision, accepted by the convention apparently without debate. The characterization of that power as a franchise meant that it could be exercised only under properly authorized processes and not affected by special legislation.

This section has little modern effect, being implemented by various statutory provisions governing rate setting and provision of services.

SECTION 7

Agency acquisition of real property in conformance to California water laws. Whenever any agency of government, local, state, or federal, hereafter acquires any interest in real property in this State, the acceptance of the interest shall constitute an agreement by the agency to conform to the laws of California as to the acquisition, control, use, and distribution of water with respect to the land so acquired. [June 8, 1976]

Section 7 was first adopted in 1954 as a new section 4 of the original Article XIV, having been proposed as a senate constitutional amendment; it was renumbered without change in the 1976 revision. The original ballot arguments suggested that the provision was needed to clarify the "long-understood" rule that government agencies must conform to the substantive law of the state in acquiring and using water rights.[44] Interestingly, the section uses the phrase "acquisition, control, use, and distribution of water," which is strikingly similar to language contained in section 8 of the federal Reclamation Act of 1902. That act provides that "nothing in this Act shall be construed as affecting . . . or to in any way interfere with the laws of any State . . . relating to the control, appropriation, use, or distribution of water."[45] Indeed, opponents of the new section charged that it was nothing more than a "subterfuge" and "an attempt to create a hidden

[44] Proposed Amendments to Constitution (ballot pamphlet) General Election of Nov. 2, 1954, pt. I, p. 14.

[45] 32 Stat. 390, codified at 43 U.S.C.A. sec. 383 (West's 1986).

veto to be used to prevent further federal reclamation projects."[46] The opponents appeared to have discerned the essential issue, for only four years later the U.S. Supreme Court (*Ivanhoe Irrigation District v. McCracken*, 1958) specifically relieved the secretary of the interior from complying with state laws regarding use of water and held that that official was instead obliged to comply with specific congressional policy directives. Within a short time, additional opinions of the Court (*City of Fresno v. California*, 1963; *Arizona v. California*, 1963) extended that holding to a general statement that the secretary was not bound by state law in disposing of water from federal projects. That result mocked the proponents of section 7, who had predicted that the provision would "have a powerful persuasive effect upon Congress and the Federal Government . . . to recognize our citizens' rights to water under California's just and reasonable water laws."[47] After the strong expressions from the Supreme Court, section 7 fell into utter ignominy; it has been overlooked by commentators and never considered or interpreted in litigation.

The section purported to force government agencies to accept, perhaps as an implied contract, their obligation to conform to state law. In that, it is unquestionably ineffective as against the federal government, which is generally recognized as having "plenary constitutional power to override any state regulation of" a federal project (*U.S. v. State of California, State Water Resources Control Board*, 1982). To the extent it merely restates California's desire that state substantive rules of water rights be respected, the section is little more than precatory.

Subsequent events, however, have transformed section 7 into quaint surplusage; the earlier language of the *Ivanhoe* opinion was expressly disavowed by the Supreme Court in 1977 in *California v. United States*, an opinion that strongly reasserted the Reclamation Act's policy that a state indeed may impose any condition on "control, appropriation, use, or distribution of water" that is "not inconsistent with" clear congressional directives contained in the authorizations of the project. The Court concluded that Congress indeed intended to defer generally to the substance of state water law, thus potentially subjecting federal projects to numerous conditions imposed by state authorities to ensure compliance with state policies and laws. Although Congress retains the authority to impose preemptive directives, the desires of section 7's proponents apparently have been vindicated.

[46] Proposed Amendments to Constitution (ballot pamphlet) General Election of Nov. 2, 1954, pt. I, p. 14.

[47] Proposed Amendments to Constitution (ballot pamphlet) General Election of Nov. 2, 1954, pt. I, p. 14.

Article XA

Water Resources Development

This article was proposed to the electorate by the legislature and adopted as part of the constitution in November 1980. By its own terms, however, it was "to have no force or effect" unless a related senate bill authorizing a proposed Peripheral Canal and other units of the State Water Project became effective. Although that bill was later enacted by the legislature, it was subsequently rejected by the voters in a referendum on June 8, 1982, thus rendering Article XA ineffective. It is not reproduced here.

Article XB

Marine Resources Protection Act of 1990

Article XB was added to the constitution by a citizens' initiative in November 1990, becoming effective immediately. It prohibits the commercial use of certain types of "indiscriminate" fishing nets that are believed harmful to various seabirds and marine mammals, particularly dolphins and sea otters.[48] The article gives constitutional status to a preexisting statutory regulation of nets in northern and central California waters and imposes a new ban on nets in southern California, to become fully effective on January 1, 1994. The restrictions generally apply only to a narrow band of near-shore ocean waters.

SECTION 1

Title. This article shall be known and may be cited as the Marine Resources Protection Act of 1990. [Nov. 6, 1990]

Section 1 provides a uniform name of the article for purposes of citation. This article is unusual in that it purports to be an act, which is usually understood to be a law enacted by a legislative body rather than a part of a constitution.

---

[48] A preface to Art. X B, although included within the text of the initiative, was not made part of the language of the article. The preface included "findings" that explained the intent and purpose of the article. See the Ballot Pamphlet, General Election of November 6, 1990, p. 116.

The article was subsequently codified in, and implemented by, statutory amendments to the California Fish and Game Code.

SECTION 2

Definitions. (a) "District" means a fish and game district as defined in the Fish and Game Code by statute on January 1, 1990.
(b) Except as specifically provided in this article, all references to Fish and Game Code sections, articles, chapters, parts, and divisions are defined as those statutes in effect on January 1, 1990.
(c) "Ocean waters" means the waters of the Pacific Ocean regulated by the state.
(d) "Zone" means the Marine Resources Protection zone established pursuant to this article. The zone consists of the following:
(1) In waters less than 70 fathoms or within one mile, whichever is less, around the Channel Islands consisting of the Islands of San Miguel, Santa Rosa, Santa Cruz, Anacapa, San Nicolaus, Santa Barbara, Santa Catalina, and San Clemente.
(2) The area within three nautical miles offshore of the mainland coast, and the area within three nautical miles off any manmade breakwater, between a line extending due west from Point Arguello and a line extending due west from the Mexican border.
(3) In waters less than 35 fathoms between a line running 180 degrees true from Point Fermin and a line running 270 degrees true from the south jetty of Newport harbor. [Nov. 6, 1990]

This section provides the definitions used elsewhere in the article and in related statutes. The reference in subsections (a) and (b) to the Fish and Game Code as it existed in 1990 is critical to the overall effect of the article, because it incorporates those sections in a static condition and raises them to constitutional authority. The physical area under the state's regulatory jurisdiction is limited by both international and federal law, as reflected by subsection (c).

Subsection (d) defines the protected zone as the waters immediately surrounding the offshore Channel Islands (which comprise the Channel Islands National Park), the narrow coastal waters extending northward from the Mexican border to Point Arguello (near Santa Barbara), and a triangular section seaward of the Los Angeles Harbor—Long Beach—Newport Beach area. The new zone is thus exclusively in southern California waters.

SECTION 3

Prohibition of gill or trammel nets. (a) From January 1, 1991, to December 31, 1993, inclusive, gill nets or trammel nets may only be used in the zone pursuant to a

nontransferable permit issued by the Department of Fish and Game pursuant to Section 5.
(b) On and after January 1, 1994, gill nets and trammel nets shall not be used in the zone. [Nov. 6, 1990]

Section 3 creates a transition or phase-out period for the net prohibition from 1991 to 1993 and, in subsection (b), an absolute prohibition beginning on January 1, 1994. (A gill net traps fish by the gills; a trammel net captures fish by entangling them.)

SECTION 4

Regulation of gill or trammel nets. (a) Notwithstanding any other provision of law, gill nets and trammel nets may not be used to take any species of rockfish.
(b) In ocean waters north of Point Arguello on and after the effective date of this article, the use of gill nets and trammel nets shall be regulated by the provisions of Article 4 (commencing with Section 8660), Article 5 (commencing with Section 8680) and Article 6 (commencing with Section 8720) of Chapter 3 of Part 3 of Division 6 of the Fish and Game Code, or any regulation or order issued pursuant to these articles, in effect on January 1, 1990, except that as to Sections 8680, 8681, 8681.7, and 8682, and subdivisions (a) through (f), inclusive of Section 8681.5 of the Fish and Game Code, or any regulation or order issued pursuant to these sections, the provisions in effect on January 1, 1989, shall control where not in conflict with other provisions of this article, and shall be applicable to all ocean waters. Notwithstanding the provisions of this section, the Legislature shall not be precluded from imposing more restrictions on the use and/or possession of gill nets or trammel nets. The Director of the Department of Fish and Game shall not authorize the use of gill nets or trammel nets in any area where the use is not permitted even if the director makes specified findings. [Nov. 6, 1990]

Subsection (a) prohibits the use of gill or trammel nets under any circumstances for taking rockfish, thus establishing a uniform rule that supersedes a confusing variety of earlier statutory directives. Unlike sections 2 and 3, this provision is not specifically limited to a designated zone or area and has been interpreted by the Department of Fish and Game to be a general prohibition within the full 200-mile fisheries limit recognized under federal law. That interpretation was promptly contested in federal court and remains unresolved.

Subsection (b) adopts the complex and extensive statutory restrictions on the use of nets in northern and central California waters and continues them in effect as a constitutional directive. When the preexisting statutory restrictions are combined with the absolute prohibition of subsection 3(b) applicable to the new zone in the southern waters, gill or trammel netting is prohibited in much of the state's coastal waters. (The 4(b) reference to waters "north of Point Arguello," although not clearly stated, includes the central coast areas in which some gill or trammel netting might still be allowed to occur under the terms of the statutory provisions.)

The constitutional adoption of the statutory system prevents the legislature from weakening the statutes and specifically prohibits the director of the Department of Fish and Game from allowing gill netting. Rather than imposing a complete prohibition on further legislative involvement, however, subsection 4(b) specifically allows the legislature to impose more restrictive measures on nets. That provision, like section 15, forestalls concerns that the article might be interpreted to preclude supplemental legislative regulation.

SECTION 5

Permits for gill or trammel nets. The Department of Fish and Game shall issue a permit to use a gill net or trammel net in the zone for the period specified in subdivision (a) of Section 3 to any applicant who meets both of the following requirements:

(a) Has a commercial fishing license issued pursuant to Sections 7850–7852.3 of the Fish and Game Code.
(b) Has a permit issued pursuant to Section 8681 of the Fish and Game Code and is presently the owner or operator of a vessel equipped with a gill net or trammel net. [Nov. 6, 1990]

During the phase-out period 1991–1994, only the holders of existing commercial fishing licenses who already own or operate boats equipped with gill or trammel nets remain eligible for permits to use the nets within the zone in southern waters. No new permit system is established for the northern or central waters described in section 4(b). Any person who holds such a permit must pay the fees specified in section 6 and then becomes eligible for compensation upon surrender of the permit and the nets during the last six months of the phase-out period, as provided in sections 7 and 8.

SECTION 6

Permit fees. The Department of Fish and Game shall charge the following fees for permits issued pursuant to Section 5 pursuant to the following schedule:

Calender Year	Fee
1991	$250
1992	$500
1993	$1,000

[Nov. 6, 1990]

This section is self-explanatory; the new fees are in addition to the $250 fee already in effect as of the time of adoption of the article.

SECTION 7

Compensation for surrender of permit. (a) Within 90 days after the effective date of this section, every person who intends to seek the compensation provided in subdivision (b) shall notify the Department of Fish and Game, on forms provided by the department, of that intent. Any person who does not submit the form within that 90-day period shall not be compensated pursuant to subdivision (b). The department shall publish a list of all persons submitting the form within 120 days after the effective date of this section.
(b) After July 1, 1993, and before January 1, 1994, any person who holds a permit issued pursuant to Section 5 and operates in the zone may surrender that permit to the department and agree to permanently discontinue fishing with gill or trammel nets in the zone, for which he or she shall receive, beginning on July 1, 1993, a one time compensation which shall be based upon the average annual ex vessel value of the fish other than any species of rockfish landed by a fisherman, which were taken pursuant to a valid general gill net or trammel net permit issued pursuant to Sections 8681 and 8682 of the Fish and Game Code within the zone during the years 1983 to 1987, inclusive. The department shall verify those landings by reviewing logs and landing receipts submitted to it. Any person who is denied compensation by the department as a result of the department's failure to verify landings may appeal that decision to the Fish and Game Commission.
(c) The State Board of Control shall, prior to the disbursement of any funds, verify the eligibility of each person seeking compensation and the amount of the compensation to be provided in order to ensure compliance with this section.
(d) Unless the Legislature enacts any required enabling legislation to implement this section on or before July 1, 1993, no compensation shall be paid under this article. [Nov. 6, 1990]

This section authorizes compensation, in the form of a one-time lump sum payment, to persons who had come to rely on income from gill and trammel netting. Appropriate enabling legislation and appropriations were enacted in June 1992. That legislation implements the administration and disbursement of a special account to be established under the authority of section 8.

The actual compensation received by any permit holder is computed under the terms of subsection (b), which requires permit holders to have been fishing during the years 1983 to 1987 and to be included on the list created under the terms of section 7(a). More than 130 persons notified the department of their intent to seek compensation. The compensation offer is available until January 1, 1994, when the complete prohibition of section 3(b) becomes effective. An additional year is provided under subsection 8(f) for payments to be completed.

SECTION 8

Marine Resources Protection Account. (a) There is hereby created the Marine Resources Protection Account in the Fish and Game Preservation Fund. On and after January 1, 1991, the Department of Fish and Game shall collect any and all fees required by this article. All fees received by the department pursuant to this article shall be deposited in the account and shall be expended or encumbered to compensate persons who surrender permits pursuant to Section 7 or to provide for administration of this article. All funds received by the department during any fiscal year pursuant to this article which are not expended during that fiscal year to compensate persons as set forth in Section 7 or to provide for administration of this article shall be carried over into the following fiscal year and shall be used only for those purposes. All interest accrued from the department's retention of fees received pursuant to this article shall be credited to the account. The accrued interest may only be expended for the purposes authorized by this article. The account shall continue in existence, and the requirement to pay fees under this article shall remain in effect, until the compensation provided in Section 7 has been fully funded or until January 1, 1995, whichever occurs first.

(b) An amount, not to exceed 15 percent of the total annual revenues deposited in the account excluding any interest accrued or any funds carried over from a prior fiscal year may be expended for the administration of this article.

(c) In addition to a valid california sportfishing license issued pursuant to sections 7149, 7149.1 or 7149.2 of the Fish and Game Code and any applicable sport license stamp issued pursuant to the Fish and Game Code, a person taking fish from ocean waters south of a line extending due west from Point Arguello for sport purposes shall have permanently affixed to that person's sportfishing license a marine resources protection stamp which may be obtained from the department upon payment of a fee of three dollars ($3). This subdivision does not apply to any one-day fishing license.

(d) In addition to a valid California commercial passenger fishing boat license required by Section 7920 of the Fish and Game Code, the owner of any boat or vessel who, for profit, permits any person to fish from the boat or vessel in ocean waters south of a line extending due west from Point Arguello, shall obtain and permanently affix to the license a commercial marine resources protection stamp which may be obtained from the department upon payment of a fee of three dollars ($3).

(e) The department may accept contributions or donations from any person who wishes to donate money to be used for the compensation of commercial gill net and trammel net fishermen who surrender permits under this article.

(f) This section shall become inoperative on January 1, 1995. [Nov. 6, 1990]

Between 1991 and 1995, the Marine Resources Protection Account will be established to receive fees that provide the compensation payments established by section 7. Sources of funding for the special account include the fees established by section 6, stamp revenues established under subsections (c) and (d), and contributions established under subsection (e). The legislative analyst estimated at the time of the article's adoption that fee and license stamp revenues under section 8 would provide approximately $5 million to the account.

SECTION 9

Marine Resources Protection Account Grants. Any funds remaining in the Marine Resources Protection Account in the Fish and Game Preservation Fund on or after January 1, 1995, shall, with the approval of the Fish and Game Commission, be used to provide grants to colleges, universities and other bonafide scientific research groups to find marine resource related scientific research within the ecological reserves established by Section 14 of this act. [Nov. 6, 1990]

This section is self-explanatory.

SECTION 10

Report to legislature. On or before December 31 of each year, the Director of Fish and Game shall prepare and submit a report to the Legislature regarding the implementation of this article including an accounting of all funds. [Nov. 6, 1990]

This section requires an annual report to the legislature, an obligation that apparently continues even beyond the phase-out and compensation periods.

SECTION 11

Violations. It is unlawful for any person to take, possess, receive, transport, purchase, sell, barter, or process any fish obtained in violation of this article. [Nov. 6, 1990]

In addition to the prohibitions on use of gill or trammel nets established by sections 3 and 4, this section establishes further all-inclusive prohibitions that extend to the possession, sale, or processing of fish in violation of the article. In contrast to the penalties established in section 13, however, this section makes no mention of penalties for its violation, which might instead be included within other statutory prohibitions.

SECTION 12

Monitoring of commercial fish landings. To increase the state's scientific and biological information on the ocean fisheries of this state, the Department of Fish and Game shall establish a program whereby it can monitor and evaluate the daily landings of fish by commercial fishermen who are permitted under this article to take these fish. The cost of implementing this monitoring program shall be borne by the commercial fishing industry. [Nov. 6, 1990]

The monitoring program mandated by this section is intended to provide information on the effects of the prohibitions and is related to the information to be obtained from the reserve program established under section 14. Monitoring costs will be imposed on the commercial fishing industry according to administrative regulations of the Department of Fish and Game.

SECTION 13

Penalties for violations. (a) The penalty for a first violation of the provisions of section 3 and 4 of this article is a fine of not less than one thousand dollars ($1,000) and not more than five thousand dollars ($ 5,000) and a mandatory suspension of any license, permit or stamp to take, receive, transport, purchase, sell, barter or process fish for commercial purposes for six months. The penalty for a second or subsequent violation of the provisions of sections 3 and 4 of this article is a fine of not less than two thousand five hundred dollars ($2,500) and not more than ten thousand dollars ($10,000) and a mandatory suspension of any license, permit or stamp to take, receive, transport, purchase, sell, barter, or process fish for commercial purposes for one year.
(b) Notwithstanding any other provisions of law, a violation of Section 8 of this article shall be deemed a violation of the provisions of Section 7145 of the Fish and Game Code and the penalty for such violation shall be consistent with the provisions of Section 12002.2 of said code.
(c) If a person convicted of a violation of Section 3,4, or 8 of this article is granted probation, the court shall impose as a term or condition of probation, in addition to any other term or condition of probation, that the least the minimum fine prescribed in this section. [Nov. 6, 1990]

This section, which establishes penalties for violations of various portions of the article, may be the only provision within the constitution that establishes criminal penalties, a function traditionally (and more appropriately) accomplished by statute. Essentially the same effect could have been achieved by incorporation of statutory provisions, as in subsection (b), or creation of a new statute by the same initiative.

SECTION 14

New ecological reserves. Prior to January 1, 1994, the Fish and Game Commission shall establish four new ecological reserves in ocean waters along the mainland coast. Each ecological reserve shall have a surface area of at least two square miles. The commission shall restrict the use of these ecological reserves to scientific research relating to the management and enhancement of marine resources. [Nov. 6, 1990]

The preface to the initiative had stressed the need for "increased scientific and biological research and reliable data collection," in order to provide information needed to help restore and maintain ocean resources. As part of that goal, this section mandates the establishment of four ecological reserves. The location and designation of the new reserves is within the discretion of the Department of Fish and Game, but must be accomplished before January 1, 1994. Section 9 makes available for use within those reserves any unused funds from the account established under section 8.

SECTION 15

No preemptive or superseding effect. This article does not preempt or supersede any other closures to protect any other wildlife, including sea otters, whales, and shorebirds. [Nov. 6, 1990]

This section was included as a cautionary measure, to negate any inference that the article was intended to establish an exclusive an regulatory system for marine bird or mammal protection. It specifically allows other "closures" (that is, prohibitions on harvesting of wildlife) to be implemented by other methods.

SECTION 16

Severability. If any provision of this article or the application thereof to any person or circumstances is held invalid, that invalidity shall not affect other provisions or applications of this article which can be given effect without the invalid provision or application, and to this end the provisions of this article are severable. [Nov. 6, 1990]

This section, known generally as a severability clause, is a common technique of lawmaking, designed to protect the entirety of the new law from the threat of invalidity because some portion of its provisions might be held invalid by a court. This expressed the intent of the electorate that the goals of the article might yet be attained even if some other portion of the article is held invalid.

Article XI

Local Government

Article XI establishes the arrangement of the various levels of government within the state. In comparison to Article III, which describes the legislative, executive, and judicial branches of state government, Article XI describes the relationships between the single state-level government and the many general-purpose local governments. Those governments include 58 counties and about 450 cities. (Although there are more than 5,000 additional local or regional governments of a more specialized nature, known as special districts, they are not directly treated by the constitution but instead are created and controlled by action of the legislature.) In addition to establishing the state-local relationship, Article XI sets out the basic structure and powers of cities and counties.

As enacted in 1879, Article XI was of only moderate length and established relatively cogent policies affecting local government. Numerous amendments in succeeding years expanded its detail and complexity, making it a prime example of the need for a major revision. A substantially shortened revision was rejected by the voters in 1968, but it was proposed again and adopted on June 2, 1970.

As originally drawn in 1878, Article XI was titled "Cities, Counties, and Towns" and reflected the delegates' mistrust of state government in several ways. The article attempted to minimize the methods by which the legislature could alter or affect the structure of local governments, and it gave the local governments certain rights and protections against legislative power. The basic arrangement adopted in 1879 was altered in major amendments of 1896, 1911, and 1914, each of which expanded aspects of local control. Recent decades have generated new demands for the creation of regional governmental arrangements that can deal with problems of transportation, environmental management, financing, and urban growth.

SECTION 1

Counties: formation and powers. (a) The State is divided into counties which are legal subdivisions of the State. The Legislature shall prescribe uniform procedure for county formation, consolidation, and boundary change. Formation or consolidation requires approval by a majority of electors voting on the question in each affected county. A boundary change requires approval by the governing body of each affected county. No county seat shall be removed unless two-thirds of the qualified electors of the county, voting on the proposition at a general election, shall vote in favor of such removal. A proposition of removal shall not be submitted in the same county more than once in four years.

(b) The Legislature shall provide for county powers, an elected county sheriff, an elected district attorney, an elected assessor, and an elected governing body in each county. Except as provided in subdivision (b) of Section 4 of this article, each governing body shall prescribe by ordinance the compensation of its members, but the ordinance prescribing such compensation shall be subject to referendum. The Legislature or the governing body may provide for other officers whose compensation shall be prescribed by the governing body. The governing body shall provide for the number, compensation, tenure, and appointment of employees. [June 7, 1988]

Counties are the most elemental of local governments in California, responsible for the provision of basic governmental services to all areas of the state. They also serve as regional agencies and instrumentalities of some state-level functions and are thus treated as legal and operational subdivisions of the state government itself. Section 1 establishes only the basic structure of counties and leaves it to the legislature to explain their dual local-state role and to specify their powers.

It was common practice in the mid-nineteenth century for state legislatures to create new counties in response to particular political requests, making unique rules to govern each county. Section 1 instead requires uniform procedures (now in statutory form in the state Government Code) to govern the creation of new counties, consolidation of existing counties, or changes of county boundaries.

The entire state is divided into counties; necessarily, therefore, a new county can be created only by altering the territory of already existing counties, either by relocation of existing county boundaries or by consolidation of existing counties. Both methods have substantial political implications, affecting the jurisdictional reach of the government and the voting patterns of its citizens. Section 1(a) therefore requires that formation or consolidation receive political approval by a popular vote held within each county. However, if only a change of the boundary between existing counties is proposed, the only approval necessary is by a vote of the representative governing bodies. Modern proposals for the creation of more responsive local or regional general-purpose governments continue to raise problems of county formation.

County seats are the primary location of county government offices. Many political battles were waged in the nineteenth century over the choice of their location, or relocation to other sites, because they were thought to represent economic and political advantage to the town or city that received the coveted designation (*County of Calaveras v. Brockway*, 1866). Delegates to the 1878 convention had complained that without safeguards such as those contained in section 1, county seats would be constantly migratory, as though "moving about on wheels,"[49] and clearly intended to "take the county seat question out of politics."[50] Section 1(a) makes changes of a county seat more difficult to achieve, since the requirement of a vote of the electorate prevents the legislature itself from relocating the seats, and the requirement of a favorable two-thirds "su-per-majority" vote of the electorate before a change can occur guards against changes occasioned by a short-term narrow majority. That requirement, combined with the four-year limitation on relocation proposals, has effectively eliminated proposals for change.

Section 1(b) requires the legislature to enact laws establishing county powers; most of those powers are set out in the state Government Code. The legislature can thus control nearly all aspects of a county's operation; it may define, expand, or contract those powers at legislative discretion, subject to limitations presented by county charters as described in section 4.

Subsection (b) also establishes the basic county officers to be provided for by legislative acts, including an elected sheriff (the law enforcement officer for county territory), district attorney (to prosecute criminal laws), assessor (to set and levy county taxes), and popularly elected governing body, called a board of supervisors. Under this section, that board is required to set the compensation of its own members, as well as the compensation and employment terms of each of the county's officers and employees. The compensation issue is thus relegated to local control, preventing interference by the legislature, despite the county's role as a subdivision of state government.

---

[49] Debates, p. 1041.

[50] Debates, p. 1042. The same prohibition existed in former Art. IV, sec. 25 prohibitions on special legislation; the twenty-first clause prohibited "changing county seats." See now Art. IV, sec. 16.

SECTION 2

Cities: formation and powers. (a) The Legislature shall prescribe uniform procedure for city formation and provide for city powers.
(b) Except with approval by a majority of its electors voting on the question, a city may not be annexed to or consolidated into another. [June 2, 1970]

Section 2 is a deceptively simple recognition of the existence of cities, which are legally considered municipal corporations, as distinguished from private corporations. Unlike counties, cities are not subdivisions of the state government (see sec. 1(a)) but instead enjoy relatively independent governmental status and are created at the request of their citizens, whereas the constitution mandates that all parts of the state are within a county.

Every city needs basic governing rules and provisions, which may be provided for by general statutes enacted by the state legislature or by unique local charters (discussed in sec. 3 and 5). Individual charters were formerly drafted for each city (just as a private corporation has a charter) and approved (or altered) by specific action of the legislature. That practice led to extensive legislative involvement in local matters and over time proved inefficient and redundant. The requirement of uniform procedure was created in 1879 as essentially another form of prohibition on the use of special laws (see Art. IV, sec. 16) and resulted in detailed statutory provisions that allow California cities to be organized and created by a greatly simplified process. The powers to be exercised by cities are set out in the Government Code in a relatively uniform fashion, thus avoiding widely discrepant powers among cities.

The law of many states holds that cities, because they are authorized or created by the legislature, may also have their boundaries, or even their existence, altered by legislative action (*Hunter v. City of Pittsburgh*, 1907). Subsection (b) protects cities, preventing their annexation by, or consolidation with, another city without a vote by that city's electorate. (Consolidation of cities with a county is discussed in sec. 6.)

SECTION 3

County and city charters. (a) For its own government, a county or city may adopt a charter by majority vote of its electors voting on the question. The charter is effective when filed with the Secretary of State. A charter may be amended, revised, or repealed in the same manner. A charter, amendment, revision, or repeal thereof shall be published in the official state statutes. County charters adopted pursuant to this section shall supersede any existing charter and all laws inconsistent therewith. The provisions of a charter are the law of the State and have the force and effect of legislative enactments.
(b) The governing body or charter commission of a county or city may propose a charter or revision. Amendment or repeal may be proposed by initiative or by the governing body.

(c) An election to determine whether to draft or revise a charter and elect a charter commission may be required by initiative or by the governing body.
(d) If provisions of 2 or more measures approved at the same election conflict, those of the measure receiving the highest affirmative vote shall prevail. [Nov. 5, 1974]

Any city or county has the option of adopting a charter, thus creating, without the need to solicit permission of the legislature, a specialized and unique document controlling many of its activities. A charter represents a substantial factor of local independence and autonomy and serves to insulate a local government from various actions of the legislature. Sections 3, 4, and 5 govern aspects of the charter option; section 3 is a general provision concerning the process of adopting a charter, section 4 concerns charters for counties, and section 5 deals with cities. A city or county that does not choose to adopt a charter will govern itself under the provisions of general laws, that is, under the ordinary statutory controls established by the legislature. There are some political and financial advantages to charter status; about one-fifth of California cities and twelve of the fifty-eight counties have chosen to adopt charters.

Charters may now be adopted, approved, and revised as described in section 3(a), thus abolishing the former procedures that required specific approval of individual charters by a special act of the legislature. Although section 3(a) overtly declares that "charters are the law of the state" and have the same effect as any state statute, its effect is not well understood, especially when compared to the similar provisions of sections 4 and 5; it thus raises complicated issues requiring judicial interpretation of conflicts between state and local power.

Section 3(b) allows the proposal of a charter to be made by either the local government's governing body (city council or county board of supervisors) or a special charter commission created for that purpose. In contrast, the amendment or repeal of a charter may be accomplished either by action of the governing body or by citizen initiative; this provision probably reflects the general concern that the initiative process (see Art. II, sec. 11), although probably too cumbersome to allow efficient initial drafting of a charter, could still be used for its amendment or repeal. Section 3(c) allows either the governing body or the citizens through their initiative power to call an election for the purpose of determining whether to draft or revise a charter. Because there may be several proposals for charter provisions competing in the same election campaign, subsection (d) dictates which measures should prevail.

SECTION 4

County charter provisions. County charters shall provide for:

(a) A governing body of 5 or more members, elected (1) by district or, (2) at large, or (3) at large, with a requirement that they reside in a district. Charter counties are subject to statutes that relate to apportioning population of governing body districts.

(b) The compensation, terms, and removal of members of the governing body. If a county charter provides for the Legislature to prescribe the salary of the governing body, such compensation shall be prescribed by the governing body by ordinance.

(c) An elected sheriff, and elected district attorney, an elected assessor, other officers, their election or appointment, compensation, terms and removal.

(d) The performance of functions required by statute.

(e) The powers and duties of governing bodies and all other county officers, and for consolidation and segregation of county officers, and for the manner and filling all vacancies occurring therein.

(f) The fixing and regulation by governing bodies, by ordinance, of the appointment and number of assistants, deputies, clerks, attaches, and other persons to be employed, and for the prescribing and regulating by such bodies of the powers, duties, qualifications, and compensation of such persons, the times at which, and terms for which they shall be appointed, and the manner of their appointment and removal.

(g) Whenever any county has framed and adopted a charter, and the same shall have been approved by the Legislature as herein provided, the general laws adopted by the Legislature in pursuance of Section 1(b) of this article, shall, as to such county, be superseded by said charter as to matters for which, under this section it is competent to make provision in such charter, and for which provision is made therein, except as herein otherwise expressly provided.

(h) Charter counties shall have all the powers that are provided by this Constitution or by statute for counties. [June 7, 1988]

The basic organizational structure required for any county was described in section 1(b). This section, added in 1911, allows individual counties to opt for a charter structure for their government and establishes minimum elements that such a charter must contain. Only twelve counties in California have chosen to take charter status.

Subsection (a) allows a charter county a choice of three patterns of representation in election of its board of supervisors. (In contrast, statutes require that all noncharter counties must elect their county supervisors by districts.)

The governing bodies of charter counties have long had the power to set their own compensation, a power specifically recognized by subsection (b). (A similar power was extended to the boards of supervisors of noncharter counties by section 1(b).) The second sentence of subsection (b) recognizes that some older county charters, although having the authority to set their own salaries, nevertheless chose to adopt the general salary scale set by the legislature under the former system. This subsection now requires a county with such a charter provision to set its own salary by ordinance.

Subsections (c), (d), (e), and (f) require the charter to address a variety of important concerns regarding the role and powers of county officers and bodies.

The provisions of section 4 are important because they allow a county to adopt those organizational patterns and practices that appear most appropriate to its circumstances rather than to operate under the requirements otherwise imposed by the legislature in the general statutes. The county charter provisions, however, do not appear to give a charter county any general autonomy regarding local matters, an outcome that is in sharp contrast to the extensive home role powers that can be enjoyed by a charter city under section 5. County charter provisions instead appear to be restricted in subject to structural and organizational matters of county government. Thus, subsection (g) provides that the basic statutory provisions regarding governmental organization that are established under section 1(b) are to be superseded by county charter provisions, but only as to those matters, such as public employee concerns, for which the charter is made "competent" by the terms of section 4 itself (*Pearson v. County of Los Angeles*, 1957). A charter might still address other concerns, but as to those concerns it would have to yield to conflicting state law. (Compare the somewhat different result as to the police power authorization available to any county under sec. 7, below.)

The nature of a charter county's home rule, in fact, is quite indistinct. A county's status as an administrative subdivision of state government, as provided by section 1(a), implies that it ought to be controlled by the larger government of which it is an inherent part. But the philosophy of home rule suggests the existence of a sphere of county activities or powers within which an autonomous role might still exist, protected from legislative control by a protective charter status.

Finally, subsection (h) clarifies that charter counties share, as a minimum authorization, the same powers that are provided generally by statute, or by the constitution, for all counties, thus reinforcing the implication that they enjoy some additional powers of their own derived from their charter status.

SECTION 5

City charter provisions. (a) It shall be competent in any city charter to provide that the city governed thereunder may make and enforce all ordinances and regulations in respect to municipal affairs, subject only to restrictions and limitations provided in their several charters and in respect to other matters they shall be subject to general laws. City charters adopted pursuant to the Constitution shall supersede any existing charters, and with respect to municipal affairs shall supersede all laws inconsistent therewith.

(b) It shall be competent in all city charters to provide, in addition to those provisions allowable by this Constitution, and by the laws of the State for: (1) the constitution, regulation, and government of the city police force, (2) subgovernment in all or part of a city, (3) conduct of city elections, and (4) plenary authority is hereby granted, subject only to the restrictions of this article, to provide therein or by amendment thereto, the manner in which, the method by which, the times at which, and the terms for which the several municipal officers and employees whose compensation is paid by the city shall be elected or appointed, and for their removal, and for their compensation, and for the number of deputies, clerks and other employees that each shall have, and for the compensation, method of appointment, qualifications, tenure of office and removal of such deputies clerks, and other employees. [June 2, 1970]

Section 3 allows any California city to choose charter status; this section explains the effect that a charter has on city powers and specifies some of the permitted content of the charter provisions. In contrast to section 4 (regarding the mandatory content of county charters), section 5 employs permissive language ("it shall be competent") that allows cities to choose the breadth of their charter provisions. Section 5 also establishes plenary authority to set out the manner of election, terms of office, and similar details regarding city officers and management, thus creating a form of municipal autonomy that is of much greater scope than the charter county powers of section 4.

City charter powers are perhaps the most noteworthy feature of local government law in California. They represent the heart of the concept of home rule, a philosophy of local government autonomy employed in many states as a coun-terforce to the powers of a state legislature. The original 1879 antecedents of the current section 5 allowed a city to adopt "a charter for its own government"; but those new "freeholder's charters" remained "subject to and controlled by" any general legislative act. That pattern was abruptly changed in 1896 by amendments that exempted "municipal affairs" from control by the general laws, thereby creating for the first time the potential of autonomous home rule.

The purpose of the 1896 amendments was to prevent interference by the legislature in the government and management of the municipality (*Ex parte Braun*, 1903) and "to enable municipalities to conduct their own business and control their own affairs . . . upon the principle that the municipality itself knew better what it wanted and needed than did the state at large, and to give that municipality the exclusive privilege and right to enact direct legislation which would carry out and satisfy its wants and needs" (*Fragley v. Phelan*, 1899). The change of policy was completed in 1914, when the rule was rephrased affirmatively in essentially the language retained today: charter cities could "make and enforce all laws and regulations in respect to municipal affairs . . . and in respect to other matters, they shall be subject to and controlled by general laws." Under those revisions, a charter city could acquire "full control over its municipal affairs unaffected by general law on the same subject-matters" (*West Coast Advertising Co. v. San Francisco*, 1939). The current phrasing of section 5, adopted in 1970, has condensed the complex and redundant wording of the former sections, while accurately retaining their essential policies.

The charter city's full control is reflected in the last sentence of subsection (a), which provides that a city charter "shall supersede all laws" that are inconsistent with its provisions; the reference to "all laws" includes the general statutes passed by the legislature. Conversely, as to all matters that are not municipal affairs, subsection (a) clearly provides that cities remain "subject to general laws," thus allowing their powers to be limited by legislative actions. The phrase "municipal affairs" thus provides the measure of the sphere of activities in which the city enjoys autonomy from the legislature, and its precise definition becomes a critical test.

On several matters, the constitution itself appears to imply a definition of municipal affairs. The supreme court has held that subsection (b) provides "direct guidance" in resolving the question whether a subject of local regulation is a municipal affair and hence within the home rule power (*Sonoma County Organization of Public Employees v. County of Sonoma*, 1979). Even as to matters specifically listed within subsection (b) however, the supreme court has upheld state legislation that "impinges only minimally on the specific directives" of that section, especially where the legislation is asserted to affect a "matter of statewide concern" (*Baggett v. Gates*, 1982). More recently, the supreme court has cautioned against the "error of compartmentalization" that could result from declaring particular areas of governmental activity as categorically within or without the definition (*California Federal Savings & Loan Association v. City of Los Angeles*, 1991), which suggests that a more searching analysis may no longer guarantee autonomy to the subjects listed within subsection (b).

In addition to the specific subjects listed in subsection (b), the primary attraction to cities of municipal affairs authority is the potential breadth of the concept. As the constitution was originally written, charters had to include, with great specificity, any power that a city might expect to exercise. After amendments in 1914, the charter simply had to declare its intention to avail itself of the full power, using the language of current section 5(a)—"to make and enforce all ordinances and regulations in respect to municipal affairs." Once having done so, the city has full control over any aspect of its municipal affairs, "whether or not its charter specifically provides for the particular power sought to be exercised, so long as the power is exercised within the limitations or restrictions placed in the charter" (*West Coast Advertising Co. v. San Francisco*, 1939). Ultimately, that power of "complete autonomous rule with respect to municipal affairs" represents a vast residuum of power, able to be used without the need for direct authorization (*Bellus v. City of Eureka*, 1968; *Miller v. City of Sacramento*, 1977), thus giving to a charter city a potentially much greater range of power than that available to the "general law" cities, which operate under specific statutory authorizations.

The resulting breadth of municipal affairs powers exercised by cities provides ample opportunities for conflicts to occur between those powers and various directives and prohibitions contained in legislative statutes. In some instances, the powers can coexist without interference with one another or operate in a complementary fashion. In such cases, neither must necessarily supersede the other (*The Pines v. City of Santa Monica,* 1981). Where conflict between the exercise of state and local power is unavoidable and direct, "one or the other must give way," and courts must decide which power will supersede the other—that is, whether the matter is an invulnerable municipal affair or whether it instead must yield to paramount state authority (*Professional Fire Fighters, Inc. v. City of Los Angeles,* 1963). In making those decisions, the judiciary has developed a general distinction between matters that are primarily local in interest or effect (the municipal affairs) and matters that are no longer essentially local but instead have "statewide significance," or are of "statewide concern." No easy analytical test exists. "Municipal affairs" initially included such categories as salaries of city employees (*Popper v. Broderick,* 1899), the "internal business affairs" of a city (*Fragley v. Phelan,* 1899), contracting for city construction projects (*Smith v. City of Riverside,* 1973), and local matters of revenue and taxation (*Ex parte Braun,* 1903; *The Pines v. City of Santa Monica,* 1981). In contrast, the phrase "statewide concern" is generally recognized as involving matters of regional or statewide interest whose impact extends beyond the boundaries of the charter city. Early examples included motor vehicle regulation (*Ex parte Daniels,* 1920), public improvements that transcend the boundaries of a single city (*Wilson v. City of San Bernardino,* 1960), and the regulation of utility franchises that have obvious multicity, even interstate, connections (*Pacific Telephone and Telegraph Co. v. City and County of San Francisco,* 1959). Subsequent decisions have found statewide concern in general laws establishing such things as organizational rights for city firefighters (*Professional Fire Fighters, Inc. v. City of Los Angeles,* 1963) and providing procedural protections to police officers (*Baggett v. Gates,* 1982) and in state statutes that integrate and unify the state and local taxes applied to certain financial institutions, thus precluding municipal taxation (*California Federal Savings and Loan Association v. City of Los Angeles,* 1991).

In many circumstances, the legislature itself—rather than the courts—has attempted to establish the boundary between municipal and statewide powers by overtly declaring that a new statute involves a "matter of statewide concern," as to which local powers are invalid. The supreme court has recognized its ultimate responsibility to resolve such disputes, holding that the legislature's attempt to deal with a particular subject on a statewide basis "is not determinative of the issue" (*Bishop v. City of San Jose,* 1969) and that attempts to preclude local powers would require "the identification of a convincing basis for legislative action originating in extramunicipal concerns, one justifying legislative supersession based on sensible, pragmatic considerations" (*California Federal Savings & Loan Association v. City of Los Angeles,* 1991).

Unfortunately, the difficult issues of section 5 involving supersession of state authority by local autonomy have been confused by the opposing doctrine of "state preemption," which more properly arises under the similar home rule powers discussed below in regard to section 7. In true preemption situations, once "direct conflict" in exercise of the powers has been demonstrated, the legislative intent to prohibit exercise of power by local governments is nearly conclusive of the question, and state legislation will preempt local power. In contrast, if a matter is truly a municipal affair, it will supersede even direct state legislation intended to control it. Thus, some courts have confused legislative attempts to preempt local powers with the similar attempt to declare a matter to be of statewide concern.[51] The conflict between supersession and preemption has yet to be definitively resolved.

SECTION 6

Charter city and county. (a) A county and all cities within it may consolidate as a charter city and county as provided by statute.
(b) A charter city and county is a charter city and a charter county, its charter city powers supersede conflicting charter county powers. [June 2, 1970]

The "consolidation" of local government entities means their combination or merger into a single entity. The usual effect is that some of the entities cease to exist; consolidation is therefore frequently suggested by proponents of government reform as a means of achieving simplification of governmental structure or economic efficiencies of scale.

This section, in contrast to the related provisions of section 2, is silent on the question of voter approval. Because approval is not otherwise constitutionally required, voters will have the safeguard of withholding consent to a consolidation proposal only where their approval is statutorily required. The last phrase of subsection (a) implies that county-city consolidation may occur "as provided by statute"; thus, the questions of consolidation and voter approval remain dependent on legislative discretion.

Under subsection (a), if a county and all cities within it were to consolidate, only one city would retain its identity as part of the new consolidated entity; the other cities would cease to have separate corporate existence. Experience has shown, however, that the citizens of small cities frequently wish to retain their political identity and are reluctant to lose that identity through merger.

[51] In re Hubbard, 62 Cal. 2d 119, 396 P.2d 809 (1964); Bishop v. City of San Jose, 1 Cal. 3d 56, 360 P.2d 137 (1969); Alioto's Fish Co., Ltd. v. Human Rights Comm'n of San Francisco, 120 Cal. App. 3d 594, cert. den. 102 S. Ct. 1441, 71 L. Ed. 2d 657, 455 U.S. 944 (1981); Cox Cable San Diego, Inc. v City of San Diego, 188 Cal. App. 3d 952, 233 Cal. Rptr. 735 (1987). Compare Professional Fire Fighters, Inc. v. City of Los Angeles, 60 Cal. 2d 276, 292, 384, P.2d 158, 168 (1963), and Birkenfeld v. City of Berkeley, 17 Cal. 3d 129, 550 P.2d 1001 (1976).

Subsection (b) specifies the character of the new hybrid entity as a "charter city and a charter county," impliedly with a governmental structure somewhat like San Francisco's, which is the only such "charter city and county" within the state. Other consolidation options, such as treating the new entity as a charter city only or as a charter county, might still be possible if subsection (a) is not considered an exclusive method of consolidation.

Although section 6 was intended to apply to any consolidation proposals within the state, a special provision concerning cities in Sacramento County was added as section 1 of Title XX in 1974. Buttressed by implementing sections of the Government Code, unique procedures were established to govern proposals for consolidation of the several cities in the county. No consolidation has yet occurred there; proposals were rejected at popular elections in 1974 and 1990.

SECTION 7

Local ordinances and regulations. A county or city may make and enforce within its limits all local police, sanitary, and other ordinances and regulations not in conflict with general laws. [June 2, 1970]

Section 7 presents the most widely used of the home rule provisions of the California Constitution. In contrast to sections 4 and 5, it applies equally to all cities and counties, regardless of their charter status; however, it has no application to other forms of local government entities, such as special districts. Section 7 empowers cities and counties to use their general authority, called the police power, to control and regulate any matter or activity that is otherwise an appropriate subject for governmental concern. That power may be exercised only within the city or county territorial boundaries; it cannot extend across the lines and into the territory of an adjoining government.

The language of section 7 remains almost completely unchanged from the original draft prepared in the constitutional convention of 1878–1879. The drafters intended that local authorities "ought to be left to do all those things that in their judgment are necessary to be done, and that are not in conflict with the general laws of the state."[52] The decision was made then not to restrict local governments narrowly to those specified powers that are overtly granted to them by the legislature but to allow them to exercise whatever powers appeared necessary, without the need to request legislative authorization before taking action.

The local power recognized by section 7 is potentially broad in scope and is frequently used by cities and counties to address a variety of problems that are unusual in nature or of particular concern only in some local area. In practice,

[52] Debates, p. 1052, remarks of Mr. Blackmer.

the section 7 powers serve as a vast reservoir of potential authority that can be utilized whenever a local government body, by local legislative acts (called "ordinances"), decides to employ its powers to address a problem. Any power exercised locally, however, can potentially conflict with similar powers exercised under state statutes; thus, complicated rules have developed to determine when a local ordinance conflicts with state powers.

Under the specific language of section 7, the local powers have effect only if they are exercised in a manner that is "not in conflict with" the state powers represented by general laws. That means that the state legislature can enact new legislation that purposely conflicts with some local ordinances and thereby preempt those ordinances, depriving them of further authorization. Similarly, a local government may not enact new ordinances when state statutes already address a particular concern, thus occupying the field to the exclusion of local regulatory efforts. In practice, however, it can be extremely difficult to determine in specific cases whether local and state laws conflict or whether a purported state preemption is in fact effective to prevent local ordinances from having effect. Courts have employed many different tests to try to analyze conflict and preemption problems, including such considerations as legislative intent, whether the local ordinances appear to supplement, or instead hinder, state regulatory goals, and whether local controls might be detrimental to a coordinated or uniform regulatory program.

SECTION 8

Counties'performance of municipal functions. (a) The Legislature may provide that counties perform municipal functions at the request of cities within them.
(b) If provided by their respective charters, a county may agree with a city within it to assume and discharge specified municipal functions. [June 2, 1970]

Section 8 allows limited forms of transfer of functions among certain local government units but does not foreclose other forms of collaboration that might be authorized by the legislature.

Subsection (a) was derived from several closely related amendments, first adopted in 1914, that authorized the legislature to "provide for the performance by county officers of certain . . . municipal functions." Initially at least, the provisions were used widely by cities to avail themselves of a county's fiscal apparatus, allowing the duties of city assessors, treasurers, or tax collectors to be taken over by county officers. The full potential of transfers was revealed in the mid–1950s with the advent of the "Lakewood plan," which utilized the extensive administrative and labor resources of county government to provide a much greater range of municipal-style services to small cities. The availability of such services, provided by contract between a county and one or more of the cities within it, made possible the incorporation and fiscal stability of numerous cities that otherwise might not have been able to afford independent status. The arrangement also served to elevate the county to a more dominant political and economic role as an area-wide provider of services and, in some areas, to foster a "functional consolidation" among local government units. Many areas of the state now use similar arrangements to provide a comprehensive array of services to cities, whether of a highly technical or specialized nature not suitable to smaller cities or simply where to do so represents an efficient utilization of resources. Over an extended period, the legislature has passed numerous statutory authorizations for the transfer of particular forms of services.

The 1970 version of subsection (a), unlike earlier versions, was careful to specify that the counties would perform municipal functions not when "provided for by the Legislature" but only "at the request" of the cities, thus giving the city government, and not the state or the county, the ultimate decision to allow county performance of a city function.

Subsection (b) addresses only those cities and counties organized under charters as provided by section 3. It permits charter governments to make their own arrangements among themselves, freeing them from the need to rely on the legislative authorization in subsection (a). These provisions too were used to shift tax assessment responsibilities from cities to counties and were implemented by specific authorization in each city's charter (e.g., *Brill v. County of Los Angeles*, 1940). As to charter cities, the powers appear unnecessary because they are redundant of those normally enjoyed under the "municipal affairs" power of section 5; nevertheless, as to charter counties, sub-section (b) represents a broader form of affirmative power than that available under the restrictive authorization provided by section 4. The most important aspect of subsection (b) is thus to ensure charter counties, such as Los Angeles, a flexibility and freedom to contract not otherwise available to counties generally.

The potential flexibility and advantages resulting from cooperative undertakings extend beyond the limited patterns fostered by section 8. The narrow phrasing of subsections (a) and (b) authorizes cooperative activity only as between an individual county and one or more of the cities within that county; it does not authorize agreements among other forms of local government, such as among cities, counties, and special districts.

Despite the lack of direct constitutional authorization, several means exist to achieve greater flexibility in providing local services. Courts have validated complex arrangements by which cities and counties may transfer, and retransfer, duties among themselves, such that cities are sometimes the actual providers of the services at issue (*City of Pasadena v. County of Los Angeles*, 1965). Other forms of interlocal transfers can be authorized directly by statute. The outstanding example of legislative authorization was the enactment, in 1921, of the Joint Exercise of Powers Act, which allows joint undertakings by counties, cities, other public agencies, or even units of adjoining states (*City of Oakland v. Williams*, 1940). Agreements under the Joint Powers Act are widespread, with more than

620 entities currently operating under that authority,[53] and have been liberally interpreted by the courts (*County of Amador v. Huberty*, 1962; *Beckwith v. County of Stanislaus*, 1959). The collaborative efforts that result, and the independent financing made available under their authority, are widely believed to represent a highly effective solution to area- or region-wide problems, achieved without the intrusion of legislative involvement and only after the violitional decision to participate by the involved local governments.

SECTION 9

Local utilities. (a) A municipal corporation may establish, purchase, and operate public works to furnish its inhabitants with light, water, power, heat, transportation, or means of communication. It may furnish those services outside its boundaries, except within another municipal corporation which furnishes the same service and does not consent.

(b) Persons or corporations may establish and operate works for supplying those services upon conditions and under regulations that the city may prescribe under its organic law. [June 2, 1970]

This section is an imperfect attempt to conform the constitution to the revolutionary changes that have occurred since 1879 in the role of utilities in our society. It strengthens some aspects of local control, while shifting primary regulatory authority to the Public Utilities Commission established in Article XII.

For centuries, the common law recognized that governments had the power to grant permission, in the form of "franchises," to private businesses that wished to operate within the territory of a city. The businesses would perform valuable services for the citizenry, for which they charged appropriate fees. That relationship usually had the effect of keeping cities out of the role of directly providing services to their populace; it was also consistent with a philosophy, popular in the eighteenth and nineteenth centuries, that held it to be improper for cities to engage in those types of "proprietary" (that is, economic, or profit-producing) activities that might be performed by private corporations.

By the early twentieth century, American legal theory, spurred on by rapid advancements in utility technology, began to allow an increasing number of cities to undertake direct ownership and management of proprietary activities; indeed public works for street railways and the supply of water or gaslights were becoming commonplace. In California by 1910, nearly a dozen cities, operating under what were then called "freeholder's" charters, had given their local legislative bodies specific power variously to supply water, gas, light, heat, power,

[53] California State Controller, Annual Report of Financial Transactions Concerning Special Districts of California, Fiscal Year 1989–90, p. I–12.

transportation, or communication systems. Similarly, some general law cities had been delegated power by the legislature to acquire and operate a limited, but expanding, group of municipal utilities. Rather than rely on franchise holders to perform some services, the cities were now undertaking to do it themselves. Their legal capacity to do so, however, was not clearly established.

The constitutional theory regarding city ownership or management of utilities had been unsettled for decades. Under the terms of the 1879 version of section 19 of Article XI, from which the current section 9 was derived, in those cities "where there are no public works owned and controlled by the municipality, for supplying the same with water or artificial light," any individual or company organized under state law could be awarded the privilege of using the public streets to install distribution systems, under the direction of a municipal officer, and "upon the condition that the municipal government shall have the right to regulate the charges thereof." The original purpose of those provisions was to forestall utility monopolies by allowing any qualified entity to initiate utility service in a municipality, thus challenging already established providers (*People v. Stephens,* 1882). Unfortunately, the language chosen created at least two ambiguities. First, as to franchises, it acknowledged the existing system of state-granted franchises but nevertheless subjected them to an uncertain scope of municipal control. Second, although it did not forbid, yet neither did it clearly grant to, municipalities the power to own utilities, it only impliedly recognized that some municipally owned public works might already exist and, thus, that cities must have such a power. Because of the ambiguities, it was widely assumed that California cities had no inherent power to operate utilities (*In re Russell,* 1912; *Clark v. City of Los Angeles,* 1911) and that such power existed only where it was authorized by sporadic legislation or by very specific charter grants (*Platt v. City and County of San Francisco,* 1910).

The social and economic changes of the early twentieth century made a greater municipal role in utility management inevitable. That expanded roll was made possible by another of the sweeping changes of 1911; in contemporaneous new statutory and constitutional amendments, strong, affirmative language authorized municipal ownership and operation of public works, using terms essentially identical to the first sentence of the current section 9. At the same time, the new section clarified that those utilities could be used to supply the daily needs of the inhabitants, and not merely to perform corporate, governmental functions. Once established, the operational policies and rates of the resulting municipally owned utilities are determined by the city itself; they are generally considered to be unaffected by the Article XII, section 3 regulatory power of the Public Utilities Commission (e.g., *American Microsystems, Inc. v. City of Santa Clara,* 1982).

Other provisions of the 1911 amendment, retained currently in the important sentence regarding service "outside the boundaries," were inserted specifically to negate the arguments that such service could not be municipal in nature, since it was conducted neither within the city nor for the direct benefit of city residents. The ability to extend utilities beyond city boundaries is generally considered economically efficient and is widely practiced, but there remains a concern that noncity consumers may have insufficient political control over the municipality's policies. The validity of those arrangements has been sustained despite strong attacks that they unconstitutionally deprive voters of representation (*City of South Pasadena v. Pasadena Land and Water Co.*, 1908) or that external aspects of the service ought to be subjected to the regulatory control of the Public Utilities Commission (*County of Inyo v. Public Utilities Commission*, 1980). Nevertheless, cities that provide such service are bound by common law and statutory restraints requiring fair pricing and nondiscriminatory practices.

Subsection (b) carries forward the 1879 provisions that made franchises more readily available but incorporates the 1911 qualification that franchises were to be operated "upon such conditions, and under such regulations as the municipality may prescribe under its organic law." Although not a denial of the basic state power to grant the franchise, that language was intended to give the city authority "to prescribe when such work shall be done, and how it shall be done, and to regulate it so as to insure good work with the least public inconvenience.... The manner of using the public streets must be in accordance with such regulations as the cities may prescribe in their charters."[54] Absent from the 1911 language, and still absent currently, is a clarification whether the authority to grant franchises remains in the state or the local governments.

Municipal authorization to grant franchises is addressed in part by Article XII, section 8, a part of the 1911 provisions that revamped the role and powers of the Public Utilities Commission. That section recognizes a right of cities "to grant franchises for public utilities ... in the manner prescribed by law." The "manner prescribed by law," like the "under its organic law" provision of section 9, includes several statutory provisions, enacted at various times, that overtly authorize both cities and counties to grant certain types of franchises, generally under procedures established in the Public Utility Code. Franchise power is more securely established for charter cities, whose authority to grant franchises is not dependent on statutory power, being derived instead from section 5 charter powers (*Southern Pacific Pipe Lines, Inc. v. City of Long Beach*, 1988), so long as the particular franchise at issue can be categorized as a municipal affair. If the franchise, such as telephone communications, is considered a "statewide concern," it remains subject to statutory procedures (*Pacific Telephone & Telegraph Co. v. City and Count of San Francisco*, 1959).

Although local governments obtained a general ability to grant franchises, they simultaneously lost the ability (previously contained in the 1879 version

[54] Voter's Pamphlet, Proposed Amendments to the Constitution, General Election of Oct. 10, 1911, statement in favor of adoption of Senate Constitutional Amendment No. 49, unpaginated.

of section 19) to oversee the rates charged by franchised utilities; that role was assumed by the Public Utilities Commission under section 8 of Article XII, which allowed only a few cities to retain the rate oversight function.

SECTION 10

Local government: extra compensation, employee residence. (a) A local government may not grant extra compensation or extra allowance to a public officer, public employee, or contractor after service has been rendered or a contract has been entered into and performed in whole or in part, or pay a claim under an agreement made without authority of law.

(b) A city or county, including any chartered city or chartered county, or public district, may not require that its employees be residents of such city, county, or district; except that such employees may be required to reside within a reasonable and specific distance of their place of employment or other designated location. [June 8, 1976]

Section 10 deals with selected aspects of the relationship between local governments and their employees. These matters are distinct from the labor relations addressed in Article XIV but involve aspects of charter city autonomy otherwise established by section 5 of Article XI.

Rules prohibiting retroactive compensation of government employees are common nationally and are related to the provisions that prohibit gifts of public monies (see Art. XVI, sec. 6). Both policies are designed to protect the financial resources of the government against retroactive payments, thus encouraging proper contract, budgeting, and appropriation procedures.

Subsection (a) extends to all governments, including charter cities and counties, a general limitation on governmental powers found in section 17 of Article IV, which similarly prohibits "extra compensation" or "unauthorized agreements ." It reverses prior case law that exempted cities or counties operating under charter powers.

Many local governments historically required employees to reside within the government's jurisdictional boundaries, usually to ensure their availability in the event of an emergency, to retain their wages within the local economy, or to encourage empathy with the local area and its residents. Those requirements were unpopular with employee organizations, for whom legislation was enacted in 1970 to prohibit local agencies from imposing residency limitations. The statute was promptly challenged in the supreme court, where it was held ineffective as to charter cities, which had "plenary authority" over the qualifications of their employees under the provisions of section 5(b) of Article XI (*Ector v. City of Torrance*, 1973). Shortly after, subsection (b) was adopted; as a constitutional provision, it overcame the autonomy otherwise granted to charter cities. The magnitude of the provision's direct impact was limited; although it affected Los

Angeles, the largest city in the state, only seven other charter cities were reported to have such restrictions at the time of the election.

Local governments currently utilize the exception in subsection (b) to impose residency requirements based on reasonable grounds, such as residency within a specified mileage or travel time radius from the place of employment (*International Association of Fire Fighters v. City of San Leandro,* 1986). Some cities also offer financial incentives to key employees to encourage their residency in close proximity to city offices.

SECTION 11

Private control of public functions; deposit and investment of public moneys. (a) The Legislature may not delegate to a private person or body power to make, control, appropriate, supervise, or interfere with county or municipal corporation improvements, money, or property, or to levy taxes or assessments, or perform municipal functions.

(b) The Legislature may, however, provide for the deposit of public moneys in any bank in this state or in any savings and loan association in this state or any credit union in this state or in any federally insured industrial loan company in this state and for payment of interest, principal, and redemption premiums of public bonds and other evidence of public indebtedness by banks within or without this state. It may also provide for investment of public moneys in securities and the registration of bonds and other evidences of indebtedness by private persons or bodies, within or without this state, acting as trustees or fiscal agents. [Nov. 8, 1988]

Section 11, created in the 1879 Constitution as section 13 of Article XI, was designed to protect local governments from unwanted interference by the state legislature. It was an early, but only moderately successful, attempt to establish an appropriate balance of power between the state and local levels of government.

In the 1870s, the California legislature involved itself in a wide variety of details of local government activities. A common technique of legislative domination was to create a separate new entity called a board or commission, giving it direct management and control of local police or fire departments, public works, financial, or other matters, thus removing authority and control from local citizens. This section was designed to impose limits on the legislature's authority over local government and "to emancipate municipal corporations from the authority and control formerly exercised over them by the Legislature" (*People v. Hoge,* 1880). (Closely related provisions are found today in Art. IV, sec. 16, regarding special legislation, and Art. XIII, sec. 24, regarding local taxation.)

Application of subsection (a) has involved repeated attempts to determine the nature and extent of those local government activities that are to be protected from legislative interference. (The problem is highly analogous to the attempts to discern the meaning of "municipal affairs" under sec. 5; sec. 11, however, is broader, as it concerns municipal autonomy regardless whether a city is chartered.) Some governmental functions are not considered truly municipal in nature because cities have neither the traditional nor legal authorization to undertake them. Other functions are viewed as necessarily subject to state control, such as the location of county or municipal boundary lines or operation of a state highway commission. By 1971, it was well settled that the creation of a regional entity whose purposes were "of more than purely local concern" did not violate section 11 (*People ex rel. Younger v. County of El Dorado*, 1971; *CEEED v. California Coastal Zone Conservation Commission*, 1974).

Another important exception to the prohibition occurs where "it is the local governing body, and not the legislature, that confers [on the new entity] the right to exercise its functions" (*Housing Authority of the County of Los Angeles v. Dockweiler*, 1939). That pattern probably established the model for many forms of regional cooperation—such as under the Joint Exercise of Powers Act[55]—that survive today as basic techniques for cooperative regional problem solving.

As originally enacted in 1879, section 11 consisted of the current subsection (a) only, of which the introductory phrase read: "The Legislature shall not delegate to *any special commission*, private corporation . . . or individual any power, etc." The 1970 repeal and reenactment of section 11 intentionally omitted the specific reference to "special commission," apparently because of a concern that new regional governmental agencies being proposed in the 1970s might be impeded by a formalistic prohibition of special commissions. Section 11 might now be interpreted to prohibit only the relatively narrow category of delegations made to private entities, as distinct from public or governmental bodies (*Simi Valley Recreation & Park District v. Local Agency Formation Commission of Ventura County*, 1975). Such a construction ignores the long history and purpose of the provision and would no longer serve to protect local government functions from governmental interference but would only offer protection from a private threat for which there is little historical precedent. Future application of section 11 may therefore be limited to instances of forced privatization of local government services.

The financial affairs of a local government are to a great extent a municipal function and figure importantly in the autonomy of charter cities under section 5. Over time, however, the legislature has enacted extensive laws concerning the management of local government financial affairs. Subsection (b) is a technical clarification of the power of the legislature to make detailed statutory provisions regarding the deposit and investment of money held by cities, counties, and other local governments.

---

[55] Calif. Government Code sec. 6500; see commentary in sec. 14, below.

SECTION 12

Claims against counties and cities. The Legislature may prescribe procedure for presentation, consideration, and enforcement of claims against counties, cities, their officers, agents, or employees. [June 2, 1970]

Most states require formal preliminary procedures before lawsuits may be brought against governmental entities. Those rules are regularly upheld as reasonable means to ensure that governments receive adequate notice of claims, thus giving them an opportunity to investigate the matters, settle disputes, or take appropriate action to change government facilities or practices (e.g., *Stanley v. City and County of San Francisco*, 1975).

This section, adopted in 1960, authorizes the legislature to prescribe uniform procedures for claims against local governments. It was specifically intended to eliminate the Article XI autonomy of local governments and to extend the benefits of new statutory procedures to persons who had claims against both unchartered and chartered entities. The revisions of 1970 rather inartfully rephrased the former section "without change of meaning," producing the current language.

The claims statutes now impose a highly detailed procedure for the presentation of claims against all local public entities, including cities and counties. Those procedures are sometimes assumed, incorrectly, to have been implemented under the direct authority of section 12, when in fact the broader power was inherent in the legislative authority established in Article IV and buttressed by section 5 of Article III. Section 12's true impact therefore was to validate the legislature's authority to promulgate claims measures of statewide, uniform application, thus making an explicit application of the "statewide purpose" exception to charter powers.

SECTION 13

Construction of article. The provisions of Sections 1 (b) (except for the second sentence), 3 (a), 4, and 5 of this Article relating to matters affecting the distribution of powers between the Legislature and cities and counties, including matters affecting supersession, shall be construed as a restatement of all related provisions of the Constitution in effect immediately prior to the effective date of this amendment, and as making no substantive change.

The terms general law, general laws, and laws, as used in this Article, shall be construed as a continuation and restatement of those terms as used in the Constitution in effect immediately prior to the effective date of this amendment, and not as effecting a change in meaning. [June 2, 1970]

Section 13 is a highly technical "savings clause," inserted as part of the extensive revisions of Article XI made in 1970. Although those revisions repealed the former article entirely, many of the new provisions restated earlier rules and were not intended to make substantive changes in policy. The purpose of this section was to refute any implication that significant changes were being proposed for those parts of the article affecting home rule. The significance of section 13 has diminished, and will continue to diminish, as the affected sections become further amended subsequent to section 13's effective date of June 2, 1970.

SECTION 14

Voter approval of local taxes. A local government formed after the effective date of this section, the boundaries of which include all or part of two or more counties, shall not levy a property tax unless such tax has been approved by a majority vote of the qualified voters of that local government voting on the issue of the tax. [Nov. 2, 1976]

This provision restricts the legislature's authority to create large special districts that have unrestricted property tax power.

Special districts are often created to perform local government functions that are not appropriate to cities or counties or to avoid the debt limits otherwise imposed on local governments by section 18 of Article XVI. Because there are no uniform rules controlling the political and voting structure of new special districts, the legislature may or may not grant to local voters adequate controls over the district's taxing power. This section requires that a local property tax, although authorized by the legislature, can be levied only after approval by a majority of the voters in that district. It also prevents the legislature from making an exception, by the use of special legislation, to otherwise applicable statutory restraints on property tax rates authorized by section 20 of Article XIII.

Section 14 affects only those relatively few districts large enough to include all of one county or to extend beyond a county's boundaries, such as metropolitan or regional transit, park, airport, or irrigation districts, that were formed after November 2, 1976. Because the prohibition is specifically against property taxes, it does not appear to have any impact on other forms of taxation by special districts, such as a sales tax (e.g., *Los Angeles County Transportation Commission v. Richmond*, 1982).

The practical effect of section 14, adopted in 1976, was overwhelmed by the adoption of Article XIII A only two years later. Section 1 of that article severely constrains the practice of imposing additional property tax burdens by limiting the cumulative tax that can be imposed by all the local governments in one area. The incentive to create a special district as a supplementary tax vehicle is thereby greatly diminished (*Rider v. County of San Diego*, 1991).

SECTION 15

Vehicle license fee allocations. (a) All revenues from taxes imposed pursuant to the Vehicle License Fee Law, or its successor, other than fees on trailer coaches and mobile homes, over and above the costs of collection and any refunds authorized by law, shall be allocated to counties and cities according to statute.

(b) This section shall apply to those taxes imposed pursuant to that law on and after July 1 following the approval of this section by the voters. [June 3, 1986]

This section was designed to "protect . . . local funds from raids by the Legislature."[56] For years, the state Department of Motor Vehicles collected an annual vehicle license fee, transferred the revenue to the General Fund, and then allocated those revenues to counties and cities as a subvention to local governments. As a part of the complex maneuvering related to subventions that followed the adoption of Article XIII B, the legislature had begun to reduce the amount of revenue released to local governments. This section mandates that revenues be allocated according to statute, thus restricting legislative discretion and creating a dedicated revenue source on which cities and counties could rely with greater certainty.

[56] California Ballot Pamphlet, Primary Election June 3, 1986, p. 21.

Artical XII

Public Utilities

This article provides for a Public Utilities Commission (PUC), which is authorized to regulate private corporations that provide important commodities or services to the public, such as gas or electrical utilities, and transportation or communication companies. The commission's authority has eclipsed similar regulatory powers of local governments and is analogous to many regulatory powers of the federal government.

As set out in the 1879 Constitution, Article XII was originally titled "Corporations." Most of its provisions, carried forward from the original 1849 Constitution, dealt with legal requirements regarding the creation and operation of corporations, but several sections established specific rules governing railroads and other companies involved in transportation. Concurrently, the ability to regulate railroads had become a national concern, highlighted in 1877 by a series of U.S. Supreme Court decisions endorsing the principle that states may regulate businesses "affected with a public interest" (*Munn v. Illinois*, 1877; *Chicago, B. and Q.R.R. v. Iowa*, 1877).

The 1879 version of Article XII provided for three railroad commissioners, who were empowered to set rates for transportation companies. Reform of the commission and its activities led eventually to a complex new statute, the Public Utilities Act of 1911, which was drafted in anticipation of ambitious constitutional amendments. The new act was passed shortly after the amendments were adopted, thus ensuring that the commission's unusual powers were created pursuant to constitutional authorization.

The current form of Article XII resulted from extensive revisions made in 1974 that consolidated and restated the utility regulation provisions and eliminated the general provisions regarding other types of corporations. Article XII was thus pared down from a cumbersome general corporations article to a concise statement of PUC authority.

SECTION 1

Public Utilities Commission: composition. The Public Utilities Commission consists of 5 members appointed by the Governor and approved by the Senate, a majority of the membership concurring, for staggered 6-year terms. A vacancy is filled for the remainder of the term. The Legislature may remove a member for incompetence, neglect of duty, or corruption, two thirds of the membership of each house concurring. [Nov. 5, 1974]

As first established by the 1879 Constitution, the commission was to have three elective members. That pattern was changed by the reforms of 1911, which raised the number of commissioners to five and required that they be appointive. Rather than actually creating the commission, section 1 recognizes the continued existence of the entity first created in 1879.

The changes implemented in 1911 were motivated by progressive political theory, which emphasized the need for commissioners who could be independent of improper, corrupt, or partisan political influence. Thus, appointment for staggered six-year terms ensured that no single governor could appoint a majority of the commissioners within that governor's four-year term. The staggered nature of their terms was thought to offer continuity for the commissioners, and thus greater stability of policy, as well as a chance for the commissioners to gain desirable expertise. The requirement of senate consent was added in 1946 and serves further to reduce the partisan nature of gubernatorial appointments.

Section 1 alters the general rule that allows a governor both to appoint and remove officers and specifies instead that the commissioners may be removed only by the legislature for specified reasons and with a two-thirds vote requirement. After appointment by the governor, it is thus the legislature that maintains complete control over the subsequent performance of the individual commissioners.

Section 1 makes no attempt to require specific qualifications or experience for commissioners, a requirement that is common among other state public service commissions and employed widely for other California commissions. With the exception of some statutory conflict of interest prohibitions, and similar prohibitions in section 7 against either a financial or an official relation with a regulated company, the absence of specific qualifications obviously affords a broader choice of candidates to the governor.

SECTION 2

Public Utilities Commission: procedures. Subject to statute and due process, the commission may establish its own procedures. Any commissioner as designated by the commission may hold a hearing or investigation or issue an order subject to commission approval. [Nov. 5, 1974]

This section provides the commission with a wide latitude to perform both administrative and judicial functions. The California courts have long recognized the unusual status of the commission, including the authority to depart from the usual (and often much more stringent) rules of evidence or procedure utilized by courts. Thus, unlike a court, to which controversies are brought by adversarial parties, the commission is expected to undertake investigations of facts and initiate its own proceedings. Moreover, in doing so, the commission has "a very large, if not an almost unlimited, discretion, with relation to the inception, order and conduct of proceedings before it" (*Saunby v. Railroad Commission*, 1923). Investigations or hearings by a single commissioner have been accepted by the courts as the equivalent of full hearings that afford constitutional due process to petitioners (*Southern California Edison Co. v. Railroad Commission*, 1936).

The power granted by section 2 is buttressed by statute and by detailed rules of practice and procedure promulgated by the commission itself. The commission is also exempt from the general procedural prescriptions applicable to most other state agencies involved in administrative adjudications.

SECTION 3

Legislative control of public utilities. Private corporations and persons that own, operate, control, or manage a line, plant, or system for the transportation of people or property, the transmission of telephone and telegraph messages, or the production, generation, transmission, or furnishing of heat, light, water, power, storage, or wharfage directly or indirectly to or for the public, and common carriers, are public utilities subject to control by the Legislature. The Legislature may prescribe that additional classes of private corporations or other persons are public utilities. [Nov. 5, 1974]

Section 17 of the original 1879 Constitution merely declared "all railroad, canal, and other transportation companies" to be "common carriers" and thus subject to the regulatory power of the commission. The constitutional amendments of

1911 introduced an extensive enumeration of specific examples of "public utilities," including within that broader term the earlier transportation-based category of common carriers. That expanded definition, which transformed the role of the commission from railroad regulation to full-scale utility regulation, survives in more concise form in the current section 3.

The 1911 language asserted control over a minimum catalog of utilities and also gave to the legislature a broad grant of power to expand the list of entities that could be made subject to regulation. That power, found in the last sentence of section 3, allows the legislature to extend the regulatory power of the commission by enacting ordinary statutory provisions, such as those now contained in the Public Utilities Code. The commission currently regulates the service and rates of thousands of privately owned utility and transportation companies, including all the major telephone, gas, electric, pipeline, railroad, and highway or water carriers in the state but excluding most airlines. Although the legislative power to define public utilities, common carriers, or similar categories always theoretically remains subject to review by the courts, a long series of judicial decisions has established a tradition of liberal interpretation and deference to the legislature's judgment (*Allen v. Railroad Commission*, 1918; *Greyhound Lines, Inc. v. Public Utilities Commission*, 1968). The statutory definitions added by the legislature have addressed a wide variety of industries and services that reflect emerging technology and practices, such as the recognition of activities involving heat derived from solar or geothermal resources.

The extensive jurisdiction of the commission can be narrowed by other factors, primarily the assertions of regulatory authority by other governments, whether federal, state, or local. PUC jurisdiction has also been narrowed by state law, as when the legislature created the California Energy Commission in 1974, thus shifting some authority from the PUC to the Energy Commission over certain aspects of electric energy development, the siting of thermal power plants, transmission lines, and related matters (e.g., *California Public Utilities Commission v. California Energy Resources Conservation and Development Commission*, 1984).

Section 3, in specifically authorizing regulation of private corporations, appears implicitly to exclude from PUC control any publicly owned utilities or carriers. That provision reflects a policy decision, inherent in drafting both the amendments and the new Public Utility Act, to give the commission no power over municipally owned utilities. Most public service commissions in the rest of the nation follow a similar policy, and the commission continues today to disclaim any general regulatory control over municipally owned utilities.

SECTION 4

Utility rates. The commission may fix rates and establish rules for the transportation of passengers and property by transportation companies, prohibit discrimination, and award reparation for the exaction of unreasonable, excessive, or discriminatory charges. A transportation company may not raise a rate or incidental charge except after a showing to and a decision by the commission that the increase is justified, and this decision shall not be subject to judicial review except as to whether confiscation of property will result. [Nov. 5, 1974]

Section 4 carries forward the heart of the several provisions of the 1879 Constitution that sought to control the "rates" (that is, the tolls, charges, or fares) charged by transportation companies and to prohibit the discriminatory application of those rates. (A redundant, but broader, rate-setting power applicable to "all utilities" is granted to the commission in section 6.) Since the 1911 amendments, the commission has had broad statutory powers and procedures to assess and set appropriate rates.

The commission's power to award reparation refers to its ability to order that awards be paid by carriers to shippers to compensate them for rates that were excessive or that were found to be preferential or discriminatory, such as rates that unfairly charged more to short-haul than to long-haul customers or for situations in which reduced rates were charged in order to drive competitors out of business. Statutes now extend those reparation powers to any public utility and provide that reparation orders that are not obeyed may be enforced by the courts.

The last sentence of section 4 was designed to overcome awkward features of the pre–1911 provisions. As interpreted in early judicial opinions, transportation companies were allowed to raise their rates unilaterally, and the commission's response to the increases was limited to after-the-fact challenges in the courts (*Edson v. Southern Pacific Railroad Co.*, 1904). Under section 4, rate increases must first be justified to the commission, whose decision whether to approve them is protected from second-guessing by the courts (see section 5).

SECTION 5

Public Utilities Commission: jurisdiction. The Legislature has plenary power, unlimited by the other provisions of this constitution but consistent with this article, to confer additional authority and jurisdiction upon the commission, to establish the manner and scope of review of commission action in a court of record, and to enable it to fix just compensation for utility property taken by eminent domain. [Nov. 5, 1974]

This section, distilled primarily from the 1911 constitutional amendments, clarifies the respective role and authorities of the legislature, the commission, and the state courts.

The unique role of the legislature was recognized by the California Supreme Court during its first opportunity to consider the expanded powers created in 1911.

In *Pacific Telephone & Telegraph Co. v. Eshleman* (1913), the court noted that the amended constitution had authorized the legislature to assign unusually broad judicial powers to the commission, in addition to its legislative and administrative functions, thus making the legislature the "supreme law of the land" as to "all matters touching public utilities." Concerned that the legislature might grant overly broad powers to the commission, the court imposed the limitation, considered inherent in the article's context, that the additional powers must be "cognate and germane to the regulation of public utilities." That limitation is preserved in section 5's qualification that the scope of the power must be "consistent with this article."

Section 5 now speaks directly to the allocation of constitutional powers, granting to the legislature extensive additional authority to expand the role of the PUC, subject to the "plenary power" qualification. The legislature, in turn, has directly delegated expansive powers to the commission; section 701 of the Public Utilities Code confers authority on the PUC to "do all things . . . which are necessary and convenient" to the regulation of public utilities. The resulting powers have been construed consistently by the courts in a broad, liberal manner (*Consumers Lobby Against Monopolies v. Public Utilities Commission*, 1979).

The reference to the legislature's power to establish "the manner and scope of review of commission action in a court of record" is a practical concomitant to the procedural freedom granted the commission by section 2 and is necessary in order to counter the otherwise-applicable jurisdiction of the courts established by sections 10 and 11 of Article VI, which delimit judicial powers. Thus, a vitally important political and practical objective of the unique role created for the commission in 1911 was the ability to have its decisions protected from time-consuming or too-intrusive judicial review. The first Public Utilities Act accordingly provided that only the state supreme court could "review, reverse, correct or annul any order or decision of the Commission." The California courts have consistently recognized that power, derived from section 5, as one of the few instances in which the constitutionally established jurisdiction of the courts may be restricted.[57]

The other primary power recognized in section 5 is authorization to the PUC to fix "just compensation" awards. That authority, considered of uncertain legality when first created by statute (*Marin Water and Power Co. v. Railroad Commission*, 1916), was adopted in 1914 to allow the PUC's expertise to be used in establishing the appropriate compensation to be paid for any public utility properties that the state or various local governments might wish to acquire, either by purchase or the use of condemnation proceedings (*City of North*

---

[57] Pacific Tel. etc. Co. v. Eshleman, 166 Cal. 640, 651–61, 137 P. 1119, 1122–26 (1913); Truck Owners & Shippers, Inc. v. Superior Court, 194 Cal. 146, 152–53, 228 P. 19, 21–22 (1924). Cf. Marin Water and Power Co. v. Railroad Comm'n, 171 Cal. 706, 713, 154 P. 864, 867 (1916). Cf. County of Sonoma v. Energy Resources Conser. Comm'n, 40 Cal. 3d 361, 708 P.2d 693 (1985).

Sacramento v. Citizens Utilities Co. of California, 1961). The resulting proceedings put the commission in the role of a special judicial tribunal, able to make binding findings regarding just compensation. Were it not for this provision, those proceedings arguably would conflict with the guarantee provided by section 19 of Article 1, which calls for a jury to ascertain the amount of just compensation awards, and might also affect the traditional separation of administrative and judicial powers recognized by section 3 of Article III. Those concerns are now rendered merely theoretical by section 5's express recognition of the compensation power, which is therefore "unlimited" by those other provisions.

SECTION 6

Public Utilities Commission: powers and duties. The commission may fix rates, establish rules, examine records, issue subpoenas, administer oaths, take testimony, punish for contempt, and prescribe a uniform system of accounts for all public utilities subject to its jurisdiction. [Nov. 5, 1974]

Section 6 carries forward the basic thrust of former section 22 as it was expanded in 1911, reflecting an elemental description of the operating practices of the commission under its modernized role. Those activities include, but are more expansive than, the traditional powers described in section 4 (which originally covered only transportation companies, not utilities) and are premised on the powers and procedural flexibility already established under section 2. In many respects, therefore, sections 2, 4, and 6 are interdependent and somewhat redundant. Statutes now provide for the implementation of sections 4 and 6 through the maintenance of records and accounts by utilities according to formats prescribed by the PUC, their inspection by representatives of the commission, and the filing and posting of rate schedules.

SECTION 7

Prohibition of free passes and other conflicts of interest. A transportation company may not grant free passes or discounts to anyone holding an office in this state; and the acceptance of a pass or discount by a public officer, other than a Public Utilities Commissioner, shall work a forfeiture of that office. A Public Utilities Commissioner may not hold an official relation to nor have a financial interest in a person or corporation subject to regulation by the commission. [Nov. 5, 1974]

Section 7 is a quaint anachronism whose purpose could be more readily accomplished by modern statutory proscriptions on conflict of interest or provisions for disclosure of political contributions.

The prohibition of this section, dating from 1879, was designed to inhibit certain aspects of the distribution of free passes, not to proscribe it entirely. As such, early operation of the prohibition appears to have been only partially successful, but it was rewritten in its present form in 1974. It continues to have occasional modern application because it affects airlines as well as other transportation companies.

The second sentence, which reflects a more basic prohibition on conflict of interests, is similar to that contained in section 22 of both the 1879 and 1911 versions and, although considered unnecessary by the California Constitution Revision Commission, was retained as a constitutional provision rather than transferred to statute.

SECTION 8

Prohibited local regulation of public utilities. A city, county, or other public body may not regulate matters over which the Legislature grants regulatory power to the Commission. This section does not affect power over public utilities relating to the making and enforcement of police, sanitary, and other regulations concerning municipal affairs pursuant to a city charter existing on October 10, 1911, unless that power has been revoked by the city's electors, or the right of any city to grant franchises for public utilities or other businesses on terms, conditions, and in the manner prescribed by law. [Nov. 5, 1974]

By the early twentieth century, some local governments had begun to engage in various forms of utility regulation, doing so under several powers contained in Article XI. In contrast, the expanded and strengthened role of the PUC signaled a shift away from reliance on the sporadic regulatory measures employed by some cities. Mindful of debates regarding the appropriate role of state and local government, the 1911 legislature had allowed pre–1911 forms of local regulation to continue, but that split of authority was quickly recognized as unworkable, and in 1914 a further amendment forcibly shifted to the commission "all of the rate fixing powers now exercised by incorporated cities." Under the prohibition in the first sentence of section 8, cities and counties are prohibited from regulating rates and similar matters that are within PUC jurisdiction, except for the narrow exception, represented by the second sentence of section 8, that continues to allow municipal regulatory authority in those few situations where local powers are based on a pre–1911 city charter *and* where they relate to those police and sanitary regulations that concern municipal affairs under section 5 of Article XI and are thus not subject to the legislature's powers over statewide concerns.

SECTION 9

Construction of article. The provisions of this article restate all related provisions of the Constitution in effect immediately prior to the effective date of this amendment and make no substantive change. [Nov. 5, 1974]

This provision, a "savings clause" inserted as part of the 1974 modernization of the entire article, clarifies that the complete repeal of all former sections of Article XII was not intended as a rejection of the policies or as destruction of any ongoing powers or rights of the old sections. Thus, section 9 declares that only organizational and stylistic changes were intended, and it overtly denies any substantive effect.

Article XIII

Taxation

Article XIII of the 1879 Constitution dealt generally with the subject of taxation. It was repealed entirely in 1974 and replaced with the current version, still relating to taxation generally but in substantially redrafted form. In addition to establishing general policies, Article XIII also contains highly specific and technical material creating particular exemptions from taxation. Two additional taxation articles, numbered XIII A and XIII B, have been added by subsequent initiative measures.

SECTION 1

Uniformity of taxation. Unless otherwise provided by this Constitution or the laws of the United States:

(a) All property is taxable and shall be assessed at the same percentage of fair market value. When a value standard other than fair market value is prescribed by this Constitution or by statute authorized by this Constitution, the same percentage shall be applied to determine the assessed value. The value to which the percentage is applied, whether it be the fair market value or not, shall be known for property tax purposes as the full value.
(b) All property so assessed shall be taxed in proportion to its full value. [Nov. 5, 1974]

Section 1 affirms the legislature's power to tax all forms of property, subject to concepts of federal supremacy also recognized in section 1 of Article III. Thus, imported items or those that are in interstate commerce may not be taxed by a state under sections 8 and 10 of Article I of the federal Constitution. In the absence of exemptions or exceptions, all forms of property—both real property (land, improvements, and fixtures) and personal property (addressed in detail in sec. 2)—are potentially subject to taxation.

The policy of section 1 is to spread the burden of taxation as equally as possible on all property in the state. The section's general rule that all property subject to taxation is to be assessed at the same percentage of market value establishes a principle of uniform assessment and taxation. That policy generally prohibits the use of a split role or similar other practices that impose different rates of tax on different categories of property, such as residential and business properties. However, the second sentence of subsection (a) recognizes that value standards other than market value may be imposed by the constitution, such as are utilized in several of the other sections. Similarly, "acquisition value," rather than "market value," has become the value standard applied to real property under the operation of Article XIII A.

Subsection (b), requiring that all property be taxed in proportion to its full value, derives from amendments of 1933. Assessments at full value are discussed in section 3.5.

SECTION 2

Personal property classification. The Legislature may provide for property taxation of all forms of tangible personal property, shares of capital stock, evidences of indebtedness, and any legal or equitable interest therein not exempt under any other provision of this article. The Legislature, two-thirds of the membership of each house concurring, may classify such personal property for differential taxation or for exemption. The tax on any interest in notes, debentures, shares of capital stock, bonds, solvent credits, deeds of trust, or mortgages shall not exceed four-tenths of one percent of full value, and the tax per dollar of full value shall not be higher on personal property than on real property in the same taxing jurisdiction. [Nov. 5, 1974]

Section 2 concerns only personal property and since 1933 has made its taxation subject to the discretion of the legislature. Although the general uniformity rule of section 1 applies to personal property, the classifications and exemptions established by a two-thirds vote of the legislature in practice have created many variations. Definitions and categories of personal property have been established by statute; generally, the term excludes intangibles, such as bank and savings accounts, government licenses, mortgages, and similar property interests that are difficult to define, detect, or tax effectively. Unless exempted, all tangible personal property is taxable.

Personal property is generally unaffected by the drastic changes to real property taxation represented by Article XIII A, except that the last phrase of section 2, limiting the tax rate of personal property to no higher than that for real property, automatically incorporates for personal property the 1 percent maximum rate on realty imposed by Section 1 of Article XIII A.

SECTION 3

Property tax exemptions. The following are exempt from property taxation:

(a) Property owned by the State.

(b) Property owned by a local government, except as otherwise provided in Section 11(a).

(c) Bonds issued by the State or a local government in the State.

(d) Property used for libraries and museums that are free and open to the public and property used exclusively for public schools, community colleges, state colleges, and state universities.

(e) Buildings, land, equipment, and securities used exclusively for educational purposes by a nonprofit institution of higher education.

(f) Buildings, land on which they are situated, and equipment used exclusively for religious worship.

(g) Property used or held exclusively for the permanent deposit of human dead or for the care and maintenance of the property or the dead, except when used or held for profit. This property is also exempt from special assessment.

(h) Growing crops.

(i) Fruit and nut trees until 4 years after the season in which they were planted in orchard form and grape vines until 3 years after the season in which they were planted in vineyard form.

(j) Immature forest trees planted on lands not previously bearing merchantable timber or planted or of natural growth on lands from which the merchantable original growth timber stand to the extent of 70 percent of all trees over 16 inches in diameter has been removed. Forest trees or timber shall be considered mature at such time after 40 years from the time of planting or removal of the original timber when so declared by a majority vote of a board consisting of a representative from the State Board of Forestry, a representative from the State Board of Equalization, and the assessor of the county in which the trees are located.

The Legislature may supersede the foregoing provisions with an alternative system or systems of taxing or exempting forest trees or timber, including a taxation system not based on property valuation. Any alternative system or systems shall provide for exemption of unharvested immature trees, shall encourage the continued use of timberlands for the production of trees for timber products, and shall provide for restricting the use of timberland to the production of timber products and compatible uses with provisions for taxation of timberland based on the restrictions. Nothing in this paragraph shall be construed to exclude timberland from the provisions of Section 8 of this article.

(k) $7,000 of the full value of a dwelling, as defined by the Legislature, when occupied by an owner as his principal residence, unless the dwelling is receiving another real property exemption. The Legislature may increase this exemption and may deny it if the owner received State or local aid to pay taxes either in whole or in part, and either directly or indirectly, on the dwelling.

No increase in this exemption above the amount of $7,000 shall be effective for any fiscal year unless the Legislature increases the rate of State taxes in an amount sufficient to provide the subventions required by Section 25. If the Legislature increases the homeowners' property tax exemption, it shall provide increases in benefits to qualified renters, as defined by law, comparable to the average increase in benefits to homeowners, as calculated by the Legislature.

(1) Vessels of more than 50 tons burden in this State and engaged in the transportation of freight or passengers.

(m) Household furnishings and personal effects not held or used in connection with a trade, profession, or business.

(n) Any debt secured by land.

(o) Property in the amount of $1,000 of a claimant who—

(1) is serving in or has served in and has been discharged under honorable conditions from service in the United States Army, Navy, Air Force, Marine Corps, Coast Guard, or Revenue Marine (Revenue Cutter) Service; and—

(2) served either

(i) in time of war, or

(ii) in time of peace in a campaign or expedition for which a medal has been issued by Congress, or

(iii) in time of peace and because of a service-connected disability was released from active duty; and—

(3) resides in the State on the current lien date. An unmarried person who owns property valued at $5,000 or more, or a married person, who, together with the spouse, owns property valued at $10,000 or more is ineligible for this exemption. If the claimant is married and does not own property eligible for the full amount of the exemption, property of the spouse shall be eligible for the unused balance of the exemption.

(p) Property in the amount of $1,000 of a claimant who—

(1) is the unmarried spouse of a deceased veteran who met the service requirement stated in paragraphs (1) and (2) of subsection 3(o), and

(2) does not own property in excess of $10,000, and

(3) is a resident of the State on the current lien date.

(q) Property in the amount of $1,000 of a claimant who—

(1) is the parent of a deceased veteran who met the service requirement stated in paragraphs (1) and (2) of subsection 3(o), and

(2) receives a pension because of the veteran's service, and

(3) is a resident of the State on the current lien date.

Either parent of a deceased veteran may claim this exemption. An unmarried person who owns property valued at $5,000 or more, or a married person, who, together with the spouse, owns property valued at $10,000 or more, is ineligible for this exemption.

(r) No individual residing in the State on the effective date of this amendment who would have been eligible for the exemption provided by the previous section 1 1/4 of this article had it not been repealed shall lose eligibility for the exemption as a result of this amendment. [Nov. 8, 1988]

Section 3 mandates specific exemptions from taxation for categories of both real and personal property. (In contrast, section 2 allows the legislature to classify and exempt only personal property.) The exemptions listed in this section have accrued over many years and do not represent coherent policies or practices. Many are quite technical or self-explanatory and do not merit detailed treatment. A few other exemptions occur in other articles, and all are subject to additional constitutional restrictions, such as the anachronistic section 9 of Article VII, which prohibits exemptions for subversive persons and organizations.

Property owned by the federal government is exempt from state taxation under the federal Constitution's supremacy clause. A similar exemption is established by subsections (a) and (b), which exempt generally all public property owned by the state or its local governments. The exemption extends to various agencies of government but not to property in which a governmental entity is merely a lessee. Subsection (c) exempts bonds issued by California governments, thus encouraging purchase of bonds by eliminating concern for any personal property tax liability.

The libraries and museums exemption of subsection (d) was intended to encourage the establishment and maintenance of such institutions so long as they are free to the public. This exemption overlaps substantially with the general welfare exemption of section 4(b).

Subsection (e)'s exemption for educational purposes is available only to nonprofit private institutions (public institutions are already exempt under subsections (a) and (b)). The "higher education" stipulation excludes many private schools of lower accreditations.

The exemption in subsection (f) for buildings and land used for religious worship has existed since 1900, thus avoiding the prohibition on public aid for sectarian purposes contained in section 5 of Article XVI. It requires that property actually be used for worship, although it may also be used for incidental purposes. The exemption applies whether the property is owned or rented by the religious organization and is extended in certain particulars by sections 4(d) and 5. Although some cemeteries are included within "religious" exemptions, any nonprofit cemetery property is exempted by subsection (g); buildings and lands not yet devoted to burial purposes are excluded, as are for-profit cemeteries.

Subsections (h), (i), and (j) involve agricultural products and exempt from taxation plants that are harvested or replanted annually or that are too young to bear market crops. Subsection (j) similarly exempts immature timber but also empowers the legislature to establish an alternative "timber yield tax." The resulting statutory system reflects modern resources and environmental concerns and exempts all growing timber from taxation, imposing instead a yield tax; restricted lands on which timber is grown can be taxed on its current use value (see sec. 8).

A "homeowners' property tax exemption" is established in subsection (k), applicable only to owner-occupied dwellings that do not receive another constitutional or statutory exemption. This protection is related to the provisions discussed for sections 8.5 and 9.

Subsection (l) exempts large freight or passenger vessels, a measure intended to stimulate the shipbuilding industry after the opening of the Panama Canal. Subsection (m) exempts household furnishings, essentially a waiver of personal property taxation for individuals, and subsection (n) exempts debts secured by land, thereby removing mortgages and deeds of trust from taxation, although they are already statutorily exempt as intangibles.

Subsections (o) through (r) comprise a veterans' exemption, first adopted in 1911 and revised repeatedly since then. It is subject to numerous qualifications and conditions. A more limited exemption for disabled veterans is discussed in section 4(b).

SECTION 3.5

Adjustments to assessment ratios to maintain veterans' exemptions. In any year in which the assessment ratio is changed, the Legislature shall adjust the valuation of assessable property described in subdivisions (o), (p) and (q) of Section 3 of this article to maintain the same proportionate values of such property. [Nov. 6, 1979]

The term "assessment ratio" refers to a ratio of the assessed value of property to its full market value. For many years, local assessors arbitrarily set assessed values substantially below market values, a practice that required the State Board of Equalization to equalize ratios among the various counties (see sec. 18). Although section 1(a) mandates that all property "be assessed at the same percentage of fair market value," the concept of a ratio was altered drastically by the 1978 adoption of Article XIII A. Section 2(a) of that article established "full cash value" as the assessed value of property, thus effectively establishing a ratio of one to one or 100 percent and making the concept of assessment ratio irrelevant for most properties.

This section was adopted to accompany legislation passed in 1978 in which the legislature shifted to a 100 percent ratio system. The new system effectively eliminated the use of a ratio and was urged upon the voters as a way to simplify the property tax system and make it more understandable. It also authorized the legislature to make necessary statutory adjustments to the veterans' exemptions established by several subsections of section 3.

SECTION 4

Property tax exemptions. The Legislature may exempt from property taxation in whole or in part:

(a) The home of a person or a person's spouse, including an unmarried surviving spouse, if the person, because of injury incurred in military service, is blind in both eyes, has lost the use of 2 or more limbs, or is totally disabled unless the home is receiving another real property exemption.

(b) Property used exclusively for religious, hospital, or charitable purposes and owned or held in trust by corporations or other entities (1) that are organized and operating for those purposes, (2) that are nonprofit, and (3) no part of whose net earnings inures to the benefit of any private shareholder or individual.

(c) Property owned by the California School of Mechanical Arts, California Academy of Sciences, or Cogswell Polytechnical College, or held in trust for the Huntington Library and Art Gallery, or their successors.

(d) Real property not used for commercial purposes that is reasonably and necessarily required for parking vehicles of persons worshipping on land exempt by Section 3(f). [Nov. 5, 1974]

The exemptions established in section 3 are constitutional mandates; this section authorizes the legislature, at its option, to establish and define further exemptions but only for specific categories of real or personal property. It is thus more restrictive than the general power under section 2 to classify and exempt categories of personal property.

The disabled veterans' exemption in subsection (a) is implemented by detailed statutes that establish qualifications and definitions for qualified persons and is in lieu of the exemptions established by Sections 3(o)-(r).

Subsection (b), first adopted in 1944, is known as the welfare exemption and concerns both nonprofit and religious institutions. Statutory provisions govern its application, including highly detailed definitions of religious, hospital, or charitable activities, and include conditions and qualifications for the exemptions. It is duplicative of many of the institutions listed in section 3(e). The courts have liberally interpreted how exclusively the property must be used to qualify for the exemption (*Santa Catalina Island Conservancy v. County of Los Angeles*, 1981) and have allowed a variety of reasonably necessary incidental uses as well (*Cedars of Lebanon Hospital v. Los Angeles County*, 1950).

The specific listing of institutions in subsection (c) is an anachronism dating to the early 1900s and exempts all property owned by the listed institutions, even if the property is not actually used for charitable purposes (*California Academy of Sciences v. Fresno County*, 1987).

The subsection (d) parking exemption extends the religious exemption of section 3(f) by allowing churches to use their parking lots for free or paid public parking when they are not used for religious meeting purposes.

SECTION 5

Property tax exemption for buildings under construction. Exemptions granted or authorized by Sections 3(e), 3(f), and 4(b) apply to buildings under construction, land required for their convenient use, and equipment in them if the intended use would qualify the property for exemption. [Nov. 5, 1974]

Sections 3(e) and (f) relate to exemptions for buildings used for higher education and religious worship, a category included within the general nonprofit/welfare exemption of 4(b). Those exemptions are extended by this section to include buildings under construction, an extension that apparently includes other exempted uses under construction as well (*J. Paul Getty Museum v. County of Los Angeles*, 1983). It probably does not include land in stages of planning or preparation for those uses.

SECTION 6

Exemption waivers. The failure in any year to claim, in a manner required by the laws in effect at the time the claim is required to be made, an exemption or classification which reduces a property tax shall be deemed a waiver of the exemption or classification for that year. [Nov. 5, 1974]

Section 6 establishes a firm rule requiring taxpayers to file appropriate claims for exemptions in a timely fashion. It does not affect exemptions or classifications that are self-executing. The section also prevents the occasional legislative practice of enacting retroactive relief statutes for taxpayers who failed to make timely applications (*Copren v. State Board of Equalization*, 1988).

SECTION 7

Exemption of low-value property. The Legislature, two-thirds of the membership of each house concurring, may authorize county boards of supervisors to exempt real property having a full value so low that, if not exempt, the total taxes and applicable subventions on the property would amount to less than the cost of assessing and collecting them. [Nov. 5, 1974]

Section 7 recognizes that some exemptions are desirable for purposes of administrative convenience and efficiency. Under current legislation, county boards of supervisors annually may exempt designated classes of low-value real (as well as personal) properties.

SECTION 8

Exemption for open-space land and historical property. To promote the conservation, preservation and continued existence of open space lands, the Legislature may define open space land and shall provide that when this land is enforceably restricted, in a manner specified by the Legislature, to recreation, enjoyment of scenic beauty, use or conservation of natural resources, or production of food or fiber, it shall be valued for property tax purposes only on a basis that is consistent with its restrictions and uses.

To promote the preservation of property of historical significance, the Legislature may define such property and shall provide that when it is enforceably restricted, in a manner specified by the Legislature, it shall be valued for property tax purposes only on a basis that is consistent with its restrictions and uses. [June 8, 1976]

The general requirement in section 1(a) that realty be assessed at fair market value sometimes imposed an unrealistic valuation method on golf courses, historic sites, open spaces, and similar types of land. Those properties often had a relatively low current value but a much higher potential market value. When the lands were assessed and taxed at the full market value, the result frequently was to impose taxes so high that the use made of the land had to be intensified in order to produce sufficient revenue to pay the taxes. That change was often denounced as the premature development of desirable open space land. This section, added in 1966, calls for those lands to be evaluated on a basis that is consistent with their restrictions and uses. The several "current use" programs have enjoyed relative success and generally produce more favorable valuation assessments than the acquisition-based assessments utilized after the 1978 adoption of section 2 of Article XIII A (*Shellenberger v. Board of Equalization*, 1983).

Open space lands in California may be established and enforceably restricted under statutes that authorize contracts or easements to protect agricultural, wetlands, public recreation spaces, wildlife habitat, and properties of historic importance. All of the measures described require the cooperation of local governments, a few of which have declined to participate in some of the programs. Similar programs regarding timberlands exist and under section 3(j) can also be treated under this section.

Operation of the section may result in the loss of local government property tax revenue. Statutes therefore provide for reimbursement to local governments by the payment of open space subventions from the legislature. Lands assessed at a reduced valuation under this section may later be included under one of the broader exemptions, such as the charitable purposes provisions of section 4(b) (*Santa Catalina Island Conservancy v. County of Los Angeles*, 1981).

SECTION 8.5

Postponement of property taxes. The Legislature may provide by law for the manner in which a person of low or moderate income who is 62 years of age or older may postpone ad valorem property taxes on the dwelling owned and occupied by him or her as his or her principal place of residence. The Legislature may also provide by law for the manner in which a disabled person may postpone payment of ad valorem property taxes on the dwelling owned and occupied by him or her as his or her principal place of residence. The Legislature shall have plenary power to define all terms in this section.

The Legislature shall provide by law for subventions to counties, cities and counties, cities and districts in an amount equal to the amount of revenue lost by each by reason of the postponement of taxes and for the reimbursement to the state of subventions from the payment of postponed taxes. Provision shall be made for the inclusion of reimbursement for the payment of interest on, and any costs to the state incurred in connection with, the subventions. [Nov. 6, 1984]

Section 8.5 was added by a legislative amendment in 1976 as a means of providing tax relief to senior citizens with fixed incomes. A 1984 amendment added similar protections to disabled persons. The section does not reduce taxes; rather, it allows qualified persons to defer payment of real property taxes so long as they remain in their home, with the tax and interest liability (which becomes a lien on the home) to be due and payable upon their death or the sale of the home. Definitional details regarding "low and moderate income," "disabled," and the like are contained in statutory provisions. A variety of similar tax postponement measures have since been enacted directly by the legislature.

As with some other provisions that potentially reduce local tax revenues, this section mandates that subventions be paid by the state to local governments to replace tax revenues lost because of postponements. The fiscal impact of this section on state and local governments might have been significant, but its effect was overshadowed only two years later by the substantial tax reductions mandated in sections 1 and 2 of Article XIII A.

SECTION 9

Valuation of single-family dwellings. The Legislature may provide for the assessment for taxation only on the basis of use of a single-family dwelling, as defined by the Legislature, and so much of the land as is required for its convenient use and occupation, when the dwelling is occupied by an owner and located on land zoned exclusively for single-family dwellings or for agricultural purposes. [Nov. 5, 1974]

This section provides preferential treatment for the owners of single-family residences. Adopted in 1972, it was one of the legislature's early attempts to utilize valuation methods based on current use rather than on market values that reflect the potential use and value of realty.

Because the general provisions of section 1 mandate a valuation system based on potential market value system, local assessors sometimes placed high values on single-family houses, allegedly forcing home owners out of possession. This section authorizes an alternative valuation method, a technique similar to that used in sections 8 and 10. It does not apply to duplexes or forms of housing other than owner occupied, or to many areas that have not been zoned in the most restricted categories, and it has been effectively surpassed by the broader benefits available under sections 1 and 2 of Article XIII A.

SECTION 10

Golf course valuation. Real property in a parcel of 10 or more acres which, on the lien date and for 2 or more years immediately preceding, has been used exclusively for nonprofit golf course purposes shall be assessed for taxation on the basis of such use, plus any value attributable to mines, quarries, hydrocarbon substances, or other minerals in the property or the right to extract hydrocarbons or other minerals from the property. [Nov. 5, 1974]

As with sections 8 and 9, this section provides for property tax assessment based on the current use value rather than market value of land. Golf courses were the first of the categories to receive protection as open space areas, surviving early litigation brought to challenge the validity of the use value concept and the fairness of the classification (*Stevens v. Watson*, 1971). As with other use value provisions, lower assessments may be available under section 2 of Article XIII A, essentially giving golf course operators the choice of the lower of the two values (*Los Angeles County v. Pope*, 1985).

SECTION 11

Taxation of local government real property. (a) Lands owned by a local government that are outside its boundaries, including rights to use or divert water from surface or underground sources and any other interests in lands, are taxable if (1) they are located in Inyo or Mono County and (a) they were assessed for taxation to the local government in Inyo County as of the 1966 lien date, or in Mono County as of the 1967 lien date, whether or not the assessment was valid when made, or (b) they were acquired by the local government subsequent to that lien date and were assessed to a prior owner as of that lien date and each lien date thereafter, or (2) they are located outside Inyo or Mono County and were taxable when acquired by the local government. Improvements owned by a local government that are outside its boundaries are taxable if they were taxable when acquired or were constructed by the local government to replace improvements which were taxable when acquired.

(b) Taxable land belonging to a local government and located in Inyo County shall be assessed in any year subsequent to 1968 at the place where it was assessed as of the 1966 lien date and in an amount derived by multiplying its 1966 assessed value by the ratio of the statewide per capita assessed value of land as of the last lien date prior to the current lien date to $766, using civilian population only. Taxable land belonging to a local government and located in Mono County shall be assessed in any year subsequent to 1968 at the place where it was assessed as of the 1967 lien date and in an amount determined by the preceding formula except that the 1967 lien date, the 1967 assessed value, and the figure $856 shall be used in the formula. Taxable land belonging to a local government and located outside of Inyo and Mono counties shall be assessed at the place where located and in an amount that does not exceed the lower of (1) its fair market value times the prevailing percentage of fair market value at which other lands are assessed and (2) a figure derived in the manner specified in this Section for land located in Mono County. If land acquired by a local government after the lien date of the base year specified in this section was assessed in the base year as part of a larger parcel, the assessed value of the part in the base year shall be that fraction of the assessed value of the larger parcel that the area of the part is of the area of the larger parcel.

If a local government divests itself of ownership of land without water rights and this land was assessed in Inyo County as of the 1966 lien date or in Mono County as of the 1967 lien date, that divestment shall not diminish the quantity of water rights assessable and taxable at the place where assessed as of that lien date.

(c) In the event the Legislature changes the prevailing percentage of fair market value at which land is assessed for taxation, there shall be used in the computations required by Section 11(b) of this Article, for the first year for which the new percentage is applicable, in lieu of the statewide per capita assessed value of land as of the last lien date prior to the current lien date, the statewide per capita assessed value of land on the prior lien date times the ratio of the new prevailing percentage of fair market value to the previous prevailing percentage.

(d) If, after March 1954, a taxable improvement is replaced while owned by and in possession of a local government, the replacement improvement shall be assessed, as long as it is owned by a local government, as other improvements are except that the assessed value shall not exceed the product of (1) the percentage at which privately owned improvements are assessed times (2) the highest full value ever used for taxation of the improvement that has been replaced. For purposes of this calculation, the full value for any year prior to 1967 shall be conclusively presumed to be 4 times the assessed value in that year.

(e) No tax, charge, assessment, or levy of any character, other than those taxes authorized by Sections 11(a) to 11(d), inclusive, of this Article, shall be imposed upon one local government by another local government that is based or calculated upon the consumption or use of water outside the boundaries of the government imposing it.

(f) Any taxable interest of any character, other than a lease for agricultural purposes and an interest of a local government, in any land owned by a local government that is subject to taxation pursuant to Section 11(a) of this Article shall be taxed in the same manner as other taxable interest. The aggregate value of all the interests subject to taxation pursuant to Section 11(a), however, shall not exceed the value of all interests in the land less the taxable value of the interest of any local government ascertained as provided in Sections 11(a) to 11(e), inclusive, of this Article.

(g) Any assessment made pursuant to Sections 11(a) to 11(d), inclusive, of this Article shall be subject to review, equalization, and adjustment by the State Board of Equalization, but an adjustment shall conform to the provisions of these Sections. [Nov. 5, 1974]

Many local governments own property outside their own borders and within the boundaries of another local government, such as land used for water supply systems, airports, or the extraterritorial provision of utility services (see Art. XI, sec. 9). Because property is to be assessed and taxed where it is located, those lands or improvements normally would be taxable by the local government in whose boundaries they are found. Section 3(b), however, exempts generally from taxation any property "owned by a local government." This section creates an exception to that traditional exemption by specifically permitting the taxation of property owned by a local government if it had been of a taxable nature when it was acquired. That rule is essentially a compromise, allowing local governments to retain preexisting taxing power rather than granting them an absolute power over parcels owned by another government. The retained power to tax will evaporate in the event the location of the land or improvement is later annexed to, and thus brought within the boundaries of, the owning government.

Section 11 was derived from amendments adopted in 1914 that were intended to protect the revenue-raising capacity of smaller counties, allowing them to tax property within their boundaries even though it was owned by large cities or other forms of government (*Pasadena v. Los Angeles County*, 1920; *City of San Francisco v. Alameda County*, 1936). That is particularly important in some of California's rural counties in which water rights have been acquired for export elsewhere; section 11(a) specifically includes water rights among aspects of landownership, thus preventing their loss from local tax rolls.

Subsections (b) and (c) establish specific rules for lands in Inyo and Mono counties, some of the major sources of water for the city of Los Angeles. Subsections (d), (e), and (f) establish specific formulas for valuation of those interests made taxable by this section.

Subsection (g) recognizes that disagreements that arise between the owningand taxing governments regarding assessments will have to be resolved by the State Board of Equalization (see sec. 16–18) (*City of San Francisco v. San Mateo County*, 1950).

SECTION 12

Unsecured property tax rate. (a) Except as provided in subdivision (b), taxes on personal property, possessory interests in land, and taxable improvements located on land exempt from taxation which are not a lien upon land sufficient in value to secure their payment shall be levied at the rates for the preceding tax year upon property of the same kind where the taxes were a lien upon land sufficient in value to secure their payment.

(b) In any year in which the assessment ratio is changed, the Legislature shall adjust the rate described in subdivision (a) to maintain equality between property on the secured and unsecured rolls. [Nov. 2, 1976]

A "secured roll" lists all property in a county for which the taxes are of an amount sufficient to make an effective lien on the property; an "unsecured" role exists as well. A tax rate is determined annually for the secure roll that can be expected to produce adequate revenue. Continuing a rule in effect since 1924, subsection (a) directs that property on the unsecured roll will be taxed at the prior year's secured rate. Distinctions between the tax rates are now largely obsolete under section 1 of Article XIII A.

Subsection (b) was intended to ensure that taxes on the unsecured roll would be fairly adjusted to reflect the prior year's rate whenever assessment ratios were changed, as described in section 3.5.

SECTION 13

Separate land and improvements assessment. Land and improvements shall be separately assessed. [Nov. 5, 1974]

This section, part of the original 1879 provisions, requires that land and the improvements on it be separately identified and assessed, but it does not affect the valuation method to be employed or require separate appraisals of value. The distinction was thought necessary to ensure that the assessments on each category could be identified and equalized adequately (see sec. 16 and 18).

SECTION 14

Tax situs. All property taxed by local government shall be assessed in the county, city, and district in which it is situated. [Nov. 5, 1974]

This section establishes the basic rule of tax situs, continued with little change from the 1879 Constitution. Although the rule would appear to be self-evident, its purpose is to prevent the imposition of a tax unless the property has a situs in the state and, secondarily, to prevent multiple taxation by specifying that any item of property has a single situs. The situs of real property is the county in which the property is located; the situs of tangible personal property is generally considered to be either the place where it is "permanently" located or the domicile of the owner. The problem raises numerous difficulties for items or goods in transit, such as aircraft or shipping containers, all of which are addressed by detailed statutory and administrative provisions.

SECTION 15

Disaster relief. The Legislature may authorize local government to provide for the assessment or reassessment of taxable property physically damaged or destroyed after the lien date to which the assessment or reassessment relates. [Nov. 5, 1974]

The lien date is the date on which taxes become a lien on property and operates generally as the date on which the value of personal property is determined. This section authorizes local agencies to provide tax relief when the property's value has been reduced by calamity or disaster after the lien date.

SECTION 16

County boards of equalization. The county board of supervisors, or one or more assessment appeals boards created by the county board of supervisors, shall constitute the county board of equalization for a county. Two or more county boards of supervisors may jointly create one or more assessment appeals boards which shall constitute the county board of equalization for each of the participating counties.

Except as provided in subdivision (g) of Section 11, the county board of equalization, under such rules of notice as the county board may prescribe, shall equalize the values of all property on the local assessment roll by adjusting individual assessments.

County boards of supervisors shall fix the compensation for members of assessment appeals boards, furnish clerical and other assistance for those boards, adopt rules of notice and procedures for those boards as may be required to facilitate their work and to insure uniformity in the processing and decision of equalization petitions, and may provide for their discontinuance.

The Legislature shall provide for: (a) the number and qualifications of members of assessment appeals boards, the manner of selecting, appointing, and removing them, and the terms for which they serve, and (b) the procedure by which two or more county boards of supervisors may jointly create one or more assessment appeals boards. [Nov. 5, 1974]

Sections 16 through 19 allocate local and state responsibilities for "equalization" of tax assessments. Section 16 establishes local boards for each of the counties in the state, and sections 17 through 19 describe the statewide powers of the State Board. It is the duty of the boards to review the evaluations made of property, and to provide review mechanisms for individual taxpayers.

Section 16 requires that each county has a board, comprised of either the supervisors themselves, or a separate assessment appeals board appointed by the supervisors under processes and qualifications established by statute. Each board is to "equalize the value of all property" in the county, except property owned by other governments, which is controlled by the State Board under the provisions of Section 11(g). Taxpayers may appeal to the boards, who have broad powers to raise or lower individual assessments in order to equalize the assessment role; the county board may not change the county's assessment role as an entirety, as that power is reserved to the state board.

SECTION 17

State board of equalization. The Board of Equalization consists of 5 voting members: the Controller and 4 members elected for 4-year terms at gubernatorial elections. The state shall be divided into four Board of Equalization districts with the voters of each district electing one member. No member may serve more than 2 terms. [Nov. 6, 1990]

The State Board of Equalization was created by the 1879 Constitution, replacing a board with somewhat different powers established earlier by statute. Section 17 carries forward the 1879 format, as amended in 1980 to clarify that the boundaries of the four districts must be set according to the reapportionment provisions of Article XXI. The two-term limitation was added in 1990 as part of the reforms of Proposition 140, which imposed precise term limits on many state officers. Salaries of board members are set by the Compensation Commission established in Article III, section 8. The board's duties are described under sections 18 and 19.

SECTION 18

Intercounty equalization. The Board shall measure county assessment levels annually and shall bring those levels into conformity by adjusting entire secured local assessment rolls. In the event a property tax is levied by the state, however, the effects of unequalized local assessment levels, to the extent any remain after such adjustments, shall be corrected for purposes of distributing this tax by equalizing the assessment levels of locally and state-assessed properties and varying the rate of the state tax inversely with the counties' respective assessment levels. [Nov. 5, 1974]

The primary function of the state board was to equalize on a statewide basis the assessment roles within each county, thus achieving intercounty equalization. However, as reflected in section 3.5, the causes of deviations among the counties have changed substantially due to the effect of sections 1 and 2 of Article XIII A, and the board's other duties, reflected in section 19, have become more prominent. Further, the potential of a new property tax levied by the state is severely reduced by the general prohibition on real property taxes contained in section 3 of Article XIII A.

SECTION 19

State assessment of utilities. The Board shall annually assess (1) pipelines, flumes, canals, ditches, and aqueducts lying within 2 or more counties and (2) property, except franchises, owned or used by regulated railway, telegraph, or telephone companies, car companies operating on railways in the State, and companies transmitting or selling gas or electricity. This property shall be subject to taxation to the same extent and in the same manner as other property.

No other tax or license charge may be imposed on these companies which differs from that imposed on mercantile, manufacturing, and other business corporations. This restriction does not release a utility company from payments agreed on or required by law for a special privilege or franchise granted by a government body.

The Legislature may authorize Board assessment of property owned or used by other public utilities.

The Board may delegate to a local assessor the duty to assess a property used but not owned by a state assessee on which the taxes are to be paid by a local assessee. [Nov. 5, 1974]

Privately owned utility properties, of the types listed in the first paragraph, frequently extend across many counties and cannot fairly be assessed by individual counties. Under amendments adopted in 1933, the value of utility properties is instead directly assessed by the state board, which operates as a "sole, central assessing agency," using uniform valuation procedures (*Southern California Telephone Co. v. County of Los Angeles*, 1941). Although those properties are assessed by the state, they pay the resulting taxes to local governments, as they are to be taxed to the same extent and in the same manner as other property. Section 19 does not require valuation on the same basis, or by the same procedures, as other property; the board employs complex valuation methods for utility properties, reflected by specific statutes and board rules. Those valuations and assessments are made annually, which makes the rollback and freeze provisions of Article XIII A inapplicable to utilities (*ITT World Communications v. City of San Francisco*, 1985).

The "no other tax" provision does not prohibit the use of traditional city license taxes or prohibit normal franchise fees of the type that might be levied under section 8 of Article XII.

The board's other duties include administration of the timber yield tax authorized by section 3(j) and oversight of the valuations and standards employed by local assessors and county boards of equalization.

SECTION 20

Maximum tax rates and bonding limits for local governments. The Legislature may provide maximum property tax rates and bonding limits for local governments. [Nov. 5, 1974]

Prior to 1972, most local governments had complete power to set their own tax rates; statutes enacted that year attempted to limit local rates in order to provide taxpayer relief. This section, adopted in 1974, clarifies the legislature's power to set limits on the tax and bonding rates utilized by local governments. That power was itself essentially superseded by the subsequent adoption in 1978 of Article XIII A, section 1, which imposed a 1 percent maximum rate statewide. More generally, the section continues to authorize various statutes that control the local setting of rates after establishment of budgets.

This section appears to include all local governments within its scope; it has not been tested to determine whether that includes all forms of cities and special districts, which are often treated separately elsewhere in the constitution; it appears to include school districts, as suggested by section 21.

SECTION 21

County levy of school district taxes. Within such limits as may be provided under Section 20 of this Article, the Legislature shall provide for an annual levy by county governing bodies of school district taxes sufficient to produce annual revenues for each district that the district's board determines are required for its schools and district functions. [Nov. 5, 1974]

This section is derived from an original portion of the 1879 Constitution's Article IX; it requires the legislature to ensure that county supervisors provide needed revenue for school districts, as part of the county's general authority to levy local taxes. The supervisors must set a tax rate sufficient to produce the revenue requested by the district in order to fund its annual budget (*San Francisco Community College District v. City and County of San Francisco*, 1976). The supervisors' tax power is not unrestricted but must be exercised within the limits established by section 20 and other applicable provisions of the constitution, such as the equal protection guarantees of Article I, section 7. In landmark litigation, the supreme court determined in 1976 that section 21 and other ele- ments of the public school financing system violated equal protection guarantees by making school revenues, and hence the quality of education, dependent on the varied availability of tax revenue within each school district (*Serrano v. Priest*, 1976). Complexities raised by that litigation and subsequent constitutional and statutory measures have yet to be resolved, including local funding of schools under Article XIII A, section 4, and state funding under Article XIV, section 8.5.

SECTION 22

State property tax limits. Not more than 25 percent of the total appropriations from all funds of the State shall be raised by means of taxes on real and personal property according to the value thereof. [Nov. 5, 1974]

Section 22 mandates that not more than 25 percent of the state's appropriations may come from property taxes. It thus ensures that property taxes will share the burden with other revenue sources, including the income taxes on individuals and corporations authorized by section 26, the corporate franchise tax authorized by section 27, and the insurance company taxes described in section 28. In fact, real property taxes are a primary source of revenue for *local* governments, and the *state's* revenues now depend primarily on the sales and personal income taxes.

SECTION 23

Taxation after state boundary change. If State boundaries change, the Legislature shall determine how property affected shall be taxed. [Nov. 5, 1974]

The state's boundaries are established in section 2 of Article III, as modified by statute. This section was adopted in 1956 as a cautionary response to the possibility of an alteration in boundaries. In 1980, the U.S. Supreme Court declined to change the boundary established years earlier, thus ending perhaps the last possibility of a major change (*California v. Nevada,* 1980).

SECTION 24

Taxes for local purposes. The Legislature may not impose taxes for local purposes but may authorize local governments to impose them.

Money appropriated from State funds to a local government for its local purposes may be used as provided by law.

Money subvened to a local government under Section 25 may be used for State or local purposes. [Nov. 5, 1974]

The first sentence of this section is unchanged from its original version in 1879, whose purpose was to prohibit legislative interference with local taxation and expenditures. It instead allows the legislature, by general laws, to authorize the local governments themselves to levy taxes for local purposes. It thus retains a close similarity to the policies underlying Article XI, section 11. The state remains free to levy local taxes for state or regional purposes (*People ex rel. Younger v. County of El Dorado,* 1971).

Except for the charter city home rule provisions of section 5 of Article XI, local governments generally do not have an inherent power to tax; that power must be specifically authorized by the legislature. This provision applies to all forms of taxes, including property and license taxes.

Under the second and third paragraphs of this section, where funds are derived from state rather than local taxes and are transferred to local governments for state purposes, the legislature remains able to direct the application of the funds (*Los Angeles v. Riley,* 1936).

SECTION 25

Reimbursement of local government for homeowners' tax exemptions. The Legislature shall provide, in the same fiscal year, reimbursements to each local government for revenue lost because of Section 3(k). [Nov. 5, 1974]

A program for home owners' property tax exemption was adopted in 1968. This section implements that program by requiring that payments be made by the state to local governments to reimburse them for the loss of tax revenues attributable to the home owners' exemption.

SECTION 26

Income tax. (a) Taxes on or measured by income may be imposed on persons, corporations, or other entities as prescribed by law.

(b) Interest on bonds issued by the State or a local government in the State is exempt from taxes on income.

(c) Income of a nonprofit educational institution of collegiate grade within the State of California is exempt from taxes on or measured by income if: (1) it is not unrelated business income as defined by the Legislature, and (2) it is used exclusively for educational purposes. [Nov. 5, 1974]

Subsection (a) forms the basis for the state's extensive personal income tax system, which has existed since 1935. A detailed statutory system establishes rules and procedures that closely resemble the federal income tax system; they apply to all state residents and to nonresidents to the extent those persons derive income from sources within the state (*McCulloch v. Franchise Tax Board*, 1964). A corporate income tax has been established on the income earned by those corporations that, although deriving income from sources within the state, do not "do business" there (compare sec. 27).

The section authorizes an income tax as prescribed by law; statutes explicitly restrict the power to the state government, but some uncertainty exists as to whether home rule charter cities, under section 5 of Article XI, might impose an income tax on their own authority (*Weekes v. City of Oakland*, 1978). Some local governments have experimented with other forms of local taxes that have a similar effect as an income tax (*A.B.C. Distributing Co., Inc. v. City of San Francisco*, 1975).

Bonds issued by the state or local governments are a form of intangible property that is constitutionally exempted from property taxation under section 3(c). Subsection (b) furthers the same policies by exempting the interest generated by those bonds from the income tax authorized by subsection (a).

Subsection (c) extends the general property tax exemption established in section 3(e) by establishing a tax-exempt status for the income of private colleges and universities, subject to the enumerated restrictions.

SECTION 27

Corporate franchise taxes. The Legislature, a majority of the membership of each house concurring, may tax corporations, including State and national banks, and their franchises by any method not prohibited by this Constitution or the Constitution or laws of the United States. Unless otherwise provided by the Legislature, the tax on State and national banks shall be according to or measured by their net income and shall be in lieu of all other taxes and license fees upon banks or their shares, except taxes upon real property and vehicle registration and license fees. [June 8, 1976]

Section 27, originally adopted in 1928, authorizes what is generally known as the "corporate franchise tax," which is imposed on corporations for the privilege of exercising their corporate franchise within the state. The tax is measured by the net income of entities that do business in California; the tax is applied to all general corporations, as well as to banks and financial institutions. In contrast, corporations that do not do business within California (and thus do not have a local franchise) but nevertheless derive income from sources within the state are taxed under a separate "corporate income tax" authorized by section 26. The bank and corporation franchise tax and the corporate income tax are designed to operate in a complementary fashion—one acting where the other does not.

What is now the Bank and Corporation Tax Law, administered by the Franchise Tax Board, was passed by the legislature in 1929; its complex statutory provisions provide for various exemptions and in many ways mirror the operation of the federal taxes on corporate income. The treatment of financial institutions as distinct from other corporations reflects the earlier federal immunity of nationally chartered banks, but since 1973, taxation of their property has been permitted by an express act of Congress. Thus, under current statutes, banks and most other financial institutions are taxed similarly. The taxes are imposed in lieu of other possible taxes, such as those on personal property, whether levied by state, county, or municipal government (*California Federal Savings and Loan Association v. City of Los Angeles*, 1991). The legislature thus preempted any local taxes on the activities of financial institutions, except taxes on their real property.

Both sections 27 and 28 were amended in 1976 to change the required legislative vote from two-thirds to the present majority, thus removing the special advantage previously enjoyed by those corporate interests.

SECTION 28

Taxation of insurance companies. (a) "Insurer," as used in this section, includes insurance companies or associations and reciprocal or interinsurance exchanges together with their corporate or other attorneys in fact considered as a single unit, and the State Compensation Insurance Fund. As used in this paragraph, "companies" includes persons, partnerships, joint stock associations, companies and corporations.

(b) An annual tax is hereby imposed on each insurer doing business in this state on the base, at the rates, and subject to the deductions from the tax hereinafter specified.

(c) In the case of an insurer not transacting title insurance in this state, the "basis of the annual tax" is, in respect to each year, the amount of gross premium, less return premiums, received in such year by such insurer upon its business done in this state, other than premiums received for reinsurance and for ocean marine insurance. In the case of an insurer transacting title insurance in this state, the "basis of the annual tax" is, in respect to each year, all income upon business done in this state, except:

(1) Interest and dividends.

(2) Rents from real property.

(3) Profits from the sale or other disposition of investments.

(4) Income from investments.

"Investments" as used in this subdivision includes property acquired by such insurer in the settlement or adjustment of claims against it but excludes investments in title plants and title records. Income derived directly or indirectly from the use of title plants and title records is included in the basis of the annual tax. In the case of an insurer transacting title insurance in this state which has a trust department and does a trust business under the banking laws of this state, there shall be excluded from the basis of the annual tax imposed by this section, the income of, and from the assets of, such trust department and such trust business, if such income is taxed by this state or included in the measure of any tax imposed by this state.

(d) The rate of the tax to be applied to the basis of the annual tax in respect to each year is 2.35 percent.

(e) [Deleted June 8, 1976].

(f) The tax imposed on insurers by this section is in lieu of all other taxes and licenses, state, county, and municipal, upon such insurers and their property, except:

(1) Taxes upon their real estate.

(2) That an insurer transacting title insurance in this state which has a trust department or does a trust business under the banking laws of this state is subject to taxation with respect to such trust department or trust business to the same extent and in the same manner as trust companies and the trust departments of banks doing business in this state.

(3) When by or pursuant to the laws of any other state or foreign country any taxes, licenses and other fees, in the aggregate, and any fines, penalties, deposit requirements or other material obligations, prohibitions or restrictions are or would be imposed upon California insurers, or upon the agents or representatives of such insurers, which are in excess of such taxes, licenses and other fees, in the aggregate, or which are in excess of the fines, penalties, deposit requirements or other obligations, prohibitions, or restrictions directly imposed upon similar insurers, or upon the agents or representatives of such insurers, of such other state or country under the statutes of this state; so long as such laws of such other state or country continues in force or are so applied, the same taxes, licenses and other

fees, in the aggregate, or fines, penalties or deposit requirements or other material obligations, prohibitions, or restrictions, of whatever kind shall be imposed upon the insurers, or upon the agents or representatives of such insurers, of such other state or country doing business or seeking to do business in California. Any tax, license or other fee or other obligation imposed by any city, county, or other political subdivision or agency of such other state or country on California insurers or their agents or representatives shall be deemed to be imposed by such state or country within the meaning of this paragraph (3) of subdivision (f). The provisions of this paragraph (3) of subdivision (f) shall not apply as to personal income taxes, nor as to ad valorem taxes on real or personal property nor as to special purpose obligations or assessments heretofore imposed by another state or foreign country in connection with particular kinds of insurance, other than property insurance; except that deductions, from premium taxes or other taxes otherwise payable, allowed on account of real estate or personal property taxes paid shall be taken into consideration in determining the propriety and extent of retaliatory action under this paragraph (3) of subdivision (f). For the purposes of this paragraph (3) of subdivision (f) the domicile of an alien insurer, other than insurers formed under the laws of Canada, shall be that state in which is located its principal place of business in the United States. In the case of an insurer formed under the laws of Canada or a province thereof, its domicile shall be deemed to be that province in which its head office is situated.

The provisions of this paragraph (3) of subdivision (f) shall also be applicable to reciprocals or interinsurance exchanges and fraternal benefit societies.

(4) The tax on ocean marine insurance.

(5) Motor vehicle and other vehicle registration license fees and any other tax or license fee imposed by the state upon vehicles, motor vehicles or the operation thereof.

(6) That each corporate or other attorney in fact of a reciprocal or interinsurance exchange shall be subject to all taxes imposed upon corporations or others doing business in the state, other than taxes on income derived from its principal business as attorney in fact. A corporate or other attorney in fact of each exchange shall annually compute the amount of tax that would be payable by it under prevailing law except for the provisions of this section, and any management fee due from each exchange to its corporate or other attorney in fact shall be reduced pro tanto by a sum equivalent to the amount so computed.

(g) Every insurer transacting the business of ocean marine insurance in this state shall annually pay to the state a tax measured by that proportion of the underwriting profit of such insurer from such insurance written in the United States, which the gross premiums of the insurer from such insurance written in this state bear to the gross premiums of the insurer from such insurance written within the United States, at the rate of 5 per centum, which tax shall be in lieu of all other taxes and licenses, state, county and municipal, upon such insurer, except taxes upon real estate, and such other taxes as may be assessed or levied against such insurer on account of any other class of insurance written by it. The Legislature shall define the terms "ocean marine insurance" and "underwriting profit," and shall provide for the assessment, levy, collection and enforcement of the ocean marine tax.

(h) The taxes provided for by this section shall be assessed by the State Board of Equalization.

(i) The Legislature, a majority of all the members elected to each of the two houses voting in favor thereof, may by law change the rate or rates of taxes herein imposed upon insurers.

(j) This section is not intended to and does not change the law as it has previously existed with respect to the meaning of the words "gross premiums, less return premiums, received" as used in this article. [June 8, 1976]

Section 28 creates a unique tax applicable only to insurance companies, administered by the State Board of Equalization, and exempting those companies from nearly all other state or local taxes.

This section was first adopted in 1942, and in highly detailed, technical language, it imposes a tax (in subsections (b) and (c)) measured usually by a company's gross premiums, which is the total cost of insurance coverage provided to insured parties. Separate provisions in subsections (c) and (g) establish different measuring standards for title and ocean marine insurance companies and create a retaliatory provision in subsection (f)(3) as to out-of-state companies whose states impose undue taxes on California companies (*Western and Southern Life Insurance Co. v. State Board of Equalization*, 1979). The legislature may set or change the rate of the tax by a simple majority vote (subsection (i)).

The broad tax exemption of subsection (f) protects insurance companies from normal taxes on personal property, the corporate franchise tax created by section 27, and the corporate income taxes of section 26. The application of local property taxes was retained in order to maintain those traditional revenues for local governments (*Mutual Life Insurance Co. of New York v. State Board of Equalization*, 1990).

SECTION 29

Local government tax sharing. The Legislature may authorize counties, cities and counties, and cities to enter into contracts to apportion between them the revenue derived from any sales or use tax imposed by them which is collected for them by the State. Before any such contract becomes operative, it shall be authorized by a majority of those voting on the question in each jurisdiction at a general or direct primary election. [Nov. 5, 1974]

California has had a sales and use tax since 1933, which produces revenue for the state and local governments. The State Board of Equalization administers and collects the tax on behalf of local governments, which depend on its revenue to help fund local services. When large shopping centers are introduced in an area, radical shifts in the retail sales patterns may occur, moving the resulting tax revenue from one local jurisdiction to another.

This section was adopted in 1968 as an exception to the general prohibition on the "gift" of public funds now in section 6 of Article XVI. It allows local governments, with the approval of their voters, to allocate and apportion the sales tax revenues among themselves by contract, thus preventing injurious competition or interlocal rivalries. Although statutes authorize the contracts, they are not widely employed.

SECTION 30

Tax liens and presumption of payment. Every tax shall be conclusively presumed to have been paid after 30 years from the time it became a lien unless the property subject to the lien has been sold in the manner provided by the Legislature for the payment of the tax. [Nov. 5, 1974]

Statutes provide that all taxes on realty and on most improvements become a lien against the land. Section 30, first adopted in 1932, essentially makes any liens expire automatically after thirty years, and the related taxes are then conclusively presumed to have been paid. An owner of land could redeem the property by payment of later liens, without being required to pay the taxes and interest prior to the thirty-year period.

SECTION 31

Unhindered power to tax. The power to tax may not be surrendered or suspended by grant or contract. [Nov. 5, 1974]

This section, only slightly revised from its original appearance in the 1879 Constitution, protects the taxing power as a vital, inherent power of government. Under sections 2, 3, and 4, exemptions or exceptions may be made by the constitution or by statute where authorized, but this section prohibits the state or local governments from relinquishing the power by deed or contract. Thus, deeds to realty cannot establish priorities for assessments that would impede state taxes (*Bolton v. Bella Terra Irrigation District*, 1930), but a city does not create a contractual exemption where it agrees to pay taxes on behalf of a favored lessee of city property (*Cane v. City and County of San Francisco*, 1978).

SECTION 32

Collection proceedings. No legal or equitable process shall issue in any proceeding in any court against this State or any officer thereof to prevent or enjoin the collection of any tax. After payment of a tax claimed to be illegal, an action may be maintained to recover the tax paid, with interest, in such manner as may be provided by the Legislature. [Nov. 5, 1974]

This section, sometimes called the anti-injunction provision, prohibits taxpayers from using legal or equitable procedures, such as declaratory judgments or injunctions, to restrain or inhibit the assessment or collection of taxes. The only legal avenue to resolve a tax dispute is to pay the tax and then contest it as appropriate, with the state to pay interest on any taxes wrongfully collected (*State Board of Equalization v. Superior Court*, 1985). The section incorporates a widely recognized policy allowing revenue collection to continue during litigation, in order to protect the collection processes and to prevent unnecessary interruption of governmental services dependent on revenue (*Pacific Gas and Electric Co., v. State Board of Equalization*, 1980). Some instances occur, however, in which an injunction may be appropriate to prevent an assessor from collecting improper or irrelevant information as the basis for further investigation (*Union Pacific Railroad Co. v. State Board of Equalization*, 1989).

SECTION 33

Mandate to legislature to implement. The Legislature shall pass all laws necessary to carry out the provisions of this article. [Nov. 5, 1974]

This provision, continued directly from the 1879 Constitution, empowers the legislature to enact whatever definitions or enforcement measures may be necessary to carry out the taxing powers established by this constitution.

Article XIIIA

Tax Limitation

This article was created in June 1978 by the passage of Proposition 13, a voters' tax revolt also known as the Jarvis–Gann initiative. The initiative sought primarily to reduce local real property taxes, which had risen dramatically in the years before its passage. Because those taxes were levied *ad valorem* ("according to the value") of realty, they rose in response to substantial increases in residential property values that had been fueled by inflation and speculative pressures. To the dismay of voters, many governments did not respond by lowering their tax rates but continued to tax as before, appearing unsympathetic to taxpayers' concerns. Although similar tax reform proposals had been defeated earlier, Proposition 13 was adopted in a wave of popularity, despite obvious ambiguities and inconsistencies in its wording. The general constitutionality of the article was confirmed by the supreme court only three months after its passage (*Amador Valley Joint Union High School District v. Board of Equalization*, 1978) and upheld by the U.S. Supreme Court in 1992 (*Nordlinger v. Hahn*).

SECTION 1

Maximum ad valorem tax on real property. (a) The maximum amount of any ad valorem tax on real property shall not exceed one percent (1%) of the full cash value

of such property. The one percent (1%) tax to be collected by the counties and apportioned according to law to the districts within the counties.
(b) The limitation provided for in subdivision (a) shall not apply to ad valorem taxes or special assessments to pay the interest and redemption charges on (1) any indebtedness approved by the voters prior to July 1, 1978, or (2) any bonded indebtedness for the acquisition or improvement of real property approved on or after July 1, 1978, by two-thirds of the votes cast by the voters voting on the proposition. [June 3, 1986]

Maximum Tax Rate

The primary effect of section 1 was to reduce the maximum tax rate on real property to 1 percent of the property's full cash value. Formerly, each local government with taxing power determined its own tax rate, but because the new maximum restricted the cumulative amount levied by all local governments, it represented a substantial reduction in the taxes imposed on most landowners.

Each county tax collector levies and collects taxes on behalf of all the local governments within that county. Because the proposition did not suggest how local governments were to split the 1 percent sum, the legislature immediately directed the proportional allocation of collected revenues among those local governments that had levied property taxes the previous year.[58] For most governments, the allocations represented a severe loss of revenue.

"Full Cash Value"

California traditionally utilized an ad valorem taxation system, taxing realty by applying a property tax rate to its current "assessed value." Proposition 13 changed the relevant term to "full cash value," as further defined in section 2, thereby eliminating the former practice of using assessed values that were distinct from market values—the difference between the two had produced assessment ratios whose variations required constant adjustment.

Payments on "Bonded Indebtedness"

As first adopted, section 1's limitation on ad valorem tax rates could be exceeded only to pay off certain indebtedness. Local indebtedness might include various forms of obligations, such as water delivery contracts (*Goodman v. Riverside County*, 1983) or charter provisions requiring contributions to an employee retirement system (*City of Fresno v. Superior Court*, 1984) but only if those debts

[58] See now California Revenue & Taxation Code Sections 93, 95–100 (Deering's 1992).

had been approved by the voters prior to the article's effective date of July 1, 1978 (*Carman v. Alvord*, 1982; *Patton v. Alameda*, 1985).

Local government indebtedness usually took the form of general obligation bonds, the most common and least expensive form of long-term debt used by governments. By prohibiting any creation of indebtedness after 1978, Proposition 13 thus forced cities to use more expensive methods to raise needed funds. In 1986, the passage of Proposition 46 added the phrase after subsection (b)(2), thus allowing local governments to resume the issuance of general obligation bonds and to levy taxes above the 1 percent limit as needed to pay for them. The amendment, which was unopposed, was considered consistent with the purposes of proposition 13, since a two-thirds vote to approve bonds and thereby raise taxes kept decision-making authority over local financial issues within the control of local taxpayers.

SECTION 2

Valuation of real property. (a) The full cash value means the county assessor's valuation of real property as shown on the 1975–76 tax bill under "full cash value" or, thereafter, the appraised value of real property when purchased, newly constructed, or a change in ownership has occurred after the 1975 assessment. All real property not already assessed up to the 1975–76 full cash value may be reassessed to reflect the valuation. For purposes of this section, "newly constructed" does not include real property which is reconstructed after a disaster, as declared by the Governor, where the fair market value of the real property, as reconstructed, is comparable to its fair market value prior to the disaster. Also, the term "newly constructed" shall not include the portion of reconstruction or improvement to a structure, constructed of unreinforced masonry bearing wall construction, necessary to comply with any local ordinance relating to seismic safety during the first 15 years following that reconstruction or improvement.

However, the Legislature may provide that under appropriate circumstances and pursuant to definitions and procedures established by the Legislature, any person over the age of 55 years who resides in property which is eligible for the homeowner's exemption under subdivision (k) of Section 3 of Article XIII and any implementing legislation may transfer the base year value of the property entitled to exemption, with the adjustments authorized by subdivision (b), to any replacement dwelling of equal or lesser value located within the same county and purchased or newly constructed by that person as his or her principal residence within two years of the sale of the original property. For purposes of this section, "any person over the age of 55 years" includes a married couple one member of which is over the age of 55 years. For purposes of this section, "replacement dwelling" means a building, structure, or other shelter constituting a place of abode, whether real property or personal property, and any land on which it may be situated. For purposes of this section a two-dwelling unit shall be considered as two separate single-family dwellings. This paragraph shall apply to any replacement dwelling which was purchased or newly constructed on or after November 5, 1986.

In addition, the Legislature may authorize each county board of supervisors, after consultation with the local affected agencies within the county's boundaries, to adopt an ordinance making the provisions of this subdivision relating to transfer of base year value also applicable to situations in which the replacement dwellings are located in that county and the original properties are located in another county within this state. For purposes of this paragraph, "local affected agency" means any city, special district, school district, or community college district which receives an annual property tax revenue allocation. This paragraph shall apply to any replacement dwelling which was purchased or newly constructed on or after the date the county adopted the provisions of this subdivision relating to transfer of base year value, but shall not apply to any replacement dwelling which was purchased or newly constructed before November 9, 1988. The Legislature may extend the provisions of this subdivision relating to the transfer of base year values from original properties to replacement dwellings of homeowners over the age of 55 years to severely disabled homeowners, but only with respect to those replacement dwellings purchased or newly constructed on or after the effective date of this paragraph.

(b) The full cash value base may reflect from year to year the inflationary rate not to exceed 2 percent for any given year or reduction as shown in the consumer price index or comparable data for the area under taxing jurisdiction, or may be reduced to reflect substantial damage, destruction or other factors causing a decline in value.

(c) For purposes of subdivision (a), the Legislature may provide that the term "newly constructed" shall not include any of the following:

(1) The construction or addition of any active solar energy system.

(2) The construction or installation of any fire sprinkler system, other fire extinguishing system, fire detection system, or fire-related egress improvement, as defined by the Legislature, which is constructed or installed after the effective date of this paragraph.

(3) The construction, installation, or modification on or after the effective date of this paragraph of any portion or structural component of a single or multiple family dwelling which is eligible for the homeowner's exemption if the construction, installation, or modification is for the purpose of making the dwelling more accessible to severely disabled person.

(4) The construction or installation of seismic retrofitting improvements or improvements utilizing earthquake hazard mitigation technologies, which are constructed or installed in existing buildings after the effective date of this paragraph. The Legislature shall define eligible improvements. This exclusion does not apply to seismic safety reconstruction or improvements which

qualify for exclusion pursuant to the last sentence of the first paragraph of subdivision (a).

(d) For purposes of this section, the term "change in ownership" shall not include the acquisition of real property as a replacement for comparable property if the person acquiring the real property has been displaced from the property replaced by eminent domain proceedings, by acquisition by a public entity, or governmental action which has resulted in a judgment of inverse condemnation. The real property acquired shall be deemed comparable to the property replaced if it is similar in size, utility, and function, or if it conforms to state regulations defined by the Legislature governing the relocation of persons displaced by governmental actions. The provisions of this subdivision shall be applied to any property acquired after March 1, 1975, but shall affect only those assessments of that property which occur after the provisions of this subdivision take effect.

(e) Notwithstanding any other provision of this section, the Legislature shall provide that the base-year value of property which is substantially damaged or destroyed by a disaster, as declared by the Governor, may be transferred to comparable property, within the same county, that is acquired or newly constructed as a replacement for the substantially damaged or destroyed property. This subdivision shall apply to any comparable replacement property acquired or newly constructed on or after July 1, 1985, and to the determination of base-year values for the 1985-86 fiscal year and fiscal years thereafter.

(f) For the purposes of subdivision (e):

(1) Property is substantially damaged or destroyed if it sustains physical damage amounting to more than 50 percent of its value immediately before the disaster. Damage includes a diminution in the value of property as a result of restricted access caused by the disaster.

(2) Replacement property is comparable to the property substantially damaged or destroyed if it is similar in size, utility, and function to the property which it replaces, and if the fair market value of the acquired property is comparable to the fair market value of the replaced property prior to the disaster.

(g) For purposes of subdivision (a), the term "purchased" and "change in ownership" shall not include the purchase or transfer of real property between spouses since March 1, 1975, including, but not limited to, all of the following:

(1) Transfers to a trustee for the beneficial use of a spouse, or the surviving spouse of a deceased transferor, or by a trustee of such a trust to the spouse of the trustor.

(2) Transfers to a spouse which take effect upon the death of a spouse.

(3) Transfers to a spouse or former spouse in connection with a property settlement agreement or decree of dissolution of a marriage or legal separation.

(4) The creation, transfer, or termination, solely between spouses, of any coowner's interest.

(5) The distribution of a legal entity's property to a spouse or former spouse in exchange for the interest of the spouse in the legal entity in connection with a

property settlement agreement or a decree of dissolution of a marriage or legal separation.

(h) For purposes of subdivision (a), the terms "purchased" and "change of ownership" shall not include the purchase or transfer of the principal residence of the transferor in the case of a purchase or transfer between parents and their children, as defined by the Legislature, and the purchase or transfer of the first $1,000,000 of the full cash value of all other real property between parents and their children, as defined by the Legislature. This subdivision shall apply to both voluntary transfers and transfers resulting from a court order to judicial decree.

(i) Unless specifically provided otherwise, amendments to this section adopted prior to November 1, 1988, shall be effective for changes in ownership which occur, and new construction which is completed, after the effective date of the amendment. Unless specifically provided otherwise, amendments to this section adopted after November 1, 1988, shall be effective for changes in ownership which occur, and new construction which is completed, on or after the effective date of the amendment. [Nov. 7, 1990]

As first adopted in 1978, section 2 was brief and to the point, containing essentially the first two sentences of subsection 2(a) as they appear above and most of what is now subsection 2(b). The remainder of the current section 2 was added in a series of amendments that will further reduce government revenues. Many of those changes are highly technical in nature and are grouped together below by general topic.

Rollback to 1975–1976 Tax Bill

A central feature of Proposition 13 was the rollback of assessed values of realty. Adopted in 1978, the first sentence of section 2(a) retroactively returned assessments to the lower values that had been used in the 1975–1976 tax period. By itself, that feature would have reduced taxes, but it accomplished even greater reductions when combined with the 1 percent rate limit established by section 1. The 1975–1976 values represented the "base year" valuation applicable to most realty in the state; values, and thus taxes, were frozen at those levels, subject to an increase under section 2(b) of no more than 2 percent a year to reflect inflation and further subject to reappraisal caused by later changes of ownership.

Property reassessments formerly had occurred periodically, with all parcels eventually being reassessed. Under the new system, revaluations occur only for certain classes of taxpayers, allowing others to remain free from reassessment and thereby enjoy lower taxes. This occurs through retention of the 1975–1976 base year value, which has become an important goal for any taxpayer; that phenomenon explains much of the subsequent litigation and constitutional exemptions.

"Newly Constructed"

Section 2(a) provides that the "full cash value" (the base year values plus 2 percent increments) must be replaced by "appraised value" whenever realty is "purchased, newly constructed, or a change in ownership has occurred" after 1975. Normal additions and renovations to realty therefore would require a reassessment to the newly improved value. Only five months after Proposition 13 was passed, the first of its amendments exempted from reappraisal real property erty that had been affected by a disaster; thus, the third sentence of subsection (a) allows replacement of realty damaged in large-scale disasters, and the second sentence of subsection 2(b) allows reappraisal of property whose value has declined because of substantial damage. Both changes were made to prevent "unfair" results, to "insure equal treatment," and "to prevent additional tax burdens from falling on those who have suffered major property losses."[59]

Other exemptions to "newly constructed" were adopted in succeeding years for the addition of fire sprinklers, seismic safety renovations, and seismic retrofits. Those changes, which appear in sections 2(c)(2), the last sentence of the first paragraph of section 2(a), and section 2(c)(4), were intended to provide an incentive to property owners to increase the safety of their buildings. Although some loss in property tax revenue would result in each situation, the gain in public safety represented a strong public policy rationale for the exemptions.

The provisions in section 2(c)(3), exempting from "new construction" any structural changes for severely disabled persons, were added in 1990, as were the provisions of section 2(a) regarding transfers of base year values of dwellings of severely disabled home owners. Although those amendments would reduce real property tax revenues, they reflected a conscious decision to provide tax relief to the severely disabled and thereby allow those persons to modify or move their dwellings without suffering increased tax liability.[60]

"Purchase" or "Change in Ownership"

Section 2 originally provided for reappraisal whenever realty was purchased or upon any other "change in ownership." It was expected that realty automatically would be reappraised as it was sold, thus resulting eventually in a gradual reappraisal of most real property, but other forms of ownership change, such as inheritance or change in business organizations, were not addressed by the original Proposition 13. It was foreseen that reappraisals might occur more frequently for residential property than for commercial or industrial realty, which might be expected to change ownership less frequently. Those assumptions, however, have been substantially changed by later amendments.

---

[59] California Voters Pamphlet, General Election of Nov. 7, 1978, p. 37.

[60] California Ballot Pamphlet, Primary Election June 5, 1990, p. 17.

The first major exception to "change of ownership" occurred in 1982; section 2(d) now exempts from reappraisal property owners who were involuntarily forced by government action to undergo a change in ownership. That exemption extends the base year valuation by applying it to realty acquired in subsequent years, generally at a higher market value. A similar "involuntary change" exemption was passed in 1986, adding subsections (e) and (f), allowing the base year values to be transferred to properties that replaced realty damaged or destroyed in an officially declared disaster.

Much more important exemptions were passed in a series of amendments adopted in 1986 and 1988. The first of those, Proposition 58, allowed base year values to be transferred between family members. The provisions of section 2(g), (h), and (i) operate to prevent reassessment in the case of transfers of realty between parents and their children or between spouses, although such transfers would otherwise constitute changes of ownership. As between spouses, Proposition 58 merely reflected preexisting statutory law, but the provisions regarding transfers to children were a new concept and were expected to reduce property tax revenues substantially. Such transfers would include essentially any form of transfer between parent and child, subject to certain monetary exemptions. Thus, although inheritance of real property is certainly a change of ownership, it is exempted from reappraisal when it involves transfers from parents to children that occurred after the effective date of Proposition 58 (*Larson v. Duca*, 1989).

The second major exemption to change of ownership was accomplished by Propositions 60 and 90 in 1986 and 1988. Section 2(a), in the paragraphs beginning "However," and "In addition," allows most of the senior citizens in the state to transfer the assessed value of their former homes to a replacement home. Those measures were designed to protect older home owners from the property tax increases that would result from reappraisals when they sold their home with the intent of moving to a different structure. Although such a move is certainly a change of ownership of the type apparently contemplated by Proposition 13, these provisions overtly exempt qualified persons from the increased property taxes they would otherwise pay, with a consequential loss of tax revenue to many local governments. Their former homes, of course, would be reappraised and subjected to higher taxes when acquired by new owners.

Both provisions are subject to detailed statutory implementation by the legislature, and, in the case of replacement homes located in a different county, implementation is also subject to that county's agreement to participate. Because of the impact on county tax revenues, many counties have declined to participate.

Base Year or Acquisition Price versus Current Market Value

The base year values of 1975–1976 are advantageous for many landowners. Those persons whose lands have subsequently increased in value, under the purchase, new construction, or change of ownership provisions described above, will have an assessed valuation established by that more recent event; the supreme court characterized that new value as one based on "date of acquisition" (*Amador Valley Joint Union High School District v. Board of Equalization*, 1978). The inevitable result of the divergent valuation systems is that owners of essentially identical parcels of realty may be assessed, and taxed, in different amounts—one based on a 1975–1976 base year and the other on a more recent market acquisition price. If the time interval between valuation dates is long, the differences in taxation may be substantial. Repeated attacks have been mounted against Article XIII A based on that apparent discrepancy, usually on the theory that such discrepancies are a violation of principles of equal protection, or rights of interstate travel, but the California courts have consistently upheld the acquisition value system as a legitimate basis for placing taxpayers into classifications that are based on the value of property when it was purchased rather than its increased value in later years (*Northwest Financial, Inc. v. State Board of Equalization*, 1991). That approach was accepted by the U.S. Supreme Court in 1992 (*Nordlinger v. Hahn*).

SECTION 3

Vote requirement for changes in state taxes. From and after the effective date of this article, any changes in State taxes enacted for the purpose of increasing revenues collected pursuant thereto whether by increased rates or changes in methods of computation must be imposed by an Act passed by not less than two-thirds of all members elected to each of the two houses of the Legislature, except that no new ad valorem taxes on real property, or sales or transaction taxes on the sales of real property may be imposed. [June 6, 1978]

This is the only section of Article XIII A that directly affects state government or its general power of taxation. Prior to the adoption of Proposition 13, state taxes usually could be created or increased by a majority vote of both houses of the legislature and approval of the governor. This provision raised the required margin to a two-thirds legislative vote for all general tax increases and prohibits entirely any new taxes on real property transactions or ad valorem taxes on realty itself.

Although section 3 imposes restrictions on the ability of the legislature to enact tax increases, it has no effect on tax measures or increases that are proposed and adopted by a citizens' initiative. The voters therefore can adopt a statewide tax using their powers of initiative reserved in section 1 of Article IV, without being limited by this section (*Kennedy Wholesale, Inc. v. State Board of Equalization*, 1991). Moreover, the two-thirds vote requirement of section 3 is inapplicable because section 10 of Article II requires only a majority approval of initiative measures.

SECTION 4

Imposition of special taxes. Cities, Counties and special districts, by a two-thirds vote of the qualified electors of such district, may impose special taxes on such district, except ad valorem taxes on real property or a transaction tax or sales tax on the sale of real property within such City, County or special district. [June 6, 1978]

Although it is phrased in permissive terms, section 4 was intended to *restrict* the ability of local governments to pass new "special taxes" unless they were authorized by at least a two-thirds vote of the local electorate. Because a two-thirds (supermajority) vote is considered very difficult to obtain, the provision effectively restricts the use of local tax powers, thus limiting the ability of local governments to replace property tax revenues that would be lost due to the effect of sections 1 and 2. However, the definition of both "special taxes" and "special districts" was not provided by Proposition 13 and subsequently has been variously developed by the legislature and the courts.

Supermajority Voting Requirement

The requirement of a two-thirds affirmative vote was originally attacked as a violation of democratic majoritarian principles since it allows a small group's negative vote to prevent the adoption of a tax favored by a majority of the voters. Nevertheless, two-thirds requirements have been upheld generally and, while difficult to obtain, did not invalidate the proposition (*Amador Valley Joint Union High School District v. State Board of Equalization,* 1978). The "fundamentally undemocratic" nature of the two-thirds requirement sometimes has been used as a reason to construe section 4 narrowly (*Los Angeles County Transportation Commission v. Richmond,* 1982).

Definition of "Special Taxes": Nontax Revenue Sources

An immediate effect of section 4 was to force local governments to seek out sources of revenue other than taxation to fund their local services. The legislature specifically encouraged special districts to utilize user charges and fees to replace the tax revenues eliminated by sections 1 and 2 of Proposition 13.[61] Consequently, there has been tremendous expansion in local governments' utilization of regulatory fees, user charges, special assessments, and similar cost-recovery devices, thus radically altering the mix of revenue sources used by local governments.

---

[61] Calif. Government Code sec. 16270 (Deering's 1992).

The term *special taxes* does not include conventional special assessments, which are widely used to recover the costs of making traditional public improvements that directly benefit particular real property (*Fresno County v. Malmstrom,* 1979; *City Council of San Jose v. South,* 1983). Moreover, the concept of special assessments has been expanded to include payments for diverse public improvements that benefit the public at large (*J. W. Jones Cos. v. City of San Diego,* 1984). Another major category of revenue devices excluded from special taxes is regulatory fees, which are charges levied by governments to recover the direct costs of imposing police power regulation on private activities or to offset increased demand on government facilities caused by private parties. Those fees include such devices as land use regulatory measures (*Trent Meredith, Inc. v. Oxnard,* 1981), urban transit impact fees (*Russ Building Partnership v. San Francisco,* 1987), air pollution control permit fees (*San Diego Gas & Electric Co. v. San Diego County Air Pollution Control District,* 1988), and a variety of similar measures. User charges are another form of cost-recovery device, representing charges for services that are provided directly to a consumer, such as garbage collection charges.

Regardless of the name of the charges, however, where their amount as actually levied exceeds the reasonable costs of providing the service or benefit, the excess amounts are viewed as the equivalent of taxes levied to raise general revenue and are then included within the special taxes regulated by this section (*Beaumont Investors v. Beaumont–Cherry Valley Water District,* 1985). That concept was subsequently adopted by the closely related section 8(c) of Article XIII B and in statutory provisions[62] and has served to maintain tight standards governing the use of charges and fees.

Definition of "Special Taxes": Determined by Use of the Revenues

In 1982 the supreme court narrowed the scope of section 4 by holding that when the revenue from a tax went exclusively to a city's general fund accounts, it would not be considered "special"; "special taxes" would instead be interpreted to mean those that are levied and designated for a specific purpose (*City and County of San Francisco v. Farrell,* 1982). Although apparently applicable to cities and counties that have a multitude of governmental functions to be paid for by their general funds, the special tax exemption was later declared inappropriate for those local governments, such as special districts, that collect tax revenues only for specific, narrow, or limited governmental purposes and whose general fund is applied only to those limited purposes (*Rider v. County of San Diego,* 1991). Consequently, all specific-purpose tax levies will continue to require a two-thirds supermajority approval.

[62] Calif. Government Code sec. 50076 (Deering's 1992).

An early supreme court definition of "special taxes" suggested that the term should not include taxes, such as those on retail sales, that are not levied against real property, since an apparent purpose of Proposition 13 had been to protect real property from further tax impacts (*Los Angeles County Transportation Commission v. Richmond*, 1982). That position was abandoned when it became apparent that the legislature had frequently authorized local governments to levy nonproperty taxes specifically to replace property tax revenues lost under the general provisions of Proposition 13, thus defeating the larger intent of the original proposition (*Rider v. County of San Diego*, 1991).

In 1986 the voters attempted to reinforce the strictures of section 4 by the adoption of Proposition 62. That initiative imposed new statutory sections (rather than making amendments to the constitution) that required local voter approval for all new taxes imposed for general purposes.[63] Its constitutionality remains in substantial doubt, as it appears to conflict variously with the powers of charter cities under Article XI, section 5, with a local government's general authorization to levy taxes contained in section 24 of Article XIII, and the general exemption of tax levies from referenda under sections 9 and 11 of Article II. The measure has received varied responses from the courts (*City of Westminster v. County ofOrange*, 1988; *California Building Industry Association v. Governing Body of the Newhall School District*, 1988; *Woodlake v. Logan*, 1991; *Rider v. County of San Diego*, 1991).

The power of a local government to levy special taxes usually requires specific statutory authorization; accordingly, the legislature has complied with the policy of section 4 by authorizing cities, counties, districts,[64] school districts,[65] and various other local governments to propose special taxes to take effect upon a two-thirds vote of the local electorate (*Heckendorn v. City of San Marino*, 1986; *California Building Industry Association v. Governing Board of the Newhall School District*, 1988).

Definition of "Special District"

Special districts are traditionally created to perform particular activities different from those of general purpose local governments such as cities and counties or to operate within different jurisdictional boundaries. Often they are formed as a redundant overlay of other governments, frequently to avoid various fiscal restraints (see, e.g., Art. XVI, sec. 18). Recently the supreme court has held that where special districts appear to have been created primarily for the purpose of levying taxes that would replace revenues otherwise lost to the general governments because of Proposition 13, those districts must be included within the

---

[63] Calif. Government Code sec. 53720–30 (Deering's 1992).

[64] Calif. Government Code sec. 50075, and see, e.g., sec. 53978 (Deering's 1992).

[65] Calif. Government Code sec. 50079 (Deering's 1992).

scope of section 4 and are subject to its two-thirds vote requirement (*Rider v. County of San Diego*, 1991). That decision is expected to have severe implications for many special districts, but other districts have been especially designed to accommodate section 4, and they levy special taxes to pay for particular public facilities only after receiving a two-thirds vote of the local electorate.[66]

Real Property Transaction or Sales Taxes

Although new sales or transaction taxes on the sale of real property are prohibited by section 4, where such taxes predated Proposition 13 they may continue in existence, and newly incorporated cities may share in the allocation of tax revenue to the same extent as other cities in a county (*Cathedral City v. County of Riverside*, 1985).

SECTION 5

Effective date. This article shall take effect for the tax year beginning on July 1 following the passage of this Amendment, except Section 3 which shall become effective upon the passage of this article. [June 6, 1978]

Amendments to the constitution accomplished by initiative generally become effective the day after the election (see sec. 4 of Art. XVIII). This section instead postponed the effective date of all but section 3 of the article by about three weeks, to July 1, 1978, the start of the next fiscal year. During the intervening period, several cities took the opportunity to enact new tax measures without a two-thirds approval and thereby legally avoided the prohibition of section 4 (*National Independent Business Alliance v. City of Beverly Hills*, 1982). In contrast, section 3, restricting the imposition of state taxes by the legislature, became effective immediately.

SECTION 6

Severability. If any section, part, clause, or phrase hereof is for any reason held to be invalid or unconstitutional, the remaining sections shall not be affected but will remain in full force and effect. [June 6, 1978]

This is a traditional severance clause, indicating the drafters' intention that the remainder of the article should continue in effect in the event some portion of it is invalidated by judicial action.

---

[66] See, e.g., Mello-Roos Community Facilities Act of 1982, Calif. Government Code sec. 53312–39.9 (Deering's 1992).

Article XIIIB

Government Spending Limitation

Article XIII B, adopted by the voters in 1979, was widely known as the Gann initiative, named after its primary author and sponsor. It was also called the Spirit of 13 initiative, reflecting its close relationship to the government limitation philosophy of Proposition 13 (which had become Article XIII A the previous year). It was proposed primarily as a means of limiting the rate of growth of "state and local government spending." It was incidentally intended to "close loopholes" that had been discovered in Proposition 13, curb government waste and user fees, and refund excess state tax funds to the taxpayers.[67] As such, it has become the subject of extremely contentious political maneuvering among the legislature, taxpayer groups, local governments, and a school financing reform movement.

For the first six years after its adoption, the spending limitations created by the article had little actual effect on the state or local governments, since various economic factors operated to keep government expenditures below the limits created by the article. By the 1986–1987 fiscal year, however, the gap between the limit and government revenues had narrowed, and the limit threatened to

[67] California Ballot Pamphlet, Special Election of Nov. 6, 1979, arguments in favor of Proposition 4, p. 18.

become an effective restraint on government appropriations.[68] But at that juncture, several other factors became important.

The potential impact of Article XIII B had been recognized as an opportunity by other citizens who were interested in reform of education at grade levels kindergarten through 12. As first adopted, the article had required the state government to refund excess tax revenues to the citizenry; advocates of education opposed refunds of revenue as long as schools allegedly remained inadequately funded. In 1988, they successfully urged the adoption of Proposition 98, which amended the article to require that "excess" funds be used to establish a minimum guaranteed level of funding for public schools.

Neither the original government limitation nor the school funding goals will ever be realized, however, because amendments proposed by the legislature and adopted in 1990 substantially reduced the article's impact on the budget processes of both state and local governments. Those changes were included in Proposition 111, the Traffic Congestion Relief and Spending Limitation Act of 1990, whose announced purpose was to change the spending limit in order to permit certain highway and mass transit expenditures to be made. The amendments not only made possible various expenditures for transportation but fundamentally altered the effect of the limitation on the entire state budget. As amended, the article is not expected to serve as an effective restraint on general state expenditures until "sometime during the first half of the 21st century."[69] The same 1990 amendments substantially reduced the size of the recently added guarantee of funding for schools.

Although its impact on expenditures by the state was blunted by the 1990 amendments, the article will apparently continue to limit the appropriations of local governments, which are expansively defined in section 8(d) to include effectively all forms of local government in the state. As a result, several of the sections will have a merely theoretical impact on state financing and should be analyzed instead in terms of the revenue, budgeting, and expenditure activities of local governments.

A distinct feature of the article eventually may prove to have constitutional implications that overshadow the importance of spending limits, refunds, or education budgets. Section 6 will have a major impact on the decision as to whether particular government services will continue to be performed, and paid for, by the state rather than by local levels of government. As such, it will restrain the legislature's attempts to force local governments to absorb the financial burden of new programs or other expenditures that are made necessary by state legislative action.

---

[68] California Commission on State Finance, Annual Long Term General Fund Forecast (Spring 1986), p. 7.

[69] California Commission on State Finance, Long Term General Fund Forecast (Fall 1990), p. 78.

SECTION 1

Annual appropriations limitation. The total annual appropriations subject to limitation of the state and of each local government shall not exceed the appropriations limit of the entity of government for the prior year adjusted for the change in the cost of living and the change in population, except as otherwise provided in this article. [June 5, 1990]

This section is essentially the same as when adopted in 1979, with only minor phrasing changes made in 1990. It restricts the amount of tax revenues a government entity may spend each year by limiting its appropriations, which are simply authorizations to expend funds. Previously, the constitution had placed no limits on state or local government expenditures, so long as sufficient revenues were available (compare Art. XVI, sec. 18). Section 1 creates for each governmental unit a sum termed the "appropriations subject to limitation," defined in great detail in section 8(a). That sum includes only appropriations resulting from tax revenues and does not prevent growth in appropriations that are financed from nontax revenue sources, such as bonds, grants received from the federal government, or reasonable user fees.

The primary purpose of section 1 is to restrain the growth of government expenditures by limiting each government to the same base amount of appropriations as it made in the preceding year, with adjustments made for changes in the cost of living and population (thus allowing increases in the limits to reflect inflation and population growth). It was the highly technical amendments made in 1990 to the definitions of "change in the cost of living" and "change in population," contained in sections 8(e) and (f), that affected the actual computation of the limit applicable to state government, making it far less likely that the limit would become a binding constraint on state spending. Those same changes have also given local governments slightly more flexibility in their calculation and adjustment of their respective appropriations limits. They are discussed further under section 8.

SECTION 1.5

Audit of annual appropriations limit. The annual calculation of the appropriations limit under this article for each entity of local government shall be reviewed as part of an annual financial audit. [June 5, 1990]

This section, added in 1990, inserted a new requirement that each government's annual calculation of its appropriations limit be subjected to a financial audit. That annual review will consider the adjustments made to the limit from one fiscal year to the next, determine whether the optional calculation methods in subsections (e) and (f) were properly selected, and generally review the accuracy of the documentation and the computations.

SECTION 2

Revenues in excess of limitation. (a) (1) Fifty percent of all revenues received by the state in a fiscal year and in the fiscal year immediately following it in excess of the amount which may be appropriated by the state in compliance with this article during that fiscal year and the fiscal year immediately following it shall be transferred and allocated, from a fund established for that purpose, pursuant to Section 8.5 of Article XVI.

(2) Fifty percent of all revenues received by the state in a fiscal year and in the fiscal year immediately following it in excess of the amount which may be appropriated by the state in compliance with this article during that fiscal year and the fiscal year immediately following it shall be returned by a revision of tax rates or fee schedules within the next two subsequent fiscal years.

(b) All revenues received by an entity of government, other than the state, in a fiscal year and in the fiscal year immediately following it in excess of the amount which may be appropriated by the entity in compliance with this article during that fiscal year and the fiscal year immediately following it shall be returned by a revision of tax rates or fee schedules within the next two subsequent fiscal years. [June 5, 1990]

As originally designed, section 2 of the Gann initiative was a single sentence, providing simply that any "excess revenues" that a government might receive had to be returned to taxpayers, essentially by adjusting the "tax rates or fee schedules" in subsequent years; in fact, cash refunds were made to state taxpayers in 1987. That pattern was changed radically by Proposition 98, the "School Funding Guarantee" passed in 1988. That proposition amended section 2 to provide that the excess revenues formerly required to be returned to taxpayers were instead to be transferred and allocated to a State School Fund, and to be "expended solely for the purposes of instructional improvement and accountability" as established under Proposition 98. The provisions for the school fund were contained in a new section 8.5, simultaneously added to Article XVI, which deals with public finance.

Forecasts in 1989 indicated that up to $2.5 billion potentially would become available to the school fund, but the legislature, by adjusting the ratios of state and local school spending, instead absorbed the "excess" in the form of state expenditures and quickly took additional steps to prevent a similar recurrence in the future.[70] Once step was to advocate the modification of the school funding guarantee, such that only half the "excess" would be allocated to the school fund, with the other half to remain in the budgetary process, perhaps including rebates.

[70] California Commission on State Finance, Annual Long Term General Fund Forecast (Winter 1989/90), pp. 7–8.

That change was included in the amendments of Proposition 111 in 1990 and is reflected in the current 50 percent provisions of section 2(a).

Because the educational provisions apply only to state budgeting, section 2(b) continues to require rebates for all government units other than the state. Those local jurisdictions may return revenue by suspension of taxes or granting of credits or refunds.

SECTION 3

Adjustments to appropriations limit. The appropriations limit for any fiscal year pursuant to Sec. 1 shall be adjusted as follows:

(a) In the event that the financial responsibility of providing services is transferred, in whole or in part, whether by annexation, incorporation or otherwise, from one entity of government to another, then for the year in which such transfer becomes effective the appropriations limit of the transferee entity shall be increased by such reasonable amount as the said entities shall mutually agree and the appropriations limit of the transferor entity shall be decreased by the same amount.
(b) In the event that the financial responsibility of providing services is transferred, in whole or in part, from an entity of government to a private entity, or the financial source for the provision of services is transferred, in whole or in part, from other revenues of an entity of government, to regulatory licenses, user charges or user fees, then for the year of such transfer the appropriations limit of such entity of government shall be decreased accordingly.
(c) (1) In the event an emergency is declared by the legislative body of an entity of government, the appropriations limit of the affected entity of government may be exceeded provided that the appropriations limits in the following three years are reduced accordingly to prevent an aggregate increase in appropriations resulting from the emergency.

(2) In the event an emergency is declared by the Governor, appropriations approved by a two-thirds vote of the legislative body of an affected entity of government to an emergency account for expenditures relating to that emergency shall not constitute appropriations subject to limitation. As used in this paragraph, "emergency" means the existence, as declared by the Governor, of conditions of disaster or of extreme peril to the safety of persons and property within the state, or parts thereof, caused by such conditions as attack or probable or imminent attack by an enemy of the United States, fire, flood, drought, storm, civil disorder, earthquake, or volcanic eruption. [June 5, 1990]

Subsections (a) and (b) remain unchanged from the 1979 original, but subsection (c) was amended in 1990.

Subsection (a) recognizes the constant activities among local governments that transfer the responsibilities for providing services from one government to another, whether by overt transfers (See Art. XI, sec. 8), contractual agreements, or the process of government boundary changes that accompany any annexation, incorporation, or dissolution of government bodies. This section requires that after a transfer from one entity of government to another—or one level of government to another, such as from the state to local agencies—each entity must increase or decrease its appropriations limit by the same amount.

Subsection (b) is designed to prevent agencies from shifting the financial responsibility for services to a private entity or to another source of government revenue. Drafters of the initiative feared that governments might attempt to evade the appropriations limit by abandoning a service and forcing citizens to acquire that service from a provider in the private sector. Under this section, such a change would require a proportionate reduction in the government entity's limit. Of greater concern was the fear that government entities might attempt to evade the limit by changing the source of government revenues used to pay for a service, such as from the general fund to user charges, license fees, or similar cost-recovery devices (see also sec. 8(c)). Such a shift would allow a government to use its tax revenues for new or other purposes (thus expanding "government spending") and was one of the "loopholes" that had been perceived under Article XIII A; this section reduces some of the advantage thereby gained for the appropriations limit.

Subsection (c)(1) recognizes that emergency conditions may require a government to exceed its appropriations limit, but any excess expenditures are not to become the basis for a future increase in the limit. The subsection thus requires a reduction in appropriations over the next three years to recoup the entire additional spending occasioned by that emergency.

Subsection (c)(2), added in 1990, recognizes as another category of emergencies those that are officially proclaimed by the governor. Unlike the local proclamations in (c)(1), reliance on a gubernatorial proclamation adds assurance of the significance of the emergency, and appropriations made under those conditions are not subject to the limitation and need not be recouped over the next three years.

Other adjustments to the appropriations limit will result from the population and inflation changes recognized by section 1, the voter overrides established by section 4, and certain mandated activities discussed in section 11.

SECTION 4

Establishment or change of appropriations limit by electors. The appropriations limit imposed on any new or existing entity of government by this Article may be established or changed by the electors of such entity, subject to and in conformity with constitutional and statutory voting requirements. The duration of any such change shall be as determined by said electors, but shall in not event exceed four years from the most recent vote of said electors creating or continuing such change. [Nov. 6, 1979]

Section 4, part of the original measure, allows the electorate to "override" their government's appropriations limit by majority vote for a temporary period not to exceed four years. A voters' override is consistent with the philosophy of both Articles XIII A and XIII B, since it allows the electorate to exercise direct control over the desirability of any excessive appropriations by government. In practice, votes on a proposed override may be requested directly by a local government itself but have more often been initiated by citizens interested in specific local programs. There is no guidance on the specific design of override measures, although most have specified the amounts and purpose of the excess appropriations.

SECTION 5

Management of contingency funds. Each entity of government may establish such contingency, emergency, unemployment, reserve, retirement, sinking fund, trust, or similar funds as it shall deem reasonable and proper. Contributions to any such fund, to the extent that such contributions are derived from the proceeds of taxes, shall for purposes of this Article constitute appropriations subject to limitation in the year of contribution. Neither withdrawals from any such fund, nor expenditures of (or authorizations to expend) such withdrawals, nor transfers between or among such funds, shall for purposes of this Article constitute appropriations subject to limitation. [Nov. 6, 1979]

This section concerns a large category of reserve or contingency funds and includes them within the category of "appropriations" that must be counted within the limit. Unlike many government appropriations, these funds are usually not thought of as leading to actual expenditures but nevertheless under this provision are to be considered as a type of appropriation. When the funds are withdrawn, they are not to be counted as appropriations subject to the limitation, thus avoiding a double counting. One suggested reason for this provision, which grew out of the early experience under Article XIII, was to prevent governments from allocating large amounts of excess funds to a reserve instead of refunding it to taxpayers.

SECTION 5.5

Prudent state reserve. The Legislature shall establish a prudent state reserve fund in such amount as it shall deem reasonable and necessary. Contributions to, and withdrawals from, the fund shall be subject to the provisions of Section 5 of this Article. [Nov. 8, 1988]

This section (which includes its own title), is an addition to the original article, adopted by the voters as part of proposition 98. Although a state reserve fund already existed, this section was added as a constitutional mandate, unlike the permissive wording of section 5. The section does not specify an amount to be allocated to the fund, the language of Proposition 98 suggesting only that its purpose was to enable the state "to set aside funds when the economy is strong and prevent cutbacks or tax increases in times of severe need or emergency."[71] This section's role in the larger pattern of state finance remains unclear.

SECTION 6

Mandated subventions for local services. Whenever the Legislature or any state agency mandates a new program or higher level of service on any local government, the state shall provide a subvention of funds to reimburse such local government for the costs of such program or increased level of service, except that the Legislature may, but need not, provide such subvention of funds for the following mandates:

(a) Legislative mandates requested by the local agency affected;
(b) Legislation defining a new crime or changing an existing definition of a crime; or
(c) Legislative mandates enacted prior to January 1, 1975, or executive orders or regulations initially implementing legislation enacted prior to January 1, 1975. [Nov. 6, 1979]

Section 6 requires the state to reimburse local governments for expenses they incur as a result of certain state laws, actions, or orders. As such, it essentially requires a reallocation of revenues from the state to particular local governments.

This section was modeled on an earlier property tax relief measure enacted in 1972. That law limited the power of local governments to raise taxes but, as a compensation, allowed reimbursements (called "subventions") to be paid by the state to the local governments to offset the costs of "new programs or increased levels of service" required by the state. Section 6 adapted that pattern, reflecting a concern that the state might attempt to shift the responsibility for some public service programs from itself to local governments whose tax revenues had been reduced by Proposition 13. A related concern is reflected in section 3(a), which requires the transfer of a portion of the appropriations limit whenever a

[71] Proposition 98, sec. 2, Nov. 8, 1988.

responsibility for providing services is shifted from one unit of government to another.

The reference to "mandates" in the first sentence includes legislative statutes, executive orders, and administrative agency actions (*Long Beach Unified School District v. State of California*, 1990), but not all costs necessarily require subventions. Subventions are required for the expenses or increased costs of locally administered programs to provide services that are unique to local governments but not for laws of general application that result in some incidental expenses to local agencies or that apply generally to both public and private activities in the state (*County of Los Angeles v. State of California*, 1987). Subventions are not required if the costs can be recovered from some revenue source other than taxes. Thus, where local governments have authority to levy service charges, fees, or assessments to pay for the mandated program or increased level of service, subventions are not required (*County of Fresno v. State of California*, 1991).

In 1984 the legislature enacted a detailed and comprehensive administrative system to deal with claims by local governments against the state.[72] A five-member Commission on State Mandates implements section 6 by hearing and deciding claims by local governments for reimbursement by the state. The commission adopts its own procedures, adjudicates disputes, and reports its activities to the legislature (*Kinlaw v. State of California*, 1991).

SECTION 7

Bonded indebtedness. Nothing in this Article shall be construed to impair the ability of the state or of any local government to meet its obligations with respect to existing or future bonded indebtedness. [Nov. 6, 1979]

Governments often raise funds through long-term borrowing in the form of bonds. This section was intended to allay concerns that the appropriations limits might threaten the payments necessary to service bonded indebtedness, the same general concern that prompted similar language in section 1(b) of Article XIII A. This section is also affected by the definitions in sections (8)g, 8(i), and 9(a); under those provisions, section 7 allows the payment of interest and redemption of principle on all bonds issued before January 1, 1979, but allows payments after that date only for voter-approved bonded debt.

[72] Calif. Government Code sec. 17500–630.

SECTION 8

Definitions. As used in this article and except as otherwise expressly provided herein:

(a) "Appropriations subject to limitation" of the state means any authorization to expend during a fiscal year the proceeds of taxes levied by or for the state, exclusive of state subventions for the use and operation of local government (other than subventions made pursuant to Section 6) and further exclusive of refunds of taxes, benefit payments from retirement, unemployment insurance, and disability insurance funds.

(b) "Appropriations subject to limitation" of an entity of local government means any authorization to expend during a fiscal year the proceeds of taxes levied by or for that entity and the proceeds of state subventions to that entity (other than subventions made pursuant to Section 6) exclusive of refunds of taxes.

(c) "Proceeds of taxes" shall include, but not be restricted to, all tax revenues and the proceeds to an entity of government, from (1) regulatory licenses, user charges, and user fees to the extent that those proceeds exceed the costs reasonably borne by that entity in providing the regulation, product, or service, and (2) the investment of tax revenues. With respect to any local government, "proceeds of taxes" shall include subventions received from the state, other than pursuant to Section 6, and, with respect to the state, proceeds of taxes shall exclude such subventions.

(d) "Local government" means any city, county, city and county, school district, special district, authority, or other political subdivision of or within the state.

(e) (1) "Change in the cost of living" for the state, a school district, or a community college district means the percentage change in California per capita personal income from the preceding year.

(2) "Change in the cost of living" for an entity of local government, other than a school district or a community college district, shall be either (A) the percentage change in California per capita personal income from the preceding year, or (B) the percentage change in the local assessment roll from the preceding year for the jurisdiction due to the addition of local nonresidential new construction. Each entity of local government shall select its change in the cost of living pursuant to this paragraph annually by a recorded vote of the entity's governing body.

(f) "Change in population" of any entity of government, other than the state, a school district, or a community college district, shall be determined by a method prescribed by the Legislature. "Change in population" of a school district or a community college district shall be the percentage change in the average daily attendance of the school district or community college district from the preceding fiscal year, as determined by a method prescribed by the Legislature. "Change in population" of the state shall be determined by adding (1) the percentage change in the state's population multiplied by the percentage of the state's budget in the prior fiscal year that is expended for other than educational purposes for kindergarten and grades one to 12, inclusive, and the community colleges, and (2) the percentage change in the total statewide average daily attendance in kindergarten and grades one to 12, inclusive, and the community colleges, multiplied by the percentage of the state's budget in the prior fiscal year that is expended for educational purposes for kindergarten and grades one to 12, inclusive, and the community colleges. Any determination of population pursuant to this subdivision, other than that measured by average daily attendance, shall be revised, as necessary, to reflect the periodic census conducted by the United States Department of Commerce, or successor department.

(g) "Debt service" means appropriations required to pay the cost of interest and redemption charges, including the funding of any reserve or sinking fund required in connection therewith, on indebtedness existing or legally authorized as of January 1, 1979, or on bonded indebtedness thereafter approved according to law by a vote of the electors of the issuing entity voting in an election for that purpose.

(h) The "appropriations limit" of each entity of government for each fiscal year is that amount which total annual appropriations subject to limitation may not exceed under Sections 1 and 3. However, the "appropriations limit" of each entity of government for fiscal year 1978–79 is the total of the appropriations subject to limitation of the entity for that fiscal year. For fiscal year 1978–1979, state subventions to local governments, exclusive of federal grants, are deemed to have been derived from the proceeds of state taxes.

(i) Except as otherwise provided in Section 5, "appropriations subject to limitation" do not include local agency loan funds or indebtedness funds, investment (or authorizations to invest) funds of the state, or of an entity of local government in accounts at banks or savings and loan associations or in liquid securities. [June 6, 1990]

This section, adopted as part of the original initiative, provides essential definitions for the application of the other sections of the article and has been the source of considerable technical controversy. It has undergone only minor changes except for the all-important amendments to subsections (e) and (f), which allowed changes in calculation methods that effectively removed or postponed, perhaps for many decades, the limiting effect of the article on state government.

Most of the subsections are technical and self-explanatory, with paragraph (c) generating the greatest controversy. Litigation has frequently been necessary to clarify that special assessments, user fees, impact fees, and similar cost-recovery devices that do not exceed the reasonable cost of providing the service are not included within the definition of "proceeds of taxes," as they fall outside the conventional definitions of "taxes"[73] (e.g., *County of Placer v. Corin*, 1980).

[73] See generally Calif. Government Code sec. 53715.

SECTION 9

Exceptions to appropriations limit. "Appropriations subject to limitation" for each entity of government do not include:

(a) Appropriations for debt service.
(b) Appropriations required to comply with mandates of the courts or the federal government which, without discretion, require an expenditure for additional services or which unavoidably make the provision of existing services more costly.
(c) Appropriations of any special district which existed on January 1, 1978, and which did not as of the 1977–78 fiscal year levy an ad valorem tax on property in excess of 12 1/2 cents per $100 of assessed value; or the appropriations of any special district then existing or thereafter created by a vote of the people, which is totally funded by other than the proceeds of taxes.
(d) Appropriations for all qualified capital outlay projects, as defined by the Legislature.
(e) Appropriations of revenue which are derived from any of the following:
(1) That portion of the taxes imposed on motor vehicle fuels for use in motor vehicles upon public streets and highways at a rate of more than nine cents ($0.09) per gallon.
(2) Sales and use taxes collected on that increment of the tax specified in paragraph (1).
(3) That portion of the weight fee imposed on commercial vehicles which exceeds the weight fee imposed on those vehicles on January 1, 1990. [June 6, 1990]

This section recognizes that certain types of expenditures are essentially beyond the discretionary control of a government and thus exempt from the limit; those include debt obligations (see subsec. (a) and sec. 7) and mandates from the courts or from the federal government (subsec. (b)). The last category includes a wide variety of obligations, such as labor or occupational safety laws, postage rates, unemployment insurance, social security or Medicare payments, or various environmental requirements (*City of Sacramento v. State*, 1990). The specific reference to certain special districts in subsection (c) exempts such districts from an appropriations limit, as are any districts that do not receive funding from proceeds of taxes.

This section too was amended by Proposition 111 by the addition of subsections (d) and (e); they made exemptions for some "capital outlay projects," and for revenues derived from the transportation-related measures introduced by that proposition.

SECTION 10

Effective date. This Article shall be effective commencing with the first day of the fiscal year following its adoption. [Nov. 6, 1979]

Amendments to the constitution accomplished by initiative generally become effective the day after the election (see sec. 4 of Art. XVIII), which in this case would have fallen in the middle of government budgetary periods, making immediate compliance highly impractical. This section instead postponed the effective date of the article to the more appropriate July 1, 1980, the start of the next fiscal year.

SECTION 10.5

Appropriations limit on or after July 1, 1990. For fiscal years beginning on or after July 1, 1990, the appropriations limit of each entity of government shall be the appropriations limit for the 1986–87 fiscal year adjusted for the changes made from that fiscal year pursuant to this article, as amended by the measure adding this section, adjusted for the changes required by Section 3. [June 5, 1990]

Proposition 111 made several changes in the formulas for determining the appropriations limit, necessitating that any limit established prior to the effective date of Proposition 111 would have to be recalculated. This section provides for recalculated limits under the revised terms of sections 1, 3, and 8 (e) and (f).

SECTION 11

Severability of categories added to or removed from appropriations limit. If any appropriation category shall be added to or removed from appropriations subject to limitation, pursuant to final judgment of any court of competent jurisdiction and any appeal therefrom, the appropriations limit shall be adjusted accordingly. If any section, part, clause or phrase in this Article is for any reason held invalid or unconstitutional, the remaining portions of this Article shall not be affected but shall remain in full force and effect. [Nov. 6, 1979]

Many government entities have seen fit to recalculate their base year limits; the decision to recalculate, when done with proper accounting techniques, is considered an appropriate legislative prerogative and does not violate this article (*Santa Barbara County Taxpayers Association v. Board of Supervisors of County of Santa Barbara*, 1989). Either as part of such a recalculation or as part of the annual calculations, questions arise as to the appropriate treatment of particular types of revenues or expenditures. This section recognizes that any resulting litigation will affect particular limits and perhaps similar calculations elsewhere; the provision seeks to avoid a result that might endanger the constitutionality of the article by providing that an appropriation category as defined by the courts will be respected. The second sentence is simply a severance clause, used commonly to proclaim the drafters' intention to retain as much as possible of an enactment should some portion of it be declared invalid.

SECTION 12

Tobacco tax exceptions. "Appropriations subject to limitation" of each entity of government shall not include appropriations of revenue from the Cigarette and Tobacco Products Surtax Fund created by the Tobacco Tax and Health Protection Act of 1988. No adjustment in the appropriations limit of any entity of government shall be required pursuant to Section 3 as a result of revenue being deposited in or appropriated from the Cigarette and Tobacco Products Surtax Fund created by the Tobacco Tax and Health Protection Act of 1988. [Nov. 9, 1988]

Section 12 is an addition to the article from yet a different source, the antitobacco Proposition 99, adopted by the voters in 1988. This provision allows entities of government to receive revenues from the specific tax created by the new law, without being subject to the adjustments to their appropriations limits that would otherwise occur upon the receipt of new proceeds of taxes.

Article XIV

Labor Relations

Prior to 1976, all five sections of what is now Articles XIV existed, or had their roots, in Article XX. Related in subject matter, they were transplanted to this article as part of the constitutional revision of that year. Of the five, only the last section has been subsequently amended.

SECTION 1

Minimum wages and general welfare. The Legislature may provide for minimum wages and for the general welfare of employees and for those purposes may confer on a commission legislative, executive, and judicial powers. [June 8, 1976]

Adopted in 1914 as Article XX, section 17 1/2, this section in its original form authorized the legislature to provide for the establishment of a minimum wage for women and minors and for the "comfort, health, safety and general welfare of any and all employees," and to confer on "any commission now or hereafter created such power and authority as the Legislature may deem requisite to carry out the provisions of this section." Its primary purpose was to remove constitutional doubts surrounding the legislature's creation, in the previous year, of the Industrial Welfare Commission with power to make rules, hold hearings, and issue orders specifying minimum requirements with respect to wages, hours, and working conditions for women and minors. It was also intended to ratify legislative measures that had already been taken to provide for safety in employment under the administration of what was then the Industrial Accident Commission.

Following congressional adoption of the Civil Rights Act of 1964 and its banon sex discrimination, the limitation of wage orders on the basis of sex became suspect, and in 1970 the section was amended to its current form in order to cure that problem and otherwise to bring the language of the section up to date. Shortly after, the legislature amended the applicable provisions of the Labor Code to authorize the Industrial Welfare Commission to establish minimum wages, maximum hours, and standard conditions of employment for all workers.

Courts have been deferential to the commission and its orders, recognizing that the commission acts in a quasi-legislative capacity (*Industrial Welfare Commission v. Superior Court,* 1980). Moreover, Courts have viewed this section as authorizing legislative delegation of authority, including judicial authority, to bodies other than the Industrial Welfare Commission, for purposes related to the general welfare of employees and not limited to prescribing minimum conditions of employment. On that basis, the state Agricultural Labor Relations Act, allocating judicial authority to a state agency for the supervision of a system of collective bargaining for agricultural workers, was upheld (*Perry Farms Inc. v. Agricultural Labor Relations Board,* 1978).

SECTION 2

Eight-hour workday. Worktime of mechanics or workers on public works may not exceed eight hours a day except in wartime or extraordinary emergencies that endanger life or property. The Legislature shall provide for enforcement of this section. [June 8, 1976]

This provision, formerly Article XX, section 17, derives from the Constitution of 1879 and reflects the political strength of the Workingmen's party in the 1878–1879 constitutional convention. In Its original form it declared: "Eight hours shall constitute a legal day's work on all public work." In 1902 the language was strengthened to make clear that work was to be "limited and restricted to eight hours" except in certain emergencies, that the restriction applied "whether said work is done by contract or otherwise," and that it applied to public works of the state or any of its subdivisions. At the same time, the category of employees covered by the provision was defined to include "all laborers or workmen or mechanics."

Notwithstanding its broad language, the provision received a narrow interpretation. In 1920 the supreme court held that an employee of a fire department was not within the covered category and strongly suggested that the section did not apply at all to persons directly employed by a public entity but only to the entity's contractors (*Danielson v. Bakersfield,* 1920).This narrow reading was subsequently adopted in opinions of the attorney general and has been tacitly accepted. The section was amended to its current language in 1970.

SECTION 3

Mechanics' liens. Mechanics, persons furnishing materials, artisans, and laborers of every class shall have a lien upon the property upon which they have bestowed labor or furnished material for the value of such labor done and material furnished; and the Legislature shall provide, by law, for the speedy and efficient enforcement of such liens. [June 8, 1976]

When a person furnishes labor or materials to improve another person's property, the law may give the worker or materials supplier a lien against the property, so as to ensure that the wages or materials costs will be paid. The owner of the property cannot sell it without satisfying the lien, and if necessary, the property will be sold in order for the lien amounts to be paid. This is known as a mechanic's lien, and it exists in most states through legislation. That it exists in California as a constitutional mandate is a tribute to the efforts of the Workingmen's party at the 1878–1879 constitutional convention. Reflecting distrust of both legislatures and courts, it constitutionalizes the rights of workers and material providers to a lien on property as security for payment of services or materials furnished and to statutory provisions for "speedy and efficient enforcement" thereof. Courts have held that the provision is not self-enforcing (*Spinney v. Griffith,* 1893) and have allowed the legislature substantial leeway in its implementation.

SECTION 4

Workers' compensation. The Legislature is hereby expressly vested with plenary power, unlimited by any provision of this Constitution, to create, and enforce a complete system of workers' compensation, by appropriate legislation, and in that behalf to create and enforce a liability on the part of any or all persons to compensate any or all of their workers for injury or disability, and their dependents for death incurred or sustained by the said workers in the course of their employment, irrespective of the fault of any party. A complete system of workers' compensation includes adequate provisions for the comfort, health and safety and general welfare of any and all workers and those dependent upon them for support to the extent of relieving from the consequences of any injury or death incurred or sustained by workers in the course of their employment, irrespective of the fault of any part; also full provision for securing safety in places of employment; full provision for such medical, surgical, hospital and other remedial treatment as is requisite to cure and relieve from the effects of such injury; full provision for adequate insurance coverage against liability to pay or furnish compensation; full provision for regulating such insurance coverage in all its aspects, including the establishment and management of a State compensation insurance fund; full provision for otherwise securing the payment of compensation; and full provision for vesting power, authority and jurisdiction in an administrative body with all the requisite governmental functions to determine any dispute or matter arising under such legislation, to the end that the administration of such legislation shall accomplish substantial justice in all cases expeditiously, inexpensively, and without incumbrance of any character; all of which matters are expressly declared to be the social public policy of this State, binding upon all departments of the State government.

The Legislature is vested with plenary powers, to provide for the settlement of any disputes arising under such legislation by arbitration, or by an industrial accident commission, by the courts, or by either, any, or all of these agencies, either separately or in combination, and may fix and control the method and manner of trial of any such dispute, the rules of evidence and the manner of review of decisions rendered by the tribunal or tribunals designated by it; provided, that all decisions of any such tribunal shall be subject to review by the appellate courts of this State. The Legislature may combine in one statute all the provisions for a complete system of workers' compensation, as herein defined.

The Legislature shall have power to provide for the payment of an award to the state in the case of the death, arising out of and in the course of the employment, of an employee without dependents, and such awards may be used for the payment of extra compensation for subsequent injuries beyond the liability of a single employer for awards to employees of the employer.

Nothing contained herein shall be taken or construed to impair or render ineffectual in any measure the creation and existence of the industrial accident commission of this State or the State compensation insurance fund, the creation and existence of which, with all the functions vested in them, are hereby ratified and confirmed. [June 8, 1976]

This complex section derives from two amendments designed to ensure the constitutional validity of workers' compensation legislation. The first amendment was adopted in 1911 to validate a statute enacted earlier that year. That statute, the Roseberry Act, established a system of no-fault liability for industrial injuries through insurance, but it was permissive only, and few employers participated. The amendment, formerly section 21 of Article XX, authorized the legislature to establish such a system and to provide for its administration "by arbitration, or by an industrial accident board, by the courts, or by either, any or all of these agencies, anything in this Constitution to the contrary notwithstanding." The reason for including such authorization was to remove constitutional doubts.

In 1913 the legislature adopted a compulsory workers' compensation law, and four years later that was expanded and strengthened through the comprehensive Workmen's Compensation Act of 1917, which (with numerous amendments) forms the basis for California's current statutory scheme. To ensure its validity, Article XX, section 21 was amended the following year to substitute the more specific (and expansive) provisions that appear in paragraphs 1, 2, and 4 of this section. Among other things, the 1918 amendment prescribed minimum requirements for a "complete system of workmen's compensation." The third paragraph, making clear the authority of the legislature to require payment of the equivalent of death benefits for employees without dependents and use the proceeds to augment other funds, was added in 1972.

SECTION 5

Inmate labor. (a) The Director of Corrections or any county Sheriff or other local government official charged with jail operations, may enter into contracts with public entities, nonprofit or for profit organizations, entities, or businesses for the purpose of conducting programs which use inmate labor. Such programs shall be operated and implemented pursuant to statutes enacted by or in accordance with the provisions of the Prison Inmate Labor Initiative of 1990, and by rules and regulations prescribed by the Director of Corrections and, for county jail programs, by local ordinances.

(b) No contract shall be executed with an employer that will initiate employment by inmates in the same job classification as non-inmate employees of the same employer who are on strike, as defined in Section 1132.6 of the Labor code, as it reads on January 1, 1990, or who are subject to lockout, as defined in Section 1132.8 of the Labor Code, as it reads on January 1, 1990. Total daily hours worked by inmates employed in the same job classification as non-inmate employees, of the same employer who are on strike, as defined in Section 1132.6 of the Labor Code, as it reads on January 1, 1990, or who are subject to lockout, as defined in Section 1132.8 of the Labor Code, as it reads on January 1, 1990, shall not exceed, for the duration of the strike, the average daily hours worked for the preceding six months, or if the program has been in operation for less than six months, the average for the period of operation.

(c) Nothing in this section shall be interpreted as creating a right of inmates to work. [Nov. 7, 1990]

The Constitution of 1879 provided, in Article X, section 6, that "the labor of convicts shall not be let out by contract to any person, copartnership, company or corporation, and the Legislature shall, by law, provide for the working of convicts for the benefit of the State." That provision was later moved to Article X, section 1 and in 1976 to its current location, but its language, prohibiting the privatization of convict labor, remained intact until 1990. In that year, an initiative measure amended the section to its present form and at the same time enacted an implementing statute. The backers of the initiative argued that the measure was a desirable means of ensuring that prisoners would pay part of their own upkeep and compensate victims.

As amended, subsection (a) allows state prison and local jail officials to contract with private organizations (profit or nonprofit) for the use of inmate labor subject to statutes enacted by or in accordance with the measure and in accordance with rules established, in the case of prisons, by the director of corrections and, in the case of local jails, by local ordinance. Subsection (b)limits the use of convict labor as a substitute for workers who are on strike or locked out by their employer. Subsection (c) makes clear that the section does not create a constitutional right of inmates to work.

The statutory provisions enacted by the measure are more specific. They require the state to establish inmate labor contracts through joint venture programs to be coordinated by the Joint Venture Policy Advisory Board consisting of the director of corrections, the director of the Employment Development Department, and five members appointed by the governor (one representing industry, one organized labor, and three public members). Companies that participate in such a program may lease real property on prison grounds at or below market rates and may receive tax incentives in the form of tax credits for their participation. Products and services produced by the programs are available for sale to the public. Inmates are to be paid prevailing wages, but up to 80 percent of their wages may be used to pay for their prison room and board, for restitution of victims, and for support of the inmate's family.

Article XV

Usury

This article, consisting of a single section, contains the constitutional limitations on usury, the charging of interest in excess of a permissible maximum. California's usury restrictions are a curious and confusing blend of this constitutional article, statutory law, and case law pertaining to both Article XV and the relevant usury statutes. In addition, some federal laws operate to preempt the operation of contrary provisions either in Article XV or in other sources of California law.

SECTION 1

Rate of interest and exemptions to usury limits. The rate of interest upon the loan or forbearance of any money, goods, or things in action, or on accounts after demand, shall be 7 percent per annum but it shall be competent for the parties to any loan or forbearance of any money, goods or things in action to contract in writing for a rate of interest:

(1) For any loan or forbearance of any money, goods, or things in action, if the money, goods, or things in action are for use primarily for personal, family or household purposes, at a rate not exceeding 10 percent per annum; provided, however, that any loan or forbearance of any money, goods or things in action the proceeds of which are used primarily for the purchase, construction, or improvement of real property shall not be deemed to be a use primarily for personal, family or household purposes; or

(2) For any loan or forbearance of any money, goods, or things in action for any use other than specified in paragraph (1), at a rate not exceeding the higher of (a) 10 percent per annum or (b) 5 percent per annum plus the rate prevailing on the 25th day of the month preceding the earlier of (i) the date of execution of the contract to make the loan or forbearance, or (ii) the date of making the loan or forbearance established by the Federal Reserve Bank of San Francisco on advances to member banks under Sections 13 and 13a of the Federal Reserve Act as now in effect or hereafter from time to time amended (or if there is no such single determinable rate of advances, the closest counterpart of such rate as shall be designated by the Superintendent of Banks of the State of California unless some other person or agency is delegated such authority by the Legislature).

No person, association, copartnership or corporation shall by charging any fee, bonus, commission, discount or other compensation receive from a borrower more than the interest authorized by this section upon any loan or forbearance of any money, goods or things in action.

However, none of the above restrictions shall apply to any obligations of, loans made by, or forbearances of, any building and loan association as defined in and which is operated under that certain act known as the "Building Loan and Association Act," approved May 5, 1931, as amended, or to any corporation incorporated in the manner prescribed in and operating under that certain act entitled "An act defining industrial loan companies, providing for their incorporation, powers and supervision," approved May 18, 1917, as amended, or any corporation incorporated in the manner prescribed in and operating under that certain act entitled "An act defining credit unions, providing for their incorporation, powers, management and supervision," approved March 31, 1927, as amended or any duly licensed pawnbroker or personal property broker, or any loans made or arranged by any person licensed as a real estate broker by the State of California and secured in whole or in part by liens on real property, or any bank as defined in and operating under that certain act known as the "Bank Act," approved March 1, 1909, as amended, or any bank created and operating under and pursuant to any laws of this State or the United States of America or any nonprofit cooperative association organized under Chapter 1 (commencing with section 54001) of Division 20 of the Food and Agricultural Code in loaning or advancing money in connection with any activity mentioned in said title or any corporation, association, syndicate, joint stock company, or partnership engaged exclusively in the business of marketing agricultural, horticultural, viticultural, dairy, live stock, poultry and bee products on a cooperative nonprofit basis in loaning or advancing money to the members thereof or in connection with any such business or any corporation securing money or credit from any federal intermediate credit bank, organized and existing pursuant to the provisions of an act of Congress entitled "Agricultural Credits Act of 1923," as amended in loaning or advancing credit so secured, or any other class of persons authorized by statute, or to any successor in interest to any loan or forbearance exempted under this article, nor shall any such charge of any said exempted classes of persons be considered in any action or for any purpose as increasing or affecting or as connected with the rate of interest hereinbefore fixed. The Legislature may from time to time prescribe the maximum rate per annum of, or provide for the supervision, or the filing of a schedule of, or in any manner fix, regulate or limit, the fees, bonuses, commissions, discounts or other compensation which all or any of the said exempted classes or persons may charge or receive from a borrower in connection with any loan or forbearance of any money, goods or things in action.

The rate of interest upon a judgment rendered in any court of this state shall be set by the Legislature at not more than 10 percent per annum. Such rate may be variable and based upon interest rates charged by federal agencies or economic indicators, or both.

In the absence of the setting of such rate by the Legislature, the rate of interest on any judgment rendered in any court of the state shall be 7 percent per annum.

The provisions of this section shall supersede all provisions of this Constitution and laws enacted there under in conflict therewith. [Nov. 6, 1979]

Article XV and the statutes it authorizes are riddled with exemptions from usury limitations. As a result, California's usury restrictions do little more than purport to establish maximum rates for loans. Because almost all lenders in the business of making loans are wholly or partially exempt from usury limits, the only persons likely to be subjected to usury limits are those who make an occasional loan without the assistance of skilled legal counsel.

California usury law began as an attempt to prevent lenders from using what was perceived to be their collective monopoly power to take advantage of borrowers. In 1918, California voters approved an initiative measure that enacted a statute designated as the "usury law."[74] The usury law established 7 percent per annum as the legal rate of interest but permitted parties to establish, by written agreement, rates of interest as high as 12 percent per annum. Although the statute remains in effect except to the extent that its provisions are contradicted by the California Constitution,[75] events subsequent to its adoption have rendered it effectively obsolete.

By a voter initiative, California voters added Article XX, section 22 to the California Constitution in 1934. Article XX, section 22 established a legal interest rate of 7 percent per annum with the further proviso that, by written contract, parties might validly establish interest rates as high as 10 percent per annum. The section also exempted certain classes of lenders from its interest rate restrictions.

---

[74] Calif. Civil Code sec. 1916–1 to 1916–5 (West's 1985). These sections are to be found following Calif. Civil Code sec. 1916.12 (West's 1985).

[75] See Nuckolls v. Bank of California, 10 Cal. 2d 266, 74 P.2d 264 (1938); Penziner v. West American Finance Co., 10 Cal. 2d 160, 74 P.2d 252 (1938); Barnes v. Hartman, 246 Cal. App. 2d 215, 54 Cal. Rptr. 514 (1966).

As a result the statutory limits created in 1918 were partially overridden, and some classes of lenders were entirely exempted from usury limits.

A 1976 voter initiative repealed Article XX, section 22 and added in its place Article XV. Article XV was amended in 1978 and 1979.

Article XV establishes a 7 percent per annum legal interest rate but permits higher limits to be established by written contract. Article XV distinguishes loans by purpose, establishing separate usury limits for each class. The first class consists of loans primarily for personal, family, or household purposes, excluding loans primarily for the purchase, construction, or improvement of real property. The usual nomenclature applied to such loans is "consumer loans." The maximum interest rate applicable to consumer loans is 10 percent per annum. The second category is all other loans, or "nonconsumer loans." For these loans, the parties may agree in writing to an interest rate that is the higher of (1) 10 percent per annum or (2) five percentage points over the San Francisco Federal Reserve Bank's discount rate prevailing on the twenty-fifth day of the month preceding the earlier of the loan contract or the loan itself. Interest on legal judgments is limited to 7 percent per annum unless the legislature acts to increase that limit to no more than 10 percent per annum.

Article XV exempts virtually anyone regularly engaged in the business of making loans from the usury limits it establishes. Moreover, Article XV gives the legislature the power to exempt other categories of persons from the constitutional usury limits and specifically exempts any successor in interest to a loan made by a member of an exempt class. Thus, for example, should an exempt lender make a loan at the rate of 250 percent per annum and assign that loan to, say, his brother-in-law, a nonexempt lender, the loan in the hands of the brother-in-law would remain exempt."[76] Perhaps as a counterweight to these sweeping exemptions, Article XV authorizes the legislature to prescribe by statute maximum annual interest rates that may be charged by constitutionally exempt lenders.

There are three main categories of exemption to California's constitutional law of usury: those contained in Article XV or by statute pursuant to Article XV's delegated authority, exemptions mandated by federal law that preempts contrary California constitutional or statutory law, and those created by judicial manufacture of the "time-price" doctrine. Loans or lenders exempt by reason of Article XV or statutory action are either totally or partially exempt, the difference being dependent on whether the legislature has seen fit to use its authority to prescribe by statute a usury limitation. Federal law exempts from state usury laws virtually any institutional loan secured by a first lien on residential real property.[77] Since federal laws preempt any contrary state statutory or

[76] Cf. Garcia v. Wetzel, 159 Cal. App. 3d 1093, 206 Cal. Rptr. 251 (1984).

[77] 12 C.F.R. sec. 590.3(a) (1986). The regulations implement sec. 501 of the Depository Institutions Deregulation and Monetary Control Act of 1980, P.L. No. 96–221, 94 Stat. 161 (1980). See also 12 C.F.R. sec. 590.2(b).

constitutional law,[78] none of California's usury restrictions has any effect with respect to such loans.

Finally, usury is inapplicable when a seller finances the purchase of property by extending payments over time. The transaction is regarded as a credit sale rather than a loan because there is no loan or forbearance of money but, rather, a transfer of property in exchange for a price, albeit deferred in part. This time-price doctrine has been accepted by the supreme court as applicable to all such transactions, without respect to their commercial or personal nature.[79]

Judgment creditors remain as a significant nonexempt class of lenders. The economic result is that, to the extent that the maximum rate on judgments (7 to 10 percent) is less than prevailing market rates for unsecured demand notes, judgment debtors have an incentive to employ the legal system purely for the purpose of delay. Although other regulatory measures can be adopted to penalize such litigation tactics, a simpler method would have been the adoption of an unlimited interest rate on judgments that would fluctuate with some recognized measure of prevailing market rates for unsecured demand notes. It is incongruous that judgment creditors remain as perhaps the only significant class of lender in California that fails to enjoy exemption from California's usury limits.

As California's constitutional law of usury now stands, Article XV's usury limits apply to very few lenders and offer almost no protection to borrowers (even granting the debatable assumption that usury limits are, in fact, in the interest of borrowers). It may be that it is good social policy to abandon usury limits, but it is assuredly terrible legal policy to go about that project in the contorted, complex, and obtuse manner fashioned by Article XV.

---

[78] U.S. Constitution, Art. VI, cl. 2 (supremacy clause).

[79] Southwest Concrete Products v. Gosh Construction Corp., 51 Cal. 3d 701, 798 P.2d 1247, 274 Cal. Rptr. 404 (1990).

Article XVI

Public Finance

In 1879 Article XVI was titled "State Indebtedness" and contained a single section. It was renamed "Public Finance" in 1974 but deals primarily with borrowing and public expenditures; other aspects of finance are encompassed by Articles XIII, XIII A, and XIII B.

Sections have been transferred to Article XVI from other articles over many years, resulting in an uncoordinated arrangement of topics and a few overt errors. Nevertheless, major revisions proposed in 1970 by the California Constitution Revision Commission were not adopted. The current sections serve various functions; some are restrictions on the general processes of state financing, while others establish borrowing and revenue systems or authorize specific types of expenditures.

SECTION 1

Limitations on creation of state indebtedness. The Legislature shall not, in any manner create any debt or debts, liability or liabilities, which shall, singly or in the aggregate with any previous debts or liabilities, exceed the sum of three hundred thousand dollars ($300,000), except in case of war to repel invasion or suppress insurrection, unless the same shall be authorized by law for some single object or work to be distinctly specified therein which law shall provide ways and means, exclusive of loans, for the payment of the interest of such debt or liability as it falls due, and also to pay and discharge the principal of such debt or liability within 50 years of the time of the contracting thereof, and shall be irrepealable until the principal and interest thereon shall be paid and discharged, and such law may make provision for a sinking fund to pay the principal of such debt or liability to commence at a time after the incurring of such debt or liability of not more than a period of one-fourth of the time of maturity of such debt or liability; but no such law shall take effect unless it has been passed by a two-thirds vote of all the members elected to each house of the Legislature and until, at a general election or at a direct primary, it shall have been submitted to the people and shall have received a majority of all the votes cast for and against it at such election; and all moneys raised by authority of such law shall be applied only to the specific object therein stated or to the payment of the debt thereby created. Full publicity as to matters to be voted upon by the people is afforded by the setting out of the complete text of the proposed laws, together with the arguments for and against them, in the ballot pamphlet mailed to each elector preceding the election at which they are submitted, and the only requirement for publication of such law shall be that it be set out at length in ballot pamphlets which the Secretary of State shall cause to be printed. The Legislature may, at any time after the approval of such law by the people, reduce the amount of the indebtedness authorized by the law to an amount not less than the amount contracted at the time of the reduction, or it may repeal the law if no debt shall have been contracted in pursuance thereof.

Notwithstanding any other provision of this Constitution, Members of the Legislature who are required to meet with the State Allocation Board shall have equal right and duties with the nonlegislative members to vote and act upon matters pending or coming before such board for the allocation and apportionment of funds to school districts for school construction purposes or purposes related thereto.

Notwithstanding any other provision of this constitution, or of any bond act to the contrary, if any general obligation bonds of the state heretofore or hereafter authorized by vote of the people have been offered for sale and not sold, the Legislature may raise the maximum rate of interest payable on all general obligation bonds authorized but not sold, whether or not such bonds have been offered for sale, by a statute passed by a two-thirds vote of all members elected to each house thereof.

The provisions of Senate Bill No. 763 of the 1969 Regular Session, which authorize an increase of the state general obligation bond maximum interest rate from 5 percent to an amount not in excess of 7 percent and eliminate the maximum rate of interest payable on notes given in anticipation of the sale of such bonds, are hereby ratified. [June 2, 1970]

Section 1, which contains the entirety of the original article, prescribes the manner in which the legislature may create state debt. It was a reaction to the crude public finance and accounting methods of the 1850s and reflects the citizens' desire to place detailed restrictions on legislative extravagance directly into the constitution (*People ex rel. the Attorney General v. Johnson,* 1856).

Beyond a now-insignificant threshold figure of $300,000, or exceptions in case of war, section 1 requires that debts or liabilities can be created only in the form of a statute that must be approved by a two-thirds vote of each house of the legislature and subsequently approved by a majority of the state electorate, a process that includes the procedures later added by section 2. It establishes a number of other basic requirements for legislation that authorizes bonds.

In addition to these constitutional restraints, the issuance of state bonds is further regulated by statutes and, as a practical matter, must comply with federal regulation to ensure that the bonds achieve tax-exempt status under the Internal Revenue Code.

The section constrains the methods of financing undertaken by the state, preventing any attempts to employ other forms that deviate from its strictures (*Pooled Money Investment Board v. Unruh,* 1984). Despite its broad tone, however, section 1 does not apply to all forms of public debt. Certain obligations, such as those imposed on the state by federal law, federal courts, or state courts, are exempt from the section since they are not dependent on the control of the legislature or the review of the electorate. The same exception pertains in section 18, below, and section 9(b) of Article XIIIB.

The concept of "debt" has been narrowly interpreted. The courts have excepted from the requirement of voter approval some long-term financing measures, such as lease-purchase or installment contracts that extend over many years, since they do not obligate the state for the entire amount of the contract immediately (*Dean v. Kuchel,* 1950). Similarly, financing techniques that create only short-term liabilities, including interest-bearing registered warrants (*Riley v. Johnson,* 1933; *Riley v. Johnson II,* 1936) or short-term notes (*Flournoy v. Priest,* 1971), are allowed as well.

Nor does section 1 encompass all elements of the state's governments. Borrowing by many local governments is instead directly controlled by the provisions of section 18, and other entities of government, such as local authorities for housing or ports, are considered beyond the reach of section 1 entirely because their debts are paid from special-purpose funds and not from the general funds of the state (*Board of State Harbor Commissioners v. Dean,* 1953; *California Educational Facilities Authority v. Priest,* 1974). Thus, although the section restricts the issue of general obligation bonds secured by the state's general fund, it does not restrict the issue of revenue bonds, which are to be repaid from a specific project or special fund (*In re California Toll Bridge Authority,* 1931; *California Housing Finance Authority v. Elliott,* 1976).

The second paragraph was added in 1960 in order to allow legislators to sit on an administrative board whose purpose is to allocate precisely state expenditures for local uses. The State Allocation Board, created by statute, consists of two state senators, two members of the assembly, and three senior executive officers.

The third and fourth paragraphs, added in 1970, empowered the legislature to increase the maximum interest rate on unsold state general obligation bonds and, at the same time, ratified specific legislation (Senate bill 763) that effectuated that rate change. Later statutory amendments have further increased the maximum rate, thus allowing the state treasurer to offer the market rate of interest for general obligation bonds or bond anticipation notes.

SECTION 1.5

General Obligation Bond Proceeds Fund. The Legislature may create and establish a "General Obligation Bond Proceeds Fund" in the State Treasury, and may provide for the proceeds of the sale of general obligation bonds of the State heretofore or hereafter issued, including any sums paid as accrued interest thereon, under any or all acts authorizing the issuance of such bonds, to be paid into or transferred to, as the case may be, the "General Obligation Bond Proceeds Fund." Accounts shall be maintained in the "General Obligation Bond Proceeds Fund" of all moneys deposited in the State Treasury to the credit of that fund and the proceeds of each bond issue shall be maintained as a separate and distinct account and shall be paid out only in accordance with the law authorizing the issuance of the particular bonds from which the proceeds were derived. The Legislature may abolish, subject to the conditions of this section, any fund in the State Treasury heretofore or hereafter created by any act for the purpose of having deposited therein the proceeds from the issuance of bonds if such proceeds are transferred to or paid into the "General Obligation Bond Proceeds Fund" pursuant to the authority granted in this section; provided, however, that nothing in this section shall prevent the Legislature from re-establishing any bond proceeds fund so abolished and transferring back to its credit all proceeds in the "General Obligation Bond Proceeds Fund" which constitute the proceeds of the particular bond fund being re-established. [Nov. 6, 1962]

This section was added in 1962 to streamline the state's accounting practices and financial analysis by eliminating the use of separate bond funds. It provides instead for separate accounts for the proceeds of each bond issue to be maintained in a single new fund. The proceeds are to be paid out in accordance with the particular bond act under which the bonds were issued.

SECTION 2

Form of voter approval of bond issues. (a) No amendment to this Constitution which provides for the preparation, issuance and sale of bonds of the State of California shall hereafter be submitted to the electors, nor shall any such amendment to the Constitution hereafter submitted to or approved by the electors become effective for any purpose.

Each measure providing for the preparation, issuance and sale of bonds of the State of California shall hereafter be submitted to the electors in the form of a bond act or statute.

(b) The provisions of this Constitution enumerated in subdivision (c) of this section are repealed and such provisions are continued as statutes which have been approved, adopted, legalized, ratified, validated, and made fully and completely effective, by means of the adoption by the electorate of a ratifying constitutional amendment, except that the Legislature, in addition to whatever powers it possessed under such provisions, may amend or repeal such provisions when the bonds issued thereunder have been fully retired and when no rights thereunder will be damaged.

(c) The enumerated provisions of this Constitution are: Article XVI, Sections 2, 3, 4, 4 1/2, 5, 6, 8, 8 1/2, 15, 16, 16.5, 17, 18, 19, 19.5, 20 and 21. [Nov. 6, 1962]

This section, newly adopted in 1962 in conjunction with related amendments to section 1, changed the basic method by which bond measures are approved. Prior to its adoption, every bond issue had to be individually authorized by a constitutional amendment, thus creating numerous amendments of little general import. This section prohibits the former practice, thereby reducing the bulk of the constitution. The previous specific authorizations for bond issues enumerated in subsection (c) were repealed and relegated to statutory status. All bond measures are now submitted for the voters' approval under the ballot pamphlet provisions detailed in section 1.

SECTION 3

Limits on appropriations to benefit private entities. No money shall ever be appropriated or drawn from the State Treasury for the purpose or benefit of any corporation, association, asylum, hospital, or any other institution not under the exclusive management and control of the State as a state institution, nor shall any grant or donation of property ever be made thereto by the State, except that notwithstanding anything contained in this or any other section of the Constitution:

(1) Whenever federal funds are made available for the construction of hospital facilities by public agencies and nonprofit corporations organized to construct and maintain such facilities, nothing in this Constitution shall prevent the Legislature from making state money available for that purpose, or from authorizing the use of such money for the construction of hospital facilities by nonprofit corporations organized to construct and maintain such facilities.

(2) The Legislature shall have the power to grant aid to the institutions conducted for the support and maintenance of minor orphans, or half-orphans, or abandoned children, or children of a father who is incapacitated for gainful work by permanent physical disability or is suffering from tuberculosis in such a stage that he cannot pursue a gainful occupation, or aged persons in indigent circumstances—such aid to

be granted by a uniform rule, and proportioned to the number of inmates of such respective institutions.

(3)The Legislature shall have the power to grant aid to needy blind persons not inmates of any institution supported in whole or in part by the State or by any of its political subdivisions, and no person concerned with the administration of aid to needy blind persons shall dictate how any applicant orrecipient shall expend such aid granted him, and all money paid to a recipient of such aid shall be intended to help him meet his individual needs and is not for the benefit of any other person, and such aid when granted shall not be construed as income to any person other than the blind recipient of such aid, and the State Department of Social Welfare shall take all necessary action to enforce the provisions relating to aid to needy blind persons as heretofore stated.

(4) The Legislature shall have power to grant aid to needy physically handicapped persons not inmates of any institution under the supervision of the Department of Mental Hygiene and supported in whole or in part by the State or by any institution supported in whole or part by any political subdivision of the State.

(5)The State shall have at any time the right to inquire into the management of such institutions.

(6) Whenever any county, or city and county, or city, or town, shall provide for the support of minor orphans, or half-orphans, or abandoned children, or children of a father who is incapacitated for gainful work by permanent physical disability or is suffering from tuberculosis in such a stage that he cannot pursue a gainful occupation, or aged persons in indigent circumstances, or needy blind persons not inmates of any institution supported in whole or in part by the State or by any of its political subdivisions,or needy physically handicapped persons not inmates of any institution under the supervision of the Department of Mental Hygiene and supported in whole or in part by the State or by an institution supported in whole or part by any political subdivision of the State; such county, city and county, city, or town shall be entitled to receive the same pro rata appropriations as may be granted to such institutions under church, or other control.

An accurate statement of the receipts and expenditures of public moneys shall be attached to and published with the laws at every regular session of the Legislature. [Nov. 5, 1974]

This section was derived from another article in the original 1879 Constitution and reflects both the drafters' recognition of the need for charitable relief and their fear of inappropriate legislative largess. Its role is best understood in conjunction with section 5, which prohibits state support of religious organizations, section 6, which prohibits gifts of state funds for other than public purposes, and the later-enacted grants of charitable powers in sections 4, 11, and 13. Thus, the first sentence generally forbids the legislature to appropriate money for charitable institutions whenever that institution is not under the control of the state.

Despite the apparent breadth of that prohibition, courts later excused its application where money was spent for a "public purpose." That phrase is modernly interpreted to allow state appropriations for a broad range of activities, thus removing many of the earlier restrictions on the types of entities that can receive state aid (*California Housing Finance Agency v. Elliott*, 1976). As long as a private institution performs a public purpose, any benefit that it receives is merely incidental to the public benefit, and the spending will be constitutional. The last paragraph simply requires the legislature to provide an accurate accounting of receipts and expenditures each year.

Despite the general prohibitions, the six subsections of the first paragraph are the core of this section and are the only parts of the original Constitution of 1879 that explicitly authorized expenditures for charitable purposes; without express authorization, those expenditures would have been considered a form of prohibited gift.

Paragraph 1 of this section authorizes five very specific types of charitable support, notable to modern eyes because of their limitations, not their inclusiveness. Subsection (6) makes clear that a local government that provides support is eligible for the same state aid that a similar private institution would receive. The expressly reserved right to inquire into the management of private institutions that receive relief, contained in subsection (5), is today unnecessary, because inspections would be considered a proper condition of the monetary grants, as well as an appropriate exercise of the state's general police power.

Although this section was doubtless considered expansive when adopted in 1879, it omits many types of relief that are considered appropriate for a modern state. Since its adoption, the courts and legislature have greatly expanded the power to grant relief authorized under the state's general police power and the additional powers under section 11.

SECTION 4

Loan guarantees to nonprofit hospitals. The Legislature shall have the power to insure or guarantee loans made by private or public lenders to nonprofit corporations and public agencies, the proceeds of which are to be used for the construction, expansion, enlargement, improvement, renovation or repair of any public or nonprofit hospital, hospital facility, or extended care facility, facility for the treatment of mental illness, or all of them, including any outpatient facility and any other facility useful and convenient in the operation of the hospital and any original equipment for any such hospital or facility, or both.

No provision of this Constitution, including but not limited to, Section 1 of Article XVI and Section 14 of Article XI, shall be construed as a limitation upon the authority granted to the Legislature by this section. [Nov. 5, 1974]

Adopted in 1968, this section was specifically designed to remove the restrictions imposed on the legislature by sections 1 and 18; it restored to the legislature the power to guarantee loans made for the construction of nonprofit and public health facilities (*Methodist Hospital of Sacramento v. Saylor*, 1971). The legislature promptly responded by passing various statutory measures to implement this section.

The second paragraph's reference to the former section 14 of Article XI is erroneous; it refers instead to section 18 of this article. By thus removing restrictions regarding either state or local government guarantees, this section was intended to stimulate the flow of private capital into health facilities construction.

SECTION 5

Grants to religious institutions prohibited. Neither the Legislature, nor any county, city and county, township, school district, or other municipal corporation, shall ever make an appropriation, or pay from any public fund whatever, or grant anything to or in aid of any religious sect, church, creed, or sectarian purpose, or help to support or sustain any school, college, university, hospital, or other institution controlled by any religious creed, church, or sectarian denomination whatever; nor shall any grant or donation of personal property or real estate ever be made by the state, or any city, city and county, town, or other municipal corporation for any religious creed, church, or sectarian purpose whatever; provided, that nothing in this section shall prevent the Legislature granting aid pursuant to Section 3 of Article XVI. [Nov. 5, 1974]

Sections 3, 5, and 6 restrict state expenditures for charitable causes; section 5 prohibits any form of aid or promotion for religious purposes or entities. As a spending prohibition, it is broader than the similar prohibition in section 8 of Article IX, which prohibits appropriations for sectarian schools, but is of narrower scope than section 6 of this article, which establishes a general prohibition on gifts by the state or local governments. The section is therefore viewed as a general prohibition on state support of religion and is considered similar to, but more comprehensive than, the establishment clause of the First Amendment of the U.S. Constitution.

Section 5 traditionally has been used to maintain a separation between church and state, forbidding such activities as the use of public high school facilities by a voluntary student Bible study club (*Johnson v. Huntington Beach Union High School District*, 1977) or prohibiting prayers at a public school graduation (*Sands v. Morongo Unified School District*, 1991) but allowing "incidental" benefits to accrue to religious entities from statutes that have a secular primary purpose (*California Educational Facilities Authority v. Priest*, 1974).

SECTION 6

Prohibition of gifts, loans, or pledging of public credit. The Legislature shall have no power to give or to lend, or to authorize the giving or lending, of the credit of the State, or of any county, city and county, city, township or other political corporation or subdivision of the State now existing, or that may be hereafter established, in aid of or to any person, association, or corporation, whether municipal or otherwise, or to pledge the credit thereof, in any manner whatever, for the payment of the liabilities of any individual, association, municipal or other corporation whatever; nor shall it have power to make any gift or authorize the making of any gift, of any public money or thing of value to any individual, municipal or other corporation whatever; provided, that nothing in this section shall prevent the Legislature granting aid pursuant to Section 3 of Article XVI; and it shall not have power to authorize the State, or any political subdivision thereof, to subscribe for stock, or to become a stockholder in any corporation whatever; provided, further, that irrigation districts for the purpose of acquiring the control of any entire international water system necessary for its use and purposes, a part of which is situated in the United States, and a part thereof in a foreign country, may in the manner authorized by law, acquire the stock of any foreign corporation which is the owner of, or which holds the title of the part of such system situated in a foreign country; provided, further, that irrigation districts for the purpose of acquiring water and water rights and other property necessary for their uses and purposes, may acquire and hold the stock of corporations, domestic or foreign, owning waters, water rights, canals, waterworks, franchises or concessions subject to the same obligations and liabilities as are imposed by law upon all other stockholders in such corporation; and

Provided, further, that this section shall not prohibit any county, city and county, city, township, or other political corporation or subdivision of the State from joining with other such agencies in providing for the payment of workers' compensation, unemployment compensation, tort liability, or public liability losses incurred by such agencies, by entry into an insurance pooling arrangement under a joint exercise of powers agreement, or by membership in such publicly-owned nonprofit corporation or other public agency as may be authorized by the Legislature; and

Provided, further, that nothing contained in this Constitution shall prohibit the use of State money or credit, in aiding veterans who served in the military or naval service of the United States during the time of war, in the acquisition of, or payments for, (1) farms or homes, or in projects of land settlement or in the development of such farms or homes or land settlement projects for the benefit of such veterans, or (2) any business, land or any interest therein, buildings, supplies, equipment, machinery, or tools, to be used by the veteran in pursuing a gainful occupation; and

Provided, further, that nothing contained in this Constitution shall prohibit the State, or any county, city and county, city, township, or other political corporation or subdivision of the State from providing aid or assistance to persons, if found to be in the public interest, for the purpose of clearing debris, natural materials, and wreckage from privately owned lands and waters deposited thereon or therein during a period of a major disaster or emergency, in either case declared by the President. In such case, the public entity shall be indemnified by the recipient from the award of any claim against the public entity arising from the rendering of such aid or assistance. Such aid or assistance must be eligible for federal reimbursement for the cost thereof.

And provided, still further, that notwithstanding the restrictions contained in this Constitution, the treasurer of any city, county, or city and county shall have power and the duty to make such temporary transfers from the funds in custody as may be necessary to provide funds for meeting the obligations incurred for maintenance purposes by any city, county, city and county, district, or other political subdivision whose funds are in custody and are paid out solely through the treasurer's office. Such temporary transfer of funds to any political subdivision shall be made only upon resolution adopted by the governing body of the city, county, or city and county directing the treasurer of such city, county, or city and county to make such temporary transfer. Such temporary transfer of funds to any political subdivision shall not exceed 85 percent of the anticipated revenues accruing to such political subdivision, shall not be made prior to the first day of the fiscal year nor after the last Monday in April of the current fiscal year, and shall be replaced from the revenues accruing to such political subdivision before any other obligation of such political subdivision is met from such revenue. [Nov. 2, 1982]

The first paragraph of this section (as far as "provided, further,") represents the original prohibition adopted in 1879. Various qualifications were added in succeeding years to avoid a too-stringent application. The essence of this section is to bar the state or any of its political subdivisions from making gifts to private parties. It bars support in any form: the extension of credit, credit guarantees, subscription of stock, and outright grants of property.

The definition of a gift is of greater significance than the prohibition; state programs and services were often considered to be unauthorized gifts unless explicitly authorized by the constitution. For this reason, many types of expenditures, such as the provision for aiding purchase of lands by veterans in paragraph 3 of this section, are explicitly authorized by the constitution. Gradually the courts developed the general rule that an expenditure is not a proscribed gift if it satisfies a public rather than private purpose. The benefit to the public serves as "consideration," and the funds expended are therefore not a gift.

The courts show great deference to a legislative declaration that an expenditure is for a public purpose and will not overturn a statute as long as the legislature has any reasonable basis for a "public purpose" determination, even if a private party is incidentally benefited. Thus, a public purpose was easily found in credit and subsidies for construction and rental of low-income housing (*Board of Supervisors v. Dolan,* 1975) and for retroactive application of state tax exemptions (*County of Sonoma v. State Board of Equalization,* 1987).

Although the section explicitly restricts gifts made by the legislature, the prohibition is uniformly applied to all political subdivisions of the state (*Albright v. South San Francisco,* 1975; *County of Riverside v. Idyllwild County Water District,* 1978). Special exceptions have therefore been created to allow irrigation districts to acquire stock or water rights.

The second paragraph, added in 1978, allows local governments to exchange funds by joining pooled financing arrangements for workers' compensation, insurance, or similar financial arrangements. The fourth paragraph, added in 1980, allows the state or local governments, subject to conditions, to participate with private parties in federal disaster relief programs, thus overcoming the former rule that such activities were a gift of public funds.

In 1926 the fifth paragraph was added, allowing county treasurers, subject to procedural safeguards, to shift monies among the funds they hold for other local governments while awaiting receipt of tax revenues, thus avoiding paying interest on short-term borrowing.

SECTION 7

Controller's warrants. Money may be drawn from the Treasury only through an appropriation made by law and upon a Controller's duly drawn warrant. [Nov. 5, 1974]

The legislature has the exclusive power to appropriate money from the state treasury by passing an appropriation bill; funds are then disbursed by a warrant drawn by the state controller. Appropriation bills, which must specify the amount and purpose of an expenditure, are further limited by provisions of Article IV.

An earlier version of this section was part of the original Constitution of 1879; it has served continuously to bind all parties dealing with money in the state treasury (*Gillum v. Johnson,* 1936) and bars even the judiciary from ordering the release of unappropriated funds (*Mandel v. Myers,* 1981). It restricts the controller's ability to draw warrants strictly within the terms of appropriation bills (*California State Employees' Association v. Cory,* 1981).

SECTION 8

School funding priority. (a) From all state revenues there shall first be set apart the moneys to be applied by the state for support of the public school system and public institutions of higher education.

(b) Commencing with the 1990–91 fiscal year, the moneys to be applied by the state for the support of school districts and community college districts shall be not less than the greater of the following amounts:

(1) The amount which, as a percentage of General Fund revenues which may be appropriated pursuant to Article XIII B, equals the percentage of General Fund revenues appropriated for school districts and community college districts, respectively, in fiscal year 1986–87.

(2) The amount required to ensure that the total allocations to school districts and community college districts from General Fund proceeds of taxes appropriated pursuant to Article XIII B and allocated local proceeds of taxes shall not be less than the total amount from these sources in the prior fiscal year, excluding any revenues allocated pursuant to subdivision (a)of Section 8.5, adjusted for changes in enrollment and adjusted for the change in the cost of living pursuant to paragraph (1) of subdivision (e) of Section 8 of Article XIII B. This paragraph shall be operative only in a fiscal year in which the percentage growth in California per capita personal income is less than or equal to the percentage growth in per capita General Fund revenues plus one half of one percent.

(3) (A) The amount required to ensure that the total allocations to school districts and community college districts from General Fund proceeds of taxes appropriated pursuant to Article XIII B and allocated local proceeds of taxes shall equal the total amount form these sources in the prior fiscal year, excluding any revenues allocated pursuant to subdivision (a) of Section 8.5, adjusted for changes in enrollment and adjusted for the change in per capita General Fund revenues.

(B) In addition, an amount equal to one-half of one percent times the prior year total allocations to school districts and community colleges from General Fund proceeds of taxes appropriated pursuant to Article XIII B and allocated local proceeds of taxes, excluding any revenues allocated pursuant to subdivision (a) of Section 8.5, adjusted for changes in enrollment.

(C) This paragraph (3) shall be operative only in a fiscal year in which the percentage growth in California per capita personal income in a fiscal year is greater than the percentage growth in per capita General Fund revenues plus one half of one percent.

(c) In any fiscal year, if the amount computed pursuant to paragraph (1) of subdivision (b) exceeds the amount computed pursuant to paragraph (2) of subdivision (b) by a difference that exceeds one and one-half percent of General Fund revenues, the amount in excess of one and one-half percent of General Fund revenues shall not be considered allocations to school districts and community colleges for purposes of computing the amount of state aid pursuant to paragraph (2) or (3) of subdivision (b) in the subsequent fiscal year.

(d) In any fiscal year in which school districts and community college districts are allocated funding pursuant to paragraph (3) of subdivision (b) or pursuant to subdivision (h), they shall be entitled to a maintenance factor, equal to the difference between (1) the amount of General Fund moneys which would have been appropriated pursuant to paragraph (2) of subdivision (b) if that paragraph had been operative or the amount of General Fund moneys which would have been appropriated pursuant to subdivision (b) had subdivision (b) not been suspended, and (2) the amount of General Fund moneys actually appropriated to school districts and community college districts in that fiscal year.

(e) The maintenance factor for school districts and community college districts determined pursuant to subdivision (d) shall be adjusted annually for changes in enrollment, and adjusted for the change in the cost of living pursuant to paragraph (1) of subdivision (e) of Section 8 of Article XIII B, until it has been allocated in full. The maintenance factor shall be allocated in a manner determined by the Legislature in each fiscal year in which the percentage growth in per capita General Fund revenues exceeds the percentage growth in California per capita personal income. The maintenance factor shall be reduced each year by the amount allocated by the Legislature in that fiscal year. The minimum maintenance factor amount to be allocated in a fiscal year shall be equal to the product of General Fund revenues from proceeds of taxes and one-half of the difference between the percentage growth in per capita General Fund revenues from proceeds of taxes and in California per capita personal income, not to exceed the total dollar amount of the maintenance factor.

(f) For purposes of this section, "changes in enrollment" shall be measured by the percentage change in average daily attendance. However, in any fiscal year, there shall be no adjustment for decreases in enrollment between the prior fiscal year and the current fiscal year unless there have been decreases in enrollment between the second prior fiscal year and the prior fiscal year and between the third prior fiscal year and the second prior fiscal year.

[There is no subdivision (g).]

(h) Subparagraph (B) of paragraph (3) of subdivision (b) may be suspended for one year only when made part of or included within any bill enacted pursuant to Section 12 of Article IV. All other provisions of subdivision (b) may be suspended for one year by the enactment of an urgency statute pursuant to Section 8 of Article IV, provided that the urgency statute may not be made part of or included within any bill enacted pursuant to Section 12 of Article IV. [June 6, 1990]

Section 8, as first adopted in 1926, was a simple provision establishing a priority of funding for education; its language is retained as the current subsection (a). A greatly expanded version of section 8, and its companion section 8.5, was added by Proposition 98, a citizens' initiative adopted in 1988. Those measures were amended in turn by Proposition 111, a 1990 measure designed to reduce some of the impact of Proposition 98, including the power to suspend its operation under conditions of budget duress.

Both sections 8 and 8.5 interact with Article XIII B, which limits the amount of tax revenues that the state may appropriate each year. These sections were intended to create an exception to the strictures of Article XIII B in order to provide additional state support to California's schools.

Sections 8 and 8.5 must be read together to understand the system they create, which was designed to provide increased and stable state support to public schools. ("Public schools," for this purpose, means elementary, high school, and community college districts. The many campuses of the University of California and the California State Universities are funded separately and do not benefit from sections 8 or 8.5.) Public schools also receive some funding from their own districts, whose tax revenues were severely reduced after the adoption of Article XIII A in 1978. Since then, the state has had to provide greatly increased support for public schools.

Subdivision (b) requires a minimum level of school funding by mandating that schools be allocated not less than the greatest of the three amounts calculated under the technical rules of subsections (1)–(3).

Subsections (c)–(h) were added in 1990, reducing and limiting some aspects of the system first adopted as Proposition 98. Subsection (c) imposes a cap on the growth of allocations, thus preventing them from increasing too rapidly. Subsection (d) establishes a maintenance factor to be allocated to the school districts in periods of high personal income growth or when funding has been suspended by the legislature under subsection (h). Subsection (e) requires that the legislature must adjust, and in fact allocate, at least part of the maintenance factor in high-income years.

Subsection (h) was added by Proposition 111 as a safety valve. It allows the state to retain full control over its budgeting process and suspend some of the funding mandates created by this section. Specifically, it provides that the minimum funding provisions of subsection (b) may be suspended by an urgency statute passed by two-thirds of each house of the legislature. Further, it allows an additional sum provided by subsection (b)(3)(B) to schools in a high-income year to be suspended for one year if the suspension is passed as part of the governor's budget bill.

SECTION 8.5

Allocations to state school fund. (a) In addition to the amount required to be applied for the support of school districts and community college districts pursuant to Section 8, the Controller shall during each fiscal year transfer and allocate all revenues available pursuant to paragraph 1 of subdivision (s) of Section 2 of Article XIII B to that portion of the State School Fund restricted for elementary and high school purposes, and to that portion of the State School Fund restricted for community college purposes, respectively, in proportion to the enrollment in school districts and community college districts respectively.

(1) With respect to funds allocated to that portion of the State School Fund restricted for elementary and high school purposes, no transfer or allocation of funds pursuant to this section shall be required at any time that the Director of

Finance and the Superintendent of Public Instruction mutually determine that current annual expenditures per student equal or exceed the average annual expenditure per student of the 10 states with the highest annual expenditures per student for elementary and high schools, and that average class size equals or is less than the average class size of the 10 states with the lowest class size for elementary and high schools.

(2) With respect to funds allocated to that portion of the State School Fund restricted for community college purposes, no transfer or allocation of funds pursuant to this section shall be required at any time that the Director of Finance and the Chancellor of the California Community Colleges mutually determine that current annual expenditures per student for community colleges in this state equal or exceed the average annual expenditure per student of the 10 states with the highest annual expenditures per student for community colleges.

(b) Notwithstanding the provisions of Article XIII B, funds allocated pursuant to this section shall not constitute appropriations subject to limitation.

(c) From any funds transferred to the State School Fund pursuant to subdivision (a), the Controller shall each year allocate to each school district and community college district an equal amount per enrollment in school districts from the amount in that portion of the State School Fund restricted for elementary and high school purposes and an equal amount per enrollment in community college districts from that portion of the State School Fund restricted for community college purposes.

(d) All revenues allocated pursuant to subdivision (a) shall be expended solely for the purposes of instructional improvement and accountability as required by law.

(e) Any school district maintaining an elementary or secondary school shall develop and cause to be prepared an annual audit accounting for such funds and shall adopt a School Accountability Report Card for each school. [June 6, 1990]

This section, enacted by the voters as part of the same ballot initiative that produced section 8, provides additional revenue to schools in high-income years. Article XIII B, adopted in 1979, had established an annual limit on state appropriations and originally mandated the return of all excess state revenues to the taxpayers. This section, together with the matching amendments to section 2(a)(1) of Article XIII B, changed that pattern and now provides that half of any excess tax revenue is to be allocated to schools in accordance with section 8.5.

Subsection (a) requires the excess revenue to be allocated to the fund for elementary and high schools, and to the fund for community colleges, in proportion to their relative enrollments. Under paragraphs (1) and (2) of subsection (a), certain senior officials can suspend this allocation if they determine that expenditures per student have met established standards.

Subsection (b) reiterates the clear implication of Article XIII B, section 2(a)(1), that the excess revenues are not subject to limitation under Article XIII B.

Although it is not explicitly stated, it seems clear that these funds also do not raise the Article XIII B limit on total allowed appropriations.

Subsection (c) directs that individual elementary and high school districts and community college districts receive allocations in proportion to their enrollment. Under subsection (d), the funds are to be spent only for "instructional improvement and accountability." "Accountability" is explained by subsection (e), which calls for the creation of a School Accountability Report Card, a local report to voters whose details are set out in statutes adopted concurrently with these two sections.

There is no analogue in section 8.5 to the section 8(h) "safety valve," since this section does not impose a burden on the state, but instead applies only in years of fiscal excess when tax revenues would otherwise be returned to the taxpayers.

SECTION 9

Fish and game. Money collected under any state law relating to the protection or propagation of fish and game shall be used for activities relating thereto. [Nov. 5, 1974]

The original version of this section was adopted in 1942 to restrain the state from borrowing money held in special wildlife funds. That version specified that the protected funds included any court-imposed fines and forfeitures and were to be used "exclusively" for the preservation of wildlife and related enforcement and administrative costs. Although reworded in a repeal and revision of 1974, the section continues to carry the larger meaning and is interpreted in parallel with the provisions of the Fish and Game Preservation Fund, created by statute in 1957 (*Dittus v. Cranston*, 1959).

SECTION 10

State cooperation with federal pension assistance. Whenever the United States government or any officer or agency thereof shall provide pensions or other aid for the aged, co-operation by the State therewith and therein is hereby authorized in such manner and to such extent as may be provided by law.

The money expended by any county, city and county, municipality, district or other political subdivision of this State made available under the provisions of this section shall not be considered as a part of the base for determining the maximum expenditure for any given year permissible under Section 20 of Article XI of this Constitution independent of the vote of the electors or authorization by the State Board of Equalization. [Nov. 6, 1962]

This section was adopted in 1934 to authorize cooperation with New Deal welfare programs, particularly the social security system. Lengthy provisions in the original version were repealed in 1962 as it became evident that it was unnecessary to restrict the state's power.

The second paragraph is a nullity; the "Section 20 of Article XI" mentioned there, a provision limiting the appropriations of local governments, was repealed on June 2, 1970.

SECTION 11

Relief administration. The Legislature has plenary power to provide for the administration of any constitutional provisions or laws heretofore or hereafter enacted concerning the administration of relief, and to that end may modify, transfer, or enlarge the powers vested in any state agency or officer concerned with the administration of relief or laws appertaining thereto. The Legislature, or the people by initiative, shall have power to amend, altar, or repeal any law relating to the relief of hardship and destitution, whether such hardship and destitution results from unemployment or from other causes, or to provide for the administration of the relief of hardship and destitution, whether resulting from unemployment or from other causes, either directly by the State or through the counties of the State, and to grant such aid to the counties therefor, or make such provision for reimbursement of the counties by the State, as the Legislature deems proper. [Nov. 6, 1962]

When adopted in 1938, this section gave the legislature plenary power to administer state relief programs, thus counteracting other provisions (since repealed) that restricted the legislature. That complete discretion extends to whether to grant or withhold aid, and section 11 does not require that the State or any local government provide a certain minimum level of aid (*Board of Supervisors of Butte County v. McMahon*, 1990).

The state and local governments currently have many different assistance programs, usually codified in the Health and Safety and Welfare and Institutions codes; their constitutional authorization is now generally accepted.

SECTION 12

This section was repealed November 6, 1962.

SECTION 13

Legislative power to release certain liens. Notwithstanding any other provision of this Constitution, the Legislature shall have power to release, rescind, cancel, or otherwise nullify in whole or in part any encumbrance on property, personal obligation, or other form of security heretofore or hereafter exacted or imposed by the Legislature to secure the repayment to, or reimbursement of, the State, and the counties or other agencies of the State Government, of aid lawfully granted to and received by aged persons. [Nov. 6, 1962]

Section 13 was revised in 1962 concurrent with the repeal of section 12. Both sections had been adopted in 1940 to cancel various liens or encumbrances imposed by the state and counties under the provisions of a former old-age security act. Section 13 was abridged to its current form to eliminate obsolete provisions; now it merely clarifies the legislature's power to cancel those debts. Without this provision, the release and discharge of the liens would be considered an unauthorized gift of public property (*Los Angeles County v. Jessup*, 1938).

SECTION 14

Revenue bonds for environmental pollution control facilities. The Legislature may provide for the issuance of revenue bonds to finance the acquisition, construction, and installation of environmental pollution control facilities, including the acquisition of all technological facilities necessary or convenient for pollution control, and for the lease or sale of such facilities to persons, associations, or corporations, other than municipal corporations; provided, that such revenue bonds shall not be secured by the taxing power of the state; and provided, further, that the Legislature may, by resolution adopted by either house, prohibit or limit any proposed issuance of such revenue bonds. No provision of this Constitution, including, but not limited to, Section 25 of Article XIII and Sections 1 and 2 of Article XVI, shall be construed as a limitation upon the authority granted to the Legislature pursuant to this section. Nothing herein contained shall authorize any public agency to operate any industrial or commercial enterprise. [Nov. 7, 1972]

This section ensures that revenue bonds may be used to finance the construction of pollution control facilities owned by private industry. It was adopted in 1972 as a safeguard, since existing law had long recognized legislative authority to utilize revenue bonds (*In re California Toll Bridge Authority*, 1931). Revenue bonds, which generally receive tax-exempt status, are meant to be repaid from income realized from the newly constructed facilities; such bonds are not to be paid from, or secured by, the taxing power or the general credit of the state. That distinction is emphasized here by the proviso that "such revenue bonds shall not be secured by the taxing power of the state."

The legislature provided for issuance of bonds by concurrently enacting the California Pollution Control Financing Authority, which manages and issues the bonds. Notably, the act provides that the authority may issue bonds by resolution, without further authorization by the legislature, but the legislature retains the power to prohibit or limit any proposed issuance by a resolution adopted by either house. That "legislative veto" is an unusual power and is not reflected by the act.

Section 25 of Article XIII, mentioned in the second sentence, has since become the current section 6 of this article and refers to the traditional prohibition on gift of public funds. Sections 1 and 2 establish the general procedures for bond issuance, from which revenue bonds are normally exempt.

SECTION 14.5

Revenue bonds for alternative energy sources facilities. The Legislature may provide for the issuance of revenue bonds to finance the acquisition, construction, and installation of facilities utilizing cogeneration technology, solar power, biomass, or any other alternative source the Legislature may deem appropriate, including the acquisition of all technological facilities necessary or convenient for the use of alternative sources, and for the lease or sale of such facilities to persons, associations, or corporations, other than municipal corporations; provided, that such revenue bonds shall not be secured by the taxing power of the state; and provided, further, that the Legislature may, by resolution adopted by both houses, prohibit or limit any proposed issuance of such revenue bonds. No provision of this Constitution, including, but not limited to, Sections 1, 2, and 6, of this article, shall be construed as a limitation upon the authority granted to the Legislature pursuant to this section. Nothing contained herein shall authorize any public agency to operate any industrial or commercial enterprise. [June 3, 1980]

Adopted in 1980 in a period of growing environmental awareness, this section is highly similar to section 14, except that no authority was proposed for its direct implementation. Under its provisions, revenue bonds can be made available to private industry to construct alternative energy source facilities. The section also makes explicit the constitutionality of a legislature veto over issuance of bonds but requires merely a resolution (rather than a statute) of both houses of the legislature, thus making the veto marginally more difficult to achieve.

The references to sections 1,2, and 6 again refute the implication that revenue bonds should be treated as general obligation bonds, and for the same reason the section emphasizes that the bonds are not to be "secured by the taxing power of the state."

SECTION 15

Parking meter revenues. A public body authorized to issue securities to provide public parking facilities and any other public body whose territorial area includes such facilities are authorized to make revenues from street parking meters available as additional security. [Nov. 5, 1974]

This section is greatly reduced from the version first adopted in 1950, which affirmatively established the power to pledge parking meter revenues for the payment of revenue bonds. It thus overcame vague concerns regarding contractual arrangements that might constrain a local government's police and taxing powers (*La Mesa v. Freeman*, 1955).

SECTION 16

Taxation of redevelopment projects. All property in a redevelopment project established under the Community Redevelopment Law as now existing or hereafter amended, except publicly owned property not subject to taxation by reason of that ownership, shall be taxed in proportion to its value as provided in Section 1 of this article, and those taxes (the word "taxes" as used herein includes, but is not limited to, all levies on an ad valorem basis upon land or real property) shall be levied and collected as other taxes are levied and collected by the respective taxing agencies.

The Legislature may provide that any redevelopment plan may contain a provision that the taxes, if any, so levied upon the taxable property in a redevelopment project each year by or for the benefit of the State of California, any city, county, city and county, district, or other public corporation (hereinafter sometimes called "taxing agencies") after the effective date of the ordinance approving the redevelopment plan, shall be divided as follows:

(a) That portion of the taxes which would be produced by the rate upon which the tax is levied each year by or for each of those taxing agencies upon the total sum of the assessed value of the taxable property in the redevelopment project as shown upon the assessment roll used in connection with the taxation of that property by the taxing agency, last equalized prior to the effective date of the ordinance, shall be allocated to, and when collected shall be paid into, the funds of the respective taxing agencies as taxes by or for those taxing agencies on all other property are paid (for the purpose of allocating taxes levied by or for any taxing agency or agencies which did not include the territory in a redevelopment project on the effective date of the ordinance but to which that territory has been annexed or otherwise included after the ordinance's effective date, the assessment roll of the county last equalized on the effective date of that ordinance shall be used in determining the assessed valuation of the taxable property in the project on that effective date); and
(b) Except as provided in subdivision (c), that portion of the levied taxes each year in excess of that amount shall be allocated to and when collected shall be paid into a special fund of the redevelopment agency to pay the principal of an interest on loans, moneys advanced to, or indebtedness (whether funded, refunded, assumed or otherwise) incurred by the redevelopment agency to finance or refinance, in whole

or in part, the redevelopment project. Unless and until the total assessed valuation of the taxable property in a redevelopment project exceeds the total assessed value of the taxable property in the project as shown by the last equalized assessment roll referred to in subdivision (a), all of the taxes levied and collected upon the taxable property in the redevelopment project shall be paid into the funds of the respective taxing agencies. When the loans, advances, and indebtedness, if any, and interest thereon, have been paid, then all moneys thereafter received from taxes upon the taxable property in the redevelopment project shall be paid into the funds of the respective taxing agencies as taxes on all other property are paid.

(c) That portion of the taxes identified in subdivision (b) which are attributable to a tax rate levied by a taxing agency for the purpose of producing revenues in an amount sufficient to make annual repayments of the principal of, and the interest on, any bonded indebtedness for the acquisition or improvement of real property shall be allocated to, and when collected shall be paid into, the fund of that taxing agency. This paragraph shall only apply to taxes levied to repay bonded indebtedness approved by the voters of the taxing agency on or after January 1, 1989.

The Legislature may also provide that in any redevelopment plan or in the proceedings for the advance of moneys, or making of loans, or the incurring of any indebtedness (whether funded, refunded, assumed, or otherwise) by the redevelopment agency to finance or refinance, in whole or in part, the redevelopment project, the portion of taxes identified in (b), exclusive of that portion identified in subdivision (c), may be irrevocably pledged for the payment of the principal of and interest on those loans, advances, or indebtedness. It is intended by this section to empower any redevelopment agency, city, county, or city and county under any law authorized by this section to exercise the provisions hereof separately or in combination with powers granted by the same or any other law relative to redevelopment agencies. This section shall not affect any other law or laws relating to the same or a similar subject but is intended to authorize an alternative method of procedure governing the subject to which it refers. The Legislature shall enact those laws as may be necessary to enforce the provisions of this section. [Nov. 9, 1988]

This section was adopted in 1952 to authorize a local property tax system that may be used to finance redevelopment efforts. Known as tax increment financing, it establishes a tax allocation formula for the sharing of tax revenues between local taxing governments and a redevelopment agency.

Under this system, reflected in concurrent statutes titled the Community Redevelopment Law, any city or county may establish a redevelopment agency to design and administer a redevelopment project. After redevelopment has occurred, if the assessed valuation of taxable property in the project increases, the taxes levied there are divided between the new redevelopment agency and the preexisting taxing agencies. The local agencies will continue to receive the same tax revenues they would have received before the project was established, and the redevelopment agency is allocated whatever incremental tax revenue may result from the rise in assessed valuation of property within the project (*Redevelopment Agency of the City of San Bernardino v. County of San Bernardino*, 1978).

The redevelopment agency has no direct taxing power; it obtains necessary funding through borrowing, usually by issuing tax allocation bonds, and the tax revenue increments are used to pay for the acquisition and improvement of real property and the agency's loans, advances, or indebtedness, including the bonds and all the agency's operating expenses (*Marek v. Napa Community Redevelopment Agency*, 1988). Once the indebtedness of the redevelopment agency is paid, all tax revenues revert to the taxing authorities. Redevelopment agencies are also authorized by statute to levy nonproperty taxes, such as occupancy and sales taxes (*Huntington Park Redevelopment Agency v. Martin*, 1985).

The direction to the legislature in the fifth paragraph has been implemented in detailed statutory material, primarily within the Health and Safety Code. The fourth paragraph emphasizes that tax increment financing is an optional, not mandatory, system. It therefore supplements other taxing and financing powers and can work in concert with charter powers available to cities under section 5 of Article XI; in doing so, however, a redevelopment agency exercises state, not charter, powers (*Fellom v. Redevelopment Agency*, 1958).

The reference in the first paragraph to "Section 1 of this article" refers to section 1 of Article XIII, from which this section was transferred in 1974. That provision establishes the basic rule of ad valorem taxation and has been severely affected by the later adoption of Articles XIII A and XIII B, which established limits on government taxation and expenditures.

The 1978 adoption of Article XIII A created numerous uncertainties regarding tax increment financing, and the legislature responded by creating the Local Agency Indebtedness Fund to protect the credit of local agencies and, by extension, the state (*Pasadena Redevelopment Agency v. Pooled Money Investment Board*, 1982). The expenditure limitation provisions of Article XIII B do not apply to redevelopment agencies; to do so would impair the ability to repay their bonds (*Bell v. Community Redevelopment Agency*, 1985).

Subpart (c) of the second paragraph, added in 1988, adjusts the revenue allocation when local agencies have had to increase their tax rates to pay bonded indebtedness. Similar reallocations are made necessary when property within a district becomes tax exempt (*Redevelopment Agency of the City of San Bernardino v. County of San Bernardino*, 1978).

SECTION 17

State's credit and investment of public pension funds. The state shall not in any manner loan its credit, nor shall it subscribe to, or be interested in the stock of any company, association, or corporation, except that the state and each political subdivision, district, municipality, and public agency thereof is hereby authorized to acquire and hold shares of the capital stock of any mutual water company or corporation when the stock is so acquired or held for the purpose of furnishing a supply of water for public, municipal or governmental purposes; and the holding of the stock shall entitle the holder thereof to all of the rights, powers and privileges, and shall subject the holder to the obligations and liabilities conferred or imposed by law upon other holders of stock in the mutual water company or corporation in which the stock is so held.

Notwithstanding provisions to the contrary in this section and Section 6 of Article XVI, the Legislature may authorize the investment of moneys of any public pension or retirement system, subject to all of the following:

(a) The assets of a public pension or retirement system are trust funds and shall be held for the exclusive purposes of providing benefits to participants in the pension or retirement system and their beneficiaries and defraying reasonable expenses of administering the system.
(b) The fiduciary of the public pension or retirement system shall discharge his or her duties with respect to the system solely in the interest of, and for the exclusive purposes of providing benefits to, participants and their beneficiaries, minimizing employer contributions thereto, and defraying reasonable expenses of administering the system.
(c) The fiduciary of the public pension or retirement system shall discharge his or her duties with respect to the system with the care, skill, prudence, and diligence under the circumstances then prevailing that a prudent person acting in a like capacity and familiar with these matters would use in the conduct of an enterprise of a like character and with like aims.
(d) The fiduciary of the public pension or retirement system shall diversify the investments of the system so as to minimize the risk of loss and to maximize the rate of return, unless under the circumstances it is clearly prudent not to do so. [June 5, 1984]

The first lines of this section are derived directly from a complete prohibition on the pledging of state credit to private corporations that appeared in the 1879 Constitution. That prohibition eventually was interpreted as barring government agencies from acquiring water supplies through the purchase of stock in private nonprofit mutual water companies. "Mutual" water companies deliver water at cost to their members and shareholders but also can assess those shareholders for contributions to the costs of operation. A series of specific exemptions to that provision, adopted between 1926 and 1940, were consolidated in 1956, creating the remainder of the first paragraph in its current form. It allows all government agencies to buy stock in mutual water companies in order to obtain water for public use, thereby avoiding the acquisition of water rights by condemnation or other more complex methods. The section clarifies that a government agency, although acquiring all the rights of membership, is also subject to the liabilities created by stock ownership.

The second paragraph is the product of a 1984 amendment that repealed various restrictions on purchasing common stock in corporations. The current section, which concerns public employee retirement and pension funds, declares those fund assets to be "trust funds," thus protecting their status and purpose. It also clarifies the role of the fund managers and authorizes them to invest the funds in a flexible manner, but subject to specified standards of fiduciary responsibility that are reflected as well in related statutes.

SECTION 18

Limitation on local indebtedness. No county, city, town, township, board of education, or school district, shall incur any indebtedness or liability in any manner or for any purpose exceeding in any year the income and revenue provided for such year, without the assent of two-thirds of the qualified electors thereof, voting at an election to be held for that purpose, except that with respect to any such public entity which is authorized to incur indebtedness for public school purposes, any proposition for the incurrence of indebtedness in the form of general obligation bonds for the purpose of repairing, reconstructing or replacing public school buildings determined, in the manner prescribed by law, to be structurally unsafe for school use, shall be adopted upon the approval of a majority of the qualified electors of the public entity voting on the proposition at such election; nor unless before or at the time of incurring such indebtedness provision shall be made for the collection of an annual tax sufficient to pay the interest on such indebtedness as it falls due, and also provision to constitute a sinking fund for the payment of the principal thereof, on or before maturity, which shall not exceed forty years from the time of contracting the same; provided, however, anything to the contrary herein notwithstanding, when two or more propositions for incurring any indebtedness or liability are submitted at the same election, the votes cast for and against each proposition shall be counted separately, and when two-thirds or a majority of the qualified electors, as the case may be, voting on any one of such propositions, vote in favor thereof, such proposition shall be deemed adopted. [Nov. 5, 1974]

This section derives directly from an original provision of the 1879 Constitution. As with section 1, the drafters believed local governments should be operated on a pay-as-you-go basis, confining their expenditures for each year to "the income and revenue provided for such year." In apparently stringent language, the section therefore bars certain local governments from assuming any long-term debt unless it has been approved by two-thirds of the voters. The voters' approval originally was seen as a check on the local legislative body, to be exercised "in case of emergency" (*Bradford v. City of San Francisco*, 1896). If such an indebtedness is approved, the interest must be repaid annually from tax revenues, and the principal must be repaid within forty years. Financing repayable within a short term, such as warrants or anticipation notes, is not prohibited by this section (*Voorhees v. Morse,* 1934; *County of Los Angeles v. Legg,* 1936).

This section contains a limited exception to the requirement of two-thirds approval, added in 1972 to increase the chances of obtaining the necessary voter approval of school repairs deemed necessary for earthquake safety. A school district or similar entity now may incur debt with the approval of a simple majority vote if the district is authorized to issue general obligation bonds and the money is used to repair or replace buildings defined by statute as unsafe.

If bonds are approved by the voters, statutory provisions nevertheless impose a maximum ratio of debt size to the total assessed value of all property within the city or county, thus limiting the amount of debt that might be incurred. Similar ratios exist for school districts and some other local entities.

Section 18 was designed to operate as a strict debt limitation law, intended to prevent the "growing evil" of debt that was not paid from yearly revenues but was allowed to increase "like a rolling snowball as it went, until the burden of it became almost unbearable upon the taxpayers" (*McBean v. Fresno,* 1896). In the ensuing years, however, an astonishing variety of financial mechanisms has been developed to avoid the similar strictures of sections 1 and 18. Thus, despite its apparent severity, section 18 operates with two major exceptions. Its first limitation is that it restricts *only* the local governments identified in the first sentence; of those, "towns" and "townships" no longer exist. A key omission of the section is that it does not restrict financing undertaken by an independent entity or special district, such as a library board, water, or flood control district (*Eastern Municipal Water District v. Scott,* 1969). One of the traditional advantages of special districts has been their ability to acquire debt and undertake large projects unrestrained by this section. More recently, however, the strictures imposed by section 4 of Article XIII A have reduced that advantage (*Rider v. County of San Diego,* 1991). Similarly, a special district's ability to impose taxes for general obligation bonding was essentially foreclosed by section 1 of Article XIII A.

The second factor that moderates the limitations of section 18 is judicial narrowing of the definition of "indebtedness or liability." Section 18 protects only the general revenues of a local government and not money held in a "special fund." By the mid-twentieth century, "revenue bonds" had become a widely used means of financing long-;term capital improvements, with their debt to be paid from revenues of the project, held in a special fund, and thus legally insulated from the local government's general funds and credit (*City of Oxnard v. Dale,* 1955; *City of Palm Springs v. Ringwald,* 1959). The legislature accordingly enacted the Revenue Bond Law of 1941, authorizing the use of revenue bonds and specifically declaring that they do not constitute local debts (*Board of Supervisors v. Dolan,*1975). Under that statute, bonds may be issued only as authorized in the Government Code, which controls the amount, terms, and repayment provisions of revenue bonds, although it requires approval by only a majority of the electorate, not the two-thirds requirement of this section.

Nor does section 18 apply to "involuntary debts" that are imposed by law. The section operates as a limitation on the action of government officers and does not restrain debts involuntarily imposed upon a local government by state or federal law, whether statutory or as the result of litigation (*Wright v. Compton Unified School District,* 1975). Another form of excepted financing involves multiyear installment contracts, lease-purchase agreements, and rental agreements involving a contingent obligation that renders the liability not permanently binding (*County of Los Angeles v. Byram,* 1951). Only occasionally has the economic impact of such arrangements been questioned or voided by the courts (*Starr v. San Francisco,* 1977).

SECTION 19

Special assessments by chartered city or county. All proceedings undertaken by any chartered city, or by any chartered county or by any chartered city and county for the construction of any public improvement, or the acquisition of any property for public use, or both, where the cost thereof is to be paid in whole or in part by special assessment or other special assessment taxes upon property, whether the special assessment will be specific or a special assessment tax upon property wholly or partially according to the assessed value of such property, shall be undertaken only in accordance with the provisions of law governing: (1) limitations of costs of such proceedings or assessments for such proceedings, or both, in relation to the value of any property assessed therefor; (b) determination of a basis for the valuation of any such property; (c) payment of the cost in excess of such limitations; (d) avoidance of such limitations; (e) postponement or abandonment, or both, of such proceedings in whole or in part upon majority protest, and particularly in accordance with such provisions as contained in Sections 10, 11 and 13a of the Special Assessment Investigation, Limitation and Majority Protest Act of 1931 or any amendments, codification, reenactment or restatement thereof.

Notwithstanding any provisions for debt limitation or majority protest as in this section provided, if, after the giving of such reasonable notice by publication and posting and the holding of such public hearing as the legislative body of any such chartered county, chartered city or chartered city and county shall have prescribed, such legislative body by no less than a four-fifths vote of all members thereof, finds and determines that the public convenience and necessity require such improvements or acquisitions, such debt limitation and majority protest provisions shall not apply.

> Nothing contained in this section shall require the legislative body of any such city, county, or city and county to prepare or to cause to be prepared, hear, notice for hearing or report the hearing of any report as to any such proposed construction or acquisition or both. [Nov. 5, 1974]

Section 19 was added to the constitution in 1940 in order to make portions of the 1931 Special Assessment Act applicable to chartered counties and cities. It was transferred to this article in 1974.

Under sections 3–5 of Article XI, counties or cities may adopt a charter for the conduct of certain local affairs, creating a limited autonomy from legislative control. The addition of this section negated earlier case law that held a charter city's special assessments to be protected "municipal affairs" and thus unaffected by the various strictures imposed by statute.

A special assessment is a charge imposed by a local governmental entity on the owners of the realty in an identified area in order to pay for a public improvement that will benefit particular land. The 1931 act provided protection for landowners by limiting amounts of assessments and providing for public reports, hearings, and protests by affected landowners. The first paragraph of this section extends both general statutory provisions ("the provisions of law") and the specific statutory protections of the 1931 act to all special assessments undertaken by a chartered city or county. The specific sections of the act mentioned have been superseded by similar amendments, all within the Streets and Highways Code. The act itself establishes many more requirements and regulations than does this section, which imposes only limited restrictions on charter cities and counties, thus providing less inclusive protections to landowners than in the full act. Because of those limitations, the section subjects charter autonomy to only partial legislative control.

Paragraph 2 of this section provides that the legislative body imposing the special assessment can dispense with the funding limitation and majority protest provisions of the first paragraph by a vote of four-fifths of all its members. The legislative body must, however, hold hearings if required by its own law and make findings that public convenience and necessity require the project. The third paragraph provides that the legislature shall not be required to hear or publish reports concerning the project, a formality otherwise required by the codes.

ARTICLE XVII

Article XVII was repealed June 8, 1976.

Article XVIII

Amending and Revising the Constitution

SECTION 1

Legislative initiative. The Legislature by rollcall vote entered in the journal, two-thirds of the membership of each house concurring, may propose an amendment or revision of the Constitution and in the same manner may amend or withdraw its proposal. Each amendment shall be so prepared and submitted that it can be voted on separately. [Nov. 3, 1970]

The 1849 Constitution provided two methods of modifying the constitution: through amendment, proposed by a majority in both houses of the legislature and adopted by the voters, or through revision, adopted at a constitutional convention. The 1879 Constitution continued the same arrangement, except that it required a legislative proposal to be approved by two-thirds, rather than a simple majority, of both houses. It also added the requirement that amendments be submitted so that they can be voted upon separately.

Although there were no cases that tested the issue, the supreme court observed in dicta that the legislature had no power under this arrangement to propose revisions, as distinguished from amendments (*Livermore v. Waite,* 1894). In 1962, the voters approved an amendment to this section authorizing the legislature to propose constitutional revisions in the same manner as it submits proposed amendments. This change enabled the legislature to create the California Constitution Revision Commission, which proceeded to conduct studies and submit recommendations to the legislature for a series of constitutional revisions between 1966 and 1971.

The separate submission requirement of section 1 has been invoked once, in opposition to what is now Article I, section 7, which precludes state courts from mandating busing to cure racial imbalance in schools unless a federal court would be authorized to invoke that remedy under the federal Constitution. The opponents contended that the measure had an effect on six different sections of the California Constitution and that it should therefore have been divided into six parts, but the court held that because only one part of the constitution was actually amended by the measure, the separate submission requirement was satisfied (*Tinsley v. Superior Court*, 1983).

SECTION 2

Constitutional convention. The Legislature by rollcall vote entered in the journal, two-thirds of the membership of each house concurring, may submit at a general election the question whether to call a convention to revise the Constitution. If the majority vote yes on that question, within 6 months the Legislature shall provide for the convention. Delegates to a constitutional convention shall be voters elected from districts as nearly equal in population as may be practicable. [Nov. 3, 1970]

This section describes the procedure for calling a constitutional convention. While proposals within the legislature for a constitutional convention have been quite common, on only four occasions (1914, 1920, 1930, and 1933) has the requisite two-thirds vote in both houses been obtained for placing the proposal on the ballot. On the first three occasions, the ballot proposal failed to receive the necessary majority vote. The fourth proposal, in the midst of the Great Depression, managed to muster a majority, but the legislature then failed to provide for the convention as the section contemplates, and the proposal lapsed. As a consequence, there has been no constitutional convention since 1879.

SECTION 3

Popular initiatives. The electors may amend the Constitution by initiative. [Nov. 3, 1970]

The power of the electors to use the initiative as a means of amending the constitution—rare among the states—was established in 1911. (See Art. II, sec. 8.) This section was added to Article XVIII in 1970 to complete the article's description of the ways in which the constitution could be modified.

The distinction between amendment and ratification, no longer of significance in the case of legislative proposals, remains important in the case of initiative measures. In 1939, it was applied to strike down a multifarious proposal that, while it would have added only a single article to the constitution, would have had the effect of repealing or substantially altering at least fifteen of the then twenty-five articles (*McFadden v. Jordan*, 1948). It appears, however, that whether a proposal constitutes an amendment or a revision does not depend entirely on the number of provisions it affects but also on the nature of the changes it makes. For example, a measure that would have required California courts, in applying state constitutional provisions in criminal proceedings, to adhere to interpretations of similar provisions in the federal Constitution was held invalid, as affecting a fundamental change in the role of the judiciary and in the rights of criminal defendants (*Raven v. Deukmejian*, 1990). A measure that placed term limitations on legislators and limited the amounts that could be spent on legislative staff, however, was upheld as an amendment, rather than a revision, since it left the legislative branch substantially unchanged. The test is whether it appears "necessarily or inevitably . . . from the face of the challenged provision that the measure will substantially alter the basic governmental framework set forth in our Constitution" (*Legislature v. Eu*, 1991).

SECTION 4

Effective date. A proposed amendment or revision shall be submitted to the electors and if approved by a majority of votes thereon takes effect the day after the election unless the measure provides otherwise. If provisions of 2 or more measure approved at the same election conflict, those of the measure receiving the highest affirmative vote shall prevail. [Nov. 3, 1970]

This section, added to the constitution in 1970, sets forth the same rules with respect to effective date and the consequences of conflicting constitutional proposals as are set forth in Article II, section 10, for initiative statutes and referenda. As to the rule on conflicting provisions, the same problems exist.

Article XIX

Motor Vehicle Revenues

This article, first adopted in 1938 as Article XXVI, was designed to protect the state's "gasoline tax" by requiring that proceeds of the tax be spent only on highway-related matters. The article was revised and liberalized in 1974 to allow local voters to spend some of the revenues on transit systems and was renumbered as Article XIX in 1976 without amendment of its language.

SECTION 1

Use of fuel taxes. Revenues from taxes imposed by the state on motor vehicle fuels for use in motor vehicles upon public streets and highways, over and above the costs of collection and any refunds authorized by law, shall be used for the following purposes:

(a) The research, planning, construction, improvement, maintenance, and operation of public streets and highways (and their related public facilities for nonmotorized traffic), including the mitigation of their environmental effects, the payment for property taken or damaged for such purposes, and the administrative costs necessarily incurred in the foregoing purposes.

(b) The research, planning, construction, and improvement of exclusive public mass transit guide ways (and their related fixed facilities), including the mitigation of their environmental effects, the payment for property taken or damaged for such purposes, the administrative costs necessarily incurred in the foregoing purposes, and the maintenance of the structures and the immediate right-of-way for the public mass transit guideways, but excluding the maintenance and operating costs for mass transit power systems and mass transit passenger facilities, vehicles, equipment, and services. [June 4, 1974]

Section 1 was enacted to resolve a controversy regarding the use of gas tax revenues. It originally required that revenues from motor vehicle fuels taxes "be used exclusively and directly for highway purposes," thus preventing their diversion to purposes unrelated to motor vehicle transportation. That goal was served for more than three decades, withstanding repeated attempts to divert the funds. In 1974 economic and environmental concerns prompted the expansion of the approved purposes to include the construction of mass transit systems as listed in subsection (b), subject to approval of the local voters, as described in section 4. The new purposes include the construction of transit guideways such as rail systems but do not encompass special road lanes and specifically did not include the vehicles, maintenance, and operating costs of such systems. An attempt in 1990 to broaden the restrictions by allowing purchase of transit vehicles failed to receive voter approval.

SECTION 2

Use of motor vehicle fees and taxes. Revenues from fees and taxes imposed by the state upon vehicles or their use or operation, over and above the costs of collection and any refunds authorized by law, shall be used for the following purposes:

(a) The state administration and enforcement of laws regulating the use, operation, or registration of vehicles used upon the public streets and highways of this state, including the enforcement of traffic and vehicle laws by state agencies and the mitigation of the environmental effects of motor vehicle operation due to air and sound emissions.

(b) The purposes specified in Section 1 of this article. [June 4, 1974]

Section 2 relates to any registration fees and taxes on vehicles, as distinct from the taxes on fuels discussed in section 1. Paragraph (b) allows vehicle fee revenues to be used for the same purposes provided in section 1, and paragraph (a) allows the funds to be used by state administrative agencies, such as the Department of Motor Vehicles and the California Highway Patrol, for enforcement of vehicle laws.

SECTION 3

Allocation of revenues. The Legislature shall provide for the allocation of the revenues to be used for the purposes specified in Section 1 of this article in a manner which ensures the continuance of existing statutory allocation formulas for cities, counties, and areas of the state, until it determines that another basis for an equitable, geographical, and jurisdictional distribution exists; provided that, until such determination is made, any use of such revenues for purposes specified in subdivision (b) of Section 1 of this article by or in a city, county, or area of the state shall be included within the existing statutory allocations to, or for expenditure in, that city, county, or area. Any future statutory revisions shall provide for the allocation of these revenues, together with other similar revenues, in a manner which gives equal consideration to the transportation needs of all areas of the state and all segments of the population consistent with the orderly achievement of the adopted local, regional, and statewide goals for ground transportation in local general plans, regional transportation plans, and the California Transportation Plan. [June 4, 1974]

Gas tax funds are allocated statewide by the legislature, a highly political process involving rural-urban distinctions in both source and application of the revenues. Mass transit systems, being predominantly urban in nature, were seen as a threat to rural funding; this section allows the preexisting allocation patterns to continue for cities and counties, with the several areas of the state receiving their accustomed funding for section 1(a) purposes, subject to legislative adjustment. New expenditures for the mass transit purposes of section 1(b) will be taken from each area's allocated funding, thus not removing funds from the remainder of the state.

SECTION 4

Voter approval for expenditures. Revenues allocated pursuant to Section 3 may not be expended for the purposes specified in subdivision (b) of Section 1, except for research and planning, until such use is approved by a majority of the votes cast on the proposition authorizing such use of such revenues in an election held throughout the county or counties, or a specified area of a county or counties, within which the revenues are to be expended. The Legislature may authorize the revenues approved for allocation or expenditure under this section to be pledged or used for the payment of principal and interest on voter-approved bonds issued for the purposes specified in subdivision (b) of Section 1. [June 4, 1974]

This section, added in the 1974 revisions, ensures that traditional highway spending purposes will be replaced by mass transit spending only when the voters of the local area to which funds are allocated have approved the proposition, either generally or with reference to specific projects.

SECTION 5

Expenditures for bond payments. The Legislature may authorize up to 25 percent of the revenues available for expenditure by any city or county, or by the state, for the purposes specified in subdivision (a) of Section 1 of this article to be pledged or used for the payment of principal and interest on voter-approved bonds issued for such purposes. [June 4, 1974]

Section 1 was long considered to require pay-as-you-go financing, which would be violated by any attempt to allow long-term borrowing through the use of bonds. Section 5, part of the 1974 revisions, eliminated that principle by specifically expanding the highway-related purposes of section 1(a) to include payments for street and highway bonds.

SECTION 6

Loans to state general fund. This article shall not prevent the designated tax revenues from being temporarily loaned to the State General Fund upon condition that amounts loaned be repaid to the funds from which they were borrowed. [June 4, 1974]

Section 6 is a minor qualification carried forward from 1938. The original purpose of the article was to prevent any permanent deposit of the motor vehicle revenues into the state's general fund, where they would no longer be earmarked for section 1 and 2 purposes. This qualification provides fiscal flexibility by allowing loans to the general fund without endangering the restricted nature of the revenue.

SECTION 7

Scope of article. This article shall not affect or apply to fees or taxes imposed pursuant to the Sales and Use Tax Law or the Vehicle License Fee Law, and all amendments and additions now or hereafter made to such statutes. [June 4, 1974]

State and local taxes imposed on the retail sale of gasoline and other fuels are distinct from the separate state excise tax levied on the distributors of the fuel itself. The sales tax is deposited in the general fund and made available for any purposes designated by the legislature and is not affected by the restrictions imposed by this article. Vehicle license fees, levied by the state in lieu of any state or local ad valorem taxes on personal property authorized by Article XIII, are similarly unaffected.

SECTION 8

Use of excess lands for parks and recreation. Notwithstanding Sections 1 and 2 of this article, any real property acquired by the expenditure of the designated tax revenues by an entity other than the State for the purposes authorized in those sections, but no longer required for such purposes, may be used for local public park and recreational purposes. [June 8, 1976]

Section 8 was added in 1976 in order to allow real property that had been purchased with restricted funds to be used for park and recreation purposes by local governments. If the restriction had not been lifted, any excess real property (which was often small or oddly shaped) would have to be sold and the proceeds reimbursed to the local share of the motor fuels tax fund. The parcels instead may now be used for park purposes.

SECTION 9

Transfer of surplus state property located in coastal zone. Notwithstanding any other provision of this Constitution, the Legislature, by statute, with respect to surplus state property acquired by the expenditure of tax revenues designated in Sections 1 and 2 and located in the coastal zone, may authorize the transfer of such property, for a consideration at least equal to the acquisition cost paid by the state to acquire the property, to the Department of Parks and Recreation for state park purposes, or to the Department of Fish and Game for the protection and preservation of fish and wildlife habitat, or to the Wildlife Conservation Board for purposes of the Wildlife Conservation Law of 1947, or to the State Coastal Conservancy for the preservation of agricultural lands.

As used in this section, "coastal zone" means "coastal zone" as defined by Section 30103 of the Public Resources Code as such zone is described on January 1, 1977. [Nov. 7, 1978]

California's "coastal zone" is generally defined as any lands 1,000 yards inland of the Pacific shoreline or an area up to 5 miles wide in some rural coastal areas. If state agencies have used restricted funds to acquire lands in the coastal zone for the approved purposes listed in sections 1 and 2 and the lands are later found to be surplus, the lands may be transferred to other state agencies for the listed park or environmental purposes.

Under former practices, excess lands acquired with motor vehicle revenues were sold and the proceeds redeposited as earmarked funds. This section, added in 1978, allows the surplus lands to be "sold" to other state agencies at an appropriate price (at least equal to the original acquisition cost), which probably would be considerably below the current market value. The receiving agencies would acquire lands at substantial savings for use as parks, beaches, or wildlife preserves.

Article XX

Miscellaneous Subjects

Article XX is a thematically unconnected collection of sections that deal with the miscellany of the California Constitution.

SECTION 1

Sacramento County consolidation. Notwithstanding the provisions of Section 6 of Article XI, the County of Sacramento and all or any of the cities within the County of Sacramento may be consolidated as a charter city and county as provided by statute, with the approval of a majority of the electors of the county voting on the question of such consolidation and upon such other vote as the Legislature may prescribe in such statute. The charter City and County of Sacramento shall be a charter city and a charter county. Its charter city powers supersede conflicting charter county powers. [June 4, 1974]

Section 6 of Article XI establishes the general rule for consolidation of city and county governments, requiring all cities within a county to agree to join that county as a single merged government. This section, added in 1974 to accommodate proponents of local government reorganization, creates an exception for the specific case of Sacramento County by allowing consolidation of that county and "all *or any* of the cities" within it. The Government Code contains detailed special legislation allowing a new charter to be proposed for the county and an election in which the voters of each city could exercise the option of retaining their local government structure. Under the terms of those statutes, separate proposals for city-county consolidation were defeated by voters in the greater Sacramento area in 1974 and 1990.

SECTION 1.5

Homestead protection. The Legislature shall protect, by law, from forced sale a certain portion of the homestead and other property of all heads of families. [June 8, 1976]

From the first California constitutional convention until the present, the California Constitution has included a provision requiring the legislature to immunize some portion of a debtor's assets from the claims of creditors. The mandated legislation is currently codified at California Code of Civil Procedure sections 704.710–704.850 and 704.910–704.990. Although California courts often recite the doctrine that homesteads are favored in law,[80] they have also upheld the constitutionality of the provisions of the homestead statutes that permit sale of a judgment debtor's home unless a declaration of homestead has been recorded before the judgment lien has been created by recordation of an abstract of judgment.[81] The constitutional provision vests wide discretion in the legislature, including the power to impose reasonable regulations as to the amount, manner, and method of perfecting and preserving the homestead exemption. The current amount of the homestead exemption varies from $50,000 to $100,000, depending on the characteristics of the judgment debtor.[82]

SECTION 2

Tax exemptions for Stanford University and Huntington Library. Except for tax exemptions provided by Article XIII, the rights, powers, privileges, and confirmations conferred by Sections 10 and 15 of Article IX in effect on January 1, 1973, relating to Stanford University and the Huntington Library and Art Gallery, are continued in effect. [Nov. 5, 1974]

On November 5, 1974, the same date this section was added, sections 10 and 15 of Article IX were repealed. This section continues in effect the prior tax exemptions granted the two institutions by the repealed sections. The exemptions are quite broad. The Huntington Library is exempt from taxation on all its property,

[80] See, e.g., Lee v. Brown, 18 Cal. 3d 110, 132 Cal. Rptr. 649, 553 P.2d 1121 (1976).

[81] Taylor v. Madigan, 53 Cal. App. 3d 943, 126 Cal. Rptr. 376 (1975).

[82] Calif. Code of Civil Procedure sec. 704.730.

without regard to the use made of it.[83] Stanford University's exemption is limited to property held by it exclusively for educational purposes.[84] Stanford's exemption was adopted in 1900; the Huntington Library's exemption was adopted in 1930. Both exemptions were frankly admitted to be special legislation but were defended on the grounds that exemption from taxation would enable the entire income of the trust funds to be devoted to the charitable ends of the institution and to encourage "other public spirited citizens . . . to make similar gifts and bequests for the public welfare."

SECTION 3

Prescribed oath of office. Members of the Legislature, and all public officers and employees, executive, legislative, and judicial, except such inferior officers and employees as may be by law exempted, shall, before they enter upon the duties of their respective offices, take, and subscribe the following oath or affirmation:

> "I,______, do solemnly swear (or affirm) that I will support and defend the Constitution of the United States and the Constitution of the State of California against all enemies, foreign and domestic; that I will bear true faith and allegiance to the Constitution of the United States and the Constitution of the State of California; that I take this obligation freely, without any mental reservation or purpose of evasion; and that I will well and faithfully discharge the duties upon which I am about to enter.
>
> "And I do further swear (or affirm) that I do not advocate, nor am I a member of any party or organization, political or otherwise, that now advocates the overthrow of the Government of the United States or of the State of California by force or violence or other unlawful means; that within the five years immediately preceding the taking of this oath (or affirmation) I have not been a member of any party or organization, political or otherwise, that advocated the overthrow of the Government of the United States or of the State of California by force or violence or other unlawful means except as follows:______(if no affiliations, write in the words "No Exceptions") and that during such time as I hold the office of______ (name of office) I will not advocate nor become a member of any party or organization, political or otherwise, that advocates the overthrow of the Government of the United States or of the State of California by force or violence or other unlawful means."

And no other oath, declaration, or test, shall be required as a qualification for any public office or employment.

---

[83] Church Divinity School v. Alameda County, 152 Cal. App. 2d 496, 314 P.2d 209 (1957).

[84] Calif. Education Code sec. 94020, 94021.

"Public officer and employee" includes every officer and employee of the State, including the University of California, every county, city, city and county, district, and authority, including any department, division, bureau, board, commission, agency, or instrumentality of any of the foregoing. [Nov. 4, 1952]

Originally adopted in 1879, this provision was amended in 1952 to add the second paragraph of the oath, designed as an ironclad loyalty oath to bar from state employment members of the Communist party and others clinging to radical beliefs. In 1967, following the U.S. Supreme Court's decision in *Keyishian v. Board of Regents,* the California Supreme Court determined, in *Vogel v. Los Angeles County* (1967), that the oath was an unconstitutional violation of the federal Constitution's guarantee of free expression. Accordingly, the second paragraph of the oath is a dead letter.

SECTION 4

Franchises. The Legislature shall not pass any laws permitting the leasing or alienation of any franchise, so as to relieve the franchise or property held thereunder from the liabilities of the lessor or grantor, lessee, or grantee, contracted or incurred in the operation, use, or enjoyment of such franchise, or any of its privileges. [Nov. 5, 1974]

This provision, originally adopted as Article XII, section 10 of the 1879 Constitution, ensures that the transferee of any public franchise takes the franchise subject to all of its burdens and obligations, including the continued performance of the public service to which the franchise may be devoted.[85] The legislature is specifically disabled from altering this rule. In the 1878–1879 convention, the provision was considered sufficiently uncontroversial that it produced no debate or proposed alteration.

SECTION 5

Reservation of right to alter corporate laws. All laws now in force in this State concerning corporations and all laws that may be hereafter passed pursuant to this section may be altered from time to time or repealed. [June 6, 1972]

This provision, originally adopted as part of the 1879 Constitution, owes its genesis to the 1819 decision of the U.S. Supreme Court in *Trustees of Dartmouth College v. Woodward.* The New Hampshire legislature had enacted a series of statutes altering the governance structure of Dartmouth College as established by a royal charter of 1769. The Supreme Court concluded that the legislation

[85] See South Pasadena v. Pasadena Land & Water Co., 152 Cal. 579, 93 P. 490 (1908).

was invalid because the charter constituted a contract that the New Hampshire legislature was forbidden to impair by virtue of the contracts clause of Article I, section 10 of the federal Constitution.[86] As a result, corporate charters issued under laws permitting incorporation would be treated as contracts subject to the contracts clause. In order to preserve the ability of the state to alter the statutory conditions under which corporations conduct themselves, it became a popular practice of states to insert in the incorporation statute or state constitution a reservation of the right to alter the incorporation statute. Thus, any corporate charter issued pursuant to the state's incorporation statute implicitly carried within it the reservation. As a consequence, statutory changes were implicitly permitted by the corporate contract, and there was no impairment of the contract due to statutory alteration. This provision is California's reservation of this power in order to avoid the claims of holders of corporate charters that statutory alteration of the law governing corporations is an impairment of the contract established by the issuance of a corporate charter.

SECTION 6

Retirement benefits of legislators with reduced terms of office. Any legislator whose term of office is reduced by operation of the amendment to subdivision (a) of Section 2 of Article IV adopted by the people in 1972 shall, notwithstanding any other provision of this Constitution, be entitled to retirement benefits and compensation as if the term of office had not been so reduced. [Nov. 7, 1972]

This section was adopted at the same time that the term of office of senators and assemblypersons was adjusted in 1972 by amendment to Article IV, section 2. In order to preserve the expectation of retirement benefits and compensation inherent in the prior term of office, this section was added to the constitution.

SECTION 7

Term limits on constitutional officers. The limitations on the number of terms prescribed by Section 2 of Article IV, Sections 2 and 11 of Article V, Section 2 of Article IX, and Section 17 of Article XIII apply only to terms to which persons are elected or appointed on or after November 6, 1990, except that an incumbent Senator whose office is not on the ballot for the general election on that date may serve only one additional term. Those limitations shall not apply to any unexpired term to which a person is elected or appointed if the remainder of the term is less than half of the full term. [Nov. 7, 1990]

---

[86] U.S. Constitution, Art. I, sec. 10, reads in part, "No State shall . . . pass any . . . Law impairing the Obligation of Contracts."

This section partially implements Proposition 140, the Political Reform Act of 1990, which introduced to the constitution limitations on the number of successive terms that may be served by statewide elective officials. This section makes clear that the term limits created by Proposition 140 generally apply prospectively only.

SECTION 8

This section was renumbered Article I, section 21, effective November 5, 1974.

SECTION 9

This section was repealed November 3, 1970.

SECTION 10

This section was repealed June 8, 1976.

SECTION 11

This section was repealed June 8, 1976.

SECTION 12

This section was repealed November 3, 1970.

SECTION 13

This section was repealed November 3, 1970.

SECTION 14

This section was repealed November 3, 1970.

SECTION 15

This section was repealed June 8, 1976.

SECTION 16

This section was repealed November 7, 1972.

SECTION 17

This section was repealed June 8, 1976.

SECTION 17½

This section was repealed June 8, 1976.

SECTION 18

This section was renumbered Article I, section 8, effective November 5, 1974.

SECTION 19

This section was repealed June 8, 1976.

SECTION 20

This section was repealed June 8, 1976.

SECTION 21

This section was repealed June 8, 1976.

SECTION 22

Liquor controls. The State of California, subject to the internal revenue laws of the United States, shall have the exclusive right and power to license and regulate the manufacture, sale, purchase, possession and transportation of alcoholic beverages within the State, and subject to the laws of the United States regulating commerce between foreign nations and among the states shall have the exclusive right and power to regulate the importation into and exportation from the State, of alcoholic beverages. In the exercise of these rights and powers, the Legislature shall not constitute the State or any agency thereof a manufacturer or seller of alcoholic beverages.

All alcoholic beverages may be bought, sold, served, consumed and otherwise disposed of in premises which shall be licensed as provided by the Legislature. In providing for the licensing of premises, the Legislature may provide for the issuance of, among other licenses, licenses for the following types of premises where the alcoholic beverages specified in the licenses may be sold and served for consumption on the premises:

(a) For bona fide public eating places, as defined by the Legislature.

(b) For public premises in which the food shall not be sold or served as in a bona fide public eating place, but upon which premises the Legislature may permit the sale or service of food products incidental to the sale or service of alcoholic beverages. No person under the age of 21 years shall be permitted to enter and remain in any such premises without lawful business therein.

(c) For public premises for the sale and service of beers alone.

(d) Under such conditions as the Legislature may impose, for railroad dining or club cars, passenger ships, common carriers by air, and bona fide clubs after such clubs have been lawfully operated and for not less than one year.

The sale, furnishing, giving, or causing to be sold, furnished, or giving away of any alcoholic beverages to any person under the age of 21 years is hereby prohibited, and no person shall sell, furnish, give, or cause to be sold, furnished, or given away any alcoholic beverage to any person under the age of 21 years, and no person under the age of 21 years shall purchase any alcoholic beverage.

The Director of Alcoholic Beverage Control shall be the head of the Department of Alcoholic Beverage Control, shall be appointed by the Governor subject to confirmation by a majority vote of all the members elected to the Senate, and shall serve at the pleasure of the Governor. The director may be removed from office by the Governor, and the Legislature shall have the power, by a majority vote of all members elected to each house, to remove the director from office for dereliction of duty or corruption or incompetency. The director may appoint three persons who shall be exempt from civil service, in addition to the person he is authorized to appoint by Section 4 of Article XXIV.

The Department of Alcoholic Beverage Control shall have the exclusive power, except as herein provided and in accordance with laws enacted by the Legislature, to license the manufacture, importation and sale of alcoholic beverages in this State, and to collect license fees or occupation taxes on account thereof. The department shall have the power, in its discretion, to deny, suspend, or revoke any specific alcoholic beverage license if it shall determine for good cause that the granting or continuance of such license would be contrary to public welfare or morals, or that a person seeking or holding a license has violated any law prohibiting conduct involving moral turpitude. It shall be unlawful for any person other than a licensee of said department to manufacture, import or sell alcoholic beverages in this State.

The Alcoholic Beverage Control Appeals Board shall consist of three members appointed by the Governor, subject to confirmation by a majority vote of all the members elected to the Senate. Each member, at the time of his initial appointment, shall be a resident of a different county from the one in which either of the other members resides. The members of the board may be removed from office by the Governor, and the Legislature shall have the power, by a majority vote of all members elected to each house, to remove any member from office for dereliction of duty or corruption or incompetency.

When any person aggrieved thereby appeals from a decision of the department ordering any penalty assessment, issuing, denying, transferring, suspending or revoking any license for the manufacture, importation, or sale of alcoholic beverages, the board shall review the decision subject to such limitations as may be imposed by the Legislature. In such cases, the board shall not receive evidence in addition to that considered by the department. Review by the board of a decision of the department shall be limited to the questions whether the department has proceeded without or in excess of its jurisdiction, whether the department has proceeded in the manner required by law, whether the decision is supported by the findings, and whether the findings are supported by substantial evidence in light of the whole record. In appeals where the board finds that there is relevant evidence which, in the exercise of reasonable diligence, could not have been produced or which was improperly excluded at the hearing before the department it may enter an order remanding the matter to the department for reconsideration in the light of such evidence. In all other appeals the board shall enter an order either affirming or reversing the decision of the department. When the order reverses the decision of the department, the board may direct the reconsideration of the matter in the light of its order and may direct the department to take such further action as is specially enjoined upon it by law, but the order shall not limit or control in any way the discretion vested by law in the department. Orders of the board shall be subject to judicial review upon petition of the director or any party aggrieved by the order.

A concurrent resolution for the removal of either the director or any member of the board may be introduced in the Legislature only if five Members of the Senate, or 10 Members of the Assembly, join as authors.

Until the Legislature shall otherwise provide, the privilege of keeping, buying, selling, serving, and otherwise disposing of alcoholic beverages in bona fide hotels, restaurants, cafes, cafeterias, railroad dining or club cars, passenger ships, and other public eating places, and in bona fide clubs after such clubs have been lawfully operated for not less than one year, and the privilege of keeping, buying, selling, serving, and otherwise disposing of beers on any premises open to the general public shall be licensed and regulated under the applicable provisions of the Alcoholic Beverage Control Act, insofar as the same are not inconsistent with the provisions hereof, and excepting that the license fee to be charged bona fide hotels, restaurants, cafes, cafeterias, railroad dining or club cars, passenger ships, and other public eating places, and in bona fide clubs after such clubs have been lawfully operated for not less than one year, for the privilege of keeping, buying, selling, serving, and otherwise disposing of alcoholic beverages, shall be the amounts prescribed as of the operative date hereof, subject to the power of the Legislature to change such fees.

The State Board of Equalization shall assess and collect such excise taxes as are or may be imposed by the Legislature on account of the manufacture, importation and sale of alcoholic beverages in this State.

The Legislature may authorize, subject to reasonable restrictions, the sale in retail stores of alcoholic beverages contained in the original packages, where such alcoholic beverages are not to be consumed on the premises where sold; and may provide for the issuance of all types of licenses necessary to carry on the activities referred to in the first paragraph of this section, including but not limited to, licenses necessary for the manufacture, production, processing, importation, exportation, transportation, wholesaling, distribution, and sale of any and all kinds of alcoholic beverages.

The Legislature shall provide for apportioning the amounts collected for license fees or occupation taxes under the provisions hereof between the State and the cities,counties and cities of the State, in such manner as the Legislature may deem proper.

All constitutional provisions and laws inconsistent with the provisions hereof are hereby repealed.

The provisions of this section shall be self-executing, but nothing herein shall prohibit the Legislature from enacting laws implementing and not inconsistent with such provisions.

This amendment shall become operative on January 1, 1957. [Nov. 6, 1956]

When in 1933 the United States repealed nationwide prohibition of alcoholic beverages, it did so by adoption of the Twenty-first Amendment to the federal Constitution, section 2 of which conveyed to the states "virtually complete control over whether to permit importation or sale of liquor and how to structure the liquor distribution system.[87] This section is the California Constitution's assertion of the power conveyed to it under section 2 of the Twenty-first Amendment to the federal Constitution. It was adopted in 1932 (effectiveness being made expressly conditional upon federal repeal of prohibition) and subsequently amended in 1934, 1954, and 1956.

The power to regulate alcoholic beverages is not exclusively vested in the state of California. A series of U.S. Supreme Court decisions has established that if "the interests implicated by a state regulation are [sufficiently] closely related to the powers reserved by the Twenty-first Amendment . . . the [state] regulation may prevail, notwithstanding that its requirements directly conflict with express federal policies.[88] However, if the state regulates commerce in alcohol outside

---

[87] California Retail Liquor Dealers Ass'n v. Midcal Aluminum, Inc., 445 U.S. 97, 110 (1980).

[88] Capital Cities Cable, Inc. v. Crisp, 467 U.S. 691, 714 (1984).

those core powers, any conflicting federal regulation will displace the state regulation.

The core powers reserved to the states fall into two categories. The first is the decision whether to prohibit entirely the use of alcohol or to permit it under certain conditions as to minimum age, licensed premises, limited hours, or the like. Even these expressly prohibitory powers are subject to limitation by other parts of the federal Constitution.[89] The second category is the "structure of the liquor distribution system." But this power is not unlimited; the U.S. Supreme Court has declared that state attempts to regulate in a fashion inimical to federal antitrust law or that attempt to discriminate against out-of-state interests in violation of the implicit limits of the commerce clause are invalid.[90]

Within this shadow of federal control, this section mandates the creation of an elaborate structure of regulation of all phases of traffic in alcoholic beverages. The legislature has responded by the enactment of a detailed statute, codified at California Business and Professions Code sections 2300–25763, and accompanying regulations promulgated by the Department of Alcoholic Beverage Control.

The regulatory regime created by this section and the implementing legislation involves an agency, the Department of Alcoholic Beverage Control, which administers the statute, and a quasi-judicial body, the Alcoholic Beverage Control Appeals Board, in which is vested considerable power of judicial review over the actions of the department. This close relationship between the appeals board and the department is tempered by the fact that judgments of the appeals board are subject to review in the appellate courts of California.

SECTION 23

Speaker of the assembly declared an ex officio member of the governing board of the state college system. Notwithstanding any other provision of this Constitution, the Speaker of the Assembly shall be an ex officio member, having equal rights and duties with the nonlegislative members, of any state agency created by the Legislature in the field of public higher education which is charged with the management, administration, and control of the State College System of California. [Nov. 3, 1970]

---

[89] See, e.g., Larkin v. Grendel's Den, 459 U.S. 116, 122 n.5 (1982) (limited by the establishment of religion clause); Craig v. Boren, 429 U.S. 190,204–9 (1976) (limited by the equal protection clause).

[90] See, e.g., 324 Liquor Corp. v. Duffy, 107 S. Ct. 720, 726 (1987) (antitrust); Healy v. Beer Institute, Inc., 491 U.S. 324 (1989) (commerce clause); Bacchus Imports v. Dias, 468 U.S. 263 (1984) (commerce clause).

This section ensures that the Speaker of the assembly shall have a fully participating voice as a trustee of the California State University system. Education Code section 66600 creates the Trustees of the California State University and designates it as the body responsible for administering the California State University. Education Code section 66602 establishes the composition of the Trustees and, in so doing, recognizes and repeats the constitutionally guaranteed status of the Speaker of the assembly.

Article XXI

Reapportionment of Senate, Assembly, Congressional, and Board of Equalization Districts

Elected members of representative government bodies, such as a state legislature, are apportioned among districts of the state; periodically, that apportionment must be reallocated, and the resulting reapportionment requires an alteration of the boundaries of the districts the members represent. Both the 1849 and the 1879 Constitutions contained provisions that controlled the process of designating district boundaries.

This article, proposed by the legislature in 1978 and adopted by the voters in 1980, replaced, shortened, and combined several of the older provisions, restating the applicable standards in a manner believed to comply better with constitutional interpretations of both the U.S. and California supreme courts. The constitutional issues are complex, since any reapportionment has immediate effects on voting patterns within a redesigned district, and thus on both the electorate and incumbent politicians.

The 1879 Constitution had provided that members of both the state senate and assembly would be elected from districts "as nearly equal in population as may be," a provision that was replaced in 1926 with "the federal plan," under which the assembly districts would continue to be drawn primarily to reflect equal population, but senate districts would reflect geographical representation based on counties. That plan created a pattern of rural dominance of the senate that was to last nearly forty years. In 1964, the U.S. Supreme Court announced its opinions in *Reynolds v. Sims and Lucas v. Forty-fourth General Assembly,* declaring that the equal protection clause of the federal Constitution's Fourteenth Amendment required that the seats in both houses of state legislatures be apportioned on a population basis, not by area representation. Months later, federal courts accordingly held the California Senate's apportionment pattern unconstitutional (*Silver v. Jordan*, 1964), and the California Supreme Court ruled that not only the senate, but the assembly as well, must be reapportioned (*Silver v. Brown*, 1965). Similar rulings required the reapportionment of numerous congressional districts (*Silver v. Reagan*, 1967). Thus began a process of revising the standards for reapportionment that has continued to the present, with the supreme court stepping in repeatedly to prepare reapportionment plans when the legislature was unable to reach consensus or produce legally acceptable plans.

The contents of Article XXI were based in part on the experience derived from court adoption of a reapportionment plan based on the 1970 census. A series of decisions, culminating in *Legislature v. Reinecke* (IV) (1973), Established more detailed standards for reapportionment, supplanting them with additional concerns derived from the federal constitutional developments. The new article, containing a single section, replaced some clearly inappropriate standards but addressed only generally the various constitutional concerns and merely rearranged and consolidated many of the earlier standards.

The primary concern of the drafters of the new article was to "prepare for an orderly redistricting after the 1980 census."[91] The first test of Article XXI thus was the reapportionment of 1981, which unfortunately was widely acknowledged as having created district boundaries drawn for maximum partisan benefit.[92] It spawned bitter recriminations that culminated in litigation allowing the plan to control the 1982 elections, despite its rejection by the voters in intervening referendums (*Assembly v. Deukmejian*, 1982). Subsequent attempts to adopt a different scheme were then invalidated as violations of the once-a-decade rule implicitly contained in Article XXI (*Legislature v. Deukmejian*, 1983). As a result, the controversial 1981 apportionment nevertheless controlled the states' districts, and thus the membership of its legislature, until the succeeding reapportionment scheduled for 1991.

In late 1991, the California Supreme Court once again was "called on to resolve the impasse created by the failure of the Legislature and Governor" to adopt plans in time for the 1992 primary and general elections. Unlike the reapportionment controversies of earlier decades, in which concerns for geographical balance of power had eventually been replaced by overtly partisan motives,

[91] Arguments in Favor of Proposition 6, California Voter's Pamphlet, Primary Election of June 3, 1980, p. 22.

[92] See dissenting opinion of Mosk, J., in Assembly v. Deukmejian, 30 Cal. 3d 638, 639 P.2d 939, 973 (1982). Federal challenges to the 1982 plan were rebuffed in Badham v. Eu, 694 F. Supp. 664 (N.D. Cal. 1988), aff'd mem. 109 S. Ct. 829 (1989).

the 1991 controversy included considerations raised by recent federal law, the Voting Rights Act Amendments of 1982. Those concerns, which deal with minority voting patterns, were incorporated in a new reapportionment plan imposed and adopted by the court in January 1992 (*Wilson v. Eu (III)*). The opinion adopted a detailed group of standards similar to those used in 1973 and including aspects of the Voting Rights Act, Article XXI, and federal constitutional concerns, thus substantially supplementing the provisions of Article XXI.

SECTION 1

Reapportionment following national census. In the year following the year in which the national census is taken under the direction of Congress at the beginning of each decade, the Legislature shall adjust the boundary lines of the Senatorial, Assembly, Congressional, and Board of Equalization districts in conformance with the following standards:

Standards (a) Each member of the Senate, Assembly, Congress, and the Board of Equalization shall be elected from a single-member district.
(b) The population of all districts of a particular type shall be reasonably equal.
(c) Every district shall be contiguous.
(d) Districts of each type shall be numbered consecutively commencing at the northern boundary of the State and ending at the southern boundary.
(e) The geographical integrity of any city, county, or city and county, or of any geographical region shall be respected to the extent possible without violating the requirements of any other subdivision of this section. [June 3, 1980]

This section requires a reapportionment of the districts for the election of representatives to Congress, the two houses of the state legislature, and the Board of Equalization established by section 17 of Article XIII. Periodic redrawing of district boundaries is mandatory, and by established precedent, only one valid plan may be implemented during a decennial census period (*Legislature v. Deukmejian*, 1983).

Article XXI does not apply to other governmental entities within the state; for instance, sections 1–4 of Article XI, with attendant statutes, govern the apportionment of city and county elected representatives. Those provisions too are subject to similar constitutional concerns and the federal Voting Rights Act (*Griffin v. Board of Supervisors of Monterey County*, 1963; *Garza v. County of Los Angeles*, 1990).

This article specifies that it is the legislature's responsibility "to adjust the boundary lines" nevertheless, its actions remain subject to veto by the governor (*Legislature v. Reinecke (I)*, 1972; *Wilson v. Eu (I)*, 1991) and may be invalidated by a referendum passed by the electorate (*Assembly v. Deukmejian*, 1982).

Moreover, when reapportionment has not been accomplished in a timely fashion, the supreme court reluctantly has performed that duty, exercising its independent judicial power to "insure the electorate equal protection of the laws" (*Silver v. Brown (I)*, 1965; *Wilson v. Eu (I)*, 1991). It remains constitutionally uncertain whether the electorate could directly adopt a reapportionment plan by initiative (*Legislature v. Deukmejian*, 1983), and subsequent events have demonstrated the practical near impossibility of doing so, due to the extraordinary technical complexity of the task (*Wilson v. Eu (III)*, 1992).

The use of single-member districts avoids many of the practical and political difficulties created by multimember districts, in which voting patterns and party allegiance become much more complex. Single-member districts for the state senate and assembly have been a continuous requirement of California's constitutions since 1849, and similarly so for the Board of Equalization since 1879. Moreover, multimember state legislature districts, although not per se unconstitutional, are disfavored by federal courts on equal protection grounds (*Fotson v. Dorsey*, 1965) and under the Voting Rights Act (*Thornburg v. Gingles*, 1986). Prior California law was not explicit as to the composition of congressional districts; federal statutes were revised in 1967 to require single-member congressional districts,[93] a standard that was incorporated by the supreme court (*Legislature v. Reinecke (I)*, 1972) and is now mandated for all the districts covered by this article.

Provisions of the 1879 Constitution required districts of the assembly, senate, and Board of Equalization to be "nearly equal" in population. (Under the federal plan, applicable after 1926, senate districts were not based on population; since that plan was declared invalid in 1964 [*Silver v. Jordan*], the assembly and senate again have been held to a similar population standard.) In contrast, the only provisions regarding congressional apportionment contained little more than vague references to population ratios and relied primarily on combinations of contiguous assembly districts as their primary component parts.

The several earlier standards were combined in 1980 into the current subsection (b), requiring the population of districts to be "reasonably equal." Even that standard is considered insufficient to satisfy the more exacting federal law applicable to congressional districts, which requires population equality "as nearly as is practicable," a standard that requires a "good faith effort to achieve precise mathematical equality" (*Wilson v. Eu (III)*, 1992).

The 1879 Constitution introduced the requirement that senate and assembly districts be "composed of contiguous territory," a standard similarly applicable to congressional districts, whose component portions were to be "compact contiguous Assembly districts." Despite the pronounced intent of its proponents

[93] 2 U.S.C.A. sec. 2(c) (West's 1985), enacted Dec. 14, 1967. See Wesberry v. Sanders, 376 U.S. 1 (1964).

that the current subsection (c) would "help deter odd-shaped districts,"[94] the contiguity standard merely prevented discontinuous districts and did little to prevent irregularly shaped gerrymandered districts. The supreme court more recently has interpreted the contiguity provision to be compatible with both the goals of the federal Voting Rights Act and the requirement of subsection (e) regarding "geographical integrity." When thus combined, it requires that districts be "contained, insofar as possible, wholly within one of the major geographic regions of the state" and reflect a "functional compactness" allowing citizens "to relate to each other and their representatives," facilitated by shared interests and membership "in a political community, including a county or city" (*Wilson v. Eu (III)*, 1992).

Subsection (d) is a direct carryover from the 1879 provisions regarding the senate and assembly and has importance primarily as a means of designating the staggered election schedule among districts, based on odd- or even-numbered designations.

Subsection (e) is the only provision that overtly suggests a hierarchical ordering among the standards, clearly requiring that this standard be respected only "to the extent possible without violating" other requirements. A hierarchy has also of subsection (b) is "the primary" reapportionment criterion because it is mandated by the federal Constitution. The remaining standards appear to be of coequal stature.

A pervasive feature of the 1879 provisions had been a policy against locating district lines so as to divide cities or counties, a concern that related both to the "compact" and "contiguous" design goals of subsection (c) and to a fear that functional political areas might be divided for partisan advantage. However, as greater precision of population equality became a dominant concern, it became more difficult to maintain inviolate county and city boundaries, and the integrity of local government boundaries began to yield to the other requirements.

A similar standard of functional compactness is reflected in the Voting Rights Act's concern for protecting and enhancing the voting strength of political minority groups. Thus, the 1992 reapportionment was designed to "maximize the opportunities for meaningful minority participation in California elections," an approach that elevated minority voting populations to one of the primary considerations in designing the new district boundaries (*Wilson v. Eu (III)*, 1992).

ARTICLE XXII

Article XXII was repealed June 6, 1972.

---

[94] Arguments in Favor of Proposition 6, California Voter's Pamphlet, Primary Election of June 3, 1980, p. 22.

ARTICLE XXIII

Article XXIII was repealed June 8, 1976.

ARTICLE XXIV

Article XXIV was repealed June 8, 1976.

ARTICLE XXV

Article XXV was repealed November 8, 1949.

ARTICLE XXVI

Article XXVI was renumbered Article XIX, June 8, 1976.

ARTICLE XXVII

Article XXVII was repealed November 3, 1970.

ARTICLE XXVIII

Article XXVIII was repealed November 5, 1974.

[There are no articles numbered from XXIX to XXXIII.]

Article XXXIV

Public Housing Project Law

This article imposes on any state public body a requirement that in order to develop, construct, or acquire any federally financed low-income housing project, the proposal must first be approved by the voters in a referendum held for that purpose. The provision owes its origin to a unique set of historical circumstances.

This article was the direct result of the California Supreme Court's 1950 decision in *Housing Authority v. Superior Court* that local decisions regarding development of federally subsidized public housing projects were to be classified as executive or administrative acts rather than legislative acts, and thus exempt from the provisions of Article IV, section 1, which permitted electors of self-governing localities to veto by referendum any legislative action of local legislative bodies. As a direct result of the decision, a local housing authority was free to request federal assistance in the construction of low-income housing without overcoming the hurdle of a popular referendum on the issue.

Within six months, a voter initiative placed Proposition 10 on the November 1950 statewide ballot. Approved by a scant majority of the voters,[95] it added Article XXXIV to the constitution, overruling *Housing Authority v. Superior Court*

[95] The vote was 1,591,076 (50.8 percent) in favor and 1,542,161 (49.2 percent) opposed. A Study of Ballot Measures: 1884–1986, comp. Office of the Secretary of State, State of California (Secretary of State: Sacramento, CA., n.d.), results of election of November 7, 1950, with respect to Proposition 10.

by providing that not only was a referendum permissible in the case of local requests for federal funds for low-income housing but that such a referendum was mandatory. In 1974 the legislature placed Proposition 15 on the statewide ballot, seeking to repeal Article XXXIV. The proposition was soundly defeated.[96]

SECTION 1

Voter approval required for low-income housing projects. No low rent housing project shall hereafter be developed, constructed, or acquired in any manner by any state public body until, a majority of the qualified electors of the city, town or county, as the case may be, in which it is proposed to develop, construct, or acquire the same, voting upon such issue, approve such project by voting in favor thereof at an election to be held for that purpose, or at any general or special election.

For the purposes of this article the term "low rent housing project" shall mean any development composed of urban or rural dwellings, apartments or other living accommodations for persons of low income, financed in whole or in part by the Federal Government or a state public body or to which the Federal Government or a state public body extends assistance by supplying all or a part of the labor, by guaranteeing the payment of liens, or otherwise. For the purposes of this article only there shall be excluded from the term "low rent housing project" any such project where there shall be in existence on the effective date hereof, a contract for financial assistance between any state public body and the Federal Government in respect to such project.

For the purposes of this article only "persons of low income" shall mean persons or families who lack the amount of income which is necessary (as determined by the state public body developing, constructing, or acquiring the housing project) to enable them, without financial assistance, to live in decent, safe and sanitary dwellings, without overcrowding.

For purposes of this article the term "state public body" shall mean this State, or any city, city and county, county, district, authority, agency, or any other subdivision or public body of this State.

For the purposes of this article the term "Federal Government" shall mean the United States of America, or any agency or instrumentality, corporate or otherwise, of the United States of America. [Nov. 7, 1950]

The validity of this provision under the U.S. Constitution was placed at issue in a 1970 case, *Valtierra v. Housing Authority of San Jose*. In 1968 Santa Clara County voters had defeated, via a referendum required under Article XXXIV, the San Jose Housing Authority's application for federal funds to construct a low-rent

[96] Ibid.: results of election of November 5, 1974, with respect to Proposition 15. The vote was 2,028,964 (38.7 percent) in favor and 3,211,295 (61.3 percent) opposed.

housing project. Valtierra, a low-income resident of San Jose, brought suit, claiming that Article XXXIV violated the equal protection clause of the Fourteenth Amendment because it operated to discriminate invidiously against her on the basis of her poverty. The federal trial court agreed but the U.S. Supreme Court, in *James v. Valtierra* (1971), reversed. The Court concluded that wealth was not a legislative classification sufficiently suspect to trigger the most exacting judicial scrutiny. Nor was the claimed interest of the poor in obtaining safe and sanitary housing deemed sufficiently fundamental to mandate strict judicial scrutiny. The Court's view was that by adopting Article XXXIV, Californians merely sought to extend the reach of direct voter democracy: the referendum "procedure ensures that all the people of a community will have a voice in a decision which may lead to large expenditures of local governmental funds for increased public services and to lower tax revenues."

Among the interpretational issues surrounding section 1 is the question of thedefinition of low-rent housing projects. For example, the use of public bond proceeds to make long-term low interest loans to property owners in identified depressed residential areas was held not to constitute a low-rent housing project (*Board of Supervisors of City and County of San Francisco v. Dolan*, 1975). A more difficult issue is posed by so-called mixed income developments, in which a portion of the units are reserved at low rents for persons of low income and the remainder are offered at market rates without regard to the income of the prospective occupant. In 1976, the supreme court, in *California Housing Finance Agency v. Elliott*, declared that "the purpose underlying adoption of article XXXIV, section 1, was to permit the people of a community to have a voice in decisions which affect the future development of their community and which substantially increase their tax burden." Thus, a development undertaken by a public housing agency in which as many as 75 percent of the units would be leased to low-income tenants was deemed to be a low-rent project. The court reasoned that the addition of some units offered at market rates did "not substantially affect either the basic character of the low-rent housing program or its potential impact on the community" since the project at issue would "place some financial strain on the taxpayers whose communities must provide additional services and assistance to low-income tenants." Accordingly, the court determined that Article XXXIV applied to mixed-income projects where "the substance and primary purpose of the housing program . . . [was] to provide housing for those who cannot otherwise afford quality housing."

The supreme court in *Elliott* expressly left unresolved the question of whether "a housing project which consists of a relatively small portion of low-income tenants" was a low-rent housing project subject to Article XXXIV. Following *Elliott*, the legislature adopted the Public Housing Election Implementation Act,[97] which,

[97] Cal. Stat. 1976, ch. 1339, sec. 3, codified at Calif. Health and Safety Code sec. 37000–37002.

in part, excluded from the definition of "low rent housing project" developments that are privately owned, not tax exempt, and in which not more than 49 percent of the units are made available to persons of low income.[98] The supreme court in 1978 upheld the statutory definition as consistent with Article XXXIV in *California Housing Finance Agency v. Patitucci.*

Because Article XXXIV, section 1 applies only to low-rent housing projects undertaken by a public body, there have arisen several cases that grapple with the problem of such projects undertaken by private entities but with the assistance or supervision of public bodies. For example, where the public entity defines the project's scope and appearance, determines the financing arrangements, lends money needed for development, retains a right to buy, sell, or lease the project units, and imposes other rules of conduct on the private developer, the development has been held to be a public one subject to Article XXXIV.[99] By contrast, where the private developer designs, finances, and constructs the project, it retains its private character despite the right given to a public housing authority to lease a portion of the units and the fact that federal aid was sought to enable 30 percent of the units to be leased to low-income persons (*Winkelman v. City of Tiburon*, 1973). According to the supreme court, the Article XXXIV referendum endum procedure applies "whenever a state agency closely participates, or assists, in the development of a low-cost housing project" (*California Housing Finance Agency v. Elliott*, 1976).

It has been common practice since the adoption of Article XXXIV to submit to the voters ballot measures that simply ask whether they approve of the development of a specified maximum number of units of low-income housing within the affected locality.[100] In a 1990 decision, *Davis v. City of Berkeley*, the supreme court upheld that practice as consistent with Article XXXIV, section 1. Although the court conceded that the intent of Article XXXIV was to afford voters the opportunity to weigh the financial and aesthetic costs of public housing against the need for affordable housing, it concluded that nonspecific ballot measures that fail to describe the size, design, and location of the housing to be developed comport with the requirements of Article XXXIV.

Article XXXIV, section 1 has also been held to be inapplicable to the question of whether a county should simply establish a public housing authority (*Martinez v. Board of Supervisors of Sonoma County*, 1972). In reliance on a legislative declaration that "leased housing" should not come within the ambit of Article

---

[98] See Calif. Health and Safety Code sec. 37001(a).

[99] Redevelopment Agency of City of San Pablo v. Shepard, 75 Cal. App. 3d 453, 142 Cal. Rptr. 212 (1977). See also California Housing Finance Agency v. Elliott, 17 Cal. 3d 575, 551 P.2d 1193, 131 Cal. Rptr. 361 (1976).

[100] See, e.g., Davis v. City of Berkeley, 51 Cal. 3d 227, 240 n.7, 794 P.2d 46, 253 Cal. Rptr. 839 (1989).

XXXIV,[101] the court of appeal has concluded that the lease by a public housing authority of low-rent housing from a private developer did not constitute the "acqui[sition] in any manner" of low-rent housing by a public body (*Housing Authority of Monterey County v. Monterey County Senior Citizen Park*, 1985).

SECTION 2

Provisions declared to be self-executing. The provisions of this article shall be self-executing but legislation not in conflict herewith may be added to facilitate its operation. [Nov. 7, 1950]

This section is intended merely to make clear that the legislature was not required to take any action to implement the constitutional change effected by section 1 and to empower the legislature to implement Article XXXIV by appropriate, consistent legislation. The legislature has done so, most prominently in the Public Housing Election Implementation Act,[102] but also in other scattered sections of the California Health and Safety Code.[103]

SECTION 3

Constitutional severability. If any portion, section or clause of this article, or the application thereof to any person or circumstances, shall for any reason be declared unconstitutional or held invalid, the reminder of this article, or the application of such portion, section or clause to other persons or circumstances, shall not be affected thereby. [Nov. 7, 1950]

This technical section was inserted by the drafters for the precautionary purpose of preserving as much of Article XXXIV as possible in the event that its provisions were found partially to violate the U.S. Constitution. Since the validity of Article XXXIV under the federal Constitution was upheld in *James v. Valtierra* (1971), there has never been any need to apply this section.

---

[101] Calif. Health and Safety Code sec. 36000.

[102] Cal. Stat. 1976, ch. 1339, sec. 3, codified at Calif. Health and Safety Code sec. 37000–37002.

[103] See, e.g., Calif. Health and Safety Code sec. 36068, excluding certain housing projects subject to Art. XXXIV from treatment as farm labor centers under the Farm Labor Center Act, Calif. Stat. 1963, ch. 1515, sec. 1, codified at Calif. Health and Safety Code sec. 36050–72.

SECTION 4

Scope of article. The provisions of this article shall supersede all provisions of this Constitution and laws enacted thereunder in conflict therewith. [Nov. 7, 1950]

This section was included to preclude arguments that Article XXXIV might be invalid or limited in its application by reason of its inconsistency with some other portion of the California Constitution. It was probably unnecessary to recite that Article XXXIV supersedes the provisions of contrary existing legislation but the drafters did so to preclude arguments that Article XXXIV was either not intended to affect preexisting legislation or should be interpreted to accommodate such legislation. The lack of judicial interpretation of this section is some evidence of the effectiveness of the drafters' intent.

■ BIBLIOGRAPHY

Abrahamson, Shirley, and Gutmann, D. The New Federalism: State Constitutions and State Courts. Judicature 71 (1987): 88. Review of the trend toward judicial reliance on independent state constitutions.

Babcock, Barbara. Clara Shortridge Foltz: "First Woman." Ariz. L. Rev. 30 (1988): 673. An excellent biographical account of Clara Foltz, an important and colorful figure in the development of women's rights in the 1879 Constitution.

______. Clara Shortridge Foltz: Constitution-Maker. Ind. L.J. 66 (1991): 849. A continuation of Babcock's biography of Clara Foltz.

Bancroft, Hubert. History of California. Reprint ed., Santa Barbara, Wallace Hebberd, 1963. Still one of the principal reference works pertaining to California history.

Blume, William H. California Courts in Historical Perspective. Hastings L.J. 22 (1970): 121. An excellent history of the California court system to 1970.

Bowman, J. N. The Original Constitution of California of 1849. Calif. Hist. Soc. Q. 28 (1949). An account of the 1849 Constitution.

Brennan, William. State Constitutions and the Protection of Individual Rights. Harv. L. Rev. 90 (1977): 489. An influential article urging judicial reliance upon state constitutions.

Browne, J. Ross. Report of the Debates of the Convention of California on the Formation of the State Constitution. Washington, D.C., 1850. An indispensable primary source: the stenographic account of the 1849 convention.

______. Muleback to the Convention: Letters of J. Ross Browne, Reporter to the Constitutional Convention, Monterey, September-October, 1849. San Francisco: Book Club of San Francisco, 1950. A collection of Browne's correspondence during the 1849 convention, lending further insight into those proceedings.

California Constitution Revision Commission. Proposed Revision of Articles III, IV, V, VI, VII, VIII, XXIV of the California Constitution. Sacramento, Calif.: California Constitution Revision Commission, 1966. Report detailing proposed changes to the constitution.

______. Proposed Revision of Articles IX, X, XI, XII, XVII, XVIII of the California Constitution. Sacramento, Calif.: California Constitution Revision Commission, 1968. Report detailing proposed changes to the constitution.

______. Proposed Revision of the California Constitution, 1970. Sacramento, Calif.: California Constitution Revision Commission, 1970. Report detailing proposed changes to the constitution.

______. Proposed Revision of the California Constitution, Report to the California Legislature of the California Constitution Revision Commission. Sacramento, Calif.: California Constitution Revision Commission, 1971. Report detailing proposed changes to the constitution.

California Secretary of State. A Study of Ballot Measures: 1884–1986. Sacramento, Calif.: Secretary of State, n.d. A compilation of ballot measures and their electoral results.

Caughey, John W. California. Englewood Cliffs, N.J.: Prentice-Hall, 1953. A short general history of California.

Chapman, Charles E. A History of California: The Spanish Period. New York: Macmillan, 1921. A general history of the period.

Colantuono, M. The Revision of American State Constitutions: Legislative Power, Popular Sovereignty, and Constitutional Change. Calif. L. Rev. 75 (1987): 1473. An examination of the revision and amendment process to state constitutions.

Collins, Ronald. Reliance on State Constitutions: Away from a Reactionary Approach. Hastings Const. L.Q. 9 (1981): 1. Urging judicial reliance on state constitutions.

Conmy, Peter T. The Constitutional Beginnings of California. San Francisco: Native Sons of the Golden West, 1959. A useful but spare survey of the events leading up to and including the 1849 convention.

Crosby, Margaret. New Frontiers: Individual Rights under the California Constitution. Hastings Const. L.Q. 17 (1989): 81. Analyzing cases that accord citizens greater rights under the state constitution.

Crouch, W., et al. California Government and Politics. 4th ed. Englewood Cliffs, N.J.: Prentice–Hall, 1967. A general survey.

David, Leon. Our California Constitutions: Retrospections in This Bicentennial Year. Hastings Const. L.Q. 3 (1976): 697. An excellent survey of the 1849 and 1879 constitutions.

Davis, Winfield. History of Political Conventions in California, 1849–1892. Sacramento, Calif.: State Library, 1893. Contains accounts of the 1849 and 1879 conventions.

Deukmejian, George, and Thompson, Clifford K., Jr. All Sail and No Anchor: Judicial Review under the California Constitution. Hastings Const. L.Q. 6 (1979): 975. A criticism of judicial reliance on the California Constitution as an independent source of individual liberties.

Douglas, M. Judicial Review of Initiative Constitutional Amendments. U.C. Davis L. Rev. 14 (1980): 461. An examination of the circumstances under which the judiciary may review the legitimacy of constitutional amendments adopted by the initiative process.

Ehrman, Kenneth A., and Flavin, Sean. Taxing California Property (3d, Deerfield, Ill.: Callaghan, 1989).

Ellison, Joseph. The Struggle for Civil Government in California, 1846–1850. Calif. Hist. Soc. Q. 10 (1931): 3. A reasonably comprehensive survey of the events leading up to and including the 1849 convention.

______. California and the Nation, 1850–1869: A Study of the Relations of a Frontier Community with the Federal Government. New York: Da Capo Press reprint, 1969. A general account of the period.

Engelbert, Ernest A., and Gunnell, John G. State Constitutional Revision in California: An Analysis Prepared for the Citizens Legislative Advisory Commission. Sacramento, Calif.: 1961. A contemporaneous recommendation concerning constitutional revision.

Fischer, James. Ballot Propositions: The Challenge of Direct Democracy to State Constitutional Jurisprudence. Hastings Const. L.Q. 11 (1983): 43. A critical review of the effect of initiatives as a device to amend the California Constitution.

Friesen, Jennifer. Should California's Constitutional Guarantees of Individual Rights Apply against Private Actors. Hastings Const. L.Q. 17 (1989): 111. An examination of the legal question of the state action doctrine under the California Constitution arguing in favor of extending constitutional guarantees without requirement of state action.

Fritz, Christian. More Than "Shreds and Patches": California's First Bill of Rights. Hastings Const. L.Q. 17 (1989): 13. An excellent interpretation of the constitutional sources of the 1849 Constitution's Declaration of Rights.

Goodwin, Leonidas. The Establishment of State Government in California, 1846–1850. New York: Macmillan, 1914. A general survey of the developments leading up to the 1849 convention, the convention itself, and the first session of the California legislature convened after statehood.

Grodin, Joseph R. In Pursuit of Justice. Berkeley: University of California Press, 1989. Describing California's legal and judicial systems from the perspective of a former judge.

Hansen, Woodrow. The Search for Authority in California. Oakland, Calif.: Biobooks, 1960. An account of the early constitutional developments of California.

Harlow, Neal. California Conquered: War and Peace on the Pacific, 1846–1850. Berkeley: University of California Press, 1982. Discussion of the Mexican period and American conquest of California.

Harvey, R. The Dynamics of California Government and Politics. Monterey, Calif.: Brooks/Cole, 1985. A useful general background treatment.

Hichborn, Franklin. Story of the California Legislature of 1911. San Francisco: James H. Barry Co., 1911. A comprehensive account of the important legislative session in which many of the Progressive reforms were initiated.

Holliday, J. S. The World Rushed In: The California Gold Rush Experience. New York: Simon and Schuster, 1981. Colorful general background of the social and cultural experience of the time.

Horler, Virginia L. Guide to Public Debt Financing in California. San Francisco: Packard Press, 1987. Excellent analysis of state and local government financing techniques.

Hunt, Rockwell D. The Genesis of California's First Constitution (1846–49). New York: Johnson Reprint Corp., 1973. Useful survey of the events leading up to and including the 1849 Constitution.

Hyink, Bernard. California Revises Its Constitution. W. Pol. Q. 22 (1969): 637. A study of the revision process of the 1960s.

Johnson, David A. Founding the Far West: California, Oregon and Nevada, 1840–1890. Berkeley: University of California Press, 1992. Examines the process by which California entered the Union.

Langum, David J. Law and Community on the Mexican California Frontier: Anglo-American Expatriates and the Clash of Legal Traditions, 1821–1846. Norman, Okla.: University of Oklahoma Press, 1987. Dealing with the background to the American conquest of California and describing the relationship of American expatriates in Mexican California with Mexican legal institutions.

Law and California Society: 100 Years of the State Constitution. San Diego, Calif.: San Diego Union, 1980. A collection of very short essays pertaining to various aspects of the historical evolution of the California Constitution.

League of California Cities. Article XIII B Appropriations Limit, Uniform Guidelines. Sacramento: League of California Cities 1991. Suggested guidelines for municipal implementation of Article XIII A.

League of Women Voters. Initiative and Referendum in California: A Legacy Lost? Sacramento: The League, 1984. Discussing the history and modern shortcomings of the initiative process.

Lowenstein, Daniel. California Initiatives and the Single-Subject Rule. University of California at Los Angeles L. Rev. 30 (1983): 936. Reviewing the history of the constitutional requirement that initiatives be limited to a single subject.

Mercer, Lloyd J., and Morgan, W. Douglas. California City and County User Changes: A Post Proposition 13 Assessment. Urban Law and Policy 7 (1985): 187–205. Analysis of user charges levied by local governments to pay for certain government services.

Mowry, George S. The California Progressives. Berkeley, Calif.: University of California Press, 1951. A general account of the Progressive era.

Muir, William K. Legislature: California's School of Politics. Chicago: University of Chicago Press, 1982. A useful political and historical review of the California legislature.

Nash, Gerald D. State Government and Economic Development. New York: Arno Press, 1964. A comprehensive survey of the historical relationship between California government and economic development.

Olin, Spencer C., Jr. California's Prodigal Sons: Hiram Johnson and the Progressives, 1911–1917 Berkeley, Calif.: University of California Press, 1968. An excellent account of the Progressive movement.

Palmer, William, and Selvin, Paul. The Development of Law in California St. Paul, Minn.: West, 1983. A sketchy account of early developments in California.

Pitt, Leonard, ed. California Controversies: Major Issues in the History of the State. San Rafael, Calif.: ETRI Publishing Co., 1985. Collection of articles concerning pivotal political issues in the state's history.

Pope, Alexander H., and Goodrich, Max E. California Property Tax Exemptions, Exclusions, Immunities, and Restrictions on Fair Market Value—or, Whatever Became of Full Value Assessment? Pacific L.J. 18 (1987): 943–68. A compilation and analysis of the categories of tax exemptions and other revenue impacts.

Rabin, Edward H., and Brownlie, Robert W. Usury Law in California: A Guide Through the Maze. U.C. Davis L. Rev. 20 (1987): 397. A comprehensive explanation of California usury law.

Reid, John Phillip. Law for the Elephant: Property and Social Behavior on the Overland Trail. San Marino, Calif.: Huntington Library, 1980. A sustained examination of the de facto legal norms governing the overland migration, an experience shaping some immigrants' views of appropriate California legal norms.

Reiner, Ira, and Size, George Glenn. The Law Through a Looking Glass: Our Supreme Court and the Use and Abuse of the California Declaration of Rights. Pacific L.J. 23 (1992): 1183. A revisionist account of the drafting of the 1849 Declaration of Rights, contending that although the 1849 convention ostensibly borrowed from the Iowa and New York constitutions, they actually used the federal Constitution as their model.

Sargent, Noel. The California Constitutional Convention of 1878–79. Calif. L. Rev. 6 (1917): 1. An excellent, in-depth account of the 1879 convention.

Saxton, Alexander. The Indispensable Enemy: Labor and the Anti-Chinese Movement in California. Berkeley: University of California Press, 1971. Discussion of the political dynamics involved in the anti-Chinese movement.

Scheiber, Harry. Race, Radicalism, and Reform: Historical Perspective on the 1879 California Constitution. Hastings Const. L.Q. 17 (1989): 35. An excellent contemporary perspective pertaining to the 1879 convention.

Still, Bayrd. California's First Constitution: A Reflection of the Political Philosophy of the Frontier. Pacific Hist. Rev. 4 (1935): 221. An interpretation of the 1849 Constitution as a manifestation of the pioneer philosophy.

Stocker, Frederick D. Proposition 13: A ten year retrospective. Cambridge, Mass.: Lincoln Institute of Land Policy, 1991. An excellent collection of essays examining implementation of Article XIII A.

Sundby, Scott E. Is Abandoning State Action Asking Too Much of the Constitution? Hastings Const. L.Q. 17 (1989): 139. Arguing against extension of constitutional guarantees absent state action.

Swisher, Carl B. Motivation and Political Technique in the California Constitutional Convention of 1878–79. Claremont, Calif.: Pomona College, 1930. The leading, and still indispensable, secondary source pertaining to the 1879 convention.

Waldron, D. G. Biographical Sketches of the Delegates to the Convention to Frame a New Constitution for the State of California, 1878. San Francisco: Francis & Valentine, 1878. Succinct biographical information concerning the delegates to the 1879 convention.

Willey, Samuel H. California Constitutional Convention Held in Monterey, September 1849. A contemporaneous account of the 1849 convention.

Willis, E. B., and Stockton, P. K. Debates and Proceedings of the Constitutional Convention of the State of California. Sacramento, Calif., 1880. An indispensable primary source: the stenographic account of the 1879 convention.

■ TABLE OF CASES

A

A.B.C. Distributing Co, Inc. v. City of San Francisco, 15 Cal. 3d 566, 542 P.2d 625 (1975), **251**
Albright v. South San Francisco, 44 Cal. App. 3d 866, 1 18 Cal. Rptr. 901 (1975), **309**
Alioto's Fish Company, Ltd. v. Human Rights Commission of San Francisco, 120 Cal. App. 3d 594, cert. denied, 455 U.S. 944 (1981), **207**
Allen v. Railroad Commission, 179 Cal. 68, 175 P. 466 (1918), cert. denied, 249 U.S. 601 (1919), **224**
Amador Valley Joint Union High School District v. Board of Equalization, 22 Cal. 3d 208, 583 P.2d 1281 (1978), **259, 267**
American Civil Liberties Union v. Board of Education, 55 Cal. 2d 167, 359 P.2d 45 (1961), **47–48**
American Federation of Labor v. Eu, 36 Cal. 3d 687,686 P.2d 609 (1982), stay denied, 468 U.S. 1310 (1984), **78**
American Microsystems, Inc. v. City of Santa Clara, 137 Cal. App. 3d 1037, 187 Cal. Rptr. 550 (1982), **212**
Application of Wilson, 75 Cal. 580, 17 P. 698 (1888), **58**
Arizona v. California, 373 U.S. 546 (1963), **183**
Assembly v. Deukmejian, 30 Cal. 3d 638,639 P.2d 939 (1982), appeal dismissed, 456 U.S. 941 (1982), **79, 350, 351** (Art. XXI)
Atwood v. Hammond, 4 Cal. 2d 31, 48 P.2d 20 (1935), **177**

B

Bacchus Imports v. Dias, 468 U.S. 263 (1984), **347 n.11**
Badham **v.** Eu, 694 F. Supp. 664 (N.D. Cal. 1988), aff'd mem., 488 U.S. 1024 (1989), **350** (Art.XX1)
Baggett v. Gates, 32 Cal. 3d 128, 649 P.2d 874 (1982), **205, 206**
Baker v. City of Portland, 2 F. Cas. 472 (C.C.D. **Or.** 1879), **19**
Barnes v. Hartman, 246 Cal. App. **2d** 215, 54 Cal. Rptr. 514 (1966), **295** (Art. xv)
Bartling v. Superior Court, 163 Cal. App. 3d 186, 209 Cal. Rptr. 220 (1984), **33**
Batson v. State Personnel Board, 188 Cal. App. 2d 320, 10 Cal. Rptr. 452 (1961), **148**
Beaumont Investors v. Beaumont-Cherry Valley Water District, 165 Cal. App. 3d 227, 211 Cal. Rptr. 567 (1985), **269**
Beckwith v. County of Stanislaus, 175 Cal. App. 2d 40, 345 P.2d 363 (1959), **211**
Bell v. Community Redevelopment Agency, 169 Cal. App. 3d 24, 214 Cal. Rptr. 788 (1985), **320**
Bellus v. City of Eureka, 69 Cal. 2d 336, 444 P.2d 71 1 (1968), **205**
Bernal v. Fainter, 467 U.S. 216 (1984), **116** (Art. V)
Billings v. Hall, 7 Cal. 1 (1857), **45**
Birkenfeld v. City of Berkeley, 17 Cal. 3d 129, 550 P.2d 1001 (1976), **207**
Bishop v. City of San Jose, 1 Cal. 3d 56, **460** P.2d 137 (1969), **206, 207**
Board of Education v. Allen, 392 U.S. 236 (1968), **36, 164**
Board of State Harbor Commissioners v. Dean, 118 Cal. App. 2d 628, 258 P.2d 590 (1953), **301**

Board of Supervisors of Butte County v. McMahon, 219 Cal. App. 3d 286, 268 Cal. Rptr. 219 (1990), **315**
Board of Supervisors of City and County of San Francisco v. Dolan, 45 Cal. App. 3d 237, 1 19 Cal. Rptr. 347 (1975), **308, 324, 357**
Bolton v. Bella Terra Irrigation District, 106 Cal. App. 313, 289 P. 678 (1930), **256**
Bouvia v. Superior Court, 179 Cal. App. 3d 1 127,225 Cal. Rptr. 297 (1986), **33, 46**
Bowen v. Kendrick, 487 U.S. 589 (1988), **36**
Bowker v. Baker, 73 Cal. App. 2d 653, 167 P.2d 256 (1946), **164**
Boys' and Girls' Aid Society v. Reis, 71 Cal. 627, 12 P. 796 (1887), **164**
Bradford v. City of San Francisco, 112 Cal. 537, 44 P. 912 (1896), **322**
Brill v. County of Los Angeles, 16 Cal. 2d 726, 108 P.2d 443 (1940), **210**
Britton v. Board of Election Commissioners of City and County of San Francisco, 129 Cal. 337, 61 P. 1115 (1900), **49, 54**
Brosnahan v. Brown, 32 Cal. 3d 236, 651 P.2d 274 (1982), **70, 78**
Brosnahan v. Eu, 31 Cal. 3d 1, 641 P.2d 200 (1982), **78**
Burrows v. Superior Court, 13 Cal. 3d 238, 529 P.2d 590 (1974), **46**
Burum v. State Compensation Insurance Fund, 30 Cal. **2d** 575, 184 P.2d 505 (1947), **146**

C

C&K Engineering Contractors v. Amber Steel Co., 23 Cal. 3d 1, 587 P.2d 1 136 (1978), **63**
Calfarm Insurance Co. v. Deukmejian, 48 Cal. 3d 805, 771 P.2d 1247 (1989), **82**
California v. Nevada, 447 U.S. 125 (1980), **82, 250**
California v. United States, 438 U.S. 645 (1977), **183**
California Academy of Sciences v. Fresno County, 192 Cal. App. 3d 1436, 238 Cal. Rptr. 154 (1987), **238**
California Building Industry Association v. Governing Board of the Newhall School District, 206 Cal. App. 3d 212, 253 Cal. Rptr. 497 (1988), **265, 270**
California Educational Facilities Authority v. Priest, 12 Cal. 3d 593,526 P.2d 513 (1974), **35, 51, 164, 297, 301**
California Federal Savings and Loan Association v. City of Los Angeles, 54 Cal. 3d 1, 812 P.2d 916 (1991), **205, 206, 252**
California Housing Finance Agency v. Elliott, 17 Cal. 3d 575, 55 1 P.2d 1193 (1976), **301, 305, 357, 358**
California Housing Finance Agency v. Patitucci, 22 Cal. 3d 171, 583 P.2d 729 (1978), **357**
California Public Utilities Commission v. California Energy Resources Conservation and Development Commission, 150 Cal. App. 3d 437, 197 Cal. Rptr. 866 (1984), **224**
California Retail Liquor Dealers Association v. Midcal Aluminum, Inc., 445 U.S. 97 (1980), **346**
California State Employees' Association v. California, 199 Cal. App. 3d 840, 245 Cal. Rptr. 232 (1988), **146**
California State Employees' Association v. Cory, 123 Cal. App. 3d 888, 176 Cal. Rptr. 904 (1981), **309**
California State Employees' Association v. Flournoy, 32 Cal. App. 3d 219, 108 Cal. Rptr. 251 (1973), **167**
California State Employees' Association v. Trustees of California State Colleges, 237 Cal. App. 2d 541, 47 Cal. Rptr. 81 (1965), **149**
California State Employees' Association v. Williams, 7 Cal. App. 3d 390, 86 Cal. Rptr. 305 (1970), **146**
California Teachers Association v. Board of Trustees, 82 Cal. App. 3d 249, 146 Cal. Rptr. 850 (1978), **161**

California Teachers Association v. Riles, 29 Cal. 3d 794,632 P.2d 953 (1981), **35 n.181, 164**
California War Veterans for Justice v. Hayden, 176 Cal. App. 3d 982, 222 Cal. Rptr. 512 (1986), **152**
Cane v. City and County of San Francisco, 78 Cal. App. 3d 654, 144 Cal. Rptr. 316 (1978), **256**
Capital Cities Cable, Inc. v. Crisp, 467 U.S. 691 (1984), **346**
Cardenas v. Superior Court, 56 Cal. 2d 273, 363 P.2d 889 (1961), **44, 62**
Carman v. Alvord, 31 Cal. 3d 318, 644 P.2d 192 (1982), **260**
Carter v. Commission on Qualifications of Judicial Appointments, 14 Cal. 2d 179, 93 P.2d 140 (1939), **109**
Cathedral City v. County of Riverside, 163 Cal. App. 3d 960, 210 Cal. Rptr. 60 (1985), **270**
Cedars of Lebanon Hospital v. Los Angeles County, 35 Cal. 2d 729,221 P.2d 31 (1950), **238**
CEEED v. California Coastal Zone Conservation Commission, 43 Cal. App. 3d 306, 118 Cal. Rptr. 315 (1974), **216**
Chapman v. California, 386 U.S. 18 (1968), **137**
Chicago, Burlington, and Quincy Railroad Company v. Iowa, 94 U.S. 155 (1877), **221**
Church Divinity School v. Alameda County, 152 Cal. App. 2d 496,314 P.2d 209 (1957), **339** (Art. XX)
Chy Lung v. Freeman, 92 U.S. 275 (1875), **18**
Cimpher v. City of Oakland, 162 Cal. 87, 121 P. 374 (1912), **177**
City and County of San Francisco v. Farrell, 32 Cal. 3d 47, 648 P.2d 935 (1982), **269**
City Council of San Jose v. South, 146 Cal. App. 3d 320, 194 Cal. Rptr. 1 10 (1983), **268**
City of Berkeley v. Superior Court of Alameda County, 26 Cal. 3d 515, 606 P.2d 362 (1980), cert. denied, 449 U.S. 840 (1980), **176, 178**
City of Fresno v. California, 372 U.S. 627 (1963), **183**
City of Fresno v. Superior Court, 156 Cal. App. 3d 1 137, 202 Cal. Rptr. 313 (1984), **260**
City of Long Beach v. Bozek, 33 Cal. 3d 727, 661 P.2d 1072 (1983), **50**
City of Long Beach v. Mansell, 3 Cal. 3d 462, 476 P.2d 423 (1970), **178**
City of North Sacramento v. Citizens Utilities Co. of California, 192 Cal. App. 2d 482, 13 Cal. Rptr. 538 (1961), **227**
City of Oakland v. Oakland Water-Front Co., 1 18 Cal. 160, 50 P. 277 (1897), **177**
City of Oakland v. Williams, 15 Cal. 2d 542, 103 P.2d 168 (1940), **210**
City of Oxnard v. Dale, 45 Cal. 2d 729, 290 P.2d 859 (1955), **323**
City of Palm Springs v. Ringwald, 52 Cal. 2d 620, 342 P.2d 898 (1959), **323**
City of Pasadena v. County of Los Angeles, 235 Cal. App. 2d 153, 45 Cal. Rptr. 94 (1965), **210**
City of Sacramento v. State, 50 Cal. 3d 5 1, 785 P.2d 522 (1990), **284**
City of San Francisco v. Alameda County, 5 Cal. 2d 243, 54 P.2d 462 (1936), **244**
City of San Francisco v. San Mateo County, 36 Cal. 2d 196, 222 P.2d 860 (1950), **244**
City of Santa Barbara v. Adamson, 27 Cal. 3d 123, 610 P.2d 436 (1980), **33, 46**
City of South Pasadena v. Pasadena Land and Water Co., 152 Cal. 579, 93 P. 490 (1908), **213**
City of Westminster v. County of Orange, 204 Cal. App. 3d 623, 251 Cal. Rptr. 511, review denied (1988), **269**
City of Woodlake v. Logan, 230 Cal. App. 3d 1058, 282 Cal. Rptr. 27 (1991), **270**
Clark v. City of Los Angeles, 160 Cal. 30, 116 P. 722 (191 l), **212**
Colberg, Inc. v. California ex rel. Department of Public Works, 67 Cal. **2d** 408, 432 P.2d 3 (1967), **173**
Committee to Defend Reproductive Rights v. Myers, 29 Cal. 3d 252, 625 P.2d 779 (1981), **33, 46**
Communist Party v. Peek, 20 Cal. 2d 536, 127 P.2d 889 (1942), **75**
Conservatorship of Drabick, 200 Cal. App. 3d 185, 245 Cal. Rptr. **840** (1988), cert. denied, Drabick v. Drabick, 188 U.S. 958 (1988), reh'g denied, 488 U.S. 1024 (1989), **33**

Consumers Lobby Against Monopolies v. Public Utilities Commission, 25 Cal. 3d 891, 603 P.2d 41 (1979), **226**
Copren v. State Board of Equalization, 200 Cal. App. 3d 828,246 Cal. Rptr. 361 (1988), **238**
County of Amador v. Huberty, 203 Cal. App. 2d 664, 21 Cal. Rptr. 816 (1962), **210**
County of Calaveras v. Brockway, 30 Cal. 325 (1866), **199**
County of Fresno v. State, 53 Cal. 3d 482, 808 P.2d 235 (1991), **281**
County of Inyo v. Public Utilities Commission, 26 Cal. 3d 154, 604 P.2d 566 (1980), **213**
County of Los Angeles v. Byram, 36 Cal. 2d 694, 227 P.2d 4 (195 I), **323**
County of Los Angeles v. Legg, 5 Cal. 2d 349, 55 P.2d 206 (1936), **322**
County of Los Angeles v. State, 43 Cal. 3d 46, 729 P.2d 202 (1987), **281**
County of Placer v. Corin, 113 Cal. App. 3d 443, 170 Cal. Rptr. 232 (1980), **284**
County of Riverside v. Idyllwild County Water District, 84 Cal. App. 3d 655, 148 Cal. Rptr. 650 (1978), **308**
County of Sonoma v. State Board of Equalization, 195 Cal. App. 3d 982, 241 Cal. Rptr. 215 (1987) review denied, (1988), **308**
County of Sonoma v. State Energy Resources Conservation and Development Commis-' sion, 40 Cal. 3d 361, 708 P.2d 693 (1985), **226** (Art. **XII**)
Cox Cable San Diego, Inc. v. City of San Diego, 188 Cal. App. 3d 952, 233 Cal. Rptr. 735 (1987), **207**
Craig v. Boren, 429 U.S. 190 (1976), reh'g denied, 429 U.S. 1124 (1977), **347**
Crawford v. Board of Education, 17 Cal. 3d 280, 551 P. 2d 28 (1976), **55**
Crouchman v. Superior Court, 45 Cal. 3d 1167, 755 P.2d 1075 (1988), **63**
Cruzan v. Director, Missouri Department of Health, 497 U.S. 261 (1990), **33**

D

Dailey v. Superior Court, 112 Cal. 94, 44 P. 458 (1896), **47**
Danielson v. Bakersfield, 184 Cal. 262, 193 P. 242 (1920), **289**
Davis v. City of Berkeley, 51 Cal. 3d 227, 794 P.2d 46 (1989), **358, 354**
Davis v. County of Los Angeles, 12 Cal. 3d 412, 84 P.2d 1034 (1938), **79**
Dawn v. State Personnel Board, 91 Cal. App. 3d 588, 154 Cal. Rptr. 186 (1979), **146**
Dean v. Kuchel, 35 Cal. 2d 444, 218 P.2d 521 (1950), **301**
Department of Mental Hygiene v. Kirchner, 62 Cal. 2d 586, 400 P.2d 321 (1965), **55**
Dittus v. Cranston, 53 Cal. 2d 284, 347 P.2d 671 (1959), 314

E

Eastern Municipal Water District v. Scott, 1 Cal. App. 3d 129, 81 Cal. Rptr. 5 10 (1969), **323**
Ector v. City of Torrance, 10 Cal. 3d 129, 514 P.2d 433, cert. denied 415 U.S. 935 (1973), **215**
Edson v. Southern Pacific Railroad Co., 144 Cal. 182, 77 P. 894 (1904), **225**
Employment Division, Department of Human Resources of Oregon v. Smith, 494 U.S. 872 (1990), reh'g denied, 496 U.S. 913 (1990), **35**
Environmental Defense Fund, Inc. v. East Bay Municipal Utility District, 26 Cal. 3d 183, 605 P.2d 1 (1980), **174**
Evans v. Selma Union High School District, 193 Cal. 54,222 P. 801 (1924), **164**
Ex parte Ah Fook, 49 Cal. 402 (1 874), **19**
Ex parte Andrews, 18 Cal. 678 (1861), **45, 50**
Ex parte Braun, 141 Cal. 204, 74 P. 780 (1903), **204, 206**
Ex parte Curtis, 92 Cal. 188, 28 P. 223 (1891), **59**
Ex parte Daniels, 183 Cal. 636, 192 P. 442 (1920), **206**
Ex parte Felchlin, 96 Cal. 360, 31 P. 224 (1892), **55**

Ex parte Hayes, 98 Cal. 555, 33 P. 337 (1893), **56**
Ex parte Kuback, 85 Cal. 274, 24 P. 737 (1890), **45**
Ex parte Marincovich, 48 Cal. App. 474, 192 P. 156 (1920), **86**
Ex parte Quarg, 149 Cal. 79, 84 P. 766 (1906), **41, 74**

F

Fair Political Practices Commission v. Superior Court, 25 Cal. 3d 33,599 P.2d 46 (1979), cert. denied, 444 U.S. 1049 (1980), **78**
Fellom v. Redevelopment Agency, 157 Cal. App. 2d 243,320 P.2d 884 (1958), appeal denied, 358 U.S. 56 (1958), **320**
Feminist Women's Health Center, Inc. v. Philibosian, 157 Cal. App. 3d 1076, 203 Cal. Rptr. 918 (1984), hearing denied, 688 P.2d 160 (1984), cert. denied, 470 U.S. 1052 (1985), **35, 51**
First Unitarian Church v. County of Los Angeles, 357 U.S. 545 (1958), **152**
Flood v. Riggs, 80 Cal. App. 3d 138, 145 Cal. Rptr. 573 (1978), **75**
Floumoy v. Priest, 5 Cal. 3d 350, 486 P.2d 689 (1971), **301**
Forestier v. Johnson, 164 Cal. 24, 127 P. 156 (1912), **180**
Forsher v. Bugliosi, 26 Cal. 3d 792, 608 P.2d 716 (1980), **46**
Fotson v. Dorsey, 379 U.S. 433 (1965), **352**
Fox v. City of Los Angeles, 22 Cal. 3d 792, 587 P.2d 663 (1978), **37, 51**
Fragley v. Phelan, 126 Cal. 383, 58 P. 923 (1899), **204, 206**
Fresno County v. Malmstrom, 94 Cal. App. 3d 974, 156 Cal. Rptr. 777 (1979), **268**
Furman v. Georgia, 408 U.S. 238 (1972), **68**

G

Garcia v. Wetzel, 159 Cal. App. 3d 1093, 206 Cal. Rptr. 251 (1984), **292** (Art. **XV**)
Garfinkle v. Superior Court, 21 Cal. 3d 268, 578 P.2d 925 (1978), appeal dismissed, 439 U.S. 949 (1978), reh'g denied, 439 U.S. 1104 (1979), **54**
Gatza v. County of Los Angeles, 918 F. 2d 763 (9th Cir. 1990), cert. denied, 11 1 S. Ct. 681 (1991), **351**
Gay Law Students v. Pacific Telephone & Telegraph Company, 24 Cal. 3d 458, 595 P.2d 592 (1979), **55**
Genser v. State Personnel Board, 1 12 Cal. App. 2d 77, 245 P.2d 1090 (1952), **148**
George v. Ransom, 15 Cal. 322 (1860), **66**
Georgia-Pacific Corporation v. California Coastal Commission, 132 Cal. App. 3d 678, 183 Cal. Rptr. 395 (1982), **180**
Gillum v. Johnson, 7 Cal. 2d 744, 62 P.2d 1037 (1936), 309
Gin S. Chow v. City of Santa Barbara, 217 Cal. 673, 22 P.2d 5 (1933), **174**
Goodman v. Riverside County, 140 Cal. App. 3d 900, 190 Cal. Rptr. 7 (1983), **260**
Gordon v. Board of Education, 78 Cal. App. 2d 464, 178 **P.2d** 488 (1947), **164**
Gordon v. Justice Court, 12 Cal. 3d 323, 525 P.2d 72 (1974), **132**
Greyhound Lines, Inc. v. Public Utilities Commission, 68 Cal. 2d 406, 438 P.2d 801 (1968), **224**
Griffin v. Board of Supervisors of Monterey County, 60 Cal. 2d 318, 384 P.2d 421 (1963), **351**
Griswold v. Connecticut, 381 U.S. 479 (1965), **32**

H

Hall v. City of Taft, 47 **Cal.** 2d 177, 302 P.2d 574 (1956), **159**
Hancock v. Burns, 158 Cal. App. 2d 785, 323 P.2d 456 (1958), **109**
Harbor v. Deukmejian, 43 Cal. 3d 1078, 742 P.2d 1290 (1987), **105**

Harpending v. Haight, 39 Cal. 189 (1870), **115**
Harris v. McRae, 448 U.S. 297 (1980), **33**
Hartzell v. Connell, 35 **Cal.** 3d 899, 679 P.2d 35 (1984), **160**
Hawkins v. Superior Court, 22 Cal. 3d 584, 586 P.2d 916 (1978), **61**
Healy v. Beer Institute, Inc., 491 U.S. 324 (1989), **347**
Heckendorn v. City of San Marino, 42 Cal. 3d 48 1, 723 P.2d 64 (1986), **270**
Herminghaus v. Southern California Edison Co., 200 Cal. 81, 252 P. 607, appeal dismissed, 275 U.S. 486 (1926), **174**
Hill v. National Collegiate Athletic Association, 223 Cal. App. 3d 1642, 273 Cal. Rptr. 397 (1990), **34**
Housing Authority v. Superior Court, 35 Cal. 2d 550, 219 P.2d 457 (1950), 355
Housing Authority of Monterey County v. Monterey County Senior Citizen Park, 164 Cal. App. 3d 348, 210 Cal. Rptr. 497 (1985), **358**
Housing Authority of the County of Los Angeles v. Dockweiler, 14 Cal. 2d 437, 94 P.2d 794 (1939), **216**
Houston v. Williams, 13 Cal. 24 (1859), **137**
Hudgens v. NLRB, 424 U.S. 507 (1976), **36**
Hunt v. Mayor and Council of Riverside, 31 Cal. 2d 619, 191 P.2d 426 (1948), **81**
Hunter v. City of Pittsburgh, 207 U.S. 161 (1907), **200**
Huntington Park Redevelopment Agency v. Martin, 38 Cal. 3d 100,695 P.2d 220 (1985), **320**

I

Imperial Irrigation District v. State Water Resources Control Board, 186 Cal. App. 3d 1160, 231 Cal. Rptr. 283 (1986) affd on remand, 225 Cal. App. 3d 548, 275 Cal. Rptr. 250 (1991), cert. denied, 112 S. Ct. 171 (1991), **174**
In re Archy, 9 Cal. 147 (1858), **52**
In re California Toll Bridge Authority, 212 Cal. 298, 298 P. 485 (1931), **301, 316**
In re Emmett, 120 Cal. App. 349, 7 P.2d 1096 (1932), **109**
In re Fain, 145 Cal. App. 3d 540, 193 Cal. Rptr. 483 (1983), **121**
In re Hubbard, 62 Cal. 2d 119, 396 P.2d 809 (1964), **207**
In re Jennings, 133 Cal. App. 3d 373, 184 Cal. Rptr. 53 (1982), **52**
In re Lance W., 37 Cal. 3d 873, 694 P.2d 744 (1985), **70**
In re Lynch, 8 Cal. 3d 410, 503 P.2d 921 (1972), 64
In re Madera Inigation District, 92 Cal. 296 (1891), **66**
In re McCapes, 157 Cal. 26, 106 P. 229 (1909), 45
In re Miller, 162 Cal. 687, 124 P. 427 (1912), affd, 236 U.S. 373 (1915), **56**
In re Parrott, 1 F. 481 (C.C.D. Cal. 1880), **19**
In re Perkins, 2 Cal. 424 (1852), **5**
In re Perkins, 18 Cal. 60 (1861), **59**
In re Petition of Commission on the Governorship of California, 26 Cal. 3d 110, 603 **P.2d** 1357 (1979), **122**
In re Russell, 163 Cal. 668 (1912), rev'd on other grounds, Russell v. Sebastian, 233 U.S. 195 (1914), **213**
In re Underwood, 9 Cal. 3d 345, 508 P.2d 721 (1973), **59**
In re William G., 40 Cal. 3d 550, 709 P.2d 1287 (1985), **60**
Industrial Welfare Commission v. Superior Court, 27 Cal. 3d 690,613 P.2d 579 (1980), cert. denied, 449 U.S. 1034 (1980), **288**
International Association of Fire Fighters v. City of San Leandro, 181 Cal. App. 3d 179, 226 Cal. Rptr. 238 (1986), **215**

ITT World Communications v. City of San Francisco, 37 Cal. 3d 859, 693 P.2d 811 (1985), **248**
Ivanhoe Imgation District v. McCracken, 357 U.S. 275 (1958), reh'g denied, 358 U.S. 805 (1958), **183**

J

J. Paul Getty Museum v. County of Los Angeles, 148 Cal. App. 3d 600, 195 Cal. Rptr. 916 (1983), **238**
J. W. Jones Cos. v. City of San Diego, 157 Cal. App. 3d 745, 203 Cal. Rptr. 580 (1984), **268**
James v. Valtierra, 402 U.S. 137 (1971), **356, 359**
Johnson v. Huntington Beach Union High School District, 68 Cal. App. 3d 1, 137 Cal. Rptr. 43 (1977), cert. denied, 434 U.S. 877 (1977), **301**
Joslin v. Marin Municipal Water District, 67 Cal. 2d 132, 429 P.2d 889 (1967), **174**

K

Kaplan v. Superior Court, 6 Cal. 3d 150,491 P.2d 1 (1971), appeal dismissed, 407 U.S. 917 (1972), **29**
Katz v. Fitzgerald, 152 Cal. 433, 93 P. 1 12 (1907), **75**
Kennedy v. Miller, 97 Cal. 429, 32 P. 558 (1893), **159**
Kennedy Wholesale, Inc. v. State Board of Equalization, 53 Cal. 3d 245, 806 P.2d 1360 (1991), **267**
Kern River Public Access Committee v. City of Bakersfield, 170 Cal. App. 3d 1205, 217 Cal. Rptr. 125 (1985), **179**
Keyishian v. Board of Regents, 385 U.S. 589 (1967), **151, 340**
Kinlaw v. State, 54 Cal. 3d 326, 814 P.2d 1308 (1991), **281**
Kruger v. Wells Fargo, 11 Cal. 3d 352, 521 P.2d 44 (1974), **53**

L

La Mesa v. Freeman, 137 Cal. App. 2d 813, 291 P.2d 103 (1955), **318**
Lane v. City of Redondo Beach, 49 Cal. App. 3d 25 1, 122 Cal. Rptr. 189 (1975), **179**
Lansing v. Board of Education, 7 Cal. App. 2d 21 1, 45 P.2d 1021 (1935), **159**
Larkin v. Grendel's Den, 459 U.S. 116 (1982), **347**
Larson v. Duca, 213 Cal. App. 3d 324, 261 Cal. Rptr. 559 (1989), 266
Le Tourneux v. Gillis, 1 Cal. App. 546, 82 P. 627 (1905), **109**
Lee v. Brown, 18 Cal. 3d 110, 553 P.2d 1121 (1976), **338** (Art. **XX**)
Legislature v. Deukmejian, 34 Cal. 3d 658, 669 P.2d 17 (1983), **350, 351**
Legislature v. Eu, 54 Cal. 3d 492, 816 P.2d 1309 (1991) cert. denied, 112 S. Ct. 1292 (1992), **98, 102, 329**
Legislature v. Reinecke (I), 6 Cal. 3d 595, 492 P.2d 385 (1972), **351, 352**
Legislature v. Reinecke (IV), 10 Cal. 3d 396, 516 **P.2d** 6 (1973), **350**
Liberty v. California Coastal Commission, 113 Cal. App. 3d 491, 170 Cal. Rptr. 247 (1980), **180**
Livermore v. Waite, 102 Cal. 113, 36 P. 424 (1894), **25, 327**
Lloyd Corp. v. Tanner, 407 U.S. 551 (1972), **36**
Long Beach City Employees Association v. City of Long Beach, 41 Cal. 3d 937, 719 P.2d 660 (1986), **46**
Long Beach Unified School District v. State, 225 Cal. App. 3d 155, 275 Cal. Rptr. 449 (1990), **281**
Los Angeles v. Riley, 6 Cal. 2d 621, 59 P.2d 137 (1936), **250**
Los Angeles County v. Jessup, 11 Cal. 2d 273, 78 P.2d 1131 (1938), **316**

Los Angeles County v. Pope, 175 Cal. App. 3d 278, 220 Cal. Rptr. 584 (1985), **241**
Los Angeles County Transportation Commission v. Richmond, 3 1 Cal. 3d 197, 643 P.2d 941 (1982), **218, 268,269**
Lucas v. Forty-Fourth General Assembly, 377 U.S. 713 (1964), **325**
Luck v. Southern Pacific Railway, 218 Cal. App. 3d 1,267 Cal. Rptr. 618 (1990), cert. denied, 111 S. Ct. 344 (1990), **34, 46**
Lund v. California State Employees Association, 222 Cal. App. 3d 174, 271 Cal. Rptr. 425 (1990), **147**
Lungren v. Deukmejian, 45 Cal. 3d 727, 755 P.2d 299 (1988), **33, 118**

M

Mandel v. Hodges, 54 Cal. App. 3d 596, 127 Cal. Rptr. 244 (1976), **51**
Mandel v. Myers, 29 Cal. 3d 531, 629 P.2d 935 (1981), **309**
Mapp v. Ohio, 367 U.S. 643 (1961), **31**
Marek v. Napa Community Redevelopment Agency, 46 Cal. 3d 1070, 761 P.2d 701 (1988), **320**
Marin Water and Power Co. v. Railroad Commission, 171 Cal. 706, 154 P. 864 (1916), **226**, (Art. XII)
Marks v. Whitney, 6 Cal. 3d 251, 491 P.2d 374 (1971), **176, 180**
Martin v. Riley, 20 Cal. 2d 28, 123 P.2d 488 (1942), **119**
Martin v. Waddell, 41 U.S. 367 (1842), **176**
Martinez v. Board of Supervisors of Sonoma County, 23 Cal. App. 3d 679, 100 Cal. Rptr. 334 (1972), **358**
Matter of Maguire, 57 Cal. 604 (1881), **68**
McBean v. Fresno, 112 Cal. 159,44 P. 358 (1896), **323**
McCauley v. Brooks, 16 Cal. 11 (1860), **115**
McCulloch v. Franchise Tax Board, 61 Cal. 2d 186, 390 P.2d 412 (1964), appeal dismissed, 379 U.S. 133 (1964), reh'g denied, 379 U.S. 984 (1965), **251**
McFadden v. Jordan, 32 Cal. 2d 330, 196 P.2d 787 (1948), cert. denied, 336 U.S. 918 (1949), **25, 328**
McHugh v. Santa Monica Rent Control Board, 49 Cal. 3d 348, 777 P.2d 91 (1989), **63, 128**
McKinney v. Board of Trustees, 31 Cal. 3d 79, 642 P.2d 460 (1982), **55**
Melvin v. Reid, 112 Cal. App. 285, 297 P. 91 (1931), **46**
Merryman v. Bourne, 76 U.S. 592 (1869), **5**
Messenger v. Kingsbury, 158 Cal. 611, 112 P. 65 (1910), **178**
Methodist Hospital of Sacramento v. Saylor, 5 Cal. 3d 685, 488 P.2d 161 (1971), **300**
Middleton v. Low, 30 Cal. 596 (1866), **115**
Miller v. Board of Public Works, 195 Cal. 477,234 P. 381 (1925), error dismissed, 273 U.S. 781 (1927), **46**
Miller v. City of Sacramento, 66 Cal. App. 3d 863, 136 Cal. Rptr. 315 (1977), **205**
Mitchell v. Superior Court, 37 Cal. 3d 268, 690 P.2d 625 (1984), **49, 63**
MUM v. Illinois, 94 U.S. 1 13 (1877), **221**
Muskopf v. Corning Hospital District, 55 Cal. 2d 211, 359 P.2d 457 (1961), **88**
Mutual Life Insurance Co. of New York v. State Board of Equalization, 50 Cal. 3d 402, 787 P.2d 996 (1990), **255**

N

National Audubon Society v. Superior Court of Alpine County, 33 Cal. 3d 419, 658 P.2d 709, cert. denied, 464 U.S. 977 (1983), **174, 180**
National Independent Business Alliance v. City of Beverly Hills, 128 Cal. App. 3d 13, 180 Cal. Rptr. 59 (1982), **271**

National Treasury Employees Union v. Von Raab, 489 U.S. 656 (1989), **33**
Neely v. California State Personnel Board, 237 Cal. App. 2d 487, 47 Cal. Rptr. 64 (1965), **148**
New York Times Co. v. Sullivan, 376 U.S. 254 (1964), **153**
Newcomb v. Newport Beach, 7 Cal. 2d 393, 60 P.2d 825 (1936), **178**
Nollan v. California Coastal Commission, 483 U.S. 825 (1987), **180**
Nordlinger v. Hahn, 1 12 S. Ct. 2326 (1992), **259, 267**
Northwest Financial, Inc. v. State Board of Equalization, 229 Cal. App. 3d 198, 280 Cal. Rptr. 24 (1991), cert. denied, 112 S. Ct. 3026 (1992), **267**
Nuckolls v. Bank of California, 10 Cal. 2d 266,74 P.2d 264 (1937), **295** (Art. XV)

O

Olson **v.** Cory, 27 Cal. 3d 532, 636 P.2d 532 (1980), **57, 87**
Olson v. Cory, 134 Cal. App. 3d 85, 184 Cal. Rptr. 325 (1982), **88**
Otsuka v. Hite, 64 Cal.2d 596, 414 P.2d 412 (1966), **74**

P

Pacific Gas and Electric Co., v. State Board of Equalization, 27 Cal. 3d 277, 61 1 P.2d 463 (1980), **257**
Pacific Legal Foundation v. Brown, 29 Cal. 3d 168, 624 P.2d 1215 (1981), **146, 147, 142** (**Art.** VII)
Pacific Telephone and Telegraph Co. v. City and County of San Francisco, 51 Cal. 2d 766, 336 P.2d 514 (1959), **206**
Pacific Telephone & Telegraph Co. v. Eshleman, 166 Cal. 640, 137 P. 11 19 (1913), **226** (**Art.** XII)
Pasadena v. Los Angeles County, 182 Cal. 171, 187 P. 418 (1920), **244**
Pasadena Redevelopment Agency v. Pooled Money Investment Board, 136 Cal. App. 3d 290, 186 Cal. Rptr. 264 (1982), **320**
Pass School District v. Hollywood City School District, 156 Cal. 416, 105 P. 122 (1909), **159**
Patton v. Alameda, 40 Cal. 3d 41, 706 P.2d 1135 (1985), **260**
Payton v. City of Santa Clara, 132 Cal. App. 3d 152, 183 Cal. Rptr. 17 (1982), **33**
Pearson v. County of Los Angeles, 49 Cal. 2d 523, 319 P.2d 624 (1957), **203**
Penziner v. West American Finance Co., 10 Cal. 2d 160, 74 P.2d 252 (1937), **295** (Art. XV)
People v. Adcox, 47 Cal. 3d 207, 763 P.2d 906 (1990), cert. denied, 494 U.S. 1038 (1990), **121**
People v. Anderson, 6 Cal. 3d 628, 493 P.2d 880 (1972), cert. denied, 406 U.S. 958 (1972), **30, 44**, 64, **68**
People v. Beggs, 178 Cal. 79, 172 P. 152 (1918), **58**
People v. Brisendine, 13 Cal. 3d 528, 531 P.2d 1099 (1975), **60**
People v. Brophy, 49 Cal. App. 2d 15,'120 P.2d 946 (1942), **115**
People v. Cahan, 44 Cal. 2d 434, 282 P.2d 905 (1955), **33, 44**
People v. Castro, 38 Cal. 3d 301, 696 P.2d 11 1 (1985), **71**
People v. Clark, 62 Cal. 2d 870, 402 P.2d 856 (1965), **32**
People v. Cook, 33 Cal. 3d 400, 658 P.2d 86 (1983), **135**
People v. Cook, 41 Cal. 3d 373, 710 P.2d 299 (1985), **60**
People v. Copsey, 71 Cal. 548, 12 P. 721 (1887), **51**
People v. Dillon, 34 Cal. 3d 441, 668 P.2d 697 (1983), **64**
People v. Enriquez, 173 Cal. App. 3d 990, 219 Cal. Rptr. 325 (1985), **121**
People v. Gutierrez, 45 Cal. 429 (1873), **57**
People v. Hoge, 55 Cal. 612 (1880), **216**
People v. Krivda, 8 Cal. 3d 623, 504 P.2d 157 (1973), **60**

People v. Laiwa, 34 Cal. 3d 71 1, 669 P.2d 1278 (1983), **60**
People v. Lucero, 44 Cal. 3d 1006, 750 P.2d 1342 (1988), **121**
People v. Modesto, 59 Cal. 2d 722, 382 P.2d 33 (1963), **137**
People v. Mortimer, 46 Cal. 1 14 (1873), **57**
People v. New Perm Mines, Inc., 212 Cal. App. 2d 667, 28 Cal. Rptr. 337 (1963), **124**
People v. Odle, 37 Cal. 2d 52, 230 P.2d 345 (1951), **121**
People v. Oppenheimer, 156 Cal. 733, 106 P. 74 (1909), **64**
People v. Ramirez, 25 Cal. 3d 260, 599 P.2d 622 (1979), **54**
People v. Reclamation District No. 551, 1 17 Cal. 1 14, 48 P. 1016 (1897), **66**
People v. Shirokow, 26 Cal. 3d 301, 605 P.2d 859 (1980), **174**
People v. Shults, 87 Cal. App. 3d 101, 150 Cal. Rptr. 747 (1978), **124**
People v. Soto, 171 Cal. App. 3d 1158, 217 Cal. Rptr. 795 (1985), **110**
People v. Steelik, 187 Cal. 361, 203 P. 78 (1921), **64**
People v. Stephens, 62 Cal. 209 (1882), **212**
People v. Watson, 46 Cal. 2d 818, 299 P.2d 243 (1956), cert. denied, 355 U.S. 846 (1957), **136**
People v. Woody, 61 Cal. 2d 716, 394 P.2d 813 (1964), **51**
People v. Zelinski, 24 3d 357, 594 P.2d 1000 (1979), **60**
People ex rel. Deukmejian v. Brown, 29 Cal. 3d 150,624 P.2d 1206 (1981), **116, 123**
People ex rel. Mattison v. Nye, 9 Cal. App. 148, 98 P.2d 241 (1908), **118**
People ex rel. the Attorney General v. Johnson, 6 Cal. 499 (1856), **300**
People ex rel. Webb v. California Fish Company, 166 Cal. 576, 138 P. 79 (1913), 68, **177**
People ex rel. Younger v. County of El Dorado, 5 Cal. 3d 480, 487 P.2d 1193 (1971), **216, 250**
Perpich v. Department of Defense, 496 U.S. 334 (1990), **119**
Perry Education Association v. Perry Local Educators' Association, 460 U.S. 37 (1983), **36**
Perry Farms v. Agricultural Labor Relations Board, 86 Cal. App. 3d 448, 150 Cal. Rptr. 495 (1978), **288**
Personnel Administrator of Massachusetts v. Feeney, 442 U.S. 256 (1979), aff'd after remand, 445 U.S. 901 (1980), **150**
Peterson v. City of San Diego, 34 Cal. 3d 225, 666 P.2d 975 (1983), 77
Phelps v. Prussia, 60 Cal. App. 2d 732, 141 P.2d 440 (1943), **159**
Phillips Petroleum Co. v. Mississippi, 484 U.S. 469 (1988), **176**
Planned Parenthood Affiliates v. Van **de** Kamp, 181 Cal. App. 3d 245, 226 Cal. Rptr. 361 (1986), **33**
Platt v. City and County of San Francisco, 158 Cal. 74, 110 P. 304 (1910), **212**
Pollard's Lessee v. Hagen, 44 U.S. 212 (1845) **176**
Pooled Money Investment Board v. Uwh, 153 Cal. App. 3d 155, 200 Cal. Rptr. 500 (1984), **301**
Popper v. Broderick, 123 Cal. 456, 56 P. 53 (1899), **206**
Porten v. University of San Francisco, 64 Cal. App. 3d 825, 134 Cal. Rptr. 839 (1976), **33, 34, 46**
Prisoners Union v. Department of Corrections, 135 Cal. App. 3d 930, 185 Cal. Rptr. 634 (1982), **48**
Professional Fire Fighters, Inc. v. City of Los Angeles, 60 Cal. 2d 276, 384 P.2d 158 (1963), **205, 206, 207**

R

Ramirez v. Brown, 9 Cal. 3d 199, 507 P.2d 1345 (1973), cert. denied, 418 U.S. 904 (1974), **151**
Rankins v. Commission on Professional Competence, 24 Cal. 3d 167, 593 P.2d 852 (1979), appeal dismissed, 4-44 U.S. 986 (1979), **56**
Raven v. Deukmejian, 52 Cal. 3d 336, 801 P.2d 1077 (1990), **32, 67, 329**
Rebstock v. Superior Court, 146 Cal. 308, 80 P. 65 (1905), **75**

Redevelopment Agency of City of San Pablo v. Shepard, 75 Cal. App. 3d 453, 142 Cal. Rptr. 212 (1977), **358**
Redevelopment Agency of the City of San Bernardino v. County of San Bernardino, 21 Cal. 3d 255, 578 P.2d 133 (1978), **319, 320**
Reese v. Kizer, 46 Cal. 3d 996, 760 P.2d 495 (1988), **87**
Regents of the University of California v. Santa Monica, 77 Cal. App. 3d 130, 143 Cal. Rptr. 276 (1978), **167**
Regents of the University of California v. Superior Court, 17 Cal. 3d 533, 551 P.2d 844 (1976), **167**
Renne v. Geary, 111 S. Ct. 2331 (1991), **76**
Reynolds v. Sims, 377 U.S. 533 (1964), **100, 349**
Richardson v. Ramirez, 418 U.S. 24 (1974), **151**
Rider v. County of San Diego, 1 Cal. 4th 1, 820 P.2d 1000 (1991), **218, 269, 270,323**
Riley v. Johnson, 219 Cal. 513, 27 P.2d 760 (1933), **301**
Riley v. Johnson 11, 6 Cal. 2d 529, 58 P.2d 631 (1936), **301**
Robbins v. Superior Court, 38 Cal. 3d 199, 695 P.2d 695 (1985), **46**
Robins v. Pruneyard Shopping Center, 23 Cal. 3d 899, 592 P. 2d 341 (1979), aff'd, 447 U.S. 74 (1980), **28, 44, 46, 50**
Robinson v. Magee, 9 Cal. 81 (1858), **57**
Roe v. Wade, 410 U.S. 113 (1973), **33**
Rojo v. Kliger, 52 Cal. 3d 65, 801 P.2d 373 (1990), **57**
Russ Building Partnership v. San Francisco, 199 Cal. App. 3d 1496, 246 Cal. Rptr. 21, appeal dismissed, 484 U.S. 909 (1987), **268**

R

Sail'er Inn Inc. v. Kirby, 5 Cal. 3d 1, 485 P.2d 529 (1971), **56**
San Diego Gas & Electric Co. v. San Diego County Air Pollution Control District, 203 Cal. App. 3d 1132, 250 Cal. Rptr. 420 (1988), **268**
San Francisco Community College District v. City and County of San Francisco, 58 Cal. App. 3d 387, 129 Cal. Rptr. 918 (1976), **249**
San Francisco Pioneer Woolen Factory v. Brickwedel, 60 Cal. 166 (1882), **182**
San Pedro, Los Angeles and Salt Lake Railroad Company v. Hamilton, 161 Cal. 610, 119 P. 1073 (1911), **178**
San Pedro v. Hamilton, 161 Cal. 610, 119 P. 1073 (191 I), **177**
Sands v. Morongo Unified School District, 53 Cal. 3d 863, 809 P.2d 809 (1991), cert. denied, 1 12 S. Ct. 3026 (1992), **51, 301**
Santa Barbara County Taxpayers Association v. Board of Supervisors of County of Santa Barbara, 209 Cal. App. 3d 940, 257 Cal. Rptr. 615 (1989), **285**
Santa Catalina Island Conservancy v. County of Los Angeles, 126 Cal. App. 3d 221, 178 Cal. Rptr. 708 (1981), **237, 240**
Saunby v. The Railroad Commission of The State of California, 191 Cal. 226, 215 P. 904 (1923), **223**
Schlesinger v. Reservists Committee to Stop the War, 418 U.S. 208 (1974), **117**
Sema v. Superior Court, 40 Cal. 3d 239, 707 P.2d 793 (1985), **62**
Serrano v. Priest (I), 5 Cal. 3d 584, 487 P.2d 1241 (1971), **159**
Serrano v. Priest (II), 18 Cal. 3d 728, 557 P.2d 929 (1976), cert. denied, 432 U.S. 907 (1977), **55, 159, 161, 249**
Shellenberger v. Board of Equalization, 147 Cal. App. 3d 510, 195 Cal. Rptr. 168 (1983), **239**
Silver v. Brown (I), 63 Cal. 2d 270, 405 P.2d 132 (1965), **350, 352**
Silver v. Jordan, 241 F. Supp. 576 (1964), affd, 381 U.S. 415 (1965), **350, 352**

Silver v. Reagan, 67 Cal. 2d 452, 432 P.2d 26 (1967), **350**
Simi Valley Recreation and Park District v. Local Agency Formation Commission of Ventura County, 5 1 Cal. App. 3d 648, 124 Cal. Rptr. 635 (1975), **216**
Skelly v. State Personnel Board, 15 Cal. 3d 194, 539 P.2d 774 (1975), **148**
Skinner v. Railway Labor Executives' Association, 489 U.S. 602 (1989), **33**
Slivkoff v. California State University and Colleges, 69 Cal. App. 3d 394, 137 Cal. Rptr. 920 (1977), **149**
Smith v. City of Riverside, 34 Cal. App. 3d 529, 110 Cal. Rptr. 67 (1973), **206**
Sonoma County Organization of Public Employees v. County of Sonoma, 23 Cal. 3d 296, 591 P.2d 1 (1979), **205**
South Pasadena v. Pasadena Land & Water Co., 152 Cal. 579, 93 P. 490 (1908), **340**
Southern California Edison Company v. Railroad Commission of the State of California and City of Tulare, 6 Cal. 2d 737, 59 P.2d 808 (1936), **223**
Southern California Telephone Co. v. County of Los Angeles, 45 Cal. App. 2d 11 1, 113 P.2d 773 (1941), **248**
Southern Pacific Pipe Lines, Inc. v. City of Long Beach, 204 Cal. App. 3d 660, 251 Cal. Rptr. 411 (1988), **213**
Southern Pacific Transportation Co. v. Public Utilities Commission, 18 Cal. 3d 308, 556 P. 2d 289 (1976), **87**
Southwest Concrete Products v. Gosh Construction Corp., 51 Cal. 3d 701, 798 P.2d 1247 (1990), **297** (Art. XV)
Special Assembly Interim Committee v. Southard, 13 Cal. 2d 497, 90 P.2d 904 (1939), **107**
Speiser v. Randall, 357 U.S. 513 (1958) (Art. VII), **152**
Spinney v. Griffith, 98 Cal. 149, 32 P. 974 (1893), **289**
Spring Valley Water Works v. Bryant, 52 Cal. 132 (1877), **182**
Spring Valley Water Works v. City and County of San Francisco, 82 Cal. 286, 22 P. 910 (1890), **182**
Stanley v. City and County of San Francisco, 48 Cal. App. 3d 575, 121 Cal. Rptr. 84 (1975), **217**
Starr v. City of San Francisco, 72 Cal. App. 3d 164, 140 Cal. Rptr. 73 (1977), **324**
State v. McCauley & Tevis, 15 Cal. 429 (1860), **64**
State v. San Luis Obispo Sportsman's Association, 22 Cal. 3d 440, 584 P.2d 1088 (1978), **68**
State v. Steamship "Constitution," 42 Cal. 578 (1872), **19**
State Board of Equalization v. Superior Court, 39 Cal. 3d 633, 703 P.2d 1131 (1985), **257**
State Compensation Insurance Fund v. Riley, 9 Cal. 2d 126, 69 P.2d 985 (1937), **146**
State of California v. Superior Court of Lake County (Lyon), 29 Cal. 3d 210, 625 P.2d 239 (1981), **180**
State Personnel Board v. Fair Employment & Housing Commission, 39 Cal. 3d 422, 703 P.2d 354 (1985), **147**
Stevens v. Watson, 16 Cal. App. 3d 629, 94 Cal. Rptr. 190 (1971), cert. denied, 407 U.S. 925 (1972), **241**
Stevenson v. Colgan, 91 Cal. 649, 27 P. 1089 (1891), **111**
Stimson Mill Company v. Braun, 136 Cal. 122, 68 P. 481 (1902), **45**
Stockburger v. Riley, 21 Cal. App. 2d 165, 68 P.2d 741 (1 937), **146**
Sugarman v. Dougall, 413 U.S. 634 (1973) (Art. V), **116**

T

Tarpey v. McClure, 190 Cal. 593 (1923), **66**
Taxpayers to Limit Campaign Spending v. Fair Political Practices Commission, 51 Cal. 3d 744, 799 P.2d 1220 (1990), **81**

Taylor v. Madigan, 53 Cal. App. 3d 943, 126 Cal. Rptr. 376 (1975) (Art. XX), **338**
Taylor v. Underhill, 40 Cal. 471 (1871), **176**
The Pines v. City of Santa Monica, 29 Cal. 3d 656, 630 **P.2d** 521 (1981), **205, 206**
Thornburg v. Gingles, 478 U.S. 30 (1986), **352**
324 Liquor Corp. v. Duffy, 479 U.S. 335 (1987), **347**
Tinsley v. Superior Court, 150 Cal. App. 3d 90, 197 Cal. Rptr. 643 (1983), **328**
Tolman v. Underhill, 39 Cal. 2d 708, 249 P.2d 280 (1952), **167**
Trent Meredith, Inc. v. Oxnard, 1 14 Cal. App. 3d 317, 170 Cal. Rptr. 685 (1981), **268**
Truck Owners and Shippers, Inc. v. Superior Court, 194 Cal. 146, 228 P. 19 (1924) (Art. XII), **222**
Trustees of Dartmouth College v. Woodward, 17 U.S. 518 (1819), **340**

U

Unger v. Superior Court, 37 Cal. 3d 612,692 P.2d 238 (1984), **76**
Union Pacific Railroad Co. v. State Board of Equalization, 49 Cal. 3d 138, 776 P.2d 267 (1989), **257**
United States v. State of California, State Water Resources Control Board, 694 F. 2d 1171 (1982), **183**
United States v. State Water Resources Control Board, 182 Cal. App. 3d 82, 227 Cal. Rptr. 161 (1986), **174**
University of California Nuclear Weapons Labs Conversion Project v. Lawrence Livermore Laboratory, 154 Cal. App. 3d 1157, 201 Cal. Rptr. 837 (1984), 37

V

Valley Bank v. Superior Court, 15 Cal. 3d 652, 542 P.2d 977 (1975), **33**
Valtierra v. Housing Authority of San Jose, 313 F. Supp. 1 (1970), rev'd sub nom., James v. Valtierra, 402 U.S. 137 (1971), **356**
Veterans' Welfare Board v. Riley, 188 Cal. 607, 206 P. 631 (1922), **111**
Village of Belle Tern v. Boraas, 416 U.S. 1 (1974), **33**
Vinson v. Superior Court, 43 Cal. 3d 833, 740 P.2d 404 (1987), **33**
Vogel v. Los Angeles County, 68 Cal. 2d 18, 434 P.2d **961** (1967), **151, 340**
Voorhees v. Morse, 1 Cal. 2d 179, 34 P.2d 153 (1934), **322**

W

Walnut Creek Manor v. Fair Employment & Housing Commission, 54 Cal. 3d 245, 814 P.2d 704 (1991), **128**
Warner v. Kenny, 27 Cal. 2d 627, 165 P.2d 889 (1946), **81**
Way v. Superior Court, 74 Cal. App. 3d 175, 141 Cal. Rptr. 383 (1977), **120**
Weekes v. City of Oakland, 21 Cal. 3d 386, 579 P.2d 449 (1978), **251**
Wesberry v. Sanders, 376 U.S. 1 (1964), (Art. XXI), **352**
West Coast Advertising Co. v. City and County of San Francisco, 14 Cal. 2d 516, 95 P.2d 138 (1939), **204, 205**
Western and Southern Life Insurance Co. v. State Board of Equalization, 99 Cal. App. 3d 410, 159 Cal. Rptr. 539, aff'd, 451 U.S. 648 (1979), **255**
Westside Sane1Freez.e v. Ernest W. Hahn, Inc., 224 Cal. App. 3d 546, 274 Cal. Rptr. 51 (1990), 36
Whalen v. Roe, 429 U.S. 589 (1977), 33

White v. Davis, 13 Cal. 3d 757, 533 P.2d 222 (1975), **46**
Whitmore v. Brown, 207 Cal. 473, 279 P. 447 (1929), **159**
Wilkinson v. Times Mirror Corp., 215 Cal. App. 3d 1034, 264 Cal. Rptr. 194 (1989), **36**
Wilks v. Mouton, 42 Cal. 3d 400, 722 P.2d 187 (1986), cert. denied, 479 U.S. 1066 (1987), **77**
Wilson v. City of San Bernardino, 186 Cal. App. 2d 603, 9 Cal. Rptr. 431 (1960), 206
Wilson v. Eu (I), 54 Cal. 3d 471, 816 P.2d 1306 (1991), **351**
Wilson v. Eu (**In**), 1 Cal. 4th 707, 823 P.2d 545 (1992), **351, 352, 353**
Winkelman v. City of Tiburon, 32 Cal. App. 3d 834, 108 Cal. Rptr. 415 (1973), **357**
Woodlake v. Logan, 230 Cal. App. 3d 1058, 282 Cal. Rptr. 27 (1991), **270**
Woodmansee v. Lowery, 167 Cal. App. 2d 645, 334 P.2d 991 (1959), **118**
Wright v. Compton Unified School District, 46 Cal. App. 3d 177, 120 Cal. Rptr. 115 (1975), **323**

Y

Younger v. Superior Court, 21 Cal. 3d 102, 577 P.2d 1014 (1978), **120**

■ INDEX

Abortion, 33
Absentee voting, 74, 77
Adjournments during session of legislature, 96
Administrative agencies, limits on powers of, 86–7, 227
Agricultural products, taxation exemption, 233, 236
Alcoholic beverages, 343–7
Aliens, property rights, 18
Amendments. *See also* Revisions
  effective dates of, 329
  initiative process, legislative proposals, 24–9, 31, 327–8
  initiative process, proposals by, electors, 328–9
  mechanisms for submission and approval of, 25, 32, 77–9
  publication of proposed, 80–1
Appellate jurisdiction of Supreme Court, 135
Appointment power of governor
  alcoholic beverage control, appeals board, 344, 347
  alcoholic beverage control, director of, 343–7
  citizens compensation commission, 90
  filling of vacant offices, 117–19
  fish and game commissioners, 112
  generally, 117–19
  judges, 138–9
  judicial performance, commission on, 133–4
  personnel board, state, 146–8
  public utilities commissioners, 222
  University of California, regents of the, 164–7
Appropriation, definition of, 87, 275, 282
Appropriation bills
  and controller's warrants, 309
  debt limitations: local governments, 301, 322–4; state, 299–302
  two-thirds majority, 103
Appropriation of water, 172, 180–1
Appropriations limit, 274–5
  annual calculations: audit, 275
  appropriations subject to limitation, exceptions to, 282, 284, 286
  categories added or removed by judgment of court, 285–6
  definition, 283
  emergency, exceeding limit in event of, 277–8
  establishment or change by electors, 278–9
  transfer of services, 277–8
Article I. *See titles of specific articles*
Assemble, right to, 49
Assembly. *See also* Legislature
  caucus, 101
  compensation of members of, 101
  districts, 100
  election to, 95
  impeachment, 111
  reapportionment of districts, 349–53
Assessments. *See also* Taxation
  appeals boards, county, 245–6
  disaster damage, 245
  equalization of assessed property, 247
  fair market value, 231
  lands and improvements separately assessed, 245
  open space lands, practices re, 239–40
  place of assessment, 244–5
  public utilities, 248
  single family dwellings, 241
  special assessments by chartered governments, 324–5
  state board of equalization, 242–4
Assessors, elected in counties, 198, 201–2
Attainder, bill of, 57
Attorney General, 118, 122–6
  commission on judicial appointments, 132
  initiative and referendum measures, 80
Attorneys, 134

Bail
  capital offenses, 58
  excessive bail, 58–9
  public safety, 69
  right to, 58–9
"Ballot propositions," voting on. *See* Initiatives; Referendum
Banks
  deposit of public funds within, 215, 217
  exemption from usury prohibitions, 294–7
  taxation of, 251
Bar of California. *See* State Bar of California
Bill of Rights. *See* Declaration of Rights
Bills and statutes. *See also* Legislative procedures
  appropriations, vote required, 107
  budget, 107
  effective date, 103
  printing and distribution, 103
  reading, 102
  single subject, 104
  30-day waiting period, 102
  titles, 104
  uniform application, 104
  urgency statutes, 103
  veto, 105
Bills of attainder, 57. *See also* Legislative procedures
Bonds. *See also* Indebtedness
  form of vote approval, 302–3
  General Obligation Bond Proceeds Fund, 302
  general obligation bonds, 261
  impairment by appropriations limitations, 281–4
Borrowing, 281, 299, 322–4
Boundaries
  alteration by reapportionment, 349–53
  county, 198–9
  state, 85
  taxation outside local government boundaries, 242–4
  tax changes, 250
Bribery of legislators, 109
Budget
  bill, 102–3, 107–8
  Governor's budget submission, 107
  veto, 105–6
Busing, limitations on power of courts, 55
California Citizens Compensation Commission, 90–2
Capital, state, 86
Capital offenses, bail, 58
Capital punishment. *See* Death penalty
Capitol, state, maintenance, 113–4
Certiorari, original jurisdiction of courts, 134
Charters. *See* Cities; Counties
Chief Justice of Supreme Court
  acting Chief Justice, 128
  appointments to Judicial Council, 131–2
  assignment of judges, 137
  Commission on Judicial Appointments, 132–3
Children, state aid not prohibited, 303–4
Churches. *See also* Religion
  prohibition of grants to, 36, 306
  taxation of, 235
  tax exemption, 237
Cities
  alcoholic beverage license fees, 345
  assessments, special, by chartered cities, 324–5
  charter city, 200–1, 203–7
  charter city and county, 207
  churches, aid to, prohibited, 35, 306
  claims against, 217
  consolidation of cities, 200, 207–8
  credit, giving or lending of, prohibited, 307–9
  debt limitations; on local governments, 322; re special assessments, 324–5
  formation of, 200
  funds, temporary transfer of, resolution re, 308–9
  general law: cities, 201, 208; construction of term, 205–7, 217
  governing body: charter proposal or revision, 201–2; extra compensation prohibited, 214–5
  insurance pooling arrangement: joint powers agreement, etc., 307–9
  motor vehicle revenues: allocations to cities, 332
  officers and employees: charter city provisions, 201, 203–7; nonpartisan nature, 76; oath of office, 339–40; residence location, 214–5; subversives, disqualification of, 151–2

ordinances, 208–9
powers of, 200, 208–9
pro rata share of state support to needy, 303–5
public improvements, special assessments for, 269, 283, 324–5
religious sects, aid to, prohibited, 35, 306
sales or use tax revenues, apportionment of, 255
tidelands, sales to, 175–8
Civil cases, right to jury trial in, 62–3
Civil liberties. *See* Declaration of Rights
Civil service system, state. *See* Personnel board, state
Claims against cities or counties, 217
Clemency, executive, 120–1
Commissioners, court, 144, 223
Commissions
Citizens Compensation, 90
exempt from civil service, 148–9
Fish and Game, 112
Judicial Appointments, 132–3
Judicial Performance, 133
minimum wages and, 268
Public Utilities, 221–3, 225–6
state mandates, 90
workers' compensation, 289–91
Common carriers, 224
Community colleges
charter city provisions, 169
creation, 168
funding, 309–14
tax exemption, 233, 235
Community redevelopment, 318–20
Compensation. *See also* Salaries
California Citizens Compensation Commission, 90–2
judges, 142–3
legislators, limitations on, 96–8
limits on reduction during term, 87–8
local officials and employees, 199, 202, 204, 206, 214–5
state officers, 90–2
Condemnation, 65, 226
Confrontation of witnesses, right to, 61–2
Congressional districts, reapportionment, 349–51
Conscience, liberty of, 50
Constitution
amendment by initiative, 328–9
amendment or revision, 328–9
constitutional convention, 327
interpretation, 68
Constitutional Conventions
authority to call, 328
Convention of 1849, 7–13
Convention of 1878–1879, 13–23
Constitution of 1849, history of, 7–13
Constitution of 1879, history of, 13–23
Contempt of court
jury trial, 62–3
newspersons, immunity from, 49
Contracts, laws impairing, 57
Controller, state, 118, 122–3, 125
Corporations, 8, 14, 16–17, 23, 222, 340–1
regulation by Public Utilities Commission, 223
Counsel, right to in criminal proceedings, 61
Counties
boards of education, 169
boundaries, 198
charters, 200–3, 337
claims against, procedure, 217
consolidations, approval by majority of electors, 198
consolidation with city, 207
formation, 198, 337
indebtedness or liability, limitations on, 322–4
liability losses: payment through insurance pooling arrangement, 307–9
motor vehicle revenues, 332
officers and employees: designated by county charter, 200–3; designated by legislature, 198; nonpartisan nature, 76; residential restrictions prohibited, 214–5
ordinances and regulations, enforcement of, 208–9
performance of municipal functions, 209–11
powers of, 198–9
sales or use tax revenues, apportionment of, 255
school taxes, levy of, 249
seat of government, 113, 198–9
superior court in each county, 129–30
vehicle license fees: allocation to counties, 219

Courts. *See also* Judges; Judicial Article; Judicial Council; Jurisdiction
  Administrative Director of courts, 131–2
  Court of appeal: districts and divisions, 129; presiding Justice, 128
  jurisdiction, appellate, 135
  jurisdiction, original, 134–5
  Municipal and Justice Courts, establishment and organization, 130
  publication of opinions, 137
  Superior Courts: county clerk as ex officio clerk, 130; establishment in counties, 129–30
  Supreme Court: Chief Justice, 128–9; composition, 128; limitation on power of appellate court to reverse judgment, 136; power to review, 135; transfer of causes, 135–6
Credit of local government or state, prohibition, 307–9
Criminal proceedings
  bail, right to, 58
  cruel or unusual punishment, 63–4
  death penalty, 68
  discovery, 72
  felony prosecutions, by indictment or information, 60–1
  joinder of criminal cases, 72
  jury trial, right to, 62–3
  prior convictions, use of, 70
  Public Safety Bail, 69
  restitution, 69
  right of people to speedy and public trial, 71–2
  rights of defendants in, 61–2
  treason, 64
  Truth-in-Evidence, 69
  Victims' Bill of Rights, 68–71

Death penalty
  not unconstitutional, 68
  proposed abolition, 11
Debt, imprisonment for, 58
Debt limits. *See also* Indebtedness
  local government, 322
  state appropriations, 274, 299–302
Declaration of Rights. *See also specific rights*
  generally, 43–5
  independent interpretation of, 44
Defamation, 47, 152–3
Defendants, criminal. *See* Criminal proceedings
Disabled persons, tax exemptions, 234, 237, 262, 265
Disasters
  legislative powers during, 112
  public disaster aid not a prohibited "gift," 307, 309
  taxation relief, 245, 263–6
Discrimination
  prohibition, generally, 56
  religious, 50
Distribution of powers of government, 86, 197. *See also* Executive Article; Judicial Article; Legislative Article; Local Government Article
District attorneys, 123, 198
Districts
  Board of Equalization, 246, 349–54
  community college, 168
  congressional, 349–54
  employee residence requirements, 214–5
  fish and game, 112
  legislative (Senate and Assembly), 100, 349–54
  local government entities, 197, 282
  municipal and justice courts, 130
  school, 168
  special districts, taxes on, 268, 270
Divorce, 8, 58
Double jeopardy, 62
Dual office holding, limitations on, 150–1
Due process of law
  criminal prosecutions, 61–2
  deprivation of life, liberty, or property, 52–4
  right of the people to, in criminal cases, 71

Education. *See also* Finance Article; Tax limitation
  boards of education, 158, 162, 169
  California State University, 346–7
  common public schools, 159–161
  community colleges, 169, 233, 235, 309–12
  county superintendent of schools, 157–8
  free textbooks, 163
  prohibition of aid to sectarian schools, 163–4
  school districts, 161, 168

Stanford University, 338–9
superintendent of public instruction, 118, 125, 156
University of California, 164–7
Elections. *See also* Initiatives; Recall; Referendum
free elections, 74
of governor, 116–7
improper practices, 74–5
judicial, 138
legislative, 95
nonpartisan offices, 76
primary, 75–6
secret voting, 76–7
Eligibility requirements
for executive officers, 117, 119, 147
for governor, 116, 157–8
for judges, 137–8
for state legislative seats, 95, 152
Eminent domain, power of, 64–5
Employees, public, 145–54. *See also* Cities; Counties
Equalization, State Board of, 246–7
Equal protection of law, 53–6
Evidence. *See also* Searches and seizures
authority of judges to comment on, 134–5
"Truth in Evidence," right to, 69, 71
Excessive fines, 63–4
Executive Article, 115–26. *See also* Governor
conflicts of interest, 124–6
executive clemency and parole system, 120–1
executive power vested in Governor, 115
executive reorganization, 119
militia, provision for, 119
reporting to legislature, 117
term limits, 122–3
vacancies, 117–19
Exemptions, tax. *See* Taxation
Ex Post Facto Laws, 57

Federal supremacy, 85
Fees, distinct from "special taxes," 268–71
Felons, disqualification from voting, 74–5
Felony, prosecutions for. *See* Criminal proceedings
Finance Article, 299. *See also* Cities; Counties; Indebtedness; Taxation; Tax limitation
appropriations, limit on, 273–86
local indebtedness, 322
public schools, 273–7, 309–12
urban redevelopment, 318–20
Fines. *See* Excessive fines
Fish, right to, 67
Fish and Game Commission, 112
responsibilities regarding marine mammals, 187–195
restriction on use of funds, 314
Freedoms. *See* Declaration of Rights
Free speech. *See* Speech, liberty of

Gambling. *See* Lotteries
Gasoline tax, 331
Government
distribution of powers of, 86, 197
purpose of, 73–4
Governor. *See also* Appointment power of governor; Executive Article
appointment of executive officers, 117, 119
appointment of judges, 138
election of, 116
eligibility requirements, 116
impeachment of, 122
powers and duties of, 115–6
salary of, 90–2
special session of legislature and, 96
supervision of executive branch, 117–9
term of office, 116, 122–3
vacancy in office of, 122
veto power, 105–6
Grand jury
indictment of, 60
summons of, 66

Habeas corpus, 58
Happiness, right to pursue and obtain, 45, 47
Historical property, taxation exemptions, 239
History, constitutional, 3–37
Homeowner's property tax exemption, 234, 236
Homesteads, 10, 338
Horse racing, 111–2
Hospitals, tax exemption, 237
Huntington Library, 237, 338

Impeachment
of public officers and employees, 111
of Supreme Court justices and other judges, 111
Imprisonment for debt, 57–8
Inalienable rights, 45
Income taxes, 251
Indebtedness
bonded, 260–1, 281
city, county, etc., limitations on, 322–4
evidences of: taxation, 232
government spending limitation: indebtedness as of January 3, 1979, 281, 283
local government, limitations on, 260
state, limitations on, 299–302
Independence of state constitutional rights, 21, 29–37
Indictment of grand jury, 60–1
Indictments. *See* Criminal proceedings
Initiatives. *See also* Referendum
cities and counties, 81
conflicting measures, 80
effective date, 80
legislative authority over procedure, 81
legislative repeal or amendment, 80
limitations on, 82
title and summary, 81
Investigations, by Public Utilities Commission, 223
Involuntary servitude, prohibition, 52
Item veto, 105

Jeopardy, double, 62
Judges. *See also* Courts
appointment by governor, 138–9
appointment of appellate judges, 132–3
authority to comment on evidence, 134–5
compensation, 142–3
disqualification, discipline, removal, 140–2
election of, 138–9
eligibility, 137–8
restrictions on employment, benefits, 139–40
retirement, 143
temporary, 143–4
Judicial Appointments, Commission on, 132
Judicial Article, 127
Judicial Council, 131–2
Judicial Performance, Commission on, 133–4
Judicial power, 127
Jurisdiction
appellate, 135
original, 134–5
Jury
number of jurors, 63
right to trial by jury, 62
Jury, grand. *See* Grand jury
"Just compensation," notion of, 64–5

Labor relations
eight-hour day on public works, 288–9
general, 287–92
inmate labor, 291–2
mechanic liens, 289
minimum wages and general welfare, 287
Lands, riparian, 173–4
Language, English as official, 88
Laws
ex post facto, 57
governor's power and duty to execute, 115–21
local or special, 110, 208–9, 216
uniform application of, 110
Legal profession. *See* State Bar of California
Legislative accountability, 113
Legislative Article, 93
Legislative power. *See* Legislature
Legislative procedures. *See also* Bills and statutes
caucus, 101
committees, 106–7
journals, 101
power of each house to adopt rules, 101
quorum, 101
recess, 101
roll call votes, 104
sessions, 96, 101
Legislators. *See also* Legislature
compensation for, 90–2
conflict of interest, 96–8
eligibility, 95
expulsion by two-thirds vote, 98–9
impeachment of, 111
improper influence of, 109
ineligibility for certain offices, 108–9

limitations on dual office holding, 150
lobbying, limitation on, 98–9
oath or affirmation of office, 339–40
prohibited compensation and activities, 96–8
protection from civil process, 108–9
qualifications determined by each house, 97
retirement, 97–8
term limits, 95
travel and living expenses, 97
Legislature, structure and power of. *See also* Legislative procedures; Legislators
assembly, 95
budget bills, 107
committees, 106–7
districts for Senate and Assembly, 100, 349–54
expenditures, limitation on, 102
governor's annual message to, 117–8
limitation on power to grant extra compensation or allowance, 110–1
officers, 101
regulation of elections, 74
senate, 95
vacancies, 95
Libel. *See* Defamation
Liberties. *See* Declaration of Rights
Liberty, right to enjoyment and defense of, 45
Lieutenant Governor, 121–3
Life, right to enjoyment and defense of, 45
Local government, 282, 197–219
Local Government Article, 197
Local laws, 110, 208, 216
Lotteries, 111–2
Low rent housing, 356–9

Marine mammals, 187
Marine Resources Protection Act, 187–94
Marriage
marital property, history, 10
separate property, how acquired, 65–6
Mass transit, 331–3
Mechanic's liens, 289
Military
quartering of soldiers, 52
subordination to civil power, 52, 119
Militia, provision for, 119
Motor vehicle fuel tax, 331
lands used for park and recreation, 334–5
loans to State General Fund, 334
Municipal corporations, interpretation of powers of, 203–8, 217–8
Municipalities. *See* Cities

Natural rights, 11
Navigable waters
access to, 178–80
control and ownership of tidelands, 175–8
eminent domain to acquire frontage, 172–3
Newspersons sources, protection for, 49
Noncitizens, property rights of, 65
Nonpartisan offices, 76

Oath of office for state officers, 339–40
Officers, public, 145–54. *See also* Cities; Counties

Pardons, governor's power to grant, 120–1
Pensions. *See* Retirement benefits
Personal income taxation, 251
Personal property
exemptions from taxation, 233–7
taxation, 232
Personnel board, state, 147–8
Petition, right to, 49
Police force, 204, 206
Police power, 208–9
Pollution control, revenue bond issuance for, 316–7
Popular initiative, amendment by, 328–9
Power
distribution of government, 86, 197
gubernatorial, 115–21
judicial, 127
legislative, 94
Power of eminent domain, 64
Preamble, 42
Press, liberty of, 47
Primary elections, 75–6
Prior convictions, admissibility of, 69
Privacy, right to, 32–5, 45–6
Private property for public use, 65
Privilege and newspersons, 49
Privileges or immunities, 54
"Probable cause," issuance of warrant and, 60

Property
inalienable right of, 45
noncitizens, property rights of, 65
private, for public use, 65
prohibition on property qualification for vote or office, 66
separate property, 66
tidal, title to, 176
Property taxation, 218, 259. *See also* Finance Article; Taxation; Tax limitation
Proposition 13. *See* Tax limitation
Prosecution, by indictment or information, 60
Prosecutors, county. *See* District attorneys
Public employees, 145–54. *See also* Cities; Counties
Public Finance Article, 299
Public housing, 355–60
Public officers and employees. *See also* Cities; Counties
city, 200–8, 214
county, 200, 214
impeachment of, 111
state, 145–54
"Public purpose" doctrine
in eminent domain, 64
in expenditures, 303
in public gifts, loans, or credit, 306
Public school system, free, 159
Public trial, right to
defendant's right, 61
public's right, 71
Public utilities, 211–4, 221–9
Public Utilities Commission, 221
appointment of by governor, 222
eminent domain, fixing of compensation re, 225
examination of books and records of transportation companies, 227
powers and duties, 221–9
regulation of public utilities, 221, 223
transportation fares and charges, 224–5
utility rates, fixing of, 224–5
Public works, eight-hour day, 288–9
Punishment, cruel and unusual, 63–4

Quartering of soldiers, 52
Quorum, in legislature, 101

Racial discrimination, 54–6
Railroads, 221, 224
Reapportionment, 349–53
Recall
defined, 82
elections, 82–3
of Governor or Secretary of State, 83
legislative power to provide for, 83
local officers, 83–4
reimbursement for expenses, 83
Referendum. *See also* Initiatives
defined, 79
proposal for, 79–80
submission to electorals, 79
Release on own recognizance, 58
Religion
establishment of, 35, 50
free exercise and enjoyment of, 35
prohibition of government aid to, 306
Religious freedom. *See* Religion
Renters, tax benefits, 234
Reprieves, governor's power to grant, 120
Restitution of crime victims, 69
Retirement benefits
elected constitutional officers, 89–90
judges, 143
legislators, restrictions on, 94, 98
Revisions, constitutional, 327–9
Rights, affirmative. *See also* Happiness; Privacy; Safe schools; Safety
education, 159, 163–4
women's, 9, 20–1
Riparian
lands, 173–4
rights, 173
Roll-call votes, 103
Rule making power of Judicial Council, 131

Safe schools, right to, 69
Safety, right to pursue and obtain, 45
Salaries. *See* Compensation
Sales or use taxes, 249, 255
Schools, 155–69
finance, 274–7, 309–14
limitation on judicial power to order busing, 52–3
safety, 69
Searches and seizures, freedom from unreasonable, 59–60
Secretary of State, 118, 122

Seismic safety real property valuation, 262, 265
Self-incrimination, right against, 70
Senate. *See also* Legislative procedures; Legislators; Legislature
districts, 100
election to, 95
impeachment trial in, 111
term of office for senators, 95
Senior citizens
postponement of taxes, 240
transfer of assessed value, 261, 266
Separate property of husband and wife, 10, 65–6
Separation of powers, 86. *See also* Executive Article; Judicial Article; Legislative Article
Sex discrimination, 20, 56
Sheriffs, 123, 198–9
Single-family dwellings
homestead, 338
taxation assessment, 241
Slander. *See* Defamation
Slavery prohibited, 12, 52
Solar power
revenue bonds to finance facilities, 317
taxation of added solar systems, 262
Soldiers, quartering of, 52
Sovereign immunity, 88
Special assessments, 165, 347–8
distinct from special taxes, 268–9
not affected by appropriations limits, 284
procedures by chartered governments, 324–5
Special session of legislature, 96
Speech, liberty of, 46–7
Speedy trial, right to
right of the people, in criminal cases, 72
rights of criminal defendant, 62
Spending limits, 273–86. *See also* Appropriations limit
Stanford University, 338–9
State
boundaries, 86, 250
capital, 86
language, 88–9
suits against, 88
State Bar of California, 134
Statutes. *See* Bills and statutes
Subventions
historic properties, 240
homeowners tax exemption, 250–1
mandated local services, 280–1
open space, 239
postponed taxes, 240
transfers to local governments for state purposes, 250
Succession in office of governor, 122
Suffrage
absentee voting, 74
change of residency and, 74
exclusions from, 75
qualifications for, 74
women's right to, 20–1
Suits against the state, 88
Superintendent of Public Instruction, 118, 125, 156–7
Superior Court. *See* Courts
Supremacy of federal government, 19, 22, 85
Supreme Court. *See* Courts

"Taking" of private property for public use, 64
Taxation. *See also* Finance Article; Indebtedness
ad valorem, 259
exemptions, 233–40, 250–1
gasoline, 331–3
personal income, 251
property, 231–2
uniformity principle, 231–2
vote requirements for state tax changes, 267
Tax limitation
assessed valuation limits, 261–4
base year values, 266–7
base year values, transfer of, 262, 266
bonded indebtedness allowed, 260–1
disaster, reconstruction after, 261, 265
effective date of tax limitation, 270
full cash value, definition, 260
improvements or renovations to realty, 265
inflationary increases allowed, 262, 264
maximum ad valorem rate, 259–60
ownership change due to eminent domain, 263, 265–6
real property sales or transaction tax prohibited, 267

senior citizen's transfer of base value, 262, 266–7
severability of provisions, 271
special districts, effect on, 270–1
special taxes allowed, 269–70
state school fund, 273–7, 312–4
state tax changes, vote requirement, 267
transfers of base value among family members, 265–6
two-thirds vote required for special taxes, 268
Teachers, 160–1
Terms of office
of elective offices, commencement of, 84
of governor, 116, 122–3
of judges, 138–9
of members of the assembly, 95
of public officers, 122, 147, 156–7, 165
of senators, 95
Tidal properties, title to, 175–8
Transportation
allocation of motor vehicle revenues, 332–3
local government operation of transportation utilities, 211–4
prohibition on free passes, 227–8
regulation by public utilities commission, 221, 224
Treason, 64
Treasurer, State, 122, 125
Trial, speedy public, right to
criminal defendant, 61
of public, 71
Trial by jury, right to. *See* Jury
"Truth-in-Evidence," 69

Unalienable rights. *See* Inalienable rights
Uniformity principle of property taxation, 231–2
University of California, 164–7
Urban redevelopment, 318–20
Usury, 293–7
Utilities
limited regulation by cities, 228
owned by cities, 211–14
regulation by Public Utilities Commission, 221–9

Vacancies
in executive offices, 117
in legislature, 95
in office of governor, 122
Veterans
not included within 'gift' prohibitions, 307
property tax exemptions, 234, 236
Veto power
of governor, 106
item, 106
Victims' Bill of Rights, 68–9
Voting rights. *See* Suffrage

War- or enemy-caused disasters, 112–3
Warrants, search, 59–60
Water
government agencies to conform to California law, 182–3
public access, 178–80
public trust doctrine, 175
reasonable and beneficial use requirement, 173–5
subject to state regulation, 180–1
Witnesses
compulsory process of, 61
confrontation of, right to, 61
detention of, 57–8
disqualification by religion prohibited, 56–7
Women
rights of, 10, 20
suffrage for, 20
Workers' compensation, 289
Writs, 133

Zoning, as local ordinance, 208–9

About the Authors

JOSEPH R. GRODIN, former Associate Justice, California Supreme Court, and Professor of Law, Hastings College of Law, University of California, is also the author of *In Pursuit of Justice* (1989), among many other works dealing with state constitutional practice.

CALVIN R. MASSEY, Associate Professor of Law, Hastings College of Law, teaches state constitutional law and American constitutional history and has written at length on constitutional issues.

RICHARD B. CUNNINGHAM, Professor of Law, Hastings College of Law, is a former attorney with the federal Office of Chief Engineers and has written at length on regulations dealing with resources and environmental matters.

Printed in the USA/Agawam, MA
April 4, 2011

557497.006